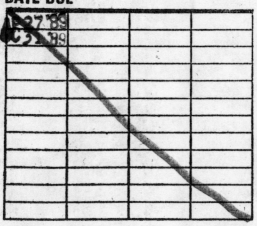

WHITE SUPREMACY

WHITE
SUPREMACY

A Comparative Study
in American and South African History

George M. Fredrickson

New York   Oxford
OXFORD UNIVERSITY PRESS
1981

Copyright © 1981 by George M. Fredrickson

Library of Congress Cataloging in Publication Data

Fredrickson, George M   1934-
White supremacy.

Bibliography: p.
Includes index.
1. United States—Race relations. 2. South
Africa—Race relations. 3. Afro-Americans—Civil
rights. 4. Blacks—South Africa—Civil rights.
5. Indians of North America—Civil rights.
I. Title.
E184.A1F73   305.8'00973   80-12559
ISBN 0-19-502759-0

Printed in the United States of America

For My Children
Anne Hope, Caroline, Laurel, and Tom

Acknowledgments

The National Endowment for the Humanities supported this project generously, first by granting me a Senior Fellowship to do sustained research in 1973–74, and then by providing part of the resources that enabled me to spend a year at the Center for Advanced Study in the Behavioral Sciences at Stanford, California, in 1977–78. The Center itself offered ideal facilities for writing a first draft of the book; and I would like to thank its staff for innumerable contributions to my comfort and productivity. The Northwestern University Grants Committee helped to finance my research trip to South Africa in 1974 and later subsidized the typing of a final draft of the manuscript.

Of the many individuals who have assisted me in one way or another I can name only a notable few. Gwendolen Carter encouraged me to begin the project and helped me to find my initial bearings in the field of South African studies. Hans Panofsky guided me in the use of the South African materials in the Northwestern Library's superb Africana Collection. While doing research in Cape Town, I benefited especially from the assistance and hospitality of Hendrik van der Merwe and Christopher Saunders. During a brief stay in England, I was stimulated and enlightened by extended conversations with Martin Legassick. Various drafts of all or part of the manuscript were read by T. H. Breen, Elizabeth Eldredge, Hermann Giliomee, Glenna Matthews, David Roediger, Leonard Thompson, and C. Vann Woodward. (Professor Thompson deserves a special mention here for his unusually close and exacting critique of the South African sections of my final draft.) Without the expert advice and criticism provided by these scholars of U.S. or South African history this would not be half the book it is. I am, of course, fully responsible for any errors of fact or interpretation that remain. Sheldon Meyer of Oxford University Press was a profound source of encouragement and help during all stages of the project, and Stephanie Golden of Oxford did an excellent job of copy-editing. Hélène Fredrickson came to my rescue in the final and (for me) excruciating stage of proof-reading printed copy. The first smooth draft was typed by Kate Hughes of the Behavioral Sciences Center and the final manuscript by Joan Stahl.

Evanston, Ill.   G. M. F.
July 1980

Contents

MAPS

Introduction

The phrase "white supremacy" applies with particular force to the historical experience of two nations—South Africa and the United States. As generally understood, white supremacy refers to the attitudes, ideologies, and policies associated with the rise of blatant forms of white or European dominance over "nonwhite" populations. In other words, it involves making invidious distinctions of a socially crucial kind that are based primarily, if not exclusively, on physical characteristics and ancestry. In its fully developed form, white supremacy means "color bars," "racial segregation," and the restriction of meaningful citizenship rights to a privileged group characterized by its light pigmentation. Few if any societies that are "multi-racial" in the sense that they include substantial diversities of physical type among their populations have been free from racial prejudice and discrimination. But white supremacy implies more than this. It suggests systematic and self-conscious efforts to make race or color a qualification for membership in the civil community. More than the other multi-racial societies resulting from the "expansion of Europe" that took place between the sixteenth century and the twentieth, South Africa and the United States (most obviously the southern United States during the era of slavery and segregation) have manifested over long periods of time a tendency to push the principle of differentiation by race to its logical outcome—a kind of *Herrenvolk* society in which people of color, however numerous or acculturated they may be, are treated as permanent aliens or outsiders.[1]

I was tempted at one time to use the term "racism" to denote the processes of establishing and rationalizing white privilege and dominance in the two societies. But after weighing this option carefully, I concluded that racism is too ambiguous and loaded a word to describe my subject effectively. Narrowly defined, racism is a mode of thought that offers a particular explanation for the fact that population groups that can be distinguished by ancestry are likely to differ in culture, status, and power. Racists make the claim that such differences are due mainly to immutable genetic factors and not to environmental or historical circumstances. Used in this way, the concept of racism is extremely useful for describing a trend in Western thought between the late eighteenth century and the twentieth that has provided *one* kind of rationale for racially repressive social systems. But nonwhites have at times been subjugated or treated as inferiors in both the United States and South Africa without the aid of an explicit racism of this sort. In recent years, racism has commonly been used in a broader sense, as a blanket term for all discriminatory actions or policies directed at groups thought to be physically distinct from a dominant or "majority" element. But this usage leaves us without a separate word for the overt doctrine of biological inequality and inhibits a sense of the role that this ideology has played in specific historical situations.[2]

Racism (in the broad, modern sense) has the further terminological disadvantage of having been used so frequently as an epithet. No one, at least in our time, will admit to being a racist. The phrase white supremacy, on the other hand, is relatively neutral; both defenders and opponents of a fixed racial hierarchy have been willing to invoke it. Until recently, Alabama proclaimed the virtues of "white supremacy" in its state motto; and the upholders of South African apartheid will more readily admit to being white supremacists than racists. Egalitarians have also used this phrase to sum up the blatant forms of discrimination existing in the South before desegregation and still prevailing in South Africa today. Although I have my own feelings of moral revulsion against racial prejudice and discrimination—and I trust that these will be evident but unobtrusive in the chapters that follow—I believe that the principal contribution of a study of this kind should be to increase understanding of the processes examined rather than to make direct moral judgments. In general, I leave it to my readers to make such judgments for themselves on the basis of the facts and analysis provided. Hence I thought it advisable to avoid sustained use of the term racism in its broad and strongly perjorative sense.

Since this work is not only a study of the phenomenon of white supremacy but also an attempt to write a particular kind of comparative history, some discussion of my method or approach would seem to be in order. What follows does not pretend to be a thorough and systematic essay on method, because I hope that the reader will be able to comprehend the way I do comparative history and see the usefulness of such an enterprise primarily through his or her direct immersion in the substantive chapters. It is far more important, in my view, to *illustrate* how comparative history can be written than to talk about it in abstract terms. But because this is a study of a somewhat special and experimental kind, it may be helpful to say something, by way of introduction, about the theoretical and historiographic assumptions on which it is based.

Interest in the use of cross-cultural approaches and perspectives has increased markedly among historians in recent years. But surprisingly little sustained comparative history has actually appeared.[3] A large portion of the most ambitious comparative work on past societies published since the 1950s has actually been written by scholars who consider themselves political scientists, sociologists, or anthropologists rather than historians.[4] There is nothing ultimately sacred about disciplinary boundaries. Much of this scholarship has drawn on the work of historians, and has in turn influenced some historians in a very creative way. One of the leading exponents and practitioners of comparative studies from within the historical profession has emerged as an interdisciplinary social scientist working in close collaboration with comparativists from other fields.[5] Clearly, then, comparative history can readily be viewed as a form of cross-disciplinary, social-scientific investigation in which historians can play a contributing role.

But there is another way to do comparative history that would make it clearly distinguishable from comparative sociology or politics as usually practiced and thus keep it within the bounds of an essentially humanistic discipline that has its own characteristic concerns and perspectives. It is possible, in my opinion, to write comparative history in a manner that retains the peculiar virtues of the more imaginative kind of orthodox historical scholarship while at the same time escaping from some of its limitations.

One reason why so few historians have actually produced thoroughly comparative works is that the typical aim or inclination of historians tends to differ from that of most social scientists. The latter are quite properly concerned with discovering and testing general hypotheses about human behavior and social organization. The former are likely to be fascinated by variety and concerned with the special features of individual societies. Hence social scientists usually look at a range of cases to test or demonstrate a general theory or "model" of human action or organization; while historians, if they employ a comparative perspective at all, normally do it to illuminate some special feature of the single society or civilization with which they are primarily concerned. Historians are therefore likely to find that the comparative generalizations of sociologists and political scientists are often too abstract or "macrocosmic" to do justice to the messy, complex, and ambiguous reality that they confront in their own research and that, to some extent, they positively relish. If they invoke social theories and models, historians are likely to use them as heuristic devices for illuminating the particular rather than as instances illustrating the universal.

Although I share many of the biases and inclinations of the orthodox historian, I do not believe that these attitudes provide an excuse for avoiding sustained comparative work. Quite the contrary—they make comparison absolutely essential to the enterprise of historical interpretation. How is one to know if a process or development is really the unique product of a special constellation of forces and influences within a given society unless one has actually compared it with analogous cases elsewhere? To the extent that historians persist in looking for causes or explanations for the phenomena they describe and are not simply content to be mere chroniclers or storytellers, they must perforce develop comparative perspectives.

But comparative history in the fullest sense is more than comparative perspective. In my view, the greatest shortcoming of much of the historical work being done in the United States is not its lack of the methodological or theoretical rigor that is found in the "hard" social sciences—history has its own quite defensible methods and theoretical assumptions—but rather its parochial vision. Historians of the United States in particular characteristically know little in depth about the history of other societies, unless, like Early Modern England, they can be directly linked to the American experience. The value of comparison is that it permits us to escape, at least to some extent, from the provincialism and limiting set of tacit assumptions that tend to result from perpetual immersion in the study of a single culture, a preoccupation that is especially constricting if that culture happens to be our own. One threshold of genuinely comparative insight is passed when one begins to find the "other" case or cases inherently interesting or absorbing in their own right and not merely the sources of analogies that help to make a new point about the society of one's original concern. A higher stage is reached when one acquires the ability to make back-and-forth comparisons that will illuminate *equally* the special features or particularities of both or all of the cases examined. Ideally, therefore, comparative history should be genuinely multi-national or multi-cultural, and its results should be of equal interest to specialists on all of the societies examined. Because of the comparative historian's concern for detail and specificity, however, it is unlikely that he or she will be able to handle more than two or at the most three societies in a single study. Doing the job properly means mastering the historiography and at least sampling the primary sources for each instance.

Comparative history of this type differs from characteristic forms of comparative social science in several ways. Most obviously, it retains much of the historian's interest in particularity or individuality. If some general theories of human action and social development are given added credibility, well and good; but the principal aim should be better understanding of the individual cases, each of which will presumably look different in the light of the other or others. The historian's penchant for narrative need not be sacrificed, but it will have to be subordinated to conceptual schemes that permit comparison; otherwise one will find oneself writing parallel histories rather than comparative ones.

It follows from this persistent concern for what is special or unique in each situation that the comparative historian will be drawn at least as much to differences as to similarities. Similitude must first be established to make comparison meaningful—it is essential to show that one is dealing with the same type or category of phenomena in each case, and that the larger historical contexts are sufficiently alike to make comparison more than forced analogy or obvious contrast. But after a firm common ground is established, it is differences that will compel most of the historian's attention because of the way that they can suggest new problems of interpretation and point to discrete patterns of causation.[6]

Furthermore, what is actually being compared will be historical processes or changes over time and not "structures" that are frozen in time for the purposes of social-scientific analysis.[7] The dimension of change and development is central to the historical consciousness and imagination; hence the historian should be uniquely qualified to deal with the kind of flux, contingency, and temporality that cannot be adequately subsumed under rigid structural categories or incorporated into simplified and static models. But this not need mean, as it does for some radical historical empiricists, that history has no direction or governing tendencies. Plausible theories of social change that are based on the actual study of a range of human societies can be called upon to help give resonance and meaning to historical comparisons, provided they are not applied *a priori* and in a mechanistic or overly deterministic way.

My own attempt to do the kind of comparative history that I have just tried to describe in prescriptive terms was initially inspired by a desire to gain a deeper understanding of the history of race relations in the United States. I was strongly impressed by the new questions and insights that had emerged from comparative studies of slavery and race relations in Latin America and the United States and wondered how the American pattern might look if viewed from another, and rather different, external vantage point. The comparison with Latin America has provided strong evidence of peculiar rigidities that developed over time in the North American mode of black-white relations. The original tendency of Frank Tannenbaum and his followers to associate this rigidity with milder or harsher forms of slavery has been seriously questioned and probably discredited.[8] But Tannenbaum's thesis that Latin American societies provided a readier access to freedom and citizenship for freedmen of African descent both during and after slavery has generally been sustained, although recent studies focusing on differences in classification and status of mixed groups have suggested some important qualifications. (It was the mulattoes and not those of unmixed African descent who normally benefited most from this relative fluidity, and even mulattoes could suffer at times from debilitating forms of discrimination in Latin American societies.)[9] The comparison with Iberian America, and to a lesser extent with the "plural societies" of the non-Hispanic West Indies, has thus drawn attention to the peculiar "two-category" system of race relations, with its attendant caste-like distinctions between whites and blacks, that emerged in the United States. Something that had previously been taken for granted now required special explanation, and the effort to account for this apparent anomaly has given a new and fertile direction to the historical study of North American racial attitudes and policies.[10]

Shifting the perspective from Latin America to South Africa necessarily puts the American inter-racial experience in a somewhat different light. As the case of a white settler regime that has gone even further than the United States during the segregation era in erecting artificial barriers against social mobility and citizenship rights for nonwhites, the South African example might readily be used, or misused, as a way of showing the relatively benign or malleable side of American race relations, in much the way that comparison with Latin America has tended to bring out their harshness and rigidity. But the South African racial configuration has been so complex, and has changed so markedly over time, that such an evaluation, valid though it may be for the 1970s, does not necessarily hold true for earlier periods. In fact the great advantage of comparison with South Africa is that it compels recognition that race relations are not so much a fixed pattern as a changing set of relationships that can only be understood within a broader historical context that is itself constantly evolving and thus altering the terms under which whites and nonwhites interact.

In comparisons between the United States and Latin America, the basic similarity that makes a cross-cultural analysis of race relations fruitful is the common history of massive slave importations from Africa, the employment of many of these slaves in plantation agriculture, and the emergence of the processes of manumission and emancipation that raised the issue of how freedmen of African origin and their descendants were to be incorporated into the larger society. It has been the differences in the last phase or aspect of this similar history—the transition from slavery to freedom and what it meant—that have raised the best questions for comparative analysis. To help explain the variance in rates of manumission, circumstances of final emancipation, and modes of group adjustment to post-emancipation society, comparativists have invoked such variables as inherited religious and legal traditions of Old World origin, demographic and environmental pressures, ruling class ideologies, cultural values associated with modernization or traditionalism, and forms of color consciousness arising from the differing "somatic norms" of the dominant groups. A lively debate has developed over which of these variables should be given priority and for what purposes.[11]

Comparing the evolution of race patterns in the United States and South Africa is a rather different kind of enterprise. Although some of the same questions and concerns are relevant, others are not; and some new ones have to be confronted. Slave transfers, agrarian servitude, emancipation, and post-emancipation adjustments are also part of the South African story; but this framework for analysis does not do justice to the full complexity of South African race relations. The most numerous and significant nonwhite group in South Africa has been the indigenous African majority, not the imported slaves or their descendents. In some ways, therefore, South Africa is more comparable to the highland societies of Latin America, with their Amerindian majorities, than to the lowland plantation societies. What makes comparison with the United States possible in the first instance is not the origin and demographic significance of nonwhite populations—although for certain times and places analogies can be made—but rather broad similarities in the kinds of white attitudes, ideologies, and policies that have emerged. The fact that the white settlers of both areas of colonization were northwest European Protestants provides a point of departure obviously lacking in the U.S.–Latin American comparison. It is tempting, therefore, to attribute the subsequent growth of intense racial consciousness to an original mind-set of the colonists deriving from similar cultural antecedents. Such an assumption would be congruent with the thesis of the "Tannenbaum school" that the Catholic-Protestant dichotomy explains the main differences in the race patterns of the Americas.

But it became clear as my study progressed that this hypothesis was inadequate and even misleading. The vagaries and variations that I have found in the actual evolution of racial attitudes and policies in North America and South Africa drew my attention away from common cultural influences and toward differing environmental circumstances and political contingencies. I have not therefore found it possible to treat "white supremacy" as a kind of seed planted by the first settlers that was destined to grow at a steady rate into a particular kind of tree. On the contrary, I have found it more plausible to regard it as a fluid, variable, and open-ended process. Major shifts in both societies in the forms of white dominance and the modes of consciousness

associated with them bely any notion of a fixed set of attitudes and relationships. What justifies comparison, therefore, is not a primordial
and predetermined aptitude for "racism" common to American and
South African whites, but rather the emergence of long-term, historically conditioned tendencies leading to more self-conscious and rigorously enforced forms of racial domination—trends that were similar in
general direction but surprisingly variable in rate of development,
ideological expression, and institutional embodiment.

To achieve a coherent organization and analysis of a vast body of
subject matter, I have broken down the history of white supremacy in
the United States and South Africa into parallel phases or aspects, associated more or less with specific periods and sometimes with individual sections or provinces. The history of frontier expansion at the
expense of indigenous peoples in the Cape Colony bears enough resemblance to what occurred in the United States, at least up to the time of
Indian removal in the 1830s, to be worthy of close comparative scru-
tiny.[12] Similarly, the parallel rise of racial slavery in the colonial South
and the Cape raised many of the same issues—how, for example, to
legitimize the resulting social order. The phenomenon of miscegenation and the problem of the subsequent status of people of mixed origin also lend themselves to cross-cultural treatment because early race
mixture took place under similar conditions. Also fruitful is a juxtaposition of the roughly analogous political conflicts and assertions of
national identity among whites in the period from 1776 to 1910 in
terms of their effect on the status and expectations of nonwhites. More
clearly than most contrasts with Latin America this comparison reveals
the crucial relevance of white political activity to the fate of nonwhites
in a settler state. The impact of industrialization on race relations, and
more specifically the ways in which the problem of inter-racial competition for industrial jobs was resolved, is an obvious subject for analysis
that has begun to attract the attention of sociologists.[13] Finally, the
growth of racial segregation or apartheid in the modern era positively
cries out for cross-cultural examination; although here I have found
that the extent of difference between the Afro-American and African
experiences creates a serious problem of comparability. But the history
of discrimination against another population group in South Africa—
the Coloreds—provides fertile ground for sustained comparisons with the
process of black segregation in the United States after emancipation.

To make my comparisons manageable and meaningful, I have not only shifted topics and angles of vision but even units of analysis. Depending on the time period and the problem at hand, my geographical reference points are the southern United States, the United States as a whole, the Cape Colony or Province of South Africa, or modern South Africa in its entirety. Similarly, the specific nonwhite groups that are the main object of white supremacist concern and activity vary from chapter to chapter. Attitudes toward Amerindians, Khoikhoi (or "Hottentots"), Afro-Americans, Bantu-speaking Africans, and Cape Coloreds are each treated within the specific contexts that have given them meaning. The advantage of this topical and segmental approach is that it does some justice to the enormous complexity of race relations in both societies. It has strengthened my sense that race relations can best be understood in the terms of the interaction of specific groups in particular historical situations and that attempts to generalize broadly about entire societies over long periods of time usually distort more than they illuminate.

What gives the book thematic unity is the persistent focus on the attitudes, beliefs, and policies of the dominant whites, and the cumulative understanding that such an emphasis provides about the causes, character, and consequences of white supremacy in the two societies. This approach has its obvious limitations. Comparative studies of nonwhite responses and resistance movements would be enormously valuable and should be done. But a useful prelude to such a work is awareness of what nonwhites were up against, and this is what I have tried to convey.

The modes of interpretation that run throughout the book may help to clarify some major issues that have emerged from the historiography of race relations in both the United States and South Africa. Perhaps the most general and insistent of these interpretive questions involves the relationship or correlation between ethno-cultural and economic concerns as motivations for racial discrimination and subjugation. The debate over the relative significance of "race" and "class" as determinants of black or brown inequality in societies like the United States and South Africa has led some scholars to take bold and unyielding stands in favor of "idealist" or "materialist" explanations.[14] I have not done so. I have sought instead to comprehend the interaction and inter-relationship of "race" and "class"—of ethic consciousness and economic advantage—without assigning a necessary priority to either. I have concluded that the historical record in these two instances will simply not sustain a final or universally applicable ruling on which is primary and independent and which is secondary and subordinate. In most cases, the two sides of the polarity are mutually reinforcing, and where they clearly conflict the outcome is open and may depend on the intervention of some other partially autonomous force, such as a political authority or pressure group that has interests or aims of its own that can be distinguished from those of the dominant economic classes or self-conscious ethnic communities within the local society. I agree with Robert Ross, a historian of South African stratification, when he writes that "any attempt to elevate either pole of the [race-class] dichotomy to paramountcy and declare the other irrelevant must prove vain. If there were now, and always had been, economic equality between the various racial groups, with consequent parity in terms of power, then there would be nothing to argue about. Conversely, if racial criteria played no part in the identification of class patterns, then South African society and the arguments about it would have taken very different forms from those they currently do."[15] Substitute the United States for South Africa in this statement, and it retains its full persuasiveness.

A major part of my task has been to explain the variations that I found in the specific ways that white power-cum-prejudice manifested itself in the face of comparable challenges or opportunities. No preconceived formula or "model" could be advanced that would do justice to the complex patterns of causation involved. But certain crucial variables recur, and a brief general description of these factors will help set the stage for the main body of the work.

One key variable is of course demography. The ratio of white settler to indigenous nonwhite population is such an obvious and enormously significant difference between the American and South African situations as they developed historically that it can never be disregarded. The fact that nonwhites are the overwhelming majority in contemporary South Africa but a relatively small minority in the United States distinguishes the two cases in such a radical way that it might even be thought to obviate useful comparison. Indeed, I eventually came to the conclusion that a straightforward contrast of race relations in the United States and South Africa in the 1960s and 70s would risk belaboring the obvious, and the reader will thus not find such a juxtaposition in the pages that follow. But it took between 200 and 250 years for South African whites to conquer the mass of indigenous Africans within the borders of the contemporary republic, and even after that time a substantial if diminishing proportion of the black population remained in "reserves" as subsistence farmers who were in some ways outside the white social and economic system. Hence there have been many times and places in South African history where the ratio of white to nonwhite in the areas under direct European rule was not so different from that in parts of the United States, particularly the Deep South. By limiting most of my comparisons to such situations, I have prevented sheer demography from controlling my analysis, but I have nevertheless had to take it into account at several points.

A second variable that exerted an influence on the nature of race or class relationships (and also affected the demographic situation) is the physical or geographical environment and the possibilities that it has offered for economic development. In contrast to North America, South Africa presented white settlers with only a very limited and specialized opportunity for the accumulation of wealth and exploitation of natural resources. About one-sixth the size of the United States, South Africa is a naturally poor country in terms of its agricultural potential: 86 percent of the land is arid or semi-arid, and only one third receives the twenty-five inches of rain necessary for the cultivation of most crops.[16] It therefore closely resembles the United States west of the hundredth meridian—which of course leaves out the corn belt and the cotton kingdom. Lacking the extensive, rich, and well-watered farming areas of the eastern United States, South Africa's white economy and population developed at a very slow rate during the first two centuries or so of settlement, a time when the United States was undergoing the rapid increase in wealth and population that would eventually make it the richest country in the world in terms of per capita wealth and the most populous of all the "new societies" resulting from the expansion of Europe.

Another physiographic barrier to South African economic development was its lack of the kind of natural transportation system that provided a stimulus for commerce and the growth of a market economy in the United States before the advent of the railroad. It may be difficult for an American to imagine, but South Africa does not have a single navigable river or arterial lake. Furthermore, the country in many areas is criss-crossed with mountain ranges or escarpments with few natural passes. Before the mineral revolution of the 1870s and 80s, therefore, white South Africa was perhaps the least promising and most economically retarded of the settler societies of northern European origin, whereas the United States was the one that was developing most rapidly. Geography was not the only cause of this contrast, but it was surely the most important. As we will see, the early phases of race relations in the two societies were significantly affected by these differing natural environments.

The rapid industrial development of South Africa since the late nineteenth century has been due almost exclusively to the exploitation of its rich mineral resources, especially gold. Were it not the world's largest supplier of this vital and precious commodity, the contemporary republic would not be able to sustain such a large and prosperous white population and might well have reverted to African rule as the rest of Africa decolonized. For our purposes, the primacy of gold is important mainly because of the peculiar conditions under which labor was recruited and utilized in the mines. The emergence of an industrial staple economy dependent on a cheap and regimented non-white labor force had implications for modern phases of race relations that can profitably be contrasted with the effects of the more extensive and less labor-repressive forms of industrial activity that could arise in a physical environment offering more varied opportunities for economic development.

A third basic source of difference or variability might be described very broadly as the semi-autonomous realm of government and politics. During the long periods when English North America and white South Africa were the dependencies of a European metropole, the degree of self-government possessed by colonial slaveholders, or by white settlers who wanted a free hand to deal with the "natives," helped determine the extent to which local prejudices and exploitative interests could be given legal sanction and allowed to shape public policy. Furthermore, political conflicts among whites—leading to struggles for autonomy or independence by elements of the white population which felt oppressed by an external authority—differed in nature or outcome in ways that had serious consequences for the future of racial policy. Hence the major political crises associated with the rise of new nationalisms and new white nations—the American Revolution, the Great Trek, the American Civil War, and the two Anglo-Boer wars—have to be viewed to some extent as historical contingencies that had a significant impact on the role and status of nonwhites (although, as we shall see, they themselves were influenced by pre-existing interests and ideologies associated with racial dominance). These critical episodes in the emergence of white settler states helped establish the parameters of nationhood and citizenship in ways that could encourage or impede the full legitimation of white supremacy. I have found it of considerable long-term significance that both the struggle for American independence and the northern cause in the Civil War were ideologically conditioned by universalistic conceptions of human freedom and equality, whereas the Afrikaner struggle for nationhood that came to ultimate fruition in the contemporary Republic of South Africa was inspired in the main by a highly particularistic sense of ethnic identity and exclusiveness.

What I conceive to be the possible value or usefulness of this study can be summed up very briefly. First of all, I will be gratified if I have provided some raw material and new insights for scholars of comparative race relations who seek a better theoretical understanding of the processes that lead to racial or ethnic stratification. But my main concern has been to shed light on the historical development of white supremacy in two very significant places—the United States and South Africa—and I have not attempted to generalize my findings beyond these two societies. I began mainly with the object of increasing my understanding of American history by looking at it from a new perspective. To some extent, I believe that this expectation has been fulfilled. But my interest in understanding South African developments took on a life of its own, and I pursued it as I would a second field of specialization. As a result, I am bold enough to think that I have made a contribution to the historical interpretation of race relations in that society as well. I hope that neither side of the comparison will look quite the same, even to experts on the history of race relations in the United States and South Africa, after each case has been viewed in terms of the other.

Finally, I hope to reach an audience beyond social scientists and scholars or students of American and South African history because of the obvious relevance of this work to vital contemporary concerns. Although certain kinds of progress have been made in recent years toward resolving the inequalities that have long existed between whites and blacks in the United States, many serious problems remain, and this work may suggest some new ways of looking at their historical roots. It has also become essential for Americans and other outsiders to acquire a deeper understanding of the volatile and potentially tragic situation that now exists in South Africa. Although I do not attempt to analyze contemporary South African race relations in any comprehensive way or to engage in the risky business of predicting the future of that troubled society, I hope that general readers concerned with the problem of apartheid and the prospects for change in southern Africa will find in this book some of the historical background they need to understand and evaluate recent developments. For Americans, it ought to be especially illuminating to view South African issues through the lens of their own inter-racial experiences. The long perspective of three hundred years of rising white supremacy can of course lead to resignation or pessimism, and those hoping for an easy or quick resolution of the racial problems of South Africa will find little comfort in the pages that follow. But the historical record is above all a record of change and human adaptability to new circumstances, and if things can change for the worse—as has been the principal experience of nonwhites in South Africa—they can also change for the better, as shown by the recent successes of the Afro-American struggle for basic civil rights. Because of the fundamental differences in the two situations, it is doubtful that the Afro-American example provides a direct model for black liberation from apartheid; but it strongly suggests, at the very least, that human beings who struggle valiantly and persistently for freedom and equality cannot forever be denied.

WHITE SUPREMACY

I

Settlement and Subjugation, 1600-1840

Two Frontiers

In May of 1607, three small ships sailed up the James River from Chesapeake Bay in search of a site for the first permanent English colony in North America. The prospective settlers chose a peninsula that had the clear disadvantage of being low and swampy. But it did provide good anchorage, and the fact that it was a virtual island made it defensible against possible attacks by hostile Indians. By giving a high priority to their physical security, the colonizers showed an awareness that this was not an empty land but one that was already occupied by another people who might well resist their incursion. Unlike earlier attempted settlements, Jamestown was not so much an outpost as a beachhead for the English invasion and conquest of what was to become the United States of America.

Forty-five years later, another three ships, flying the flags of the Dutch Republic and its East India Company, anchored in Table Bay at the Cape of Good Hope. Their purpose was to establish a refreshment station where ships could break the long voyage between the Netherlands and the Company's main settlement at Batavia in Java. The expedition of 1652 was under the command of Jan van Riebeeck, who was instructed to build a fort, plant a garden that would provide fresh fruit and vegetables for the scurvy-ridden sailors, and obtain meat through an amicable cattle trade with the local indigenes—the yellowish-skinned herders known to the Europeans as "Hottentots." By carrying out these orders, Van Riebeeck unwittingly initiated the train of events that would result in the emergence and expansion of a white-dominated society in southern Africa.

From the perspective of the seventeenth century, these occurrences were simply two examples among many of the early penetration by Europeans into Africa, Asia, and the Americas. But for the modern historian of comparative colonization, they have the special significance that they constituted the beginnings of two of the first "white settler societies" emanating from northern Europe. Unlike the tropical "exploitation colonies" being established by the Dutch, the English, and the French in the East and West Indies, both the Cape of Good Hope and the regions claimed by the English on the eastern coast of North America were temperate in climate and potentially attractive to white colonists as permanent homes rather than uncomfortable and unhealthful places where fortunes could be made and then brought back to Europe. Furthermore, the indigenous populations, at least those encountered in the early stages of settlement, lacked the population density and the developed forms of political and economic organization that were to preserve most Asian and African societies from large-scale European settlement. Since these regions also lacked the readily available mineral resources that stimulated Spanish colonization of South and Central America, as well as the opportunities for lucrative trade in scarce commodities that existed in the East, land for agriculture and grazing quickly became the source of wealth or sustenance most desired by the European invaders. The struggle with the original occupants for possession of the land constituted the essential matrix for a phase of race relations that began when the first colonists disembarked and persisted along a moving frontier until late in the nineteenth century.

The basis for our first comparison, therefore, is the common fact of a long and often violent struggle for territorial supremacy between white invaders and indigenous peoples. Starting from the small coastal settlements of the seventeenth century, the whites penetrated into the interior of North America and southern Africa; by the end of the nineteenth century they had successfully expropriated most of the land for their own use by extinguishing the communal title of premodern native societies and transforming the soil into private property within a capitalistic economy. The indigenes were left with collective ownership of only a small fraction of their former domain in the form of special reserves. Divesting the original inhabitants of their land was essential to the material success of these settler societies. In the American case, it made available the land and resources for the economic development of what was to become the world's richest nation. In South Africa, it made possible the establishment of white minority rule over an African majority, provided access to minerals on which to base an industrial revolution, and by denying Africans the right to own land outside their over-crowded reserves insured a supply of exploitable labor for the white economy. But the purpose of this chapter is not to trace the full course of frontier expansion in the two societies or to assess the final results. The aim rather is to compare what occurred up to about 1840 as a way of establishing part of the context and demonstrating one of the preconditions for the patterns of racial dominance that had emerged by that time. Hence the story will be left at a point when the fate of the American Indian was essentially predetermined, while that of the indigenous population of much of what is now the Republic of South Africa was still unresolved, even in the minds of the white invaders.

The early struggle for control of the land was part of the competition for scarce resources that sociologists have seen as a major component in the emergence of "ethnic stratification."[1] Land hunger and territorial ambition gave to whites a practical incentive to differentiate between the basic rights and privileges they claimed for themselves and what they considered to be just treatment for the "savages" who stood in their path, and in the end they mustered the power to impose their will. But the process of stripping the indigenes of their patrimony and reducing them to subservience or marginality was, from the historian's perspective, a complex and uneven one that cannot be fully appreciated in teleological terms, or merely by looking at the final outcome as the predetermined result of white attitudes, motivations, and advantages. Not only did the indigenous peoples put up a stiff resistance that at times seemed capable of stalling the white advance indefinitely, but the lack of a firm consensus of interests and attitudes within the invading community, or between the actual settlers and the agents of a metropole or mother country, could lead to internal disagreements concerning the character and pace of expansion and even on whether it should continue at all. Ultimate white hegemony may have been virtually inevitable, especially in the American case, but this outcome was less clear to the historical actors than to future generations.

To help provide the frame for an analysis, it may be useful to distinguish between five kinds of white perspectives on the "native frontier." First in time but least in long-range historical importance was the point of view of those Europeans whose primary interest was trade. Whether the trade was in furs and skins, as in English North America, or in cattle and ivory, as in South Africa, it was clear that the traders *per se* had no incentive for dispossessing or enslaving their indigenous partners. The expansion of white farming communities and the destruction of native economies and societies was in fact directly contrary to their own economic interests. In the end, however, the traders not only lacked the power to stop the extension of settlement but unwittingly contributed to it by inducing the indigenes to exhaust the animal resources on which the commercial relationship depended.

A second and much more significant perspective was that of the frontier farmers themselves, who invariably wanted access to land still occupied by indigenous peoples and hoped for the rapid extinction of native title by any means necessary. A third point of view was that of the responsible political authorities, whether they represented a chartered company, direct imperial rule, a self-governing colony, or an independent republic. As we shall see, governments could vary greatly in their responsiveness to frontier opinion, depending to a great extent on how democratic or representative they were. But all of them had some stake in regulating contacts between settlers and indigenes in order to prevent unnecessary wars that could represent a substantial and even disastrous drain on the public purse. Hence they sometimes found themselves at odds with the frontiersmen on the issue of whether, when, and how further expansion should take place. Fourthly, there were the special concerns of missionaries and the religious and philanthropic groups that supported their work. The paramount interest of missionaries was of course the conversion and "civilization" of the indigenes. This objective could lead them to favor a protective insulation of indigenous societies from the usual kind of frontier pressures and incursions so that their "civilizing" efforts could be carried on without the demoralization they characteristically associated with encroachment by unscrupulous traders or land-hungry settlers.* When

---

* They did not, of course, normally favor the retention of full independence for the people among whom they labored; generally they welcomed the support and security provided by the extension or clarification of some form of white sovereignty or political dominance.

a certain state of economic development was reached in areas already settled, the possibility arose of a fifth perspective, that of large-scale entrepreneurs with an interest in land speculation and the control of natural resources for capitalistic accumulation.

An awareness of the interaction and relative strength of these perspectives—representing the diverse and sometimes divergent aims of trade, agrarian expansion, order, conversion, and capitalistic economic development—can help provide an understanding of the comparative dynamics of white expansion in North America and South Africa; provided, of course, that one also recognizes that the character and strength of the indigenous peoples was an autonomous force to which ambitions of all white elements or interests had to adjust themselves.

The Image of the Savage

Whatever their practical intentions or purposes, the invaders did not confront the native peoples without certain preconceptions about their nature that helped shape the way they pursued their goals. Conceptions of "savagery" that developed in the sixteenth and seventeenth centuries and became the common property of Western European culture constituted a distorting lens through which the early colonists assessed the potential and predicted the fate of the non-European peoples they encountered. Circumstances did not always allow them to act in accordance with these beliefs, nor were the ideas and images so fixed and unambiguous that they could not be modified by practical experience. But they did establish a mode of thinking about cultural and racial differences that helped set the parameters of white response. These beliefs were not yet racist in the nineteenth-century sense of the term because they were not based on an explicit doctrine of genetic or biological inequality; but they could provide an equivalent basis for considering some categories of human beings inferior to others in ways that made it legitimate to treat them differently from Europeans. Most significantly for our present purposes, this body of thought suggested some rationalizations for conquering or dispossessing precisely the kind of peoples who inhabited eastern North America and the extreme southern part of Africa at the time when the first white settlers arrived.

There were two crucial distinctions which allowed Europeans of the Renaissance and Reformation period to divide the human race into superior and inferior categories. One was between Christian and

heathen and the other between "civil" and "savage." The first reflected
the religious militancy nurtured by the long and bitter struggle for
supremacy in the Mediterranean between Christian and Islamic civilizations. The Crusades had applied the principle that a war conducted
in the name of the Church against infidels was *ipso facto* a just war.
In the fifteenth century, when Spain and Portugal were in the fore-
front of Christian resistance to Islamic power, the Pope authorized the
enslavement and seizures of lands and property of "all saracens and
pagans whatsoever, and all other enemies of Christ wheresoever
placed."[2] This harsh and unrelenting attitude toward "the enemies of
Christ" was carried by the Spanish and Portuguese empire-builders of
the sixteenth century to the New World and parts of Africa and
Southeast Asia. But it was not entirely clear that sanctions for the enslavement and dispossession of pagans applied automatically to those
heathens who, unlike the Mediterranean Muslims, were not seen as a
direct threat to Christendom. Among the Spanish there was a prolonged debate on the question of whether or not force was justified to
bring about the subjugation and conversion of the American Indians.
In 1537, Pope Paul III seemed to settle the question when he issued his
famous bull proclaiming that "The said Indians and all other people
who may later be discovered by Christians, are by no means to be deprived of their liberty and possession of their property, even though
they may be outside the faith of Jesus Christ . . . nor should they be
in any way enslaved." The Pope here made an implicit distinction between the traditional and seemingly incorrigible enemies of Christendom who were still subject to dispossession and enslavement and the
new heathen peoples "discovered" by Europeans who were considered
susceptible to peaceful persuasion because they were not "dumb brutes
created for our service," but "truly men . . . , capable of understanding the Catholic faith."[3] Hence the official position of the Catholic
church in the sixteenth century supported the view of the foremost
Spanish champion of Indian rights, the Dominican friar Bartolomé
de las Casas, who also held that the crusading anti-Islamic precedent
did not apply to American Indians and other indigenous peoples who
were being exposed to Christians and Christianity for the first time.

However this viewpoint not only failed to accord with the actual
practices of the conquistadors but was strongly challenged on intellectual grounds. In his famous debate with Las Casas at Valladolid in
1550–51, the great Spanish jurist Juan Ginés de Sepúlveda invoked

Aristotle's doctrine that some people are "natural slaves" to justify the conquest and domination of the Indians by the Spanish. In the words of Lewis Hanke, the historian of this debate, Sepúlveda found slavery to be the natural condition of "persons of both inborn rudeness and of inhuman and barbarous customs." He argued that civilized men are the "natural lords" of such savages, and that if the latter "refuse this overlordship, they may be forced to obey by arms and may be warred against as justly as one would hunt down wild beasts." The judges of the debate apparently reached no decision, and Sepúlveda's doctrine did not receive the formal approbation of the Spanish Crown. Indeed, Hanke contends, it was Las Casas' policy of peaceful persuasion that remained the official one, even if its enforcement was often half-hearted and ineffectual. But Sepúlveda helped establish a precedent for going beyond the simple Christian-heathen dichotomy by appealing to classical antiquity for justifications of European domination over "savage" peoples.[4]

It is not surprising that the Renaissance, which saw the revival of classical learning in Europe, should also witness an effort to understand the nature of new-found peoples in terms of classical precedents. The Greeks had judged men by the degree of their civility and had proclaimed themselves superior to "barbarians." Although Aristotle had maintained that even barbarians were social beings, Europeans had believed since the Middle Ages that some men were so wild and uncouth that they wandered in the forests and had no society of any kind. This category of ultra-barbarians, or pure savages, who allegedly lived more like beasts than men, seemed to many Europeans of the sixteenth and seventeenth centuries appropriate for peoples like the Cape "Hottentots" or the North American, Caribbean, and Brazilian Indians, who were commonly thought to be wilderness nomads utterly devoid of religion or culture.[5]

The Christian-heathen and civil-savage dichotomies were not necessarily identical; for it was quite possible to be civilized without being Christian. The ancient Greeks were of course the prime example, but it was also widely conceded that the representatives of the complex and urbanized societies of the Far East or even of some Islamic nations must be regarded as at least semi-civilized or as higher types of barbarians who were clearly distinguishable from unimproved savages. What most commonly differentiated civilized or semi-civilized human beings from savages was that they practiced sedentary agriculture, had political forms that Europeans recognized as regular governments, and lived to some extent in urban concentrations. If all heathens were not savages, the obverse of this—that all savages were not heathens—was clearly untenable. The axiom that Christians were necessarily civilized was related to a popular explanation for the origins of cultural diversity. Civility, it was widely believed, was the original state of mankind. But after the dispersal of the progeny of Noah after the flood some branches of the human race had in the course of their wanderings lost their awareness of God and degenerated into an uncivil state. Sometimes this descent into barbarism and savagery was linked directly to the curse on Ham, which would later be used to justify African slavery. Johan Boemus, a German Hebraic scholar, argued as early as 1521 that all barbarous peoples descended from Ham, while all civilized men were the issue of Shem and Japheth.[6]

The notion that degeneration into savagery was the result of an inherited curse that God had placed on at least some non-European or nonwhite peoples may be placed alongside Sepúlveda's association of natural slavery with "inborn rudeness" and "barbarous customs" as an early anticipation of the racist doctrines that would later emerge as a justification for slavery and colonialism. But such views could rarely be followed to their logical outcome in the sixteenth and seventeenth centuries because of the strong countervailing force of the Christian belief in the essential unity of mankind. Margaret Hodgen sums up the orthodox view in her study of early anthropology: "Doctrinally, savages were men, first, last, and always—bestial and degenerate in their behavior, perhaps, but still men and thus children of God."[7] The necessary corollary was that they could be converted to Christianity and hence raised to a civilized status. Nevertheless, as Hodgen also shows, the Renaissance was a time of intellectual ferment in which many traditional and orthodox ideas were beginning to be questioned— and among these was the doctrine of the unity of mankind. There were even some tentative suggestions of a polygenetic or pluralistic theory of the origins of human diversity. Heretical speculations that only civilized men were descendents of Adam and that "savage" peoples had been separately created were closely associated with efforts to find a niche for the savage below civilized human beings on the elaborately graded hierarchy known as the "great chain of being," a traditional device for ranking all forms of life inherited from the Middle Ages. But the case for assigning a fixed place to the savage as a permanently distinct and inferior species of humanity was not systematically made until Dr. William Petty of the English Royal Society attempted to do so in an unpublished paper of 1676–77; and its religious heterodoxy would preclude the widespread acceptance of such a mode of thinking about the "types of mankind" until the nineteenth century.[8]

On a more popular level, the medieval belief in the existence of sub-human "wild men" or monsters influenced Europeans' perceptions of the savages they encountered or expected to encounter in remote parts of the world. The literature of sixteenth- and seventeenth-century exploration and travel is filled with comments likening American Indians, Eskimos, or "Hottentots" to wild beasts. In 1586, the English explorer Thomas Cavendish described some Brazilian Indians as being "as wild as ever was a buck or any other wild beast."[9] As sophisticated an Englishman as Sir Walter Raleigh was credulous enough to believe that there were natives in Guiana who "have their eyes in their shoulders, and their mouths in the middle of their breasts."[10] Because of their use of click sounds as part of their language, a general impression existed that the "Hottentots" of the Cape were so bestial that they lacked the ordinary power of human speech.[11] Whatever the conventional religious doctrine may have been, such accounts of creatures who seemed more animal than human must have raised doubts in the minds of many Europeans as to whether they really shared "one blood" and a common ancestry with many of the types of men being brought to their attention by the explorers and travelers of the late Renaissance.

A more benign image—which was also religiously unorthodox—anticipated in some ways the eighteenth-century conception of the noble savage. Some explorers described American Indians in particular as living in a natural innocence equivalent to that of Eden before the fall. The idealization of Indians as exemplars of the natural virtues that Europeans had lost because of the corrupting effect of civilization was given its classic statement by Montaigne in his famous essay "Of Cannibals," originally published in 1580. "It seems to me," he wrote after hearing a description of Indian society in Brazil, "that what we actually see in these nations surpasses not only all the pictures in which poets have idealized the golden age and all their inventions in imagining a happy state of man, but also the conception and the very desire of philosophy."[12] But the proclivity of late-sixteenth-century humanists to idealize the primitive state as a way of criticizing their own civilization had little influence on their immediate successors. According to

J. H. Elliott's account of European opinion in the age of the Counter-Reformation and the Thirty Years' War, "A Europe newly convinced of the innate sinfulness of man, and increasingly conscious of the need for a powerful state organization to restrain the forces of disorder, had little inclination to idealize the virtues of primitive societies."[13] By the time that Virginia and the Cape of Good Hope began to be colonized, therefore, any tendency to appreciate savage society as a viable or even superior alternative to European ways of living was on the wane, and cultural and religious intolerance was clearly in the ascendancy.

If the religious intensity of the seventeenth century tended to give renewed significance to the Christian-heathen dichotomy, it did so in a way that also incorporated the full differentiating power of the civil-savage distinction, especially in colonial situations where the indigenous people were regarded as simultaneously heathen and savage. There was no possibility of tolerating, except as a matter of expediency, the way the indigenes lived; the only issue was whether they could be rescued from their degenerate state by the power of the gospel or whether they were too perverse and bestial—too far gone in their savage ways—to be worthy of sustained efforts to make them civilized Christians.

The official and orthodox view seemed, on the surface at least, to be clear and unequivocal: the Christianization and civilization of native peoples, however "wild" and savage they might be, was not only deemed possible but was enjoined on colonizers as a positive duty. In Letters Patent establishing the Virginia companies of London and Plymouth in 1606, the King endorsed a plan of colonization "which may, by the Providence of Almighty God, hereafter tend to the Glory of His divine Majesty, in propagating of Christian Religion to such people, as yet live in darkness and miserable ignorance of the true knowledge and worship of God, and may in time bring the Infidels and Savages living in these parts, to human civility and to a settled and quiet Government."[14] Despite the very limited purpose of its settlement at the Cape of Good Hope, the Dutch East India Company pressed its representatives to show a similar spirit, and in his opening prayer at the first meeting of a Council of Policy at Cape Town in 1652, Jan van Riebeeck prayed for "the propagation and extension (if that be possible) of Thy true Reformed Christian religion among these wild and brutal men."[15]

In light of the limited scope and ultimate failure of early missionary endeavors, it is important to note the suggestion of tentativeness in these statements. Propagation of the gospel "may" bring the savages to civility; wild men are to be converted "if that be possible." There was apparently an undercurrent of doubt about whether such "ignorant" and "brutal" creatures were really suitable material for Christianization. The essential attitude was experimental. The effort should be made, the early colonizers seemed to be saying; but if it failed, if the indigenes proved hostile to the extension of the gospel among them, then well-established precedents for dealing with incorrigible heathens and savages could be invoked to sanction their forced subjugation.

Rehearsals: Ireland and Indonesia

Holy wars against the heathen, involving the enslavement of captives, the confiscation of property, and even the slaughter of noncombatants, had sometimes been justified in the medieval and early Renaissance periods as necessary for the defense or propagation of the One True Faith. But the Reformation of the sixteenth century resulted in the fragmentation of Christendom and, on the Protestant side of the great divide, encouraged the marriage of various "purified" versions of Christianity with the ambitions of particular nation-states. As religion became an expression of nationalism, the history of a unified Christianity threatened by Islam became less relevant as a source of precedent for dealing with culturally alien peoples and civilizations; more to the point were prior experiences of national expansionism or empire-building associated with ethnic pride and assertiveness. A combination of the new nationalism and the new religious particularism could lead to an even greater intolerance of cultural diversity than had the universalistic Catholic tradition; but it could also be more pragmatic, particularly when palpable political and economic interests were involved. Since this was also the age of mercantilist capitalism, it was understood in emerging powers like England and the Netherlands that national prosperity, national security, and the defense of an established reformed religion were indissolubly linked. Makers of policy could not ignore this interdependence; they could not, for example, authorize religious crusades that might endanger vital political or economic interests. But when patriotism, religious conviction, and the pursuit of economic ad-

vantage all seemed to dictate aggression against peoples of alien cultural traditions, actions of extreme ruthlessness and inhumanity could
readily result.

The prior national experiences that did most to set the guidelines,
precedents, and expectations that influenced early "native policy" in
North America and South Africa were earlier expansionist efforts—
namely the English attempt in the reign of Elizabeth I to subjugate
Celtic Ireland and the establishment in the early seventeenth century
of a Dutch seaborne empire in the East Indies. These endeavors not
only reflected the growth of an enterprising spirit that was bound to
seek new outlets but led in a rather direct way to the settlement of
Virginia and the Cape. The continuity is clearest in the South African
case because the Cape settlement was intended as a complementary
appendage to an East Indian trading empire. But, as recent historians
have discovered, English plans for colonization were first tried out in
Ireland, and what happened there had an important shaping effect on
the later effort on the other side of the Atlantic.[16] Since the Irish and
Indonesian experiences were very different in their objectives and
methods, they tended to produce divergent ideologies of colonization.
The resulting contrast helps to explain why, despite the existence of a
common body of preconceptions about "savages," there were initial
differences in governing ideas about the role that the indigenous population would play in achieving the purposes of the colonizers, differences that had at least a temporary effect on the pattern of race relations in these two areas of settlement.

The English claim to sovereignty over Ireland dated from the
Norman conquest of the eleventh and twelfth centuries; but the only
area where they exercised real control in the mid-sixteenth century was
the "Pale," which included only Dublin and its immediate vicinity. In
1565, the government proclaimed its intention to bring all of Ireland
under effective English rule. Following the general pattern of Elizabethan expansionism, this task was not undertaken directly by the
Crown and its own troops but was consigned to private individuals
who were licensed to conquer and colonize for their own profit as well
as for the good of the realm. Between 1565 and 1576 a series of colonization enterprises were organized and promoted, involving many of
the same West Country gentlemen who were to be leading figures in
the earliest projects for English settlement in North America. What
distinguished Elizabethan efforts to conquer Ireland from earlier inva-

sions was that the objective was not so much to establish English lords over Irish peasants but, in some places at least, to replace them with British colonists. The rationale for expropriating their land and removing them from it was that the Celtic Irish were savages, so wild and rebellious that they could only be controlled by a constant and ruthless exercise of brute force.[17]

The application of the concept of savagery to the Celtic Irish may strike a modern reader as very peculiar, since they were both white and Christian. But in the sixteenth century savagery was not yet strongly associated with pigmentation or physical type and hence was not a "racial" concept in the modern sense. Except in the case of black Africans, whose color did impress itself with some force on European observers, the darker pigmentation of non-European peoples in the Americas, Asia, and the portions of Africa inhabited by non-Negroid populations was not usually given great weight as a differentiating characteristic by European observers of the sixteenth and seventeenth centuries. In fact, they tended to attribute brown skin to the temporary effects of the sun or to customs of greasing or oiling the body. More significant in their eyes were such cultural characteristics as nomadism, "idolatry," and rude or minimal forms of clothing, shelter, government, and economic activity.[18]

Since the Irish beyond the Pale lived in what the English regarded as a primitive fashion, often retained a tribal form of political and social organization, and engaged in the semi-nomadic practice of transhumance (seasonal migration between higher and lower pastures), there was no great difficulty in classifying their way of life as savage or barbarous. But the question of their religion was not so easily disposed of. The propaganda mills of the English colonizers worked overtime to prove that the apparent Christianity of the Irish was a superficial veneer and that they were really pagans. Once the Irish had been categorized as savage heathen, their resistance to the expansion of English control could be countered in the most brutal forms imaginable. The late sixteenth- and early seventeenth-century colonization projects were accompanied by virtually every kind of atrocity that would ever be perpetrated against American Indians—women and children were massacred, captured rebels were executed or enslaved, and whole communities were uprooted and consigned to special reservations. Such conduct was justified on the grounds that it was required for "the suppressing and reforming of the loose, barbarous and most wicked life of that savage nation." Those who condemned the severity of English conduct were answered by claims that the Irish chose to "live like beasts, voide of lawe and all good order," and were indeed "more uncivill, more uncleanly, more barbarous and more brutish in their customs and demeanures, than in any other part of the world that is known."[19]

In 1609, two years after the first colonists arrived in Virginia, King James I proclaimed a land settlement for Ulster, recently the scene of a prolonged and genocidal war of conquest, that bears an almost uncanny resemblance to later divisions of land and population between English settlers and American Indians. Four fifths of the six counties of Northern Ireland were set aside for the exclusive occupancy of English or Scottish settlers; the native Irish were either driven out of Ulster or concentrated in the residual one fifth—a series of small reservations which they were forbidden to leave on penalty of death.[20]

What was so striking about English activity in Ireland on the eve of American colonization was not only the calculated denigration and brutal treatment of the indigenous population, but also the assumptions behind the recruitment of English colonists and the displacement of Irish peasants. Mere political hegemony and the imposition of an English ruling class was not enough. Proponents of colonization seemed to be saying that nothing could be made of the country unless fully elaborated English communities were planted there. The remote cultural sources of this predilection for a literal extension of England are obscure; it may conceivably be rooted in a long history of expansion within Britain itself which apparently resulted less in the assimilation of such Celtic peoples as the Welsh and the Highland Scots than in their encapsulation in remote and mountainous regions not coveted by English cultivators or their lords.[21] The immediate and practical motives are easier to discern. The colonization of Ireland was one of the early fields of enterprise for the new merchant capitalism that was emerging in England. There were profits to be made from Irish plantations if the right kind of tenants could be found. The natives were indeed rebellious and difficult to control, whereas transplanted Englishmen or lowland Scots were likely to be more docile, willing to cultivate the right staples for export, and capable of being mobilized for defense in case of internal or external attack.[22] A penchant for settler colonization was also encouraged by the growing awareness of a population crisis in England itself. Beginning in the early sixteenth century, a rapid increase of mouths to be fed outran the ability of the economy to provide sustenance and employment—a situation that lasted until the middle of the next century. The result was pauperization, vagabondage, and fear of social upheaval. The notion that an outlet for the surplus of "sturdy beggars" could be found through planting lower-class Englishmen abroad was one motive for early interest in both Irish colonization and American settlement. The sense that there was a plethora of "masterless men" who could be put to good use elsewhere helped to make colonization proposals seem not only feasible but socially therapeutic.[23]

The Irish experience and the impulses behind it foreshadowed in some ways the ideology and practice of English colonization in North America, especially in Virginia. The main presumption that persisted was that the most profitable and useful form of colonization involved more or less self-sufficient communities of Englishmen. The treatment of indigenous peoples would depend on whether they helped the settlers by conceding land and providing labor or, like the "wild Irish," resisted encroachment. If the latter, then the image of the incorrigible savage could be invoked to justify policies of extermination or confinement to reservations on land not yet coveted by the English.

Early Dutch colonization inevitably had a different character and meaning. In contrast to England, with its long tradition of nationhood and expansionism, the Dutch Republic had just come into existence in the late sixteenth century as a loose federation of provinces in revolt against the Spanish Crown; it did not in fact win full and final recognition of its independence until the treaty of Münster in 1648. Judged by the standards of ethnic nationalism, the republic that emerged was only half a nation, because the southern Low Countries, which differed scarcely at all from the northern provinces in language and customs, remained under Spanish domination. But the triumph of Protestantism in the United Provinces and the successful Spanish defense of Counter-Reformation Catholicism in what is now Belgium fixed the permanent limits of Dutch nationality.[24] Since it had recently escaped from external domination itself and was still insecure in its independence, the truncated Dutch Republic of the early seventeenth century might have seemed an unlikely base for a new imperialism. It is in fact somewhat misleading to talk about Dutch overseas activity as if it were the same kind of phenomenon as British expansionism. The Dutch had neither the ideological proclivity nor the population surplus to establish genuine settler colonies outside their own shores. The notion of a literal "expansion of the Netherlands" thus seems absurd in a way that the expansion of England does not. What led the Dutch into overseas ventures was the prospect for lucrative trade, particularly at the expense of Spain and other Catholic powers that persisted in threatening their autonomy. Substantial territorial possessions and more Dutch colonists than were needed for the transaction of business were not regarded as desirable ends in themselves and were authorized only when they seemed necessary for the success of a commercial enterprise.[25]

From the beginning of their period of international power and influence, the Dutch excelled as middlemen rather than as colonizers. The foundation of the Dutch prosperity of the sixteenth century was their control of the carrying trade from the Baltic to western and southern Europe; but toward the end of the century they began to expand into the Mediterranean, the Levant, the South Atlantic, and finally the Indian Ocean. Since Portugal was then under the Spanish Crown, efforts to displace the Portuguese as the carriers of spice from the Far East to Europe by the Cape route could be justified on the grounds of patriotism and religion. But the main impulse for trading with the East Indies was clearly the expectation of huge profits. A number of small companies were organized at the very end of the sixteenth century to finance voyages to the East; but the competition between them threatened the profitability of the trade, and pressure from the Dutch government induced them to fuse in 1602 into a single chartered corporation. The new United Dutch East India Company was not only granted a monopoly of Dutch trade east of the Cape of Good Hope but was also authorized to maintain its own military and naval forces and to wage war or make peace within its domain. Thus, as C. R. Boxer has pointed out, it was "virtually a state within a state."[26]

By 1650, the Company had routed the Portuguese and gained a stranglehold on the spice trade. Its actual territorial holdings were modest; they consisted of a few small, spice-producing islands in the Moluccas, a main rendezvous point at Batavia in Java, and trading stations in Malaya, India, and Formosa. Rather than sustaining the expense and trouble of conquering and administering non-European societies, the Company preferred the kind of indirect control that could induce or compel native rulers to grant them a monopoly of trading privileges.[27] Despite their heathenism, some of the Asians with whom the Dutch dealt were treated with a grudging kind of respect. In part, this relatively tolerant attitude was simply good business practice, but there was also some recognition that these peoples were not savages, that their Islamic or Hindu religion, their sedentary way of life, and their complex political and social structures entitled them to be regarded as at least semi-civilized. Within their own limited jurisdictions the Dutch showed little racial prejudice, and their intolerance in matters of religion was directed more at Catholics than at non-Christians. J. H. Parry has summed up the pattern of ethnic relations that existed in the Dutch East Indies in this period: "In social life discrimination against Asiatics as such was unknown either in law or in practice, and mixed marriages were common, though the company discouraged non-Europeans and half-castes from going to Holland. There was sharp discrimination in law against non-Christians. In Batavia the public exercise of any worship except that of the Dutch Reformed Church was forbidden. In practice, despite the protest of the ministers, Hindus, Muslims, and Chinese enjoyed complete freedom of worship immediately outside the walls and—as far as the company was concerned—elsewhere in the Indies."[28] But there was also a darker side to Dutch-Asian relations before 1650; for agents of the Company could be absolutely ruthless when they encountered societies that actively resisted their efforts to monopolize the spice trade. In 1621, they settled accounts with the uncooperative inhabitants of the nutmeg-producing Banda Islands by slaughtering part of the population and deporting the rest. They later impoverished most of the Moluccans by limiting clove production to the single island of Amboyna, thus destroying the economy of the other islands of the group.[29]

The key to understanding both the harsh and the relatively benign sides of Dutch "native policy" in the East is the same. Overriding all other considerations, including those of religion, was the economic interest of a large capitalistic trading enterprise. When they felt that they had to control production as well as marketing, representatives of the Company could engage in conquest and even extirpation. But more often their interests pointed toward economic manipulation of indigenous societies by working through their established rulers; for their aim was control of what these societies produced rather than direct domination of their territories and population. Establishing permanent settler colonies that would be extensions of the Netherlands overseas was not a part of their basic vision. There were discussions from time to time about whether or not more Dutch emigration to the East

should be encouraged, but the directors of the Company were uncertain about the desirability of such a policy and knew that it would be difficult to attract many emigrants in any case. There was unemployment and a good deal of poverty in the seventeenth-century Netherlands but not in such proportions as to encourage ambitious colonization projects. After the Thirty Years' War those Netherlanders who desired to emigrate in order to improve their economic prospects had only to cross the borders into northern German states depopulated by the conflict.[30]

It seems legitimate, therefore, to distinguish an English ethos or ideology of colonization, as reflected in the Irish experience, from a Dutch perspective deriving from the commercial exploitation of the East Indies. In the first case, trade with native peoples was less significant as a motivation than the desire to establish territorial claims and expropriate land. Such ambitions required forceful domination of the natives and repression of their culture, policies that could only be rationalized during this period by loudly proclaiming their abject cultural inferiority as savage heathen. In the second instance, a trading motive was paramount which did not require large-scale conquest of territory and provided some practical incentives for the toleration of cultural diversity and respect for the formal independence of indigenous societies so long as they held up their end of a commercial relationship.

From the broad theoretical perspective recently set forth by Immanuel Wallerstein, this difference can be seen as reflecting the nature and limits of the European "world-system" that emerged in the sixteenth century and was extended in the seventeenth. Ireland, like the Americas, might be regarded as one of those regions that was being directly integrated into a capitalistic "world-economy" as part of the colonized "periphery" or "semi-periphery"—an expanding hinterland for the "core" European states that functioned as a source of essential commodities that could usually be produced most profitably by repressive labor systems. East Asia, on the other hand, remained an "external area"—a separate "world-economy"—with which the main relationship was one of trade in luxuries. In this early stage of the expansion of European capitalism, the "core" nations had neither the power nor the incentive to conquer or colonize major Asian societies and thus directly involve them in the geographical division of labor within their own "system." Among the major European states, Spain and later England

were the most successful practitioners of the kind of direct subjugation and colonization that enlarged the system itself, both on the fringes of Europe and in the Americas. The Portuguese of the sixteenth century and the Dutch of the seventeenth excelled less in conquest and the planting of colonies than in playing the role of middlemen, which they did most successfully by dominating the Indies trade. Although they ended up establishing their own "peripheral" colonial societies, Portugal and the Netherlands did so in an almost accidental way and never manifested the expansionist zeal and territorial ambitions of the Spanish and the English. Their true vocation, as befitted small maritime nations with limited population resources, was international trade and commerce. The Dutch who established the outpost at the Cape of Good Hope (again like the Portuguese who had earlier penetrated Mozambique) initially viewed activity in southern Africa in the context of commercial exploitation of an "external" area rather than as a prelude to the colonization or enlargement of the "periphery." Such a perspective dictated an approach to relations with indigenous peoples that was bound to deviate in some respects from an English policy inspired in part by efforts to conquer and colonize Ireland.[31]

The Dispossession of the Coastal Indians and the Cape Khoikhoi

Although they were influenced by the ethos of Irish colonizationism, the Elizabethan Englishmen who cast covetous eyes on the New World were not at first entirely clear in their own minds about how best to profit from this new sphere of activity and what role the indigenous peoples would play in their enterprises. For some, North America was regarded as a geographical obstacle to be overcome by the finding of a "northwest passage" to the Orient and its precious commodities. Only after the fruitless attempts of Martin Frobisher and John Davis to discover such a passage in the 1570s and 80s did their attention focus on the establishment of settlements in the coastal areas between Canada and Florida that were claimed by England. Colonization of this region would break the Spanish monopoly on the New World and give the English a base from which to counter the expansionism of an arch-rival in the struggle for world power.

The individuals and companies that showed an interest in exploiting this opportunity saw two possible ways to do it. Some of the early promotional literature emphasized trade as the greatest source of potential profit. Entrepreneurs who sought to encourage investment in expeditions designed to establish mercantile relationships with the American Indians envisioned the barter of English woolens for a variety of desirable commodities that indigenous societies might be capable of producing, including perhaps the gold and silver that the Spanish had extracted from Indians elsewhere in the Americas. The trading ambitions of some of the promoters of American development encouraged them to soften the stereotyped image of the bestial savage and to portray the Indians as gentle, tractable, and open to the blandishments of a mutually advantageous commerce.[32] But some of the most influential proponents of colonization saw native society as too primitive and limited in economic capacity to produce what the English wanted. The elder Richard Hakluyt, who, along with his nephew of the same name, was one of the principal spokesmen for expansion to America, wrote a paper for the guidance of Sir Walter Raleigh in 1585 arguing that the development of American resources required the English to "conquer a countrey or province in climate & soil of Italie, Spaine, or the Islands, from whence we receive our Wines and Oiles, and to man it, to plant it, and to keepe it, and to continue the making of Wines and Oiles able to serve England."[33]

This image of an English agricultural colony producing crops that England could not raise at home and was currently forced to import from its enemies was flawed in its notion of what could actually be grown in places like Virginia but prophetic in its anticipation of the principal role that New World colonies would play, or were supposed to play, in the development of a mercantilist empire. In such a scheme, the Indians could serve only two conceivable functions—either they would be exterminated and driven away to make room for an exclusively English agricultural population or they would be converted and "civilized" so that they could become productive workers under English supervision. The elder Hakluyt and his contemporaries clearly anticipated the latter result; the only question in their minds was whether or not it would be necessary to use force to bring the Indians "in subjection and to civilitie."[34] But what if the indigenes proved unwilling or unable to shed their own way of life and adopt that of the English? Then presumably they would suffer the fate of some of the "wild Irish" and have an Ulster-type settlement imposed on them.

The dreams of the Elizabethan promoters came to fruition in the early seventeenth century when a permanent colony was established in

Virginia. Unlike the earlier and abortive settlement of the 1580s on Roanoke Island, the Jamestown colony soon came to be regarded as "a permanent community"—"an extension of England overseas."[35] After the failure of early attempts to find precious minerals, the struggling settlement turned primarily to agriculture carried on by the colonists. The local Indians—a confederation of Algonkian tribes under the paramount chieftainship of Powhatan—were the object of confused and conflicting attitudes and policies during the first fifteen years of settlement. During the early "starving times," the indigenes sometimes offered a model of cooperation by providing food from their own reserves that enabled the colony to survive. But the recipients of their charity manifested an early version of the stereotype of "the Indian giver" by suspecting some ulterior motive or treachery in this generosity. As a cosmopolitan man of the Renaissance who had observed cultural diversity in many parts of the world, Captain John Smith manifested an intelligent and sometimes sympathetic interest in the Indian way of life, but he was also an early advocate and practitioner of the view that the native Americans were inherently untrustworthy and responded better to force and intimidation than to friendly persuasion. Other early spokesmen for the colony deplored the Indians' "gross defection from the true knowledge of God," but conceded that their culture showed the rudiments of a "civilized" existence.[36]

The belief that Indians were potential raw material for assimilation into an English-dominated society was an influential viewpoint in Virginia before 1622, and a process of acculturation actually began that might conceivably have led to a bi-racial community if conflicts of interest had not intervened. Plans were made for Indian conversion and education that went so far as to encourage the adoption of Indian children by white settlers. Indians were permitted to work in white settlements as day laborers, and some Englishmen—in defiance of the law—equipped themselves to be cultural intermediaries by fleeing from the settlement and taking up residence in Indian villages. But the spirit of voluntarism and persuasion that could have made for some form of accommodation was counteracted by a belief that Powhatan was too strong and independent for the safety and security of the colony and that his power must be broken. In 1609, Sir Thomas Gates was dispatched to Virginia as governor with instructions to conquer the Chesapeake area and make the Indian tribes direct tributaries of the English, who could then use essentially feudal precedents to require

chieftains to make annual payments of corn, skins, and other commodities and also submit to labor requisitions. The smallness of the English settlement made this policy difficult to enforce, but it did provide
the stimulus for such coercive and unfriendly actions as the kidnapping of Powhatan's daughter Pocahontas in 1613 as a way of bringing
the paramount chief to tolerate the English presence. Pocahontas' subsequent marriage to the colonist John Rolfe created the basis for an
uneasy peace that lasted until the Indian uprising of 1622.[37]

The vacillation between accommodation and coercion that characterized this earliest phase of Indian-white relations in British North
America was due less to confusion about whether the "savages" were
well-disposed and tractable or naturally hostile and unreliable than to
the actual state of power relationships between the two peoples. The
dominant view was that the Indians, however friendly they might
seem, were not to be trusted. A member of the first expedition up the
river from Jamestown in 1607 showed the power of prejudice to master
direct experience when he wrote that the Indians were "naturally given
to trechery, howbeit we could not finde it in our travell up the river,
but rather a most kind and loving people."[38] Perhaps the fact that Indians had apparently wiped out the earlier English settlement on
Roanoke Island had strengthened the stereotype of savage treachery
that already had a strong hold on the European mind. But so long as
the English lacked the numbers to impose their will directly on the
Indians, they had good reason to deal cautiously and pragmatically
with communities that still had the potential strength and cohesion to
drive them into the sea.* But the "Great Migration" of 1618–23, which
reportedly increased the population of the colony from 400 to 4,500,
altered the balance of power. Furthermore, the simultaneous rise of tobacco cultivation gave the colony an economic foundation in the form
of a profitable staple for export and stimulated rapid territorial expansion at the expense of the Indians.[39] As a result, the earlier acceptance of a limited degree of coexistence and interdependence was
replaced by a growing sense of the Indian as intolerable obstacle to
white ambitions.

The Indians quite naturally viewed the rapid expansion of white

---

* The English were fortunate that Powhatan refrained from making a full-scale
attack on the settlement while he still had the probable advantage. It appears
that he hoped to use an alliance with the whites to extend his own authority over
tribes of the Chesapeake region that remained outside his confederacy.

settlement with alarm. Their own hopes for cooperation and coexistence were being shattered by the encroachment of tobacco farms on their hunting lands and by the increasing arrogance and disrespect manifested by the colonists. Consequently, they struck back in 1622 by attacking the settlements and wiping out about a third of the total population of the colony. But the "massacre" of 1622 turned out to be more disastrous for the Indians than for the colonists; for the colony survived and launched a devastating counterattack on Indian society. Thereafter, all thoughts of "civilizing" the natives and sharing the land with them on some mutually agreeable basis were jettisoned in favor of a naked policy of aggression. According to one colonial spokesman, "Our hands which before were tied with gentlenesse and fair usage are now set at liberty by the treacherous violence of the Sausages [savages]. . . . So that we . . . may now by right of Warre, and law of Nations, invade the Country, and destroy them who sought to destroy us: whereby we shall enjoy their cultivated places. . . . Now their cleared grounds in all their villages . . . shall be inhabited by us, whereas heretofore the grubbing of woods was the greatest labour."[40]

As in parts of Ireland, therefore, the resistance of the indigenous people to English encroachment and domination was countered by policies of extermination and expropriation, and once again the image of the treacherous savage who perversely resisted the benefits of civilization could be invoked to justify genocide and disposession. The events in Virginia were to be recapitulated in most of the other English colonies of North America. An early phase during which the beginning of white agricultural activity was accompanied by trade, mutual assistance, and diplomacy was quickly superseded by a period of accelerated white expansion which threatened the territorial base of the indigenous societies. The fact that land was sometimes acquired by methods that met European standards for legitimate purchase did not alter the destructive nature of the process from the Indian perspective.

The intensely ethnocentric English community that was planted in New England in the 1630s went further and subjected the Indians to a peculiarly harsh disparagement and repression of their culture and way of life. More than other colonists, Puritans were animated by the belief that Indian religion was not simply an unfortunate error of the unenlightened but quite literally worship of the Devil. Hence they believed that they had a God-given duty to stamp it out wherever possible. This repression of ungodliness was not necessarily the same

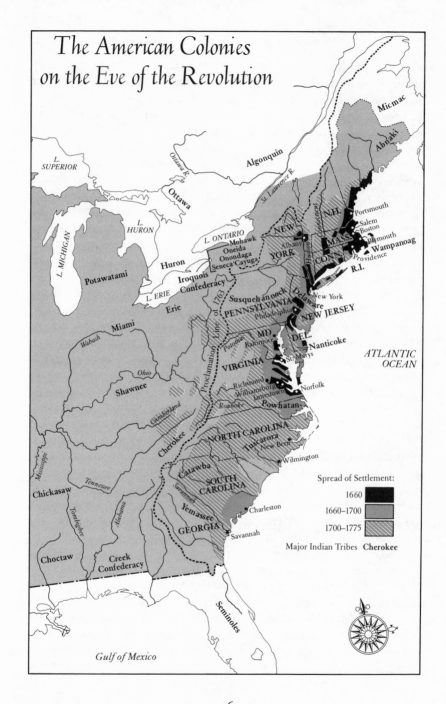

The American Colonies on the Eve of the Revolution

L. SUPERIOR

Ottawa R.

Algonquin

Ottawa

L. MICHIGAN

L. HURON

Micmac

Abnaki

Huron

L. ONTARIO

St. Lawrence R.

Mohawk
Oneida
Onondaga
Seneca Cayuga

N.H.

Portsmouth
Salem
Boston
Plymouth

Iroquois
Confederacy

NEW
YORK

MASS.

CONN.

Wampanoag

Potawatami

L. ERIE

Erie

Hudson

Providence

R.I.

Connecticut

Miami

Susquehannock

Delaware

New York

Wabash

PENNSYLVANIA

Philadelphia

NEW JERSEY

Proclamation Line of 1763

Ohio

MD.

DEL.

Shawnee

Potomac

Baltimore

Nanticoke

ATLANTIC
OCEAN

Cumberland

VIRGINIA

St. Marys

Richmond
Williamsburg Jamestown
Roanoke

Norfolk

Mississippi

Tennessee

Cherokee

Powhatan

NORTH CAROLINA

Tuscarora

New Bern

Chickasaw

Catawba

SOUTH
CAROLINA

Wilmington

Alabama

Savannah

Yemassee

Charleston

Spread of Settlement:

1660

1660–1700

1700–1775

Tombigbee

GEORGIA

Savannah

Choctaw

Creek
Confederacy

Major Indian Tribes **Cherokee**

Seminoles

Gulf of Mexico

thing as evangelization; for as strict Calvinists the Puritans believed that genuine conversion was limited to the elect and the majority of human beings were capable of nothing more than forced submission to the outward forms of Christian behavior. A few Indians might be saved—the Puritans did not believe that God's awful majesty in choosing his elect was limited by a material fact such as physical appearance —but the fate of most who fell under colonial jurisdiction or control was simply to be governed by laws forbidding the heathenish and "sinful" practices that were in fact integral to Indian culture.[41] In other colonies threats to the integrity of the Indians' way of life came less from systematic cultural intolerance than from the ravages of European diseases against which they had no immunity and the demoralizing effect of contact with traders who plied native Americans with alcohol, made them dependent on European trade goods, and induced them to carry on the disastrous practice of extirpating the wildlife within their territories to provide furs and skins for the white market. These epidemiological and economic pressures were not lacking in New England, but at times they were overshadowed by a more direct assault on Indian culture.

As elsewhere, the resistance of the New England Indians to territorial loss and cultural disintegration was severely limited by tribal rivalries that inhibited common action against the invaders; but when Plymouth authorities executed three Wampanoags accused of murdering another Indian in 1675, they touched off an uprising in which four tribes cooperated in a last desperate effort to preserve what remained of their independence and traditional way of life. The Narragansetts and others joined the Wampanoags partly because the Puritans were attempting to enforce laws requiring observance of the Sabbath and prescribing capital punishment for blasphemy. "King Phillip's War" of 1675–76 resulted in the total destruction of twelve New England towns and the death of over a thousand whites, but approximately five thousand Indians were killed, and the ultimate white victory signaled the end of the last vestiges of Indian autonomy in Massachusetts, Connecticut, and Rhode Island.[42] Furthermore, it resulted in the virtual abandonment of a peculiarly Puritan Indian policy that might be described as acculturation without assimilation. Unwilling to absorb Indians directly into their own society, the Puritans had nevertheless felt an obligation to bring the message of reformed Christianity and the discipline of a "civil" existence to as many Indians as possible.

To accomplish this purpose they had organized the Indians directly under their control into fourteeen separate "praying towns" where the gospel was preached and the inhabitants encouraged to imitate the practices of the white colonists. As a result of the stresses of King Phillip's War, most of these villages were disbanded, and the missionary impulse that had brought them into existence waned perceptibly, both because there were so few Indians left to proselytize in the vicinity of the white settlements and because the racial animosities stirred by the conflict encouraged a conviction that all Indians were incorrigible slaves of the Devil whose sole function had been to serve as a vehicle for divine wrath against the backsliding of the colonists.[43]

The general pattern of settler encroachment and increasing friction leading to a major war of extirpation was repeated in North and South Carolina in the early eighteenth century. Here again, the Indians' resistance resulted in the destruction of their societies and the loss of their land.[44] By the 1720s, all the coastal tribes from Massachusetts to South Carolina had either been exterminated by warfare and European diseases, pushed westward, or reduced to more or less detribalized fragments surviving on the fringes of white society.

The story of early indigene-white relations in the Dutch colony at the Cape of Good Hope is a simpler one because of the smaller scale of settlement and the existence of a single native policy dictated by relatively modest territorial ambitions. Any comparison with the American experience requires a recognition that this was, or at least was meant to be, colonization of a different type. While American settlement represented an effort to plant English communities that would produce important commodities for the mother country, the colony at the Cape of Good Hope had no other purpose than to serve as a provisioning station for the ships of the Dutch East India Company. Where the English Crown claimed much of North America by the right of discovery, the Dutch had neither a basis for such claims in southern Africa nor an interest in acquiring more land than they needed for the maintenance and protection of their fort and garden in the shadow of Table Mountain. All the manpower the founders anticipated needing was a relatively small number of company servants and slaves. In 1657 the directors of the Company instructed Commander van Riebeeck to keep the establishment "as confined and . . . small . . . as possible." But in that same year a decision was made that would have unforeseen expansionist consequences. To increase agricultural production to a level that would enable the colony to fulfill its mission, a small number of company servants were freed and allowed to take up land as freehold farmers. Thus a class of free burghers was created that would gradually grow in number as company servants and soldiers fulfilled their terms of service and were induced to remain at the Cape as free colonists.[45]

In accordance with the general policies of the East India Company, the founders of the settlement were enjoined not to conquer or enslave the indigenous inhabitants. The primary relationship was to be one of trade; for the people Europeans called Hottentots—but who are more properly designated as Khoikhoi, the name they gave themselves—had vast herds of cattle and sheep which could be a vital source of fresh meat for the ships that put into Cape Town. The Company's oft-repeated instructions were to treat them with gentleness and forbearance in order to encourage the cattle trade. As we have seen, there were also the usual professions of an intention to convert them to true Christianity, but almost nothing was done along these lines—partly because of a lack of clergymen and partly because there was no practical advantage in it since the Khoikhoi did not have to be Christians to fulfill their role as suppliers of livestock.[46]

The Khoikhoi did not initially regard the Dutch intrusion with alarm because they had a long experience of trading with ships of various European nations that had put into Table Bay in search of fresh provisions. Only gradually did they begin to realize that the Dutch, unlike the earlier visitors, had come to stay and were slowly increasing in numbers and enlarging their land holdings. Tension developed in what might otherwise have been a successful symbiotic relationship when the expansion of white farming began to encroach on Khoikhoi pasture lands. The first Khoikhoi-Dutch war of 1659-60 resulted in part from this expansion and was resolved by a treaty acknowledging white rights to occupancy of the disputed territory. Despite their limited numbers and the low morale and disloyalty of the Company's white servants and imported African and Asian slaves, the Dutch were able to gain a firm foothold by the end of Van Riebeeck's tenure in 1662 because the Khoikhoi in the immediate vicinity of the original settlement were divided into small and loosely organized tribes whose mutual jealousies and animosities could be manipulated by the invaders for their own advantage. Furthermore, their transhumant way of life offered them a relatively painless alternative to direct confrontation with the Dutch; they could simply walk away. Indeed a main source of Dutch grievance in the early years was not the presence of the Khoikhoi but their absence. They were not always available to provide livestock at the right time and in the quantities that the Company desired.[47]

What the Dutch failed to understand was that the Khoikhoi valued their cattle as permanent sources of wealth and status rather than as articles of commerce and were usually willing to part only with their older and less healthy animals. The failure of the neighboring tribes to provide adequate numbers of cattle induced Commander Van Riebeeck to contemplate seizing their herds and enslaving the herdsmen. But the directors of the Company rejected such drastic and inhumane policies, so the governor was compelled to try to establish contact with inland tribes whose larger herds promised a more substantial commerce. At first, Company officials could only gain access to the cattle of the inland Khoikhoi by working through local native intermediaries who were astute enough to limit the supply in order to keep the prices high. Although ways were eventually found to eliminate these middlemen from the neighboring tribes and deal directly with the source, the more remote tribes also refused to part with most of their healthy breeding stock, and the process of exhausting the surplus quickly repeated itself.

The continued unreliability of the Khoikhoi cattle trade encouraged two important deviations from the original policy of reliance on peaceful trade. The first was to encourage cattle-raising by the colonists themselves, thereby setting up a competing livestock economy. The second was to use coercion to divest the Khoikhoi of their remaining cattle. The Khoikhoi-Dutch war of 1673–77 was provoked by the alleged murder of some white elephant hunters by a tribe known as the Cochoqua, but the result of this conflict was the Company's seizure of at least 1,765 cattle and 4,930 sheep. The Dutch did not again declare war on any Khoikhoi tribes, but their well-armed trading expeditions increasingly resorted to intimidation or threat of force to compel the exchange of cattle. At the same time, the growth of a private white interest in cattle-raising and the cattle trade encouraged illegal expeditions by burghers which further depleted Khoikhoi holdings by methods ranging from unequal barter to outright raiding.[48]

Under such pressures the Khoikhoi economy and way of life disintegrated. By the early eighteenth century the indigenes of the southwestern Cape had not only lost much of their cattle but were unable to prevent white graziers from occupying their best interior pasture lands. Those who still had some livestock tended to migrate to remote semi-desert regions. The large proportion who had lost all their cattle either retreated to mountainous areas and adopted the hunting, gathering, and raiding habits of a closely related people, the San or "Bushmen," or hung around white farms and settlements in search of casual labor. In 1713 a devastating smallpox epidemic annihilated most of the surviving Khoikhoi population in or near the areas of white concentration.[49]

In many ways, therefore, their fate was similar to that of the coastal Indians. Again a weaker and less organized people gave way to a more powerful and unified invader. In both instances there was a pattern of trade that turned out to be destructive to the indigenes. Once the Indians had exhausted their supply of furs and skins for the white market and the Khoikhoi had lost their ability to provide cattle to the Company, their continued survival as independent societies no longer made any contribution to the success of white settlement. At that point the trading interest was overshadowed by the desire of white colonists to expropriate for their own use the land still occupied by the indigenous population. Force was employed when necessary to satisfy white territorial ambitions. The end result was dispossession of the indigenes and their loss of power, independence, and cultural cohesion.

Yet there were some differences in the precise way this process occurred and how it was rationalized. Almost from the beginning in the American case, purely commercial relationships were subordinated to the aim of establishing white settlements that would produce something on their own for the English market. Not all the colonies succeeded in doing this; settlement for religious reasons in areas like New England and Pennsylvania that lacked the capacity to produce staples needed in England led to a pattern of mixed agriculture and commerce that provided a basis for local prosperity but did not fit well into a mercantilistic imperial economy. But whatever the actual pattern of colonial economic development, the Indian trade rapidly became a marginal and sectional aspect of it that was readily dispensable. The desire for territorial expansion and land acquisition became paramount, and violent Indian resistance against gradual encroachment was made the occasion for huge land grabs.

In South Africa, on the other hand, the official ideology of the colonizers put a much greater premium on trade than on control of

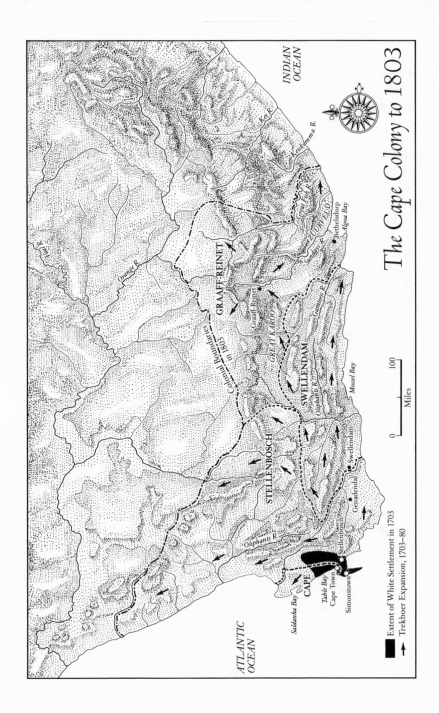

The Cape Colony to 1803

INDIAN OCEAN

ATLANTIC OCEAN

Buffalo R.

Orange R.

Ka R.

Keiskamma R.

Great Fish R.

Sundays R.

Bethelsdorp
Algoa Bay

GRAAFF-REINET

ZUURVELD

Great Brak R.

Great Karoo

GREAT KAROO

Gouritz R.

SWELLENDAM

Mossel Bay

Olifants R.

Swellendam

STELLENBOSCH

Genadendal

Oliphants R.

Saldanha Bay

CAPE

Table Bay
Cape Town
Stellenbosch
Simonstown

Colonial Boundaries
in 1803

0   100
Miles

■ Extent of White Settlement in 1703

↑ Trekboer Expansion, 1703–80

the land. The Company's original intention was to restrict the colonists to growing cereals, other foodstuffs, and wine in the immediate vicinity of Cape Town and to leave the vast and semi-arid interior to the Khoikhoi herders who would supply most of the necessary meat. This division of labor broke down by the beginning of the eighteenth century mainly because the Khoikhoi were not culturally conditioned to produce for a growing market, and because their economy and society were too fragile to sustain the pressures of an unequal commercial relationship with the Dutch.[50] Even then the Company did not encourage the migration of white graziers into the interior. They preferred to build up more intensive forms of livestock-raising as an aspect of mixed agriculture in the settled and relatively well-watered hinterland of Cape Town and to exploit what remained of the Khoikhoi trade in a controlled and monopolistic fashion. The actual displacement of most of the independent Khoikhoi by the itinerant white herdsmen known as trekboers, which took place during the eighteenth century, was, from the Company point of view, an unplanned and troublesome development that promised to weaken the cohesiveness of the colony and make it more difficult to administer. But by 1730 the destruction of the Khoikhoi economy had made the Cape market dependent on white pastoralists, and a more permissive attitude toward their movements inevitably resulted. Somewhat reluctantly, the government extended the borders of the colony when necessary to accommodate white expansion and established a system for the leasing of frontier grazing lands to trekboers. But the enlargement of the Cape Colony beyond a very limited area remained at best a necessary evil as far as the authorities were concerned. It required no official rationalization because it was more an accident than an official policy.[51]

It is even doubtful that the trekboers themselves felt much need for an ideological sanction for taking possession of territory previously occupied by Khoikhoi tribes; for they had little practical need to extinguish Khoikhoi title to it or even to recognize that such a thing had ever existed. This easy state of mind resulted from the fact that the indigenous herders were transhumant, which meant that they moved seasonally in pursuit of pasture. Although their patterns of migration took the form of regular beats that were respected by the different tribes or hordes, they lacked established villages or fixed habitations that whites would recognize as establishing any kind of possessory rights. Because of the aridity of the interior pastoral areas, the white graziers often became semi-nomadic themselves. Not allowed by the government to establish freehold farms on the frontier (as colonists had earlier been permitted to do in the vicinity of Cape Town), they held large parcels as "loan places" where they established rude homesteads. These habitations were readily deserted, either temporarily for purposes of transhumance, or permanently with the intention of acquiring a new loan place which offered the prospect of better pasture and surer supplies of water. In a thinly populated pastoral environment where migration was often necessary for survival because of the uncertainty of grass, rainfall, and wet waterholes and where most of the land was actually vacant most of the time, precise claims to land did not assume the same importance as on an agricultural frontier. Although the Dutch regarded the Khoikhoi as abject savages—indeed reports coming out of the Cape of Good Hope gave the "Hottentots" the general reputation of being the most bestial people yet encountered by Europeans in the course of discovering and conquering new lands— the circumstances were such that the concept of savagery was seldom used ideologically to rationalize territorial dispossession of the indigenous people. Such use was perhaps implied by Van Riebeeck when he proposed in 1654 to seize the persons and cattle of local tribes which he had earlier described as a "dull, rude, lazy, and stinking nation." But, as we have seen, this scheme was vetoed, and thereafter an extremely unfavorable stereotype of the Khoikhoi floated freely in the white consciousness without being linked to any calculated or comprehensive policy of dispossession and domination. In fact most Khoikhoi remained in theory members of free and independent tribes until they became an important source of servile labor during the eighteenth century.[52]

In North America, the Indians' claim to the land constituted a real obstacle to white ambition, with the result that a strong need was felt to rationalize their dispossession. Unlike the Khoikhoi, the coastal Indians lived in permanent or semi-permanent villages, cultivated crops, and had more or less fixed tribal boundaries. Although they lacked the concept of private property in the European sense, many tribes had a highly developed system of users' rights which served to allocate land to families or kinship groups for indefinite periods.[53] The very fact that the coastal Indians were an essentially sedentary people whose forms of land use and allotment actually approximated "civilized" norms created a real problem for settlers who wished to remove them and carve up their domain into freehold farms on the English model. The best solution that colonists and colonial governments could come up with was to seize on the fact that most land in Indian possession remained uncultivated and was used for hunting. According to John Winthrop, the first governor of the Massachusetts Bay Colony, almost all of the land in North America was *vacuum domicilium* because the Indians had not used it for agriculture. This meant that it was not private property in the legal or civil sense and could be expropriated by anyone who would put it under the plow. The notion that the Indians had only "savage title" because they used most of their land for hunting and therefore left it thinly populated and undeveloped became the standard rationalization for existinguishing their territorial claims and replacing them with white agriculturalists who would follow the Biblical injunction to "increase and multiply, replenish the earth and subdue it" in the way that the Indians allegedly could not. By the early eighteenth century the principle that civilized cultivators took precedence over those "savage" hunters and gatherers had become an established principle of international law as codified by the Swiss jurist Vattel. Later in the century it was incorporated into a widely accepted theory of social evolution that gauged human progress in terms of a great transformation from "barbarism" to "civilization" that was characterized primarily by the advent of sedentary agriculture.[54]

In order to make this ideology persuasive it was necessary to distort reality by exaggerating the Indians' reliance on hunting and by interpreting their occasional movements and migrations as genuine nomadism. Furthermore, the desire to seize whole blocks of Indian territory, including both cultivated and uncultivated areas, required the further argument that English political sovereignty over the "savage" inhabitants of territories the English had "discovered" had superseded tribal rights to possess or allocate land. All Indian landholding was thus without ultimate legal sanction and existed only on the sufferance of the King. The coastal Indians actually lost their land through legitimate purchase, fraud, treaties in which coercion was often involved, and land settlements resulting from wars. But behind all these policies was the settlers' conviction that they had a natural or God-given right to the soil because they were civil and the Indians were not. Hence the persistent notion that the frontier was a moving zone of conflict between "savagery" and "civilization" became central to Americans' expectations about the progress and development of their society from a very early period.

In South Africa, the trekking stock farmers who were mainly responsible for increasing the area of white occupation about tenfold between 1703 and 1780 found it more difficult to convey or project a sense of mission that could convince Europeans in general—or even their own rulers—that they were contributing to the triumph of civilization over barbarism. Eighteenth-century theories of social evolution that gave sedentary agriculture a higher claim to the land than pastoralism were obviously inapplicable. Because the classic trekboer mode of life and use of land did not appear to differ in any fundamental way from those of the Khoikhoi they were displacing, the frontiersmen were in fact liable to the charge that they were reverting to barbarism themselves. Company officials, settled and prosperous market farmers of the southwestern Cape, and European visitors to the colony all expressed the fear that the frontier might be encouraging white degeneration rather than the extension of civilization.[55] A French traveler, for example, described the trekboers he had witnessed in the 1780s as a "miserable and lazy" class of whites, "who wander on the frontiers, leading from pasture to pasture some cattle who nourish themselves as best they can; when their herds find themselves some place to stay for a time, they hastily build a rude hut which they cover with matted reeds in the manner of the Hottentots from whom they differ only in physiognomy and color."[56] One can find similar observations about American frontiersmen in the same period, but it was usually taken for granted that their way of life was a transitional one soon to be replaced by the kind of orderly and industrious society that existed in the East.[57] In South Africa, at least from the vantage point of the older, settled regions, it was an open question as to whether white expansion at the expense of indigenous "savages" would lead to an advance of civilization or to the permanent reduction of Europeans to a barbarous state.

It is, of course, highly improbable that the trekboers themselves viewed their endeavors as devoid of civilizing implications. Very little of their self-image is recoverable from historical records until the end of the century, but by that time scattered evidence begins to suggest that they had seized upon the one obvious cultural distinction between themselves and the indigenes, that of religion, and were using it to justify expropriation of the land and labor of nonwhite "heathens."[58] Presumably some notion that they were carrying Christianity into the African wilderness had been in the minds of some since the beginning of the trekboer expansion. In the nineteenth century an ethnocentric, Old Testament Christianity would help provide a cosmic meaning for further trekking of a more organized and self-conscious kind.[59] Nevertheless, the migration of semi-subsistence stock farmers never had the same favorable connotation for the educated Western mind as the kind of agricultural settlement along a broad front that occurred in North America. Because of its very nature, this characteristic South African form of settler expansion was not so readily interpreted as an extension of European civilization in all of its essential features.

For those who were the victims of white occupation of the area east of the Appalachians before the Revolution or of the trekboer movement that simultaneously divested the Khoikhoi of most of their pasture land in the northern and eastern Cape, these differences in the precise meaning that whites attributed to what was occurring could hardly have mattered very much. But there were economic and demographic influences on the South African frontier that made the ultimate fate of the Khoikhoi different from that of the Indians east of the Appalachians. Besides those who were decimated, clustered on small reservations, or impelled to migrate westward, some Indians were enslaved in the colonial period; but most of these were either shipped to the West Indies or absorbed into the Afro-American slave population. Consequently Indians as a group were not integrated into the European economy as a source of labor.[60] Once the whites had their land, they had no further use for them; for the labor needs of the colonists were met by white indentured servants and, by the eighteenth century and especially in the South, by imported African slaves.

The Cape Khoikhoi suffered a demographic disaster of equivalent proportions. As in the case of the Indians, diseases brought by the Europeans probably accounted for a greater proportion of their mortality than the wars that were fought either with the colonists or among themselves for control of the trade that the whites had inaugurated. The smallpox epidemics that broke out in 1713, 1735, and 1767 apparently resulted in the disappearance of entire tribes.[61] But the largely detribalized Khoikhoi who survived these and other disasters resulting from the white invasion did find an important niche in the settler economy. Before the coming of the Dutch, Khoikhoi who had somehow lost their cattle had customarily become clients of those who still possessed them and had acted as herdsmen in return for payment in kind that might allow them gradually to regain their status as livestock owners. When the Khoikhoi as a people had lost most of their cattle, it was quite natural for many of them to enter into similar clientage arrangements with white pastoralists. Hence they became the herdsmen, ox-trainers, and wagon drivers for the Boers, occupations for which they were eminently qualified. Indeed they became indispensable; for without their tutelage, the Boers would have had much difficulty in adjusting to a harsh environment. But their hopes for regaining independence were thwarted by white control of the land and by the tendency of the Boers to exploit their vulnerability by transforming the terms of their employment from genuine clientage, involving a voluntary and mutually advantageous exchange of labor for sustenance and protection, into a pastoral form of serfdom.[62] Hence the Khoikhoi were not simply shoved aside or exterminated like the Indians, but often became economic collaborators with the white frontiersmen.

There was also a military aspect to white-Khoikhoi interdependence. When the Boers encountered major resistance from other indigenous groups in the mid-to-late eighteenth century, they were forced to arm their Khoikhoi clients and use them as an important part of their militia. In the bitter conflicts with the hunting and gathering "Bushmen" or San, which slowed white expansion into the northern Cape in the late eighteenth century, large numbers of Khoikhoi served in the "Commandos" that meted out brutal retribution to the marauding hunters. In the wars with the Bantu-speaking Africans that began along the eastern frontier in the 1780s, they played an equally significant military role, although they did not always prove to be loyal or reliable.[63] In the course of their intimate economic and military association with frontier whites the Khoikhoi eventually lost not only their indigenous culture but even their biological identity from a process of racial mixing to be described in Chapter III. It would be misleading, however, to say that they became extinct; for their mixed descendants were the most important of the constituent elements that went into the formation of the population group that became known as the Cape Coloreds. An unflattering white stereotype of the Khoikhoi survives to this day in the use of "Hotnot" as a derogatory term applied to the Coloreds.[64]

The fact that the coastal Indians disappeared, at least from the view of most whites in the older settled areas, while the Khoikhoi persisted as a source of labor and other services in the post-frontier areas of the Cape, helps to account for the very different kinds of white images and stereotypes that became permanently attached to these two indigenous groups. When the Indian ceased to be either a military threat or a source of servile labor, he became an exotic type, no longer likely to be encountered directly. At that point he became again, as he had been for the humanists of the Renaissance, a potential symbol of natural virtue. The Enlightenment conception of the "noble savage" was carefully qualified in the American context by theories of cultural evolution that doomed the Indian's way of life to inevitable extinction; but in the meantime he could be admired for his manly stoicism, native eloquence, and, above all, as an exemplar of the great myth that America was a new Eden where man could live in harmony with a beneficent natural environment. Hence by the late eighteenth and early nineteenth centuries, there was a school of thought that portrayed the Indian as a simple child of nature who manifested the essential attributes of humanity in an uncorrupted form. The earlier image of the bestial savage persisted, but it tended to move west with the frontier.[65]

Any image of the Khoikhoi as "noble savages" was unlikely to begin with because "Hottentots" were associated with the degradation and barbarism of Africa rather than with the primal innocence of America. Furthermore, there was an important physical dimension to the image of the noble savage that seemed to disqualify them. The stereotype had to conform at least roughly to European ideas of physical beauty as derived from classical antiquity. The statuesque Indian brave excited the aesthetic admiration of Europeans from the first, and the early representations of Indians by artists drawing from nature established a tradition of portraying the Indian as a kind of bronzed European. Even the seventeenth-century observers who found nothing of value in native American culture qualified their generally disparaging assessment with admissions of admiration for the Indian as a physical type.[66] But the appearance of the "Hottentots" struck Europeans as so outlandish that there was some doubt at the beginning as to whether they were fully human. Descriptions from the seventeenth and eighteenth centuries emphasize the hollow back, the protruding buttocks, the "peppercorn" hair, and even some alleged deformities of the sexual organs. These accounts were undoubtedly exaggerated, and some of the anatomical oddities that fascinated and repelled observers were probably characteristic of only a small percentage of the population and were due to disease rather than group heredity. But the Khoikhoi physique undoubtedly differed from the European ideal to a greater extent than that of the Indian and hence failed to conform to the aesthetic requirements of the noble savage.[67]

When the noble savage image came into full fashion in the late eighteenth century, there was less reason than ever to apply it to the Khoikhoi. By that time, they had not only been stigmatized by a long tradition of adverse judgment on their appearance and character but were no longer, for the most part, independent "savages" at all, but a menial class within colonial society. Hence the contempt which precluded assigning them traits of savage nobility was not only perpetuated but strengthened by attributing to them all the demeaning characteristics associated with a servile role that the Indian had escaped.

The Trans-Appalachian and Eastern Cape Frontiers

At approximately the same time, shortly before or after 1770, the stream of white settlers in both the American colonies and the Cape began to flow across or press upon certain geographical boundaries that the authorities had hoped to maintain as at least semi-permanent dividing lines between European and native society. The movement of American pioneers across the Appalachians and of Boers into the vicinity of the Fish River in the eastern Cape inaugurated a new phase of white-indigene confrontation that increased the prospect of endemic warfare between exposed settler communities and indigenous societies with a greater potential for military resistance than those previously encountered.

In the 1760s, the land to the west of the Appalachian barrier that separated the coastal plain from the interior of eastern North America, as well as areas on its northern and southern flanks, was still in the possession of independent Indian nations or confederacies, ranging from the weakened but still intact League of the Iroquois in the North to the powerful Creek Confederacy and the battered but unconquered Cherokee nation in the South. In the Ohio Valley just west of the Alleghenies, a heterogeneous group of tribes had gathered, some of whom had migrated from east of the mountains. Despite their diversity of origin, these tribes possessed a capacity for collective resistance, as demonstrated by Pontiac's uprising against the British in 1763. It was the movement of settlers to areas just south and north of the Ohio that set off the major Indian wars of the revolutionary and post-revolutionary period. Not until the battle of Tippecanoe in 1811 was the resistance of the Ohio Valley tribes broken for good.[68]

In the eastern Cape, white settlers who crossed the Gamtoos River and pressed eastward toward the Fish in the 1770s collided directly with another expanding population, the Xhosa branch of the Nguni-speaking peoples of southeast Africa. The Nguni had occupied the area now known as the Transkei as early as the sixteenth century, if not before, and had been slowly expanding westward since that time until some Xhosa offshoots arrived in the area just east of the Fish River at about the same time as the Boers. The Nguni peoples represented the southernmost vanguard of the great population movement of pre-colonial African history, the gradual drift of black communities speaking languages of the Bantu family into most of the continent south of the Equator. The Nguni had a much more highly developed economic, social, and political structure than the Khoikhoi; they combined cattle-herding with sedentary agriculture and were divided into chiefdoms that in the early nineteenth century ranged in size from 1,000 to 35,000. These political units were not larger because of a strong tendency for chiefdoms to divide as a result of disputes over succession. This practice weakened the capacity of the Xhosa to resist the European invaders, but that disadvantage was partly counteracted by their sheer weight of numbers, which was always greatly in excess of that of the white colonists. In any case, company officials viewed with great alarm the beginnings of a conflict over land and cattle between the Boers and the numerically superior Xhosa on the eastern frontier.[69]

In both the Cape and the American colonies, the imperial or company authorities sought to avoid expensive new native wars by drawing lines on a map that would mark the limits of white settlements and protect the indigenous societies from disruptive white intrusion. When the British victory in the French and Indian War resulted in the removal of French forts in the Ohio region and raised the possibility that a flood of settlers from east of the mountains would now pour into Kentucky and the Middle West, the imperial government sought to avoid the wars that would inevitably result and preserve a regulated fur trade with the Indians by issuing the Proclamation of 1763. This edict prohibited settlement west of a line drawn roughly along the crest of the Appalachians, forbade Indians beyond the line to sell land without royal consent, and ordered colonial governors to punish white trespassers on tribal lands. Although the same desire for economy that was partly responsible for the policy in the first place prevented the imperial government from making the expenditures needed for effective implementation, even the relatively feeble enforcement efforts that were made irritated the colonists and became one of the grievances that led to the American Revolution.[70]

Although the Cape came temporarily under British rule from 1795 to 1803 and then permanently after 1806, official frontier policy remained relatively constant. Whether British or Dutch authorities were making the effort, the aim was to draw a firm line of demarcation between the Boers and the Xhosa. But here the problem was even more intractable than in North America, not only because of the government's failure to commit resources necessary for enforcement but because there was no natural boundary at all. The rapidly migrating Dutch and the slowly drifting Xhosa arrived in the pasture lands west of the Fish River known as the Zuurveld at about the same time in the 1770s. Rivalry for pasturage and cattle theft by both sides resulted in the First Frontier War of 1779–81. Victories by white militia over some of the chiefs led to efforts by the government to induce the Xhosa to withdraw from the Zuurveld and recognize the Fish River as the boundary. But this policy failed and another war broke out in 1793. Hopes for a negotiated settlement foundered because paramount chiefs east of the Fish, who were willing for reasons of their own to accept the boundary line, had no effective control over the sub-chiefs who had migrated across the river. Furthermore, the Fish was a meandering, shallow river that was easy to cross, and ejected groups could readily return. The British inherited this border problem and were forced to fight an unwelcome war in 1799, during which the hostile Xhosa were joined by rebellious Khoikhoi. It was not until 1812 that forces commanded by the British finally succeeded in driving the Xhosa out of the Zuurveld for good.[71]

The goal of Dutch and British policy on the eastern frontier was similar to that of the British in North America just before the Revolution—the government hoped to limit white expansion and regulate contacts with the indigenous people in such a way as to maintain control over the frontiersmen and prevent inter-racial violence. Left to themselves, settlers were prone to engage in aggressive behavior that risked provoking native wars because they assumed that government forces would bail them out and that the resulting peace treaties would open up additional land for their own use. The attempts of the authorities to limit expansion and their failure to provide adequate protection from native attacks or raids on the frontier farms created intense dissatisfaction with the official native policy and weakened the allegiance of the Boers to the colonial government.

The attempt of the British to arrest the moving frontier in North America contributed to a similar spirit of dissension among the colonists. This policy is not usually regarded by contemporary historians as one of the most important causes of the American Revolution, but, if we recall that the stationing of a substantial British army in America and the taxation of the colonists for its support was necessitated in part by the need to police Indian-settler relations, then the policy of frontier containment takes on added importance as a precipitating factor. Furthermore, the Quebec Act of 1774, one of the "intolerable" acts that led to open hostilities, threatened to put a permanent limit on the expansion of the northern colonies by incorporating the region north of the Ohio into an enlarged Quebec colony that the Crown would rule directly and where the laws and Catholic religion of the French-speaking inhabitants would be respected. Support for an independence that would remove actual or potential restraints on American expansionism came not only from actual pioneers but, even more significantly, from men of influence and property on the seaboard who were involved in land speculation schemes west of the mountains. From a broader perspective, the effort to limit westward movement can be seen as one aspect of a comprehensive policy of imperial regulation that threatened to stifle the ambitions of an emerging capitalistic class in the colonies.[72]

In South Africa, dissatisfaction with ineffectual or restrictive frontier policies was limited mainly to the border regions themselves, but it was sufficiently intense to provoke open rebellions that were a direct consequence of differing views on native policy. In 1795, complaints about the failure of the Company to drive the Xhosa out of the Zuurveld, provide security for frontier farms, and authorize punitive expeditions to recover stolen cattle inspired settler uprisings and abortive efforts to establish independent republics in the districts of Graaff-Reinet and Swellendam. The British, who were just taking over the colony at the time (as a war measure directed at the French and the new revolutionary republic in the Netherlands that was allied with them), quickly put down the insurrections by withholding supplies of ammunition; but a new uprising occurred in Graaff-Reinet in 1799. This one was also quickly suppressed, but not before it had unsettled conditions on the frontier to such an extent that a devastating war ensued with the Xhosa offshoots in the Zuurveld. The growth of a sectional settler consciousness thus antedated the British presence, but the imposition of foreign rule over the Dutch-speaking frontiersmen undoubtedly increased their sense of alienation from a government that seemed more interested in mediating and adjusting their conflicts with the Xhosa than in guaranteeing their safety and pushing their claims. If the American Revolution had some of the character of a white settlers' revolt against imperial native policy but involved a great deal more, the insurrections in the eastern Cape were—despite the relatively small numbers of whites involved—the first pure cases of settler rebellion against a metropole with different ideas about the treatment of indigenous peoples.[73]

The fact that the American Revolution succeeded whereas the first attempts at settler independence in South Africa failed rather ignominiously made for different patterns of subsequent interaction between frontier whites and the central government. The newly established government of the United States proclaimed its jurisdiction over all Indians in its territory but wished to avoid the expense of military action against tribes that still had the capacity for sustained resistance. Furthermore, American statesmen were conscious of the fact that the new nation's self-justifying image as a virtuous republic would be tarnished in the eyes of a skeptical world if they permitted naked aggression against the Indians; consequently they characteristically professed the most benevolent intentions toward the red "children" of the "great white father" in Washington. Laws were passed in the first Congress governing intercourse between whites and Indians and establishing the principle that Indian land could be alienated only by the Indians' own consent and as a result of compensated transfers negotiated by the federal government and formalized by treaties. During the same period, Thomas Jefferson and others proclaimed a national commitment to the "civilization" of the Indian and his incorporation into American society with full citizenship rights. But the Jeffersonian ideal of Indian acculturation and assimilation was very conveniently tied to an expectation that Indians would lose most of their land. Only when they had been divested of their "surplus" hunting lands, Jefferson believed, would they be forced to become yeoman farmers and potential American citizens. It was also Jefferson who first conceived the idea of removing most eastern Indians to the trans-Mississippi West, a policy which became a theoretical possibility after the Louisiana Purchase of 1803.[74]

The key to understanding American Indian policy between 1790 and 1830 is not the philanthropic and assimilationist rhetoric but the fact that the government was responsible to a white electorate convinced that the destiny of the nation and, in many cases, its own interests required the rapid extension of white settlement into areas still occupied by Indian nations. The extinction of Indian title and the removal of the Indians themselves were the generally accepted objectives; the only important differences of opinion were on the question of how rapidly and by what methods they should be carried out, and whether or not exceptions should be made for "civilized" Indians.

Between 1815 and 1824, a white supremacist policy of comprehensive Indian removal began to take shape. It did so in the context of growing disillusionment with Jeffersonian hopes that the Indians would voluntarily give up their "unnecessary" land and embrace white "civilization," and that white settlers would then accept them as members of their communities. These hopes were foundering as a result of the persistent and demoralizing pressure of white settlers on Indian lands, the reluctance of most Indians to abandon their traditional ways, and the refusal of state governments, particularly in the South, to give citizenship rights to "civilized" Indians who chose to accept the individual land allotments that were sometimes provided for in treaties. The state of Georgia was particularly adamant in its refusal to grant security of tenure to Indians holding land on a basis of individual ownership, despite the fact that relatively little acreage was involved. Georgia wanted nothing less than the extinguishment of all Indian land-holding within its borders in literal fulfillment of a pledge made by the federal government in 1802 that all tribal land within the state would become available for white occupancy as soon as the federal government could induce the Indians to relinquish title. Georgia's refusal signaled, according to the historian Reginald Horsman, the bankruptcy of the civilization and assimilation policy: "The logical conclusion of the civilization policy was land in fee simple and Indian citizenship, but the frontier states were unwilling to accept this." Faced with this reality, the Monroe administration proposed to Congress a plan to remove virtually all eastern Indians "whether they liked it or not, whether they had become civilized or not," to designated areas west of Missouri and Arkansas.[75]

Despite the establishment of this general policy, the pace of removal through negotiation during the 1820s remained too slow to satisfy the whites who coveted the Indian land. In 1828, Andrew Jackson, a veteran Indian fighter and long-time proponent of more coercive methods than the federal government had been willing to allow, was elected President with massive southern and western support. Between 1828 and 1831, the state of Georgia defied the clause of the Constitution giving the federal government exclusive responsibility for Indian affairs by unilaterally extending state law over the Cherokee nation within its borders and abolishing the tribal government. Jackson not only condoned this action but refused to enforce a Supreme Court decision disallowing it. Furthermore, he used his alleged inability to avert such state action as a way of bludgeoning other tribes to agree to removal treaties. The Indian Removal Act passed by Congress in 1830 gave him the funds and the authority to carry out the mass deportation of eastern Indians under federal direction, and during the next few years removal was carried out in ways that often caused great suffering to the migrating tribesmen. The refusal of the Cherokee leadership to agree to move voluntarily pricked the public conscience, particularly in the Northeast, because the Cherokees had gone further than any other Indian people in adopting the white man's way of life, even to the point of establishing a republican form of government and achieving literacy in their own language. But despite the fact that the traditional rationale for expropriating Indian land was inapplicable to the Cherokee because of the extent to which they had become agriculturalists on the white model, they were nonetheless rounded up by federal troops in 1838 and forcibly marched to Oklahoma. Because of their lack of preparation for the move and the brutal way it was carried out, an estimated 4,000 out of a total of 15,000 died on the way westward.[76]

Events unfolded very differently on the eastern Cape frontier. Slowly driven back as the consequence of a series of border wars, the Xhosa were eventually forced to open up the portion of their territory between the Fish and Kei rivers to white settlement, and they saw the rest of it fall under British sovereignty in the late nineteenth century.

But they were not displaced or removed to make way for an expansion of the kind of settler society that had developed in the western Cape. The main reason that they remained in *de facto* possession of most of their original territory and the predominant population group in the remainder was demographic. They always greatly outnumbered the white invaders and did not experience the disastrous loss of population as a result of white contact suffered by such other indigenous populations as the Khoikhoi and the American Indians. Their ability to maintain their numbers and the failure of the white population to grow rapidly as a result of the kind of massive immigration that occurred in the United States meant that they were never in danger of being overwhelmed by anything like the flood of settlers that populated much of the region between the Appalachians and the Rockies before the Civil War.[77]

Despite their relative lack of numbers, South African frontiersmen shared some of the eagerness of their American counterparts to displace the indigenes in their immediate path, although their traditional reliance on native labor meant that they did not desire anything like the kind of wholesale removal that occurred in the United States. The fact that American expansionists had an adequate supply of black slaves to work the cotton plantations of the South, or enough family members and white hired hands to carry on the mixed farming that developed in the Middle West, meant that all Indians were dispensable. But in South Africa enough of the indigenous population had to remain in newly acquired white farming areas to provide the Boers with a labor force of a size they had come to regard as adequate. Nevertheless, South African frontiersmen were as interested as American settlers in gaining access to new lands and usually had hopes of expelling or encapsulating the "surplus" natives. The first step in what many must have hoped would be a continued eastward penetration was the establishment in 1819 of a "neutral zone" between the Fish and Keiskamma rivers, which was supposed to be vacant but in fact provided scope for white encroachment. This area quickly came to be known as the "ceded territory," and the government responded to the settlers' land hunger by granting them farms there.[78]

By 1834, white farmers had occupied much of the "ceded territory" and some were intruding into areas explicitly reserved for the Xhosa. In that year the Xhosa launched a massive counterattack which involved devastating raids deep into the colony. But the British army crushed the invaders, and the settlers had good reason to anticipate a settlement that would give them access to much new territory. The British governor obliged by annexing the large area to the east of the "ceded territory" between the Keiskamma and the Kei, and he initially proposed that the hostile tribes be driven east of the Kei so that the whole region could be opened to white settlement. But the Colonial Office in London overruled the annexation itself and ordered that the entire area be retroceded to the Xhosa.[79]

This determination to break an established pattern of dispossessing some of the Xhosa after defeating them in a "defensive" war resulted from a mixture of economic and philanthropic motives. From the point of view of the Colonial Office, territorial gains from one native war simply provoked another and were part of a never-ending sequence that placed an intolerable burden on the exchequer while bringing no tangible benefits to the British Empire. Furthermore, the humanitarian movement in England had begun to shift its interest from the emancipation of slaves to the protection of aborigines from brutal treatment by white settlers. Lord Glenelg, the Secretary of State for the Colonies, who made the decision to veto the new acquisition in South Africa, was close to the philanthropic lobby and quite prepared to believe the claim of some missionaries that the war had been an unjust one resulting primarily from illicit cattle raids and other provocative acts on the part of the Boers. But his action was probably conditioned more by fiscal considerations than by humanitarian idealism.[80]

The Boer frontiersmen were bitterly disillusioned with British native policy. A number of grievances had been building up over the years concerning official interference with their own methods for controlling and disciplining the nonwhites who competed with them for land and cattle or worked as servants on their farms; the retrocession of the area that the governor had prematurely incorporated into the colony as "Queen Adelaide Province" was for some the last straw. The Great Trek—the mass migration of organized groups of Afrikaners in a northeasterly direction to regions beyond British control—had already begun, but it gained new recruits and a new sense of urgency after Glenelg's decision became known.[81]

It is a curious and ironic coincidence that the Great Trek took place at almost precisely the same time as Indian removal in the United States. In one instance the indigenous population was forced to trek to make way for white farmers and planters, and in the other it was a substantial part of the settler population that did the trekking, partly at least because the government *refused* to provide access to the lands of natives in their immediate path. An explanation of the differing outcomes of what were in some ways similar situations may reveal much about the comparative dynamics of early-nineteenth-century white expansion in the two societies.

A large part of the explanation derives from the relative population density and demographic vitality of the Xhosa, making them of course a much more formidable obstacle to white expansion than the trans-Appalachian Indians. Also significant were the differing ways in which the settlers related to the frontier environment and envisioned its future economic development. Although there were some legendary American frontiersmen who moved on as soon as they could see the smoke from their neighbor's chimney, most migrated to the newly opened territories of the West with the desire to establish permanent homesteads, engage in sedentary agriculture, and "grow up with the country" as it became more populated, town-centered, and economically diversified. To typical settlers the frontier was a passing stage on the way to a recapitulation of the civilization they had left behind in the East. But for the Boer frontiersmen of the early nineteenth century a semi-subsistence pastoralism had become a permanent way of life. They neither desired nor anticipated the kind of economic "progress" that was eagerly awaited on the American frontier.[82]

Since ecological conditions on much of the South African frontier were not only unsuitable for settled agriculture but did not even offer much promise for permanent occupation of the same pasture lands, survival often required a willingness to move on without leaving much behind except overgrazed wastelands. It was therefore quite natural for such a population of graziers to respond to any obstacle to their perpetual expansion—whether it was human or physical—by outflanking it and trekking off in a new direction. Their only ambition was to perpetuate their existing way of life wherever this could be done; for there was little sense on the South African frontier that white movement was part of a process of cultural and economic evolution that would culminate in the reproduction of a civilized society on the model of Europe or even of Cape Town. When conditions became difficult on the eastern frontier, they simply outflanked the Xhosa barrier by moving northeastward into regions where there seemed to be more open land and where they could continue their pastoral existence in a more secure environment. But that security turned out to be illusory; they soon came into conflict with other African peoples such as the Zulu, the Ndebele, and the Sotho, who were no more willing than the Xhosa to tolerate white encroachments. Consequently warfare with indigenous peoples continued to be a central element in the Boer experience.[83]

Yet the Trek was more than a response to ecological and demographic circumstances. For those migrants joining the organized parties whose leaders proclaimed their desire to escape from British jurisdiction, it was also an act of political protest against the colonial government and its native policies. The full dimensions of the ideological conflict of Boer and Briton in the early-to-mid nineteenth century will be treated in Chapter IV; here it is enough to stress that the trekkers had a different relationship to constituted political authority than the frontier whites who coveted Indian land in the United States. The United States government was strongly susceptible to pressure from frontier expansionists, especially when Andrew Jackson, one of their most ardent spokesmen, occupied the White House. Furthermore, the semi-autonomous state governments which impinged on the Indian frontier were totally dominated by the land-grabbing, Indian-removing mentality. But in the Cape effective political power was in the hands of British imperial authorities who were ethnically alien to the majority of the settlers and reluctant, in this period at least, to authorize the territorial expansion of the colony. Unlike the American frontiersmen who felt the power of a great nation behind them and considered themselves as archetypical exponents of American nationalism, the Boers were not only on their own but to some extent felt that they themselves were a persecuted ethnic group. Their constant complaint, almost inconceivable in the American situation, was that the government gave more consideration to native interests than to their own. This in fact was not strictly true, but the tendency of some British spokesmen, particularly missionaries, to blame the Boers whenever trouble broke out and to stigmatize their way of life as scarcely more civilized than that of their indigenous rivals cut deeply and made the Great Trek as much a reactive movement away from the British as a positive search for new opportunities.[84] Comparing the kind of moving frontier associated with the Indian removal with that implied by the Great Trek is to juxtapose a situation where expansion of white settlement at the expense of indigenous peoples was seen as a legitimate fulfillment of a national destiny with one where it had more of the character of a divisive sectional or ethnic interest. This contrast should not be exaggerated, because Britain did in the end make a decisive contribution to the white colonization of South Africa; but in the era of the Great Trek, between the 1820s and the 1850s, such an intention was not at all clear.[85]

These differences in the degree of commitment and legitimacy accorded to settler expansionism can be explained to some extent by noting the relative strength of missionary or humanitarian pressure groups. British policy-makers in the 1820s, 30s, and 40s paid respectful attention to a philanthropic lobby that stressed the mistreatment of the "aborigines" by the settlers and called for strong protective measures to keep native societies insulated from frontier whites so that missionaries could work for their conversion and civilization before they had been corrupted or degraded by the settlers.[86] American missionaries working among the eastern Indians subscribed to much the same philosophy, but eventually most of them gave up hope of accomplishing the civilizing mission so long as a seemingly irresistible tide of white settlement encapsulated and then pressed inward on Indian territories east of the Mississippi. Ultimately, most of them acceded to the policy of Indian removal on the grounds that this would give them a second chance to nurture civilization and Christianization, in a more gradual and controlled fashion. This decision was based on a recognition that the government was unable or unwilling to take firm action to expel white intruders who plied Indians with alcohol and swindled them out of their lands and other resources.[87]

A deeper explanation for the differing degrees of official or public support for settler expansionism in this era can be derived from the fact that South Africa and the United States were at radically different stages of economic development. The expropriation of Indian land in the Age of Jackson made a vital contribution to the growth of a dynamic capitalistic economy. Perhaps, as Michael Rogin would have it, Indian removal was an American form of what Marx called the stage of "primitive accumulation," a necessary prelude to free-market capitalism that involves the destruction by political or military means of precapitalist forms of holding land and using other natural resources so that these sources of wealth can be made available to emergent entrepreneurs.[88] It is clear enough, as Ronald Satz has pointed out, that the "expectant capitalists" of the Jacksonian period put "unremitting

pressure" on the government "to open new lands for sale and purchase."[89] Hordes of land speculators, would-be timber and mining
barons, and even slave-traders had vested interests in Indian removal
that were perhaps even more influential than those of agrarian settlers.
The strongest impulses of a market economy heading for industrial
takeoff were thus enlisted behind Indian dispossession in the 1830s.

South Africa, on the other hand, was not experiencing rapid economic development or change at the time of the Great Trek. There
was a market of sorts for agricultural commodities in Cape Town, but
before the rise of wool as an export commodity between 1835 and
1845, it was still the sale of foodstuffs to passing ships that sustained
most agricultural activity. The frontier pastoralists did send some of
their cattle to market, along with such by-products as butter and tallow,
but basically theirs was a semi-subsistence economy; such items as ammunition, coffee, sugar, and some clothing were all that they needed
to purchase from the outside world. The expansion of the frontier
opened no new sources of wealth for the enterprising; it simply extended and accentuated this pattern. Indeed, the farther the Boers
wandered the less access they had to a market and the more self-sufficient they became. Nothing like the American pattern in which new
lands were quickly exploited for commercial agriculture and tied in
with expanding markets could develop in such a situation. Furthermore, before the beginnings of diamond-digging and gold-mining in
the 1870s and 80s, South Africa had no known mineral resources to
provide a foundation for industrialization.[90]

From the vantage point of British imperialists of early to mid century, the Cape was an economically unsuccessful colony, and their only
justification for being there at all was to control the sea lanes around
the Cape of Good Hope to protect the passage to India. Consequently,
there was no strong economic motive emanating from the metropole or
even from commercial interests within the colony to expropriate native land or labor on a large scale in response to a grandiose vision of
future economic development. The interest in further native disposession or subjugation remained a local interest on the frontier, one which
might involve the government in military actions but did not crucially
concern the colony as a whole, to say nothing of the British Empire.
No generally accepted ideology of "manifest destiny"—of the kind that
sanctioned Indian removal and was central to American dreams of
progress and prosperity—yet existed; but in the 1840s and 50s a special

sense of mission began to emerge among the Afrikaner trekkers who were by then in the process of establishing their own republics. The idea that there was a divine plan to establish independent white Christian communities in what is now Natal, the Orange Free State, and the Transvaal contained the seeds of an Afrikaner nationalism that would eventually lay claim to all of South Africa in the name of ethnic and racial supremacy.

II

The Rise of Racial Slavery
in the South and the Cape

The Emergence of a Labor System

One of the more vexing problems faced by the colonizers of the Chesapeake region and the Cape of Good Hope was how to recruit a work force and establish a labor system that would meet the needs of their settlements. The decision to rely mainly on imported nonwhite slaves, made in both areas by the early eighteenth century, became fixed or irreversible only after two other options had been dismissed or rejected. One was to coerce the indigenous population—the Algonkian Indians or Cape Khoikhoi—to do most of the hard menial work under the supervision of whites, and the other was to attract lower-class immigrants from Europe who would be pressed into service through some form of contract labor or term servitude. To understand why the western Cape and the colonial South became comparable kinds of slave societies, it is necessary to have a sense of why these alternative solutions to the labor problem either miscarried or were not seriously attempted. The calculations leading to the decision for a labor force of imported bondsmen were essentially pragmatic rather than ideological, but they prepared the way for a racial division of labor and status that would provide an enduring model for institutionalized white supremacy and a seedbed for the attitudes and doctrines associated with racial inequality.

Another conceivable approach to the labor question—the extension to the colonies of the capitalistic wage-labor system already taking hold in the mother countries—was probably outside the realm of possibility and was never seriously contemplated. The prevailing assumption that some form of direct coercion would be needed to get work done in a colonial environment reflects a half-conscious awareness of a principle uncovered by modern anthropologists and sociologists that explains why involuntary labor systems tend to develop in some situations and not in others. When land is scarce and labor is plentiful, as in seventeenth-century England and the Netherlands, it is more economical for employers to hire workers by the day or for short terms at the low rates of pay that prevail in a glutted labor market than to bind them to long-term or lifetime obligations. Where labor is relatively scarce and land is plentiful, as in new settlements with expanding frontiers, the free worker usually has the option of becoming a subsistence farmer, either by purchasing cheap land or by squatting on unused acreage beyond the effective control of nominal owners whose claims often exceed the reach of their authority. Such a situation has a tendency to drive wages up to an unprofitably high level and provides a powerful incentive for legalized coercion and immobilization of the labor force. Hence in societies where resources are "open," in the sense that there is a plentiful supply of unused land, the desire to exploit opportunities for profit requiring regimented or gang-type labor almost invariably creates pressure for some kind of involuntary system. If there is an effective state apparatus responsive to the needs of profit-seeking landholders, then it is likely that some form of servitude will be introduced.[1]

Despite the small scale of the Dutch East India Company's operation at the Cape in the early years, the responsible officials had to cope with a shortage of the right kind of labor. Workers were needed, not only to raise fresh produce for provisioning ships on their way to and from the East Indies, but also for the heavy construction work necessary to make the colony defensible against attack from the sea by rival European powers, provide adequate port facilities, and insure necessary supplies of fresh water. In the immediate vicinity of the Company's fort there was a small population of cattleless Khoikhoi who had previously subsisted primarily by scavenging the beaches for shellfish. These "beachrangers" could be hired to do odd jobs, but they showed little inclination for regular or sustained work. Since company regulations prohibited the enslavement of indigenous peoples, there was no real opportunity to see how the Khoikhoi would perform under direct coercion. Although an exasperated Commander van Riebeeck recommended in 1654 that neighboring tribes be subjected to servitude after their cattle had been seized, the purpose of this aborted scheme was more to acquire livestock than to increase the labor supply. Whatever Van Riebeeck's reason may have been for assuming that the Khoikhoi could not solve his labor problem, the notion soon became prevalent in the colony that "Hottentots" would make poor slaves because of their allegedly irremediable laziness. In the early eighteenth century, a resident of the Cape expressed what had long been the settled conviction of the colonists about the work capacity of the indigenes: "They are without doubt, both in Body and Mind, the laziest people under the Sun. A monstrous Indisposition to Thought and Action, runs through all the nation of 'em. And their whole earthly happiness seems to be Indolence and Supinity."[2]

The belief that the Khoikhoi were inherently too indolent to do adequate work even under coercion was clearly an exaggeration; it was contradicted by the successful employment of a few in the early stages of settlement and later by the substantial role that they played as the clients or indentured workers of white stock farmers. But there was a grain of truth in the judgment; for sudden attempts to subject essentially nomadic peoples to regular patterns of sedentary labor have rarely been successful. The shock involved in such a radical change in the rhythm of life and work can easily result in rapid population decline and even extinction.[3] The Dutch, therefore, were probably well advised in the early years to anticipate little benefit from Khoikhoi labor. Furthermore, the fact that the Cape indigenes were initially expected to play a role as suppliers of livestock to the colony—an economic function that did not require their direct subjugation—meant that their reputation for laziness and unreliability simply confirmed a prior inclination to look elsewhere for servile workers.

Unlike the Khoikhoi, the southern coastal Indians sometimes were enslaved in the seventeenth century and put to work on English farms and plantations. But these red bondsmen, usually captives who happened to be taken in wars fought more for the purpose of killing Indians and seizing their land than to recruit unfree workers, were never an important part of the labor force in the Chesapeake colonies. In South Carolina, on the other hand, there was a period in the early eighteenth century when Indians constituted about a third of the slaves and almost 15 percent of the total population of the colony. This unique situation was the result of a flourishing slave trade that involved Indians selling their captured enemies to white traders. But even in South Carolina Indian slavery on a substantial scale was a short-lived and generally unsuccessful experiment. Indian bondage rapidly declined as planters showed their preference for Africans by exporting their native American slaves to the West Indies or New England.[4]

The question of why Indian slavery made only a minor contribution to the solution of the labor problem in the southern colonies needs more study than it has received. An alleged incapacity or culturally conditioned reluctance to perform steady agricultural labor has probably been over-emphasized as an explanation. Although there was a sexual division of labor among the Indians of the Eastern Woodlands that alloted most day-to-day agricultural tasks to women, the men were traditionally responsible for the heavy work of clearing the land and breaking the soil. Indian work patterns were obviously not those of the plantation, but imported Africans or white indentured servants from typical peasant backgrounds were scarcely better prepared for this quasi-industrial form of agricultural labor. Besides basic farming skills, the native economy required the practice of a variety of crafts that demanded considerable dexterity. Not surprisingly, as experience in South Carolina revealed, Indians could readily become skilled artisans, an aptitude that might have made them extremely useful on the largely self-sufficient plantations of the colonial period. It is hard to avoid the conclusion that cultural unreadiness or intractability was not the main reason why Indian slavery did not become more extensive.[5]

A more compelling explanation, but one that also turns out to be less than fully adequate, follows from the plausible assumption that the Indian population pool was insufficient to meet the labor needs of the colonists and that they therefore had to look for other sources of manpower. It is indeed doubtful that a plantation economy of the kind that developed in the southern colonies could have been sustained by Indian labor alone; there were simply too few Indians in the proximity of the settlements to meet the demand. But the case of South Carolina is once again instructive, because it suggests that Europeans might have involved friendly tribes in an extensive slave trade similar to that of West Africa if they had really worked at it. Encouragement of such a trade in other colonies, accompanied by more deliberate efforts to take captives in Indian wars, could, one suspects, have increased greatly the number of Indian slaves available to the colonists. Even if this did not provide a full solution to the labor problem, it would have contributed to one; and the question remains as to why this opportunity was not seized in a more deliberate and systematic way.

The answer, it would appear, is mainly that large-scale Indian servitude was regarded as incompatible with the kind of physical security and social control that the exploiters of labor demanded and colonial governments required. Unlike an imported slave or servant, the Indian was at home in the American forest and could survive in it. Consequently he was more likely to try to escape and had a better chance of succeeding. Unless his entire tribe had been enslaved, he could hope to rejoin his own people and thus had a motive for flight that did not exist for those separated from home by the wide expanse of the Atlantic. Furthermore, so long as Indian societies remained independent, the act of enslaving some of their members could provoke violent retaliation. It would seem to follow, therefore, that safe and effective Indian enslavement on a large scale could have occurred only if preceded by a thoroughgoing conquest of entire tribes. The history of colonial Indian wars shows how extraordinarily difficult such an undertaking would have been. The ability of the Indian to melt into the forest and his propensity to fight to the death when cornered meant that the value of captives brought back from massive slaving expeditions would probably have been less than the required investment of white lives and capital. And even if such hypothetical campaigns had succeeded, they would have resulted in large numbers of Indians from common tribal backgrounds being concentrated on the same farms and plantations. The prevention of rebellion under such circumstances would have required prison-like discipline rather than a normal plantation regime, once again rendering the system too expensive and troublesome to be worth the effort. Given the inherent limitations and disadvantages of Indian servitude, it is not surprising that the colonists preferred to import their unfree workers from abroad and to export even the relatively small number of Indian slaves who fell into their hands.[6]

The second option—the employment of white contract workers or term servants—was put into practice in Virginia and Maryland and was in fact the principal labor system throughout the seventeenth century. In the Cape, it was essentially a road not taken; but it was seriously considered as a possible alternative to imported slave labor as late as 1716. The failure of the Chesapeake colonies to maintain an economic system based on white labor and the unwillingness of the rulers of the Cape to introduce one when they still had the chance both need to be explained. Since these areas shared a mild climate deemed suitable for European settlement, the argument that whites could not survive or work well in the tropics could not be used, as it was in the British West Indies, to explain a transition from European to nonwhite labor.[7] There were in fact no climatic or epidemiological reasons, real or imagined, why these regions could not have developed on a white-labor basis (following the example of the northern American colonies or anticipating that of Australia and New Zealand in the nineteenth century). But instead they became the only multi-racial slave societies resulting from the white colonization of regions that were similar to parts of Europe in climate and vegetation.*

In the early years of settlement in Virginia, a choice between white servants and African slaves was not yet possible; for the international slave trade had developed only to the point where it could meet the needs of the established Spanish and Portuguese plantation colonies. But it is unlikely that the English colonizers would have opted for a labor force of black slaves even if they had been available. The ideology of English colonization assigned to American settlements the important social role of siphoning off some of the population surplus that was viewed as a threat to law and order in the mother country. When the tobacco boom of the 1620s created a surging demand for farm and plantation workers, an opportunity seemed to exist for simultaneously solving an English social problem and bolstering a colonial economy by shipping excess whites to Virginia as indentured servants. The system as it evolved in Virginia and Maryland encouraged the migration of desperate or venturesome Englishmen by offering them passage in return for a specified term of service, usually between four and seven years. Planters who paid for the transportation of their servants were given land grants or "headrights" for each person they imported. In addition to the migration of voluntary indentured servants, convicts were frequently transported for longer terms, and an indeterminate number of paupers or vagabonds were literally kidnapped in English

---

* Of course, slavery existed as an institution in other temperate regions, such as the northern English colonies and the nontropical parts of Spanish America; but in these areas it did not constitute the principal labor system for an extended period and hence did not give rise to genuine "slave societies."

ports and "spirited" on board ships bound for the colonies, where they ended up in servitude as surely as if they had chosen to indenture themselves. The economic and demographic importance of these un-free whites is reflected in the fact that in 1683 there were twelve thousand of them serving in Virginia, one sixth of a total population that also included many former servants who had done their time.[8]

The institution of indentured servitude was to some extent an invention to serve the labor needs of the American colonists; for it was not identical to any form of personal service then customary in England. The usual term for English servants was one year, and they were paid wages; whereas the indentured worker was in effect a debt bondsman serving several years without pay to cancel the obligation owed to the master for assuming the costs of passage. Where English service was usually based on voluntary contract enforced by civil action, criminal penalties were prescribed for the indentured servant who ran away or otherwise reneged on the terms of the agreement. This situation was analogous to that of parish apprentices in England who had to work to the age of twenty-one or twenty-four and did not have to be taught a trade by their masters; but apprenticeship was reserved for children, whereas indentured servants could be adults. Furthermore, unlike most English servants, American bondsmen could be bought and sold. Sometimes their masters even used them as gambling stakes. In practice, as well as in law, they appeared to have been subjected to an even crueler and more degrading regime than members of the dependent classes in England. On a day-to-day basis, they were often driven and abused in a manner normally associated with slavery rather than with milder forms of servitude. In some ways they were even more vulnerable to mistreatment than chattel slaves, because their masters did not have a lifetime stake in their health and well-being and suffered no economic loss if their work capacity was gone at the end of their terms.[9]

The degradation of the servant class that took place in the plantation colonies was not due entirely to the economic incentive for labor coercion. It is doubtful if the English government and ruling classes would have tolerated the brutality and indignity associated with colonial white servitude had it not reflected their own conviction that the poor deserved no better. A belief that the English lower classes were a pack of indolent rogues and vagabonds had been growing since the mid-sixteenth century. Proposals for disciplining the idle poor through some form of forced labor were frequently advanced during the seventeenth century and were actually implemented in a limited way through the development of such institutions as workhouses and prisons. Transportation to the colonies for term service can itself be viewed as one of many devices that were being recommended and tried out for the purpose of bringing to heel the class of "masterless men" who lacked regular employment and often turned to vagabondage, begging, and thievery. Even those who worked fairly regularly were the object of perpetual criticism for their desultory work habits, and ways were sought to make them more industrious. Serious proposals were actually made for enslaving the English poor, not merely to make them work, but in the hope that rigorous discipline would make them work efficiently. In an age when propertied Englishmen were increasingly talking about liberty, the poor were, in the words of the historian Christopher Hill, "treated as utterly rightless." Not only were beggars and starving children summarily rounded up and shipped off to Virginia, but holders of mining monopolies in the early seventeenth century were given the right to conscript the unemployed for their enterprises.[10]

In the end, of course, the advocacy and use of compulsion to discipline the poor and make them productive did not arrest the trend toward a capitalistic "free labor" system in England. The particularly intense hue and cry after the poor in the first half of the seventeenth century probably resulted partly from the fact that Protestant and capitalistic attitudes toward work and poverty had taken root among the propertied elements before they had evolved the forms of economic organization and indoctrination that would instill this new ethic into the working class. It was the development of the factory, more than anything else, that would in the long run provide the foundation for the desired combination of social discipline and economic exploitation. But contempt for the poor and laboring classes persisted into the industrial era, partly because turning laborers with a peasant heritage into efficient factory hands attuned to the work discipline and new sense of time imposed by industrial capitalism proved a difficult and prolonged process. Nevertheless, the ability of the labor market to provide sufficient wage-earners for the factories served to arrest the tendency toward overt coercion. The assumption that the poor would rather work for low wages than starve became the crux of a capitalist theory of labor procurement; and by the late eighteenth century claims were being made that reliance on a "free labor market" was more rational and profitable than any compulsory system.[11]

In the southern American colonies, as in the West Indies, the engine of economic development was not the factory but the plantation, and there was no way to induce people to work on plantations for low wages. It was too easy to survive in some less painful way, given an environment where land was readily accessible—if not always for purchase, at least for subsistence through squatting, herding, or hunting. Servitude, in one form or another, thus remained necessary for the production of the staple crops that brought wealth to a landed class. But during the middle decades of the seventeenth century, Virginia's system of indentured labor began to manifest some shortcomings that helped prepare the way for its replacement by black slavery. A major problem was that indentured servants eventually became free, thus creating a lower class that was not under the direct control of the planters. This had not been a major difficulty in the early years because the high death rate had kept down the numbers of emancipated servants and the availability of cheap land had enabled many of the survivors to become planters or yeoman farmers who quickly acquired the outlook of the privileged group. Such a society could, without thinking very much about it, adopt the practice—astonishingly radical for that day—of allowing all freemen to vote in elections for the colonial assembly. But during the 1660s and 70s a decline in the mortality rate, combined with a temporary scarcity of cheap land due to the engrossment of huge tracts by the elite, created a situation in which large numbers of servants were being freed who had no immediate prospects of becoming landowners. For the dominant class of planters this group represented a serious social problem, reminiscent of the "sturdy beggars" who had bedeviled the English upper classes earlier in the century. As T. H. Breen and Edmund Morgan have pointed out, the emergence of a "giddy multitude" of servants and ex-servants, who had no stake in the established order and were likely to be acutely disappointed with the failure of Virginia to live up to its billing as a land of opportunity, became an object of great concern to the ruling elements. The decision in 1670 to establish a property qualification for the suffrage reflected a fear of being outvoted by this new proletariat. Anticipations that the propertyless "rabble" would be prone to violence and disorder seemed borne out by their participation in Bacon's Rebellion of 1676 and other disturbances of the seventies and early eighties.[12]

One way to solve the problem would have been to lengthen the terms of indentured servitude in the direction of lifetime bondage. There were some subtle attempts to do this, but they were doomed to failure because of a gradual decline in the ability of Chesapeake planters to import servants on their own terms. Beginning in the 1660s, the growth of manufactures in England created a greater demand for labor at home and helped to deflate the notion that the country suffered from a population surplus. As the idea took hold that a large population was an economic and military asset to a nation, official and private efforts to encourage the emigration of the poor slackened perceptibly. Furthermore, the beginnings of English settlement in the Middle Atlantic region in the sixties and seventies offered a more attractive destination than Virginia or Maryland to those willing to indenture themselves in order to get to America. Large numbers consequently chose Pennsylvania or New York, because in these colonies they did not have to labor under plantation discipline. The decline in the power of the tobacco colonies to attract servants forced an improvement in the terms offered to the immigrant, but shorter terms and better treatment promised to reduce the possibilities of economic exploitation and increase the danger of social upheaval. It was fortunate for the planters that, at the very time when the shortcomings and limitations of indentured servitude were becoming painfully apparent, the English became heavily involved in the Atlantic slave trade, thus making enslaved Africans, who were already a significant minority among the plantation work force, available in greater quantity and at lower cost than previously. Economic interests and social instincts combined to make the gradual shift to a new labor system overwhelmingly attractive. By the early eighteenth century, white indentured servants were disappearing from the tobacco fields and black slaves were rapidly becoming the principal source of plantation labor.[13]

At the Cape of Good Hope, a heavy reliance on unskilled white labor characterized only the brief period of initial settlement and ended abruptly in 1658 when the first shipload of slaves arrived to provide sufficient black workers, not only for the Company, but also for the newly created class of free burghers. Commander van Riebeeck had from the beginning regarded the use of whites for menial labor as undesirable; as he reported in 1657, the work "is now rather heavy and tiresome, and it also makes the place somewhat disliked that we continue so long employing the company's servants on such hard work."[14]

His problem arose, South African historians have suggested, partly because of the character and background of those who had been recruited or impressed into term service as soldiers and servants of the East India Company. To an even greater extent than the English indentured servants who went to the Chesapeake colonies, these men came mostly from the very lowest class of society; many were representatives of the chronically unemployed and floating urban underclass of the Netherlands known as *het grauw,* and most of the rest derived from similar classes in other cities of Western Europe. Company service had a bad reputation, and company agents often had to engage almost as a matter of policy in the kind of kidnapping that was done illicitly by freelance "spirits" to augment the servant trade from England to the colonies. Servants recruited in such a manner from the poorest and least disciplined elements of society were notoriously resistant to authority and regular work. One reason why indentured servitude had achieved a modicum of success in the southern colonies, despite chronic problems of discipline and morale, was that a substantial portion of the immigrants had come voluntarily in the hope of improving their condition, and many of these were not true paupers but might even be described as lower middle class in origin. However few people with any ambition actually wanted to go to the Cape or other possessions of the Dutch East India Company; for the directors enforced monopolistic economic policies that offered little hope for future prosperity even for those who became free burghers. The type of people vulnerable to impressment were likely to have weak physical constitutions and the kind of negative social attitudes associated with what Marxists call a lumpenproletariat. It is not surprising, therefore, that those who were brought to the Cape proved to be unruly and inefficient workers and that they absconded in large numbers in the early years, often by stowing away on ships headed back to the Netherlands.[15]

Similar labor problems had already been encountered by the Company in the East Indies and had been solved in two ways—by encouraging the immigration into Dutch possessions of Chinese who would work for low wages and by importing slaves acquired from markets in India, Ceylon, Indonesia, and East Africa. Slaves were first used on a large scale between 1615 and 1619, for cultivating nutmegs on the island of Amboyna and for constructing a fort at Batavia after the governor general had decided that such an arduous task was beyond the capacity of the Company's servants and soldiers. The Chinese enjoyed a high reputation for industriousness; but since they tended to go into petty trading as soon as they had the capital, slaves from available sources in Southeast Asia and East Africa eventually became the main labor force for the Dutch settlements.[16] Commander van Riebeeck's experience in the East Indies shaped his perception of the labor problem at the Cape; consequently he had low expectations about the working capacity of white servants, a high regard for the Chinese, and a willingness to resort to Asian and African slaves if necessary. In 1652, the first year of settlement, he suggested that Chinese be induced to emigrate to the Cape; but none turned out to be willing to "leave their country for such a distant land with such uncertain prospects," and by 1656 he was calling for the introduction of slaves, "by whom we can easily imagine that the work can be more conveniently and more cheaply performed" than by the available whites.[17]

There were a few slaves in the colony from the very earliest years, mostly personal servants brought by company officials from the East; but it proved difficult to import more because the Company could not spare them from its other possessions. In 1658, however, a ship arrived with 174 Angolan slaves who had been pirated from the Portuguese, and later that year a Dutch slave trader en route from the Guinea Coast to the East Indies left part of its cargo at the Cape. Thus in 1659 the colony suddenly had 226 slaves and less than 140 whites. Consequently, the Company was able to offer the small number of ex-servants to whom it had granted land the previous year two or three slaves each to be purchased on credit. In contrast to Virginia, therefore, slavery was not only a live option but represented the path of least resistance in the early years at the Cape. Unlike Virginia and Maryland, but somewhat like South Carolina at a slightly later period, the Cape Colony was virtually born as a multi-racial slave society. But access to the West African market proved temporary, and the slave population fluctuated greatly for the rest of the century. The main source of supply was an uncertain flow from India, the East Indies, and Madagascar. In 1700 a free burgher population of 1,334 outnumbered the slaves by a ratio of about 1.5 to 1. But the subsequent growth of a more regular commerce with East Africa quickly resulted in a rough parity of free and slave populations that persisted until the closing of the slave trade in 1807.[18]

By the early eighteenth century some company officials had come to regret the introduction of slavery at the Cape, mainly because it seemed less efficient than the wage system that prevailed in the mother country, and hoped to phase it out before it became too deeply rooted by encouraging the immigration of a white laboring class. Such proposals were stimulated both by the temperate climate and by the growth simultaneously with slavery of a form of white employment that might have served as an alternative. As the number of free agriculturalists increased, irregularities in the supply of slaves induced the government to supplement the labor force on the farms by loaning out company servants who had not fulfilled their obligations, provided that their masters undertook to pay their wages. In addition, there were some freed servants who did not receive land and were encouraged to hire themselves out to private individuals. Thus a relatively small class of dependent white workers, known as *knechts,* developed in the late seventeenth and early eighteenth centuries. Most *knechts* appear to have fallen into one of two categories: some were fairly ambitious and competent young men who readily took the role of overseer and eventually earned enough to buy farms of their own or ended up marrying the widows or daughters of their masters; others were of the footloose and ungovernable temper that characterized so many of the Company's servants, and these often took advantage of lax surveillance on outlying farms by absconding. In 1696, Governor Simon van der Stel complained of the growing problem of white vagabonds, many of whom were fugitive *knechts,* who tended to subsist in the frontier areas by engaging in an illicit cattle trade with the Khoikhoi.[19]

Despite these problems, the Council of Seventeen, which ruled the Dutch East India Company from Amsterdam, decided in 1700 to authorize free passage for immigrants who desired to go to the Cape in an apparent effort to build up the white population of the colony. Previously, permanent white settlers had been obtained mainly by freeing company servants and soldiers, although the introduction of 200 free Huguenots had been subsidized by the Company in 1688. The new immigration policy was greeted unenthusiastically by the officials at the Cape, who pointed out that all the fertile land within the existing boundaries of the colony had already been taken up. It was apparently taken for granted by this time that most white immigrants would be unwilling to hire themselves out to other whites. The free-passage program was abandoned in 1707, but in 1716 the directors of the Company asked the governor and his Council of Policy at the Cape to give further consideration to the desirability of increased white immigration

and to the question of "whether European farm hands and agriculturalists would be less expensive than slaves." The ensuing discussion
resulted in a conscious and explicit decision in favor of a labor force
composed of nonwhite slaves rather than free or semi-free whites. One
member of the Council argued for the introduction of white indentured service on an expanded scale and for an end to the importation
of slaves, but all the other officials opted for a restrictive white-
immigration policy and for a continued dependence on slave labor. Besides answering the direct query of the Company about costs by contending that slaves were cheaper than farmhands, they touched on the
social problems allegedly created by the existence of a white laboring
class in a multi-racial frontier environment. According to the governor,
white agricultural workers were likely to be "more troublesome . . .
than slaves," because "all workmen, drivers, and lower classes are ad-
dicted to drink, and it is extremely difficult to restrain them and keep
them to their duties." In the opinion of one of the Council members,
lower-class white immigrants inevitably succumbed to laziness, dissipa-
tion, and vagabondage. Another noted that slaves were more obedient
than "free born servants." It was also alleged that there were many
kinds of work that whites simply refused to do because the opinion
was strongly established in the colony that hard, unskilled labor was
beneath the dignity of Europeans and must be performed by nonwhites.[20]

Twenty-five years later, Baron van Imhoff, a governor-general of
the East Indies who inspected the Cape settlement, summed up the
consequences of the decision for slavery, which had been confirmed by
the Company in 1717: "I believe it would have been for the better had
we, when this colony was founded, commenced with Europeans and
brought them hither in such numbers that hunger and want would
have forced them to work. But having imported slaves, every common or ordinary European becomes a gentleman and prefers to be
served than to serve. We have in addition the fact that the majority of
farmers in this colony are not farmers in the real sense of the word, but
owners of plantations, and that many of them consider it a shame to
work with their hands. . . ."[21]

Despite all the differences in circumstances and chronology, the
choices made in the Cape and the southern American colonies to proceed on a slave-labor basis can be seen as variations on a common
theme. Besides a sense of the real or apparent economic advantages of

nonwhite servitude over white labor, there was the promise of a more stable and cohesive social order. A large class of underprivileged and potentially discontented whites was dangerous enough in the developing metropolitan societies of the mother countries, but there the propertied classes' control of the resources necessary for subsistence meant that the capitalist prescription of work or starve could be relied upon, in the long run at least, to impel most people into productive activity. Furthermore, the growth of the modern state, with its standing armies and monopoly on the use of force, provided more effective means than had previously existed to deal with disorders resulting from lower-class discontent. But in the colonies, it proved impossible to mold white immigrants into a permanent laboring class without attempting the hazardous proceeding of subjecting people who thought of themselves as free to virtual slavery. Nor would it have been advisable, given the inadequacy of any available professional military force to provide security against indigenous resistance on the frontier and possible foreign invasion on the coastline, to deny them the arms and military training that slave status would have precluded.

These environmental pressures and military considerations meant that a servile or dependent labor force could most conveniently be provided by alien slaves, whose rightless status and regimented working conditions would set them off sharply from the European population. As we have seen, this calculation had been made almost at the outset in South Africa, although some qualms about the creation of a slave society outside the tropics persisted until 1717. In the Chesapeake colonies, a gradual shift occurred from a white labor system that proved increasingly inadequate to a rigid and rigorous form of black slavery that seemed to offer greater profits and social stability. Along the way, there was an extended period when white servants and black slaves worked side by side on the farms and plantations under day-to-day conditions that were not very different. This proved to be a particularly volatile situation from the planters' perspective because their dependents tended to fraternize across racial lines and sometimes conspired together to escape or even revolt. Seventeenth-century records contain many instances of such inter-racial cooperation.[22] Although black slaves would prove quite capable of such activity on their own, it is probable, or may have seemed so at the time, that the white servants' expectations of freedom infected their black co-workers and made them even more discontented and prone to strike for freedom than they might otherwise have been. There were some comparable examples in South Africa of collective resistance by nonwhite slaves and runaway white *knechts* or company servants. Some of the outlaw bands that lurked in the mountains around Cape Town and raided the exposed farms in the early eighteenth century were composed of European as well as nonwhite fugitives.[23] As in the South, the possible compromise of a mixed labor force must have seemed particularly unstable and dangerous to the ruling group.

Commitment to a labor regime under which non-European slaves did virtually all of the menial and subservient work had the effect of lessening the possibility of class conflict among whites by elevating all of them to a relatively privileged social status. This is the implication of Von Imhoff's comment that every white South African thought of himself as a gentleman and considered it "a shame to work with his hands." It was also the cause of what Edmund Morgan describes as a rising "populism" in early eighteenth-century Virginia, at a time when the enslavement of blacks and the decline of white servitude permitted a considerable enhancement of the political and social status of white freemen who were not members of the planter class.[24]

But the two situations were not identical. In the Cape there was apparently a wider and more equitable diffusion of actual slaveholding among the white population. Approximately half of all the free burghers in the colony owned at least one slave in 1750; of the slaveholders, 79 percent owned less than ten, only 4.7 percent owned more than twenty-five, and a mere seven individuals owned more than fifty.[25] Hence a majority or near-majority of the white population could derive a sense of status and privilege, not only from direct ownership of slaves, but also from membership in a relatively egalitarian master class that included few "big planters" in the American sense. Comparable figures do not exist for the southern colonies, but all accounts suggest a pattern in which economic and social differences among white colonists were much more substantial. Particularly significant was the gap between a dominant planter elite and the great majority who owned no slaves or only a few. If freedom and masterdom tended to go together in the Cape—in a way that could be readily understood in traditional class terms and did not require any special reinforcement—any growth of an egalitarian consciousness and sense of status among the mass of less privileged southern whites came to depend increasingly on a rigid caste division between all whites and all Negroes, whether slave or free. The implications of this difference for developing patterns of race relations remain to be explored. But the account already provided of the social circumstances surrounding the rise of racial slavery suggests a major theme of this study—that one cannot understand crucial developments in the history of white supremacy in the United States and South Africa without assigning a major causal role to tensions or divisions within the white social structure. The degradation of nonwhites frequently served to bind together the white population, or some segment of it, to create a sense of community or solidarity that could become a way of life and not simply a cover for economic exploitation.

The Ideological Origins of Slavery

The decisions that led to the emergence of slave societies in the South and the Cape were conditioned by the crucial assumption that nonwhites were enslavable while Europeans were not. This presumption is sometimes seen as evidence of a conscious racism—a belief that whites were destined by God or nature to rule over peoples whose physical characteristics denoted their innate inferiority. But the actual discourse accompanying the first introduction of slaves into North America and South Africa does not provide much support for this hypothesis. The evidence strongly suggests that Africans and other non-Europeans were initially enslaved not so much because of their color and physical type as because of their legal and cultural vulnerability.

For seventeenth-century Europeans slavery meant a total or absolute state of unfreedom. In theory, a slave had forfeited his life as a result of crime or captivity in war but his death was deferred as an act of mercy on the understanding that henceforth he could claim none of the rights associated with being a member of society or one of its constituent corporate groups. According to John Locke's, *Two Treatises of Government,* slavery was a facet of the state of nature that was not affected by the social contract establishing the philosophical and historical basis for individual claims to the rights of life, liberty, and property. It was "nothing else, but *the state of War continued, between a lawful Conquerour, and a Captive.*" Hence the slave had forfeited his natural rights and any claim to the protective jurisdiction of the state; in the eyes of the law he was property rather than a person with a social and political status.[26] In practice, of course, no slave society had ever been able to ignore, even in its slave codes, that the slave was in fact a human being with a will of his own. But legal recognition of the humanity of slaves was more likely to be a pragmatic response to their ability to resist total domination by being insubordinate or rebellious than the reflection of a humanitarian concern with their condition.

Slavery, in the sense described, did not exist as a lawful institution in England or the Netherlands at the time of colonization. But prior to the introduction of this form of servitude into their own colonies, subjects or citizens of both nations had been permitted to engage in the international slave trade. John Hawkins, the Elizabethan sea dog, had made three memorable slaving voyages during the sixteenth century in an attempt, backed by the Queen, to open up the Spanish colonial market to English slavers. His ultimate failure retarded major English participation in the commerce for another century, but the precedent was established.[27] The Dutch broke into the trade at the beginning of the seventeenth century when they began transporting Africans to the Portuguese in Brazil.[28] By this time, the "law of nations" and "custom of merchants," establishing the ground rules for international political and commercial relations between recognized states, had fully sanctioned the transportation of slaves as a legitimate activity in which Christian nations could engage.[29] It is hardly surprising that once the English and Dutch had colonies of their own they would see little objection to providing them with the same kind of human merchandise they had carried to other markets.

What made the slave trade seem a legitimate enterprise to Europeans was, first of all, the belief that slaves were in fact prisoners of war or criminals whose enslavement was an alternative to execution; or, to put the issue on a practical plane, that they were already properly condemned to slavery by the laws or customs of the African or Asian societies in which they originated, meaning that their purchase by European traders did not alter their condition. This was not, of course, an accurate picture of what occurred in places like the Guinea coast of West Africa. European slavers sometimes captured their own cargo, and they frequently inspired or provoked wars or raids that would not have occurred without the demand for human merchandise. But the fact that most slaves were acquired by purchase from native traders or rulers gave enough plausibility to the prevailing rationalization to put European consciences at ease. Relatively few whites actually observed the abominable conditions of the trade at first hand, and the traders themselves were careful not to publicize incidents of outright kidnapping and other abuses that were incompatible with the legitimizing ideology. But the seventeenth-century trade could not be adequately sanctioned solely by invoking the ancient precedent of enslaving captives in war. European nations had departed from this principle in the wars they fought among themselves by adopting the custom of ransoming prisoners rather than enslaving them. The only captives taken in wars fought by Europeans since the Middle Ages who had actually been held in bondage were heathens, particularly Moors and other Muslims. This tradition made it essential for the apologists for slave trading to emphasize that Africans were not merely captives but infidels as well. The fact of their heathenism opened the way to the ultimate in comforting rationalizations—the claim that the slave trade contributed to the propagation of Christianity by removing people from barbarous African societies inaccessible to missionaries and taking them to Christian colonies where their souls could be saved.[30]

Making heathenism a qualification for enslavement was a highly effective way to justify the trade, but it raised the serious problem of whether the colonial slaves who converted to Christianity could still be held in servitude. Traditional Christian thought on the subject did not in fact make it sinful to hold a baptized slave in bondage, because a distinction had always been made between the spiritual realm where masters and slaves could be equal in the sight of God and the temporal sphere where inequality and even despotism were accepted as manifestations of divine judgment on the human race for its original fall from grace. By the time of the Renaissance and Reformation, however, a strong antipathy had developed against enslaving fellow Christians, and the effect of conversion on the worldly status of heathen slaves was a debatable issue. This question posed particular difficulties for militant Protestants because of their stress on the individual's direct relationship to God. Although they did not repudiate slavery itself, some of the luminaries of seventeenth-century English Puritanism expressed doubt as to whether the absolute power of human masters was consistent with the obligations that the slaves owed to their master in heaven.[31]

The answer provided by the Puritans who went to New England was not to eschew slavery but to modify it by granting the slaves some of the rights of freemen, including the right to a legal marriage. The result was an institution that differed substantially from the more con-

sistent and rigorous chattel servitude that developed in the colonies to the south. Until 1664 Massachusetts slaves who became church members were theoretically eligible for membership in the company of freemen, a status that would have necessitated manumission. This policy does not appear to have been implemented in practice, but New Englanders did not follow the lead of other colonies by legalizing the principle that conversion does not require manumission—perhaps because they had real qualms about it. Although no efforts were made to compel the liberation of black Christians, the reigning theocracy did prevent masters from exerting the kind of total authority that would have prevented slaves from performing the religious and moral duties incumbent on all members of Puritan society.[32]

If Calvinists in England and New England worried about the compatibility of slavery and Christianization, those in the Netherlands made a serious attempt to resolve the issue. At the Synod of Dort, meeting in 1618 to formulate the theological and ecclesiastical doctrines of the Dutch Reformed Church, it was determined that slaves converted while in servitude "ought to enjoy equal right of liberty with the other Christians" and should not be sold. Presumably this meant that they must be emancipated, although the ruling could also be interpreted as sanctioning continued service for the same master under some form of limited servitude which, in theory at least, could also be imposed on Europeans. In any case, it gave formal sanction to a principle that English Protestants never clearly acknowledged—that Christianization and chattel slavery were incompatible.[33]

However the difficult question of the consequences of baptism might be resolved in theory or practice, it is clear from the authoritative discussions of the legal, moral, and religious foundations of slavery taking place in seventeenth-century England and the Netherlands that there was little or no overt sense that biological race or skin color played a determinative role in making some human beings absolute masters over others. The combination of heathenness and *de facto* captivity was what made people enslavable, not their pigmentation or other physical characteristics, and it is thus misleading and anachronistic to read the overt physical racism that emerged later back into the thought of this era. It is, of course, undeniable that harshly demeaning stereotypes were applied to the people who were enslaved, particularly Africans. Winthrop Jordan and others have amply demonstrated that the English in particular were strongly prone to associate the color black with evil, filth, and misfortune and were thus preconditioned to react adversely to the appearance, as well as the culture, of the Negroid peoples they encountered. But this distaste for blackness was not unanimous. David Brion Davis has uncovered some evidence of a countercurrent of admiration for African physical beauty, and some of the early English and Dutch observers of Africa and Africans mentioned color only casually or in passing before commenting extensively on cultural traits.[34]

Blackness was only one aspect, if a striking one, of the total image of the African that emerged from the literature of the time; and it could conceivably be neutralized by a strong injection of Christianity and "civilization." Along with the primitive and villainous "blackamoors" who populated the Elizabethan stage there was the noble figure of Othello, the civilized black man whose psychology transcended racial stereotyping and whose tragedy was meant to inspire compassion rather than contempt.[35] In the absence of sustained contact, the negative attitude toward Africans that Elizabethan Englishmen sometimes manifested was, in all likelihood, the casually held and somewhat fluid impression of a remote and exotic form of humanity rather than an expression of a fixed and deeply rooted colorphobia. However unflattering the usual African stereotype may have been, it was probably less derogatory and venomous than that applied at this time to the Irish, who were undeniably white.[36] Although color prejudice existed in a rudimentary form, it was, in all probability, not sufficiently salient or well-focused to have been in any significant way responsible for the initial introduction of African slaves into the colonies of northern Europeans. Perhaps a sense of their great differentness, as accentuated by their appearance, helped inure whites to the cruelties of the slave trade. But, as we have seen, Indians were also enslaved at times in the American colonies, and it was long believed that Indians were born white and became tawny as the result of artificial processes.

It is even more difficult to establish a nexus between physical prejudice and enslavement in the South African case. A large proportion of the slaves brought to the Cape by the Dutch were not Africans at all but East Asians. Although they were often referred to as "black," their dark brown pigmentation did not prevent the Dutch from generally regarding them as superior to the lighter-skinned Khoikhoi. To complicate matters further, the East African slaves, who were perhaps the darkest of all, were sometimes accorded what amounted to an intermediate place in the attitudinal hierarchy, standing somewhere between the indigenes and the Asian slaves.[37] Race is, of course, more than color, and a full examination of the European reaction to the physical appearance of various peoples would have to take hair type, facial features, physique, and other phenotypical features into account. An investigation along these lines would be useful and would shed some important light on the history of racial prejudice. What is questionable is whether it would reveal much about why some peoples were enslaved and others were not. In the American South, the fact that most slaves were black rather than red and that Indians generally seemed to the colonists more physically attractive than Africans might suggest the relevance of some sense of somatic ranking; but this would be contradicted by the Cape experience, where the indigenous peoples who remained theoretically free were characteristically regarded with great disdain, on physical as well as cultural grounds, while the slaves inspired considerably less revulsion.

Empirically speaking, the enslaved can be described as nonwhite heathens who were vulnerable to acquisition by whites as a form of property, either because they were literally captured in war or because a slave trade existed or could be inaugurated in their societies of origin. On an ideological plane, it was the combination of heathenism and captivity that was initially stressed. To prove the proposition that heathenism really *was* the most salient defining characteristic, and not merely a code word for race or color, one has to be prepared to hypothesize that white heathens available for enslavement would have been seized upon almost as readily and carried to where their labor was needed. Since there were no such populations in the seventeenth century, a definitive resolution of the issue is impossible. But what if the Irish of the sixteenth and seventeenth centuries had been true pagans rather than the obviously fictive ones of English propaganda? It strains the imagination very little to visualize heathen Irish slaves being carried in large numbers to the American colonies. As it was, hordes of Irish were massacred as the result of the policy of conquest and extirpation that was renewed in the mid-seventeenth century by Oliver Cromwell. Some revolutionaries might argue that it is better to be dead than to be a slave, but it is difficult to characterize genocidal policies against whites in the name of religion or civilization as the earmark of an age when color was a prerequisite for the most extreme forms of degradation.

From Religious to Racial Slavery in Virginia and South Africa

According to John C. Hurd, the great mid-nineteenth-century authority on the law of American slavery, heathen Africans imported into the American colonies were from the outset regarded and treated as slaves—despite the lack of positive legislation authorizing chattel servitude—because "the *law of nations* for Christian powers" sanctioned such status for "prisoners in war with heathen and infidel nations." Local legislation was nevertheless required, Hurd contended, first to qualify their status as mere property or merchandise by recognizing that for some purposes they were legal persons, and secondly to justify their continued enslavement after they had been converted to Christianity.[38] International law or the custom of nations may not have been as clear-cut as Hurd believed, but the gist of his argument deserves to be taken seriously. His thesis that original enslavement on religious grounds was followed by local action shifting the basis to ethnic or racial origin has not been accorded much respect by recent historians, mainly because doubts have arisen as to whether the first blacks to arrive in the colonies were indeed subjected to *de facto* slavery. As a result of what appears to have occurred in Virginia, a belief has grown up that the imposition of lifetime servitude developed only gradually and that the eventual sanctioning of slavery for converts was merely one aspect of the process of legalizing a unique status for blacks that had evolved over several decades.[39]

The facts are fragmentary, but this much at least is definitely known of the situation of blacks in early Virginia: of the relatively small number who arrived in the colony between 1619 and the middle of the century, some were or became free while others were serving for life—at least by the 1640s when cases involving black servitude began to appear in court records. During that decade there were approximately 300 blacks in Virginia, representing about 2.5 percent of a total population of 15,000. The fact that all blacks were not slaves makes it possible that the earliest arrivals, the handful who arrived before the 1630s, were actually considered term rather than lifetime servants, because the notion that slavery was the proper status for imported Africans had not yet taken hold.[40]

But there is another possibility, equally plausible as an interpretation of the local evidence and somewhat more persuasive in the light of international opinion concerning whom it was rightful to enslave.

The census and other data of the first decade of black immigration suggest that many of the earliest arrivals had already been baptized. The prevalence of Spanish names among them has led Wesley Frank Craven to speculate that they were "probably native to America" and that "it is possible that some or all of them were Christian," having been previously converted by the Spaniards.[41] It is known that the first twenty, who arrived in 1619, had been captured from the Spanish by a Dutch privateer cruising in the West Indies and that a child born in Virginia to one couple from this group was baptized, while his parents were not, presumably because they had already been converted. In 1624 a case came before the General Court that provides presumptive evidence of the consequence of prior conversion among Africans. A Negro named John Phillip was accorded the status of a free man and allowed to give testimony in a suit because he had been "Christened in *England* 12 years since."[42] It appears very likely, therefore, that the class of blacks who were either free or engaged as servants for a limited term originated not so much from uncertainty about the legitimacy of slavery *per se* as from the operation of the principle that baptized slaves could not be held in perpetual bondage. If, as seems probable, a greater proportion of the larger number who arrived in the 1630s were heathens, then the emergence of lifetime servitude could well have resulted primarily from a shift in the religious status of new arrivals.

If this hypothesis is valid, it bears out John C. Hurd's contention that the introduction of *heathen* slavery into an English colony caused no ideological or legal problem, and one might conclude that recent historians have made too much of the apparent confusion and inconsistency surrounding the status of imported Africans in Virginia before the formal recognition of slavery in the 1660s. No comparable uncertainty seems to have shrouded the initial process of heathen enslavement in other British colonies established in the early seventeenth century.[43] If, as Hurd suggested, heathen slavery could exist for a time without positive legal sanctions, it becomes quite conceivable that all or most of the non-Christian slaves who arrived in Virginia before the era of legislative clarification were held by their masters, as a matter of course, for just as long as their services were desired. This might in some cases have been less than their lifetimes because of the tendency existing in any slave society for masters to manumit slaves whose declining work capabilities have made them no longer worth their keep or whose unusually faithful service is deemed to merit an exceptional reward.

The important decision of the 1660s in Virginia was not that there could be slaves, for there already were, but that converted slaves could thenceforth be held in bondage. Fragmentary evidence suggests that the legislation of 1667 implementing this principle negated an enforceable right, not just a remote legal possibility. In 1644, the General Assembly determined in the case of Manuel, a baptized mulatto who had originally been purchased as a "Slave for Ever," that he was liable only "to serve as other Christians do."* In two later cases for which some records survive—Elizabeth Key's suit of 1655–56 and that of Fernando in 1667—conversion was explicitly used to support a claim for freedom. Although the final disposition and grounds for resolution of these cases remain obscure, the fact that they were entertained by the courts and seriously litigated had led Warren Billings to conclude that as late as the 1660s "a nexus existed between an African's religion and his status as a laborer in Virginia. Conversion to Christianity evidently conferred upon blacks a rank higher than that of a slave. If an African retained his native religion, in all likelihood he stayed a slave, but if he converted or were born into slavery and baptized, his conversion or baptism could provide grounds for his release from life servitude."[44] In 1667, the Assembly sought to remedy this situation by proclaiming "that the conferring of baptism doth not alter the condition of a person as to his bondage or freedom." But this first statutory sanction for Christian slavery applied directly only to slaves who had been baptized after they had arrived in the colony; the presumption of freedom for those who were Christians before their importation remained, as shown by a law of 1670 prescribing "that all servants *not* being Christians, imported into the colony by shipping, shall be slaves for life." The loophole of prior conversion was finally closed in 1682 by an enactment making slaves of all those arriving "whose parentage and native country are not Christian at the time of their first purchase . . . by some Christian." From this point on, heathen descent rather than actual heathenism was the legal basis for slavery in Virginia.[45]

Although the language was still that of religious distinctions, the

---

* But the fact that Manuel was not actually freed for twenty-one years may be an indication of ethnic discrimination among Christian servants; for his was a longer obligation than any known to have been imposed on white indentured workers.

concept of heathen ancestry was a giant step toward making racial differences the foundation of servitude. Winthrop Jordan has cogently described how the equation of whiteness with Christianity and freedom and of blackness with heathenism and slavery gradually took hold in a way that obscured any contrary facts or possibilities.[46] According to the clergyman Morgan Godwyn, who published a book in 1680 advocating increased efforts to Christianize blacks and Indians: "These two words, *Negro* and *Slave*," have "by custom grown Homogeneous and Convertible; even as *Negro* and *Christian, Englishman* and *Heathen,* are by the like corrupt nature and Partiality made *opposites;* thereby as it were implying that the one could not be *Christians,* nor the other *Infidels.*"[47] The legal developments and semantic tendencies that in effect made the disabilities of heathenism inheritable and inextricably associated with blackness laid the groundwork for what I have elsewhere called "societal racism," or the relegation of members of a racial or ethnic group to a status that implies that they are innately inferior, even though there is no explicit ideology on which to base such an assertion.[48]

It would probably confuse cause and effect, however, to view the transition to racial slavery as motivated primarily by color prejudice. There is no doubt that the blackness of Africans was an important part of what made them seem so alien and different to white Virginians. But planters also had very strong economic and social incentives to create a caste of hereditary bondsmen. For Virginia planters, slaves probably became a better long-term investment than servants by 1660.[49] Although limited availability, high prices, and the large initial outlay of capital required meant that only men who already possessed substantial wealth were able to take advantage of the opportunity—while lesser planters had to continue to rely almost exclusively on indentured servants—such a propertied elite could readily use its dominance over colonial assemblies to pass laws protecting its growing economic stake in lifetime bondage. The Maryland law of 1664 requiring all Negroes to serve *"durante vita"* so that they could not claim freedom by professing Christianity quite candidly justified this measure as necessary to protect the property interests of the masters. The Virginia law of three years later had a somewhat different rationale; its alleged intent was to encourage owners to convert their slaves free of any fear that proselytizing would lead to emancipation. But the underlying assumption was clear—masters wanted to keep their slaves in lifetime service, so the law should enable them to do so. In the words of Wilbert Moore, both laws indicated that "there was a conflict between profitable slavery and the spread of Christianity."[50] The fact that Virginia planters continued to resist baptism even after the law was passed may indicate which of the two objectives had the higher priority. Fateful as it may have been for the future of race relations, the original decision to create what amounted to a racially derived status probably arose less from a consciousness of racial privilege than from palpable self-interest on the part of members of a dominant class who had been fortunate enough to acquire slaves to supplement or replace their fluctuating force of indentured servants.

Whatever might have been the situation in Virginia, there was no uncertainty at the Cape about the initial status of imported heathens. Slavery was already an established institution in the domain of the Dutch East India Company, and nonwhite slaves were present in the colony almost from the beginning. For the Dutch, like the English, the victims of the slave trade had legitimately forfeited their status as persons under the law and custom of nations and become a form of merchandise, which meant that they had only such rights as the authorities of the colonies into which they were introduced were willing to grant them as a matter of expediency. The Dutch had the advantage of having somewhat less need than the English to spell out the full legal conditions of servitude and could make do for extended periods without elaborate slave codes. During the whole period that the Dutch occupied what later became New York, they gave no explicit recognition to the institution in statutory law despite a heavy reliance on slave labor. Pre-existing East Indian statutes could be applied at the Cape, but it remains noteworthy that a comprehensive local slave code was not promulgated for a full century. English colonies moved rapidly to formal legal sanctions when the numbers of slaves warranted such action, because the common law of England made no provision for slavery; the Dutch could be more casual, because the statutory law governing the Netherlands was based directly on Roman law, with its ample precedents for regulating slave status. Although the aspects of Roman law pertaining to slavery were held to be inapplicable to the Netherlands itself, they were customarily applied in the colonies to govern situations for which the statutes made no clear provisions.[51]

If the legal implications of slavery as an institution presented little problem for the Dutch, the question of the status of baptized slaves was even more troublesome than for the English because, as we have seen, the Synod of Dort had made it contrary to the official doctrines of the Dutch Reformed Church to hold converted heathens in chattel servitude. The Dutch East India Company and its colonies were in effect barred from following the example of Virginia and Maryland and explicitly legalizing Christian slavery. Religious authorities sometimes wished them to go further and actively enforce the principle of "Christian freedom." In 1681, the Church Council of Batavia advised the Cape government that masters who baptized their slaves were responsible for emancipating them.[52]

In the early years at the Cape, the Company did encourage the baptism of its own slaves and even established schools in which they could be instructed in Protestant Christianity. But there was no clear policy requiring that the converts be manumitted, and the majority of them were not in fact freed. In 1685, High Commissioner van Rheede of the East India Company visited the Cape and left behind a number of instructions concerning the Company's slaves, including some guidelines for the manumission of those who professed Reformed Christianity. Noting that there were a large number of slave children in the Company's lodge who had Dutch fathers, he ordered that these half-castes be raised as Dutch-speaking Christians, taught useful trades, and then emancipated and granted free burgher status when they were grown, boys to be freed at twenty-five and girls at twenty-two. As for the full-blooded slaves of the Company, they were to be considered *eligible* for manumission after thirty years of service if imported or at the age of forty if born at the Cape, provided that they had been converted and spoke Dutch. Although this policy may seem generous in its implications, it fell short of implementing the principle that Christians could not be kept in chattel slavery. The manumission of baptized slaves who had two heathen parents was made a privilege rather than a right, and the eligibility requirements applied only to slaves of the Company and not to those in private hands.[53]

Furthermore, it appears from evidence concerning subsequent manumissions by the Company that Van Rheede's plan was never actually put into effect. By the early eighteenth century, the Company was protecting its investment in a servile labor force by responding to all petitions for the emancipation of one of its adult slaves by requiring that another slave be supplied to take the place of the freedman; in the case of children substantial monetary compensation was demanded.

In 1708, a restriction was placed on the right of burghers to emancipate their own bondsmen; owners thenceforth had to provide a guarantee that their ex-slaves would not be dependent on the communal poor fund for ten years. There is no indication that the new limitations on emancipation made any exception for baptized slaves. A Dutch Reformed minister then resident at the Cape complained to church authorities in Amsterdam in 1708 that slaves who were church members were being kept in bondage and were subject to being sold or inherited, despite the fact that such practices were contrary to "Christian freedom."[54]

Although the doctrine of "Christian freedom" was not being adhered to in practice, the presumption that baptized slaves had a right to emancipation if they could somehow enforce it persisted throughout the eighteenth century. The inevitable result was that masters saw to it that few of their slaves were formally converted. A German who resided at the Cape in the 1730s later reported that "there is a common and well-grounded belief that Christians must not be held in bondage; hence only such children as are intended for emancipation are baptised."[55] A Swedish scientist visiting the Cape in the 1770s described some psalm-singing slaves who had not been christened, "since by that means, according to the law of the land, they would have obtained their freedom and [their master] would have lost them from his service."[56] Comparable resistance to Christianization persisted among American slaveholders long after the laws had made it clear that their property rights would not be affected; missionaries were seriously impeded in their proselytizing efforts until late in the eighteenth century by fears that slaves would not grasp the distinction between spiritual and temporal equality.[57] At the Cape, where a body of legal and religious precedent was actually on the side of the converted slave seeking to change his or her condition, the intensity of opposition to Christianization can readily be imagined.

This situation in fact had the remarkable effect of encouraging a tolerance for Islam as an alternative slave religion. Malays and other East Indian slaves who brought their faith with them were not only allowed to practice it, but even to proselytize among other non-Christian slaves. Although such toleration was not an official policy, the lack of active persecution and repression must have reflected a sense among the whites that there were some practical advantages in having Muslim slaves. When the British took over the colony, they were shocked at the extent to which the Dutch had allowed Islam to spread in the slave population, and in 1808 the new government called for increased missionary activity in order to counter this tendency. But in 1820, when the first survey was taken of the religious affiliations of the slaves, it was revealed that there were three times as many Muslims as Christians among them. In order to discover how such a thing could have occurred in a Christian colony, a commission listened to the testimony of a Malay priest who described how Islam had found a haven in a Christian slave society by teaching its adherents such religious obligations as obedience to masters and abstinence from alcohol. In the eighteenth century, when there were constant complaints of drunkenness among slaves—as might be expected in a colony which listed wine and brandy among its most important commodities—many masters must have welcomed the services of a teetotalling Muslim. But probably even more important in encouraging the policy of *de facto* tolerance toward the traditional enemies of Christendom was the fact that there could be no question of any obligation to free a Muslim slave.[58]

The Council of the Indies in Batavia, a governing body with jurisdiction over the Cape, finally resolved the issue of the effect of baptism on slave status in 1770 when it issued a regulation that Christian slaves could not be sold or otherwise alienated by their masters. This fell short of requiring their manumission, but it did follow the prescription of the Council of Dort to the extent that it exempted them from the full rigors of chattel servitude. To the degree that this law was enforced at the Cape—and there is some evidence from testamentary documents that it was—it probably confirmed the fears of masters that Christianization would limit their property interests and served as an added discouragement to proselytization.[59] In an effort to allay these fears by stressing that outright emancipation was still not required, a local church council of 1792 made the first explicit statement that had ever come from any official or authoritative body in the Cape to the effect that neither the law nor the Church prevented a master from retaining possession of his baptized slaves.[60] But it was the British administration of 1812 that finally removed all doubt by formally nullifying the 1770 regulation of the Council of the Indies on the grounds that any restriction on the right of a master to dispose of his slaves as he saw fit impeded the progress of Christianity. Enunciating a principle that had long been established in British slave colonies, the Chief Justice wrote to the governor that he could not "deduce from the true principles of our religion why a slave here cannot be a *slave* and at the same time a *Christian*."[61]

In a much slower and more uncertain fashion than in the southern colonies, the criterion for enslavement had thus shifted from heathenism to what could only be racial origin. The latter principle was not made explicit at the end of the process, any more than it had been in the South more than a century earlier, but it was clearly implied by the fact that it was no longer religion *and* race but race alone that was the essential distinguishing mark of the slave class.

It may have been of lasting significance that the official disassociation of heathenism and slavery took so much longer in South Africa than in the South. In the latter instance, early resolution of the issue in favor of hereditary racial slavery helped create favorable conditions for a trend toward the acceptance or encouragement of slave conversion that picked up momentum in the late eighteenth century. This new receptivity to the propagation of the gospel in the quarters was due partly to the rise of a more evangelical form of Christianity after the Great Awakening of the mid-eighteenth century and partly to the fact that an increasing majority of the slaves were American born, making them seem better raw material for baptism than the "outlandish" Africans who had predominated earlier. But what allowed the trend to persist and develop into the more substantial missionary effort of the pre–Civil War era was the growing conviction of slaveholders— and eventually even of the southern evangelical clergymen who had earlier expressed doubts about the compatibility of slavery and Christianity—that assimilation of the whites' religion did not give the blacks any claim to freedom or equality and might in fact make them better slaves by instilling the Pauline doctrine that obedience to masters was a Christian duty.[62]

No such trend of thought developed among slaveholders at the Cape before the British-imposed emancipation of the 1830s, despite the government's active encouragement of the Christianization of slaves. To some extent this difference can be explained by the fact that there was no major evangelical revival among the Dutch settlers. But the continued resistance to mission work, which left most slaves without religion of any kind or secure in their Islamic faith right up to the time they were freed, may also have represented the persistence of patterns of thought inculcated during the century and a half when Christian slavery was under a cloud. It appears that South African masters remained acutely uncomfortable with slaves or other nonwhite dependents who practiced the same religion and thus partook of the same cultural heritage as themselves. Indeed, the kind of "homogeneity" between "white" and "Christian" or "black" and "heathen" that Morgan Godwyn found in late-seventeenth-century Virginia persisted in the discourse of the Afrikaners until late in the nineteenth century.[63] What is more, they made strenuous efforts to see that these linguistic correlations mirrored reality—by neglecting and sometimes vigorously discouraging the propagation of Christianity among their nonwhite dependents. Since they craved a cultural gap as well as a racial one, they preferred to allow color and religion to remain reinforcing aspects of differentness rather than making a clear decision, such as was made in the South, as to which was to have priority. The long delay in the full legitimation of racial slavery may therefore have been one factor making the South African white-supremacist tradition more dependent on cultural pluralism than the American.

Slavery and Society in the South and the Cape

However whites may have interpreted the change, the shift in the basis of slavery from religion to ancestry was clearly crucial to the emergence of a social order based on caste-like distinctions between white and black; for it encouraged the sense that the normal condition of dark-skinned people was abject servitude. The early rise of policies designed to restrict or discourage manumission also contributed to this sense of racial determinism. At the Cape, the law of 1708 requiring a guarantee of support for freedmen was replaced by a regulation of 1767 exacting a monetary payment from the emancipator; another ten years later raised the prescribed sum fivefold.[64] Although such actions seem to have been motivated primarily by the practical aim of saving the community from the economic and social costs of maintaining a population of impoverished and unemployed ex-slaves, its effect was to slow the rate of manumission and prevent the development of a large free colored class. Only about a thousand slaves were freed between 1715 and 1791 or 92; and in 1807, the first time that a census enumerated those classified as "free blacks" separately from the rest of the free population, only 1,204 were counted, as compared to 29,303 slaves and 25,614 whites.[65] In the South, an even more strenuous effort to limit the number of free blacks began in 1691 when Virginia prohibited masters from freeing their slaves unless they were willing to "pay for the transportation of such negro or negroes out of the country within six months of setting them free."[66] Other colonies passed similar laws with the result that the free Negro population of the colonial South remained minuscule in proportion to the number of slaves and whites. According to the Maryland census of 1755, for example, free Negroes were only about 4 percent of the blacks and 2 percent of the free population. Despite the temporary operation of more permissive manumission laws in the upper South in the two decades after the Revolution, the federal census of 1820 revealed that only 8.1 percent of the black population of the South was free—a proportion that held steady through 1840 and then dropped off to 6.1 percent in 1860 as a result of a new wave of restrictive legislation.[67]

What these figures reveal is that both the South and the Cape were closed slave societies in comparison with those of the Caribbean and Latin America, where less restrictive manumission requirements enabled more sizable and socially significant free colored groups to develop. The comparative study of race patterns in the New World suggests that the absence during the slave era of a substantial intermediate group of free people of color sets the stage for a "two-category" pattern of race relations in which the essential division is a sharp dichotomy between white and black rather than a more elaborate hierarchy based on gradations of color and class. The relatively closed character of slavery in both the United States and South Africa clearly pointed in this direction.[68]

But to leave it at that would be to miss some important differences in the role slavery actually played in the evolution of social structure and status consciousness in the two situations. There were, in fact, variations in the relation of slave classes to other classes in the community that made for somewhat different patterns of social interaction during the era of servitude. The essential social structure that was emerging in the South by the mid-eighteenth century—which was strengthened and elaborated but not changed fundamentally up to the time of the Civil War—might be described as involving two racial castes, a dominant white caste and a subordinate black caste, each of which was subdivided into status groups. The caste or racial line was maintained by discriminatory legislation applicable to all blacks whether slave or free, such as the laws banning intermarriage and denying Negroes the right to vote, testify in court against whites, and bear arms. The status division among whites was determined primarily by the possession of property, especially slave property. The dominant group was the large planters, who tended to monopolize political power and social prestige; below them were the small slaveholders and land-owning yeoman farmers; and at the bottom was a class that came to be known as "poor whites," who either owned no land or had only marginal acreages barely adequate for subsistence, and of course possessed no slaves. The black caste was divided most clearly into a small minority who were nominally free and the large mass who were enslaved. Hence the main employers of labor, the substantial planters, might be described as the upper class of an upper caste, and the main work force as the lower class of a lower caste. But the racial or caste division tended to obscure the class or status differences within both the white and black categories. Whether they actually owned slaves or not, most whites could be mobilized in defense of their racial or caste privileges, thus creating a basis for inter-class solidarity and even for a kind of pseudo-equality. In the lower caste, the fact that free Negroes suffered from some of the same disabilities as slaves made them feel a greater bond with their brothers in servitude than did free colored groups in other Western Hemisphere slave societies. Clearly the institution of racial slavery was the most important determinant of this social order and the lynchpin that held it together, although the fact that a majority of the white caste held no slaves was probably a critical factor in making racial distinctions as uniquely rigid as they were. In such a society, racial privilege could and did serve as a compensation for class disadvantage.[69]

The social pattern that developed in the eighteenth-century Cape was significantly different. One cannot yet speak confidently of racial castes, as one could for the South of the same era, because there was relatively little legalized discrimination against free people of color. Before the 1790s, "free blacks" seem to have enjoyed all the basic rights and privileges of free burgher status with one major exception: beginning in 1722, some of them were conscripted for occasional duty in a segregated fire company and work batallion, a practice which developed into a prescribed alternative to the militia duty imposed on those considered to be white. Most surprisingly, there was no ban on their intermarriage with whites, and such unions not only occurred relatively often but were treated in a tolerant or off-hand way by the community. It is true that some minor ordinances of the late eighteenth century were clearly discriminatory: in 1765 free black women were enjoined not to dress like fashionable ladies; in 1771 more severe penalties were prescribed for free blacks who purchased clothing from company slaves than for whites who committed the same offense. But these were relatively trivial proscriptions in comparison to those applied to free blacks in the late colonial South.[70]

One way to comprehend the social structure of the late eighteenth- and early nineteenth-century Cape is to see it as a class society in which race mattered in the determination of status but was not all-important. The social hierarchy was composed of a white upper class of company officials and prosperous wine and grain farmers; an intermediate group of freemen, mostly white in ancestry, but including (for most purposes) some free people of color; and a servile class, entirely nonwhite but by this time subdivided into chattel slaves and Khoikhoi servants.[71] The latter were nominally free but because of their landlessness were slipping into a kind of serfdom, especially in the outlying areas; their legal status, to the extent that they had any at all, was superior to that of the slaves, but their social prestige actually tended to be lower than that of the bondsmen of East Indian and East African origin.[72] Hence the larger social setting differed from that of the Old South in its relative inchoateness or fluidity and in the extent to which social class rather than racial caste persisted as the normative basis of social organization.

The economic and ecological circumstances determining the growth and profitability of a slave labor system are also quite distinguishable. Southern servitude may have been adaptable to small agricultural units and could supply at least some of the needs of urban and industrial employers, but its main economic role was providing a work force for plantations that produced a staple crop for external markets. In the colonial period the principal crops were tobacco in the Chesapeake area and rice in South Carolina and Georgia; with the invention of the cotton gin in 1793 and the subsequent expansion westward into the fertile "black belt" areas of states like Alabama, Mississippi, and Louisiana, cotton became the South's principal export commodity and the foundation of a thriving plantation economy. Among the many factors that accounted for the rise of plantation system in the seventeenth and eighteenth centuries and its spectacular growth in the nineteenth was the South's natural transportation system—its network of navigable rivers down which inland planters could send their commodities to market.

Cape slavery, on the other hand, was much less favored by economic and geographical circumstances. No staple was found on which to base a genuine plantation economy; wine and grain—the principal crops of slaveholding agriculturalists—could not compete in the European market and were mostly used to supply passing ships or to meet the limited demand for these commodities in the Dutch possessions of the Far East. Furthermore, there were severe geographical limits on the expansion of this kind of agriculture. The Cape was totally lacking in navigable rivers, which meant that the only way to get to market was by ox-wagon, and in most directions from Cape Town this was a difficult undertaking because of mountain ranges that could be crossed only at the rare and dangerous passes known as *kloofs*. Wine-growing was limited to an area within two or three days from Cape Town by wagon, and wheat could be grown commercially in a zone only slightly larger. Also the amount of rainfall required for these crops fell only along a narrow coastal strip; the arid interior regions of the Cape, known as the Karoo, could sustain grazing, but not horticulture. Although there were a few larger holdings, most of the wine and grain farms of the limited fertile and accessible region appear to have employed between ten and twenty slaves, making them less than plantation-size according to the standard established by U.S. census-takers in the nineteenth century. A large proportion of the South African slaves were not engaged in agriculture at all but were employed in Cape Town as house servants, laborers, or skilled craftsmen. In remote areas lack of rainfall or high transportation costs so restricted the profitability of commercial farming that few whites had the capital to purchase more than one or two slaves, and many had to make do without any at all. As we have seen, the Boers in the outlying or frontier regions were developing an alternative labor system by enlisting or impressing landless Khoikhoi into their service, a process that was accelerated after the abolition of the slave trade in 1807. Whether or not southern slavery was actually approaching its "natural limits" on the eve of the Civil War—a matter of debate among American economic historians—it is clear that Cape slavery had reached its limits much earlier. Slave labor obviously could not provide the foundation for economic expansion, as it did in the antebellum South.[73]

The significance of such contrasts in the social and economic context of slavery during its mature phases should be apparent. In the South, chattel servitude was the only significant form of labor for an expanding plantation economy and the cornerstone of the entire social order. In the Cape its economic and social role, although extremely important, was somewhat more restricted. By the early nineteenth century slavery was the dominant labor system only in the southwestern hub of the colony; elsewhere it was overshadowed by the system of contract servitude for the Khoikhoi that was euphemistically described as "apprenticeship." Consequently, South African whites were accustomed to have their menial work done by nonwhites, but they were not absolutely fixated on slavery as the only way that this could be arranged. Their ability to immobilize the Khoikhoi and force them to work by apprenticing the children born on white farms until adulthood and later by enforcing the vagrancy laws that in effect required most Khoikhoi to be in the service of white farmers provided a rich experience in alternative forms of labor coercion. If the commitment to white supremacy in the South before emancipation was indissolubly linked with chattel slavery and the plantation, in South Africa it was associated more flexibly with a white economic domination that could take more than one form. When slavery eventually came under attack and emancipation became a real possibility, this difference helped account for the fact that southern slaveholders went to war to defend the institution, while a majority of those in the Cape reluctantly resigned themselves to the prospect of abolition and devoted their energies to making the best of the situation by struggling to maintain or establish other methods of labor control.[74]

These differing degrees of slaveholding militancy also reflected the fact that Cape masters were never a ruling class in the same sense as those of the South and were not used to having things their own way. During the Company era, lasting until 1795, most political power remained in the hands of company officials, and these temporary sojourners and representatives of a distant metropole had higher social status than even the most affluent slave-owning burghers. The situation did not change radically when the British took over; for they likewise ruled the colony autocratically, denying effective representative government to the settlers and imposing an alien political elite at the top of the local power structure. In the South, on the other hand, a planter oligarchy had early taken advantage of the laxity of English imperial rule and the existence of representative institutions within each colony to establish its political and social dominance. After the Revolution the planters became the ruling group of a cluster of "sovereign states" and until 1860 were able to exert considerable influence over the federal government.

At the Cape, the fact that substantial slaveholders did not clearly dominate the polity or even the society in which they were the largest possessors of private wealth also meant that the individual master-slave relationship did not have the kind of autonomy and power to shape the rest of society in its image that it acquired in the South. In the latter case, the prestige and power differential between the master and the slave class was maintained at almost any cost, whereas in the former it was sometimes violated by a higher authority that could not be fully controlled by the private owners of slaves. An example already cited was the unwelcome Batavian edict of 1770 prohibiting masters from selling their Christian slaves. Another was the practice of using company-owned slaves as constables empowered to arrest white burghers, a procedure that occasioned considerable complaint before it was gradually phased out after 1780. The right of masters to discipline and punish their slaves was also more limited than in the South. Ill-treated slaves had a right to protest to company authorities, and occasionally their masters were severely punished as a result. In an attempt to prevent slave-owners from escaping the penalties for beating or torturing a slave to death, a proclamation was issued in 1731 requiring that government permission be obtained before any deceased slave was buried so that his body could be examined for signs of brutality.[75] In the colonial South, the killing of a slave by a master was generally not considered a crime; and when it became so by the nineteenth century the refusal to accept the testimony of other slaves—usually the only witnesses to such a proceeding—made this and other new laws prescribing humane treatment virtually unenforceable. Although enforcement of protective legislation was also uncertain and sporadic at the Cape, a notoriously cruel master whose conduct came to public attention ran the risk, at the very least, of being deprived of his slaves and denied the right to purchase any more; except in the most extreme cases, usually involving flagrant sadism or multiple homicide, the worst that such a master in the Old South might reasonably anticipate was the social disapproval of his slaveholding peers.[76]

Such differences do not necessarily mean that slaves were actually treated less brutally in the Cape than in the South. The Dutch East India Company was not a humanitarian organization, and its motive for interfering in the master-slave relationship to the extent that it did was primarily to prevent cruel masters from driving discontented slaves to rebellion. The Company's own slaves were not particularly well treated, at least insofar as their material conditions were concerned, as evidenced by persistent complaints by visiting commissioners and other observers about inadequate housing, food, and clothing.[77] Furthermore, when the Company punished one of its slaves for a serious offense or fulfilled its responsibility for chastising or executing a private slave guilty of a statutory crime, it characteristically did so in a more brutal fashion than did public authorities performing a similar function in the colonial South. The laws of Holland, unlike those of England in the eighteenth century, still permitted torture and medieval methods of execution, making it possible to turn the public punishment of slaves into sadistic spectacles designed to strike terror into the heart of the slave population in general. On the whole, slaves were probably better off in the hands of private masters than under the jurisdiction of the Company.[78]

The fact that individual owners were more subject to public authority in the Cape than in the South is important, therefore, not because it denotes a kindlier regime—such judgments about the relative inhumanity of slave systems are notoriously difficult to make—but for what it suggests about the class situation of South African slaveholders.[79] To the extent that the masters themselves had masters, in the form of independent government officials empowered to intervene in the owner-slave relationship, a barrier existed to the emergence of a self-conscious and domineering slaveholding class such as existed in the antebellum South. Only on the frontier, where the influence of the central authority was weak, could masters acquire a strong sense of absolute lordship over their dependents and begin to interpret that situation as a mandate for assertive group consciousness and self-determination. But since Khoikhoi enserfment rather than chattel slavery was the main source of labor for the frontier Boers, their quest for absolute racial dominance was destined to be less a struggle for the preservation of slavery *per se* than an effort to maintain "proper relations between masters and servants" by whatever institutional means were available.

Nevertheless, the long experience of enslaving nonwhites had a broadly similar impact on the genesis of white racial attitudes in the two societies. More than any other single factor, it established a presumption that whites were naturally masters and members of a privileged group while nonwhites were meant to be their servants and social inferiors. Problems of group definition, arising from race mixture, remained to be worked out or clarified, and more elaborate and self-conscious rationalizations for white dominance emerged in response to the new intellectual trends and political developments of the nineteenth century. But a slaveholding mentality remained the wellspring of white supremacist thought and action long after the institution that originally sustained it had been relegated to the dustbin of history.

III

Race Mixture
and the Color Line

Race Mixture in Comparative Perspective

The anarchic nature of the human libido has always created serious problems for guardians of ethnic boundaries and privileges. The concerns a dominant group expresses about its sexual and marital relations with racial or ethnic "outsiders," what it actually does to regulate "miscegenation," and how it treats people of mixed parentage reveal much about a society's pattern of group stratification. Comparative studies suggest that a general strategy for managing race mixture tends to develop quite early in the history of a multi-racial society and to become deeply rooted. In both South Africa and the American colonies, the first important official acts or statements of policy that distinguished between members of society purely on grounds of ancestry involved the restriction of inter-racial sex and efforts to determine the status of mixed offspring. These actions foreshadowed the kind of color line between whites and those of mixed origin that has to some degree survived into our own time. What some readers may find surprising is the extent of divergence or dissimilarity in the kinds of attitudes and policies that emerged.

Before examining early miscegenation and white responses to it in North America and South Africa, it will be helpful to get a sense of how patterns of race mixture can vary in a range of societies with a history of enslavement and subjugation of non-Europeans by white colonists and settlers. Locating the American and South African experiences on a spectrum of possibilities will highlight some of the special characteristics of race relations in these two societies as they evolved through slavery and other face-to-face forms of racial dominance toward modern systems of segregation. It is clear, first of all, that bringing together diverse racial groups within the same social and economic system has invariably led to some intermixture. Miscegenation is likely to be especially extensive where the predominant relationship is between master and slave, because slaveholders have easy sexual access to the women of the servile class. Hence slavery and a high degree of race mixture invariably go together; other forms of contact, such as those resulting from conquest without enslavement or from the immigration of free nonwhites into a white-dominated host society, usually result in a lower incidence of inter-racial sex because the subordinate racial groups are in a better position than slaves to maintain their own family and kinship patterns, thus limiting the vulnerability of their women to sexual exploitation. It also follows that the abolition of slavery tends to result in a decline in miscegenation involving ex-slaves and their former masters. As has been suggested, most intermixture between white and nonwhite in colonial and slave situations has been hypergamous, or between men of the higher-status racial group and women of the lower.[1]

From the point of view of physical anthropology, race mixture constitutes an exchange of genes between population groups that can be distinguished by appearance but even more reliably for purposes of measurement by relative frequencies of blood types and factors. In a classic study of miscegenation, Louis Wirth and Herbert Goldhamer have distinguished between transfers that are essentially "bilateral," in the sense that they lead to a significant genetic modification of both groups involved, and those which tend to be "unilateral," meaning that the flow is mostly in one direction and substantially affects the gene pool of only one of the groups. Black-white "hybridization" in the United States, they maintain, represents a striking example of unilateral race mixing, "since the mixture may be thought of as resulting in various modifications of one of the races (the Negro) with no perceptible modification of the other (the white)." They contrast this situation with cases where a more equal exchange has meant that "both original races are submerged in a new mixed type" or where the hybrids have come to constitute a third group clearly differentiated from the "relatively pure stock" of both the parent races.[2] As Wirth and Goldhamer acknowledge, however, the *causes* of these differences are sociological; for the direction of gene flow is not determined by any biological imperative. It results rather from the social position assigned to people of mixed race. The relatively "unilateral" character of American miscegenation, in contrast to that of most other societies, has been caused by the arbitrary device of classifying all descendants of mixed unions with their black progenitors. Elsewhere the "half-white" inheritance of mulatto or mestizo groups has usually been acknowledged by granting them an intermediate status, and those whose phenotypical and cultural characteristics approach the norms of the dominant group have often been regarded as candidates for assimilation into the white stratum of society. One of the major challenges for scholars of comparative race relations has been to explain the unique "descent rule" that has been the principal basis of racial classification in the United States.[3] The anomaly will become even more striking in the light of the South African case; for not even there, despite the triumph of white supremacy and segregationism, has a rigorous ancestry principle been used to determine who is white and who is not.

According to E. B. Reuter, the pioneer sociologist of race mixture, a dominant racial group can prescribe three possible status positions for "half-castes": they may be the "lower segment of the dominant group," "members of the exploited group," or an "intermediate class or caste."[4] Comparative studies of mulatto or colored groups in Western Hemisphere societies have uncovered only the second and third types and have concentrated on contrasting the United States, with its relegation of mulattoes to "the exploited group," to Latin American or West Indian societies manifesting some variation of the white-colored-black or "three-category" system of racial stratification.[5] But in a larger comparative context there is at least one prominent case that approximates Reuter's "lower segment of the dominant group," an example that is peculiarly relevant to a comparison of the United States and South Africa.

From the earliest times in the Dutch East Indies, Eurasians who were the offspring of legal marriages between Dutch males and Asian women, or who had been formally legitimized by white fathers after being born out of wedlock, were officially classified as members of the European or Dutch population. Such a status did not always protect them from prejudice and discrimination, but it usually placed them in a more privileged position than that assigned to mulattoes in the Americas. Since there was little immigration of Dutch women and a high incidence of intermarriage and concubinage, the "Indos" became a major population group relative to the unmixed Dutch. By 1850 they accounted for more than half of those legally classified as Europeans. Although they tended to be of lower social and economic status than colonists born in the Netherlands, they had the same legal and political rights; this formal equality was clearly acknowledged in an 1842 law setting forth the prerequisites for Dutch nationality. Their role as members of the dominant racial group was further reflected in their success in obtaining positions in the colonial administration, especially after 1850. When Indonesia became independent in 1949, a majority of them joined the colonial Dutch and "repatriated" to the Netherlands, where they have been partially integrated into Dutch society.[6]

As part of a comparative spectrum, this case of an essentially "two-category" colonial society where a large proportion of the mixed population was for most purposes incorporated into the ruling group is important for two reasons: first, it draws attention to the relative exclusiveness of all the white segments in New World plantation societies, whatever the status of their mixed populations;* second, it strongly suggests that the South African case cannot be evaluated for comparative purposes simply by trying to locate it within a typology of race patterns derived from studying the slave societies of the Western Hemisphere. Neither the North American model of a two-category system with the relegation of mulattoes to the lower caste nor the three-category structures with their varying degrees of fluidity between black, colored, and white segments will do justice to the evolving South African pattern. Since South African colonization began as an offshoot of Dutch activity in the East Indies, there was an initial impulse to go the same route—namely, to incorporate a significant portion of the mixed population into the upper segment of a two-tier division between European and non-European. The persistent struggle that developed between this tendency and strong counter-trends toward a color caste

---

* But some parallels could perhaps be drawn with the situation of the acculturated offspring of Indian-white intermixture in some Latin American societies —and even in the United States—at least during certain historical periods or in particular regions.

system resembling that of the United States in its white exclusiveness helps to account for the extraordinary complexity of South African race relations from the seventeenth century to the present.

Besides comparing the long-range effects of different patterns of race mixture on the hierarchy of status groups in different societies, one can also differentiate among the policies that have sustained the varying patterns. It would be possible in theory to locate all multi-racial societies in comparable stages of development on a continuum ranging from permissive to restrictive in their official attitude toward miscegenation. The most permissive possible type would be a society where legal intermarriage was not only tolerated but positively encouraged; the most restrictive would rigidly prohibit both marital and extramarital sex between groups defined as racially different; in between would be cases where intermarriage was frowned upon but permitted and those where legal unions were out of the question but concubinage was widely condoned.[7] These policy orientations are not unchangeable: in the modern era, South Africa has shifted rather dramatically in the direction of extreme restrictiveness by banning for the first time all forms of marital and extra-marital miscegenation as part of the apartheid program enacted by the Nationalist regime after 1948; the United States, on the other hand, has moved in very recent years away from its historical pattern of restriction by eliminating laws banning intermarriage, a process completed by a Supreme Court decision of 1967. While such changes in law and public policy do not immediately alter historic patterns of racial division, they do suggest that the formal mechanisms that created such patterns are the product of particular historical circumstances and may be abandoned if those conditions cease to exist.

Restrictive miscegenation policies, and particularly bans on interracial marriage, are of great moment even in situations where few mixed unions occurred before the formal prohibition; for the passage of such laws signifies the conscious endorsement of a racial caste system. The term "caste" is used here to denote a peculiarly rigid form of social stratification and not as a direct analogue of the distinctive type of social order found in India. What distinguishes a caste society from one of "open classes" or "estates" is the virtual absence of mobility from one social stratum to another. Mobility may be very low in other hierarchical societies, but it is not ruled out in principle, and there are usually some well-sanctioned paths by which individuals from one social group can pass into another. In a typical class society the acquisition of wealth is such an avenue; in a traditional estate society—one composed of corporate groups with differentiated rights and privileges, such as that of medieval Europe—acceptance into the priesthood or some other "open elite" may permit the sons of peasants to advance to a higher status. All well-defined social groups or classes have a strong tendency to marry only with their peers, but so long as intermarriage is not prohibited it remains possible for some members of a lower group, normally women, to improve their social position by "marrying up." In a caste society, however, the enforcers of the system not only limit upward mobility by denying those of "low birth" access to higher-status professions and occupations, but must also bar social advancement through intermarriage. The most important distinguishing mark of a fully developed caste order is that social groups are completely endogamous in the sense that sexual unions between members of different castes cannot be sanctified or legalized as true marriages, and the offspring of such relationships can never be legitimized or incorporated into the kinship system of the upper-caste parent. It may be common in such societies for upper-caste males to have extra-marital liaisons with lower-caste women, but the children retain the status of the mother. It is much less likely that upper-caste women will engage in such activity because they are generally under the dominance of fathers or husbands with a strong stake in controlling their sexual behavior. The responsibilities of paternity are easily evaded, but women who have children out of wedlock, especially by lower-caste males, are subject to ostracism or worse because neither they nor their offspring have any place in the kinship or inheritance structure of their own group. It follows from such an understanding of how the caste principle operates that an examination of the attitudes and policies associated with race mixture in the early phases of American and South African history can be used to gauge the extent to which a society of racial castes was emerging.[8]

Early Race Mixture: The Restrictive American Pattern

Some Englishmen may have come to America already bedeviled by special anxieties concerning sexual relations with blacks. As Winthrop Jordan has shown, myths about the uninhibited sexuality of Africans simultaneously shocked and titillated the Elizabethans. Since some segments of English society were in the process in the late sixteenth and early seventeenth centuries of abandoning the sexual attitudes associated with late medieval village or peasant life in favor of the more repressive ethic asserted by Puritanism and the bourgeois family, this was bound to be an era of acute ambivalence about sex; a kind of freedom that was being formally rejected for its alleged sinfulness and animality but which retained its secret or subliminal attractions could easily be projected onto Africans. In *Othello,* the villainous Iago carries on his campaign of defamation against the Moor by implying that inter-racial sex is unnatural and bestial. Using animal or barnyard imagery to poison the mind of Desdemona's father against Othello, he describes their coupling as the mating of a black ram and a white ewe, "making the beast with two backs," and as the union of a woman with "a barbary horse." His companion Roderigo alludes even more directly to a stereotype of black sexuality by visualizing Desdemona in "the gross clasps of a lascivious Moor." Although these are the canards of villains with ulterior motives, such allusions would have made no sense to an audience totally lacking in qualms about miscegenation. But the handful of blacks in Elizabethan England could hardly have made race mixture a vital issue or a major social problem. Shakespeare, therefore—as his imagery suggests—may also have been playing on an opposition between the relatively open and earthly sexuality traditionally associated with rural England and the conventions of respectability and restraint that were beginning to be promulgated among the urban middle classes. As would occur in other times and other places, blacks could be used to symbolize tensions or anxieties that they had little or no role in creating.[9]

It is difficult to gauge the extent to which an unconscious connection between the repression of English sexuality and the image of African "lasciviousness" was transferred to the American colonies. What is often taken as evidence of early revulsion to miscegenation is in fact ambiguous. The unfortunate Virginia colonist Hugh Davis, who was whipped in 1630 "for abusing himself to the dishonor of God and the shame of Christians, by defiling his body in lying with a negro," may have been so castigated, as the language implies, because the black he had chosen to lie with was a heathen. Ten years later Robert Sweet was required merely "to do penance in church, according to the laws of England" because he had impregnated a Negro woman. In another case in 1649, an inter-racial couple guilty of fornication did penance together precisely in the manner of offenders of the same race.[10]

In 1662 Virginia passed a law doubling the normal fine for inter-racial fornicators, an action constituting the first clear-cut example of statutory racial discrimination in American history. In 1664 the Maryland assembly took the first step toward prohibition of inter-racial marriage when it prescribed that any English woman who married a slave should be a slave herself during the life of her husband and, in a departure from the usual rule of slave societies that children follow the condition of the mother, condemned her progeny to "be slaves as their fathers were." This law, however, had the unanticipated result of providing the masters of slaves and servants with a practical incentive to encourage exactly the type of unions the law was trying to prevent, and they apparently did so to an alarming extent. Consequently it was necessary to pass another law in 1681 providing that when marriages were permitted or instigated by the master, the "woman and her issue shall be free." In 1691, Virginia enacted the first statute that banned all forms of inter-racial marriage by providing that any white man or woman who married "a negro, mulatto, or Indian . . . bond or free" was liable to permanent banishment from the colony. Maryland, which had not previously prohibited unions between white males and black females, passed a similar law the following year.[11]

Other colonies quickly followed suit, often taking their language directly from the pioneering Virginia statute—Massachusetts in 1705, North Carolina at some point before 1715 when its laws were first published, Pennsylvania in 1725/26, and Georgia in 1750. Thus by the middle of the eighteenth century six of the thirteen colonies had made inter-racial marriage punishable by law. Of the five southern plantation colonies only South Carolina had failed to act.[12] Such legislation was not therefore all-pervasive in the colonial era, nor did it actually declare mixed marriages null and void as was done in the nineteenth century; but it does provide strong evidence of a widespread revulsion against race mixture. An examination of the circumstances and the language of the precedent-making early laws will illuminate some of the motives behind the initial erection of caste barriers in American society.

The most striking feature of the Virginia and Maryland legislation was its targeting of white women as the prime objects of concern. The Maryland law of 1664 was designed to remedy the inconvenience and shame resulting from the fact that "diverse free-born *English* women, forgetful of their free condition, and to the disgrace of our nation, do intermarry with negro slaves. . . ." Although the Virginia legislation of 1691 banned mixed marriages involving white males as well as females, its stated purpose was to prevent "that abominable mixture and spurious issue, which hereafter may increase in this dominion, as well by negroes, mulattoes, and Indians intermarrying with English or other white *women,* as by their unlawful accompanying with one another."[13] Such language implies that miscegenation involving white women and black men was fairly extensive in the Chesapeake region in the late seventeenth century. Unfortunately, the fragmentary records surviving from this period make it impossible to determine whether this was indeed the case. Only a few such unions can actually be documented, although it seems likely that there were many more. Furthermore, the laws do not always make a clear distinction between legal marriage and extended cohabitation. The latter—presumably a kind of unsanctified "slave marriage" involving a white servant as the female partner—may have been a common form of inter-racial union on the farms and plantations of the late seventeenth century (or so the Maryland legislation seems to suggest). The instances of intermarriage that have actually been uncovered by historians of the colonial period mostly involved white women and black men, and it can be assumed that this pattern prevailed for the indeterminate number of cases that were unrecorded or buried in the mass of county court records that have been lost. Whatever the actual extent or legal character of the kind of "intermarrying" that provoked Virginia and Maryland legislators to drastic action between the 1660s and the 1690s, white women and black men were obviously perceived as the principal offenders.[14]

This situation is not surprising if one considers the day-to-day relationships that could exist among the dependent classes on the farms and plantations of the period. As David Fowler has suggested, the increased importation of black slaves beginning in about 1660 did not change the practice of indenturing single English women as household servants.[15] Since the new slaves were overwhelmingly male, there must have been cases where a majority of the field workers were black men while the household staff was composed mainly of white women. Both groups would be in need of sexual partners, and some masters might connive at their living together for a variety of possible motives—keeping them contented, binding the servant partner to the plantation (especially in Maryland during the period when he had a legal right to do so)—or be simply indifferent. Since the white women came directly from the lower strata of English society, they were unlikely to be strongly deterred by racial prejudice. Repugnance to race mixture does not appear to have been a spontaneous response of lower-class English men and women who found themselves in essentially the same boat as Negroes; when male black retainers were introduced in substantial numbers into English households during the eighteenth century, they frequently intermarried with white servants.[16]

The early concern about miscegenation, therefore, was directed primarily at a particular form of intermixture that was the temporary consequence of the transitional stage between indentured servitude and slavery. The majority of white masters found these unions objectionable and felt impelled to stop them, initially at least for reasons that probably had less to do with ideals of racial purity than with more practical considerations. The Maryland law of 1664 referred to the danger of "divers suits . . . touching the offspring" of the white women who were marrying or cohabiting with black slaves. The obvious aim was to make slaves out of the children of slaves. Intermarriage with free people was hindering the efforts to solve the labor problem by creating a class of hereditary bondsmen. A lesser practical concern addressed by the legislation was the inconvenience and loss of work associated with pregnancy and motherhood among white servants. Nonracial laws punishing sexual activity and maternity among indentured servant women were also being passed at this time to protect the interest of masters in the fullest possible exploitation of white female labor; to some extent, the anti-miscegenation legislation was directed at a particular facet of this larger problem.[17]

But this passion to exploit the full labor potential of the living and the unborn is not the whole story behind the initial campaign against race mixture. References in the laws to the pairing of white woman and black man as a "shameful" action leading to "the disgrace not only of the *English* but also of many other Christian nations" and to the propagation of "an abominable mixture and spurious issue" imply a deeper and less calculated kind of anxiety. The shifting of the basis of slavery in the 1660s from heathenism to heathen ancestry and the beginnings of discrimination against free Negroes—in Virginia they were barred from owning white servants in 1670—were signs of the deteriorating social position of all people of African descent. The miscegenation laws reflected a desire to cordon off the "white Christian" community by relegating all or most blacks to a lower status. But their focus on the transgressions of white women while ignoring or dealing in a much more perfunctory way with the liaisons of white men and black women exposes a more specific kind of concern. Although the great disproportion of the sexes that had existed earlier in Virginia had begun to even out, white women were still in relatively short supply—in a sense they were a scarce resource.* If they mated with blacks they would be lost to their own ethnic community, and hopes to reproduce the family-centered society of England would be hindered. If male colonists hoped, half-consciously at least, to monopolize the women of their own nation, they were also likely to see the females who intermarried with black aliens as rebels against the principle of male dominance and patriarchal authority. Since individual Englishmen were accustomed to determining the marital and sexual lives of their wives and daughters, they could readily be induced to feel a sense of collective responsibility for unattached white females arriving from England and to consider themselves personally affronted when these women married outside the group. Such an attitude, of course, would have made no sense if blacks had not been regarded as too alien and outlandish to be absorbed into the established community. This consciousness of blacks as permanent strangers was undoubtedly strengthened and hardened as they arrived in growing numbers directly from Africa and were condemned to a life-long and hereditary bondage from which they could not claim exemption even if they embraced the religion and culture of their masters.[18]

It is likely as well that the myth of black hyper-sexuality also played a role in the origins of the American miscegenation complex. If lower-class white women had heard the stories circulating in Europe about the sexual endowments and prowess of black males, some of them might have been attracted by the prospect. If white males were familiar with these fables, they might have been provoked to a kind of jealous rage by even a small number of well-publicized incidents of miscegenation involving white women. Such a reaction would have been intensified by the seventeenth-century belief that women, like blacks, had passionate sexual natures. The Maryland law of 1681 provides a strong hint that both of these complexes were at work in its characterization of the white women who "intermarry with negroes and slaves" as doing so "always to the satisfaction of their lascivious and lustful desires."

---

* As late as 1700, the ratio of white men to white women in Virginia was roughly 1.5 to 1. Sexual balance was not achieved until about 1750.

The later introduction in some colonies of castration as a legal punishment reserved for blacks may provide further evidence of the growth of male sexual anxiety as a source of racial injustice.[19]

Fears that white women would disgrace their nation and humiliate their menfolk were equaled or exceeded in intensity by an aversion to accepting their free mulatto offspring as full-fledged members of society or even as members of an intermediate group more privileged than unmixed blacks. As we have seen, the purpose of the Virginia law of 1691 was "the prevention of that abominable mixture and spurious issue." The resistance that first developed in the late seventeenth and early eighteenth centuries to the growth and recognition of a relatively privileged free mulatto class was stronger than that manifested by any other slave society in the Americas.[20] Finding the sources of this early antipathy to mulatto aspirations may provide the key to explaining why a unique two-category system of race relations developed in the United States.

There were two special characteristics of the free mulattoes of colonial North America that distinguished them from similar groups elsewhere in the hemisphere. First, they were usually the sons and daughters of lower-class whites rather than of rich planters and their slave concubines, as was generally the case in other New World slave societies. Hence, in addition to the burdens of slave ancestry and (in most cases) illegitimacy, they also carried the stigma of descent from a lowly and despised class of whites.[21] This latter aspect of their provenance was stressed by Lieutenant Governor Gooch of Virginia when asked by the British government to justify the disfranchisement of free Negroes by the Virginia Assembly in 1723: ". . . as most of them are the Bastards of some of the worst of our imported Servants and Convicts, it seems in no way Impolitick, as well for discouraging that kind of Copulation, as to preserve a decent distinction between them and their Betters, to leave this mark on them, until time and Education has changed the Indication of their spurious Extraction, and made some Alteration in their Morals."[22] Ethnic and class prejudice against mulattoes were thus mutually reinforcing. The second unique feature of this group was that it had no useful function to perform for the slaveholders. In the West Indies, where relatively small numbers of whites had to control slave populations that outnumbered them as much as ten to one, free mulattoes were needed as part of the militia, particularly in times of slave rebellion or unrest. Their loyalty could only be commanded if they were granted a status significantly higher than that of the slaves. In the colonial South, on the other hand, there were enough free whites to meet the security needs of the planters, and it was the white lower class rather than the free mulattoes who had to be accommodated and elevated in status in order to make slavery safe for the slaveholders.[23]

The combination of the free Negroes' low social origin and the fact that there was no apparent role they could play in the maintenance of the system gave the ruling class an incentive to keep down their numbers both by discouraging the kinds of intermixture that added to their ranks and by making manumission difficult. The few who were born or became free were depressed and degraded almost to the level of the slaves, thus raising white fears that they would use their limited freedom to sow seeds of discontent among the bondsmen with whom they shared so many legal and social disabilities. This in turn provoked further white hostility against them. Another reason provided by Lieutenant Governor Gooch for depriving them of the ballot was that free Negroes were suspected of being involved in "a Conspiracy discovered among the Negroes to Cutt off the English." Such anxieties would persist into the antebellum period and provide one rationale for further assaults on their rights.[24]

The early legislation aimed at preventing miscegenation and the growth of an intermediate class of free people of color did not effectively prevent casual and covert relationships between white men and black women. Restrictions on the right of Negroes and mulattoes to testify in court against whites meant that it was almost impossible to bring white males to account for engaging in inter-racial sex and fathering mulatto children out of wedlock. But this was not a matter of great consequence to the governing elements because the main purpose of the restrictive policy was not so much to prevent race mixture *per se* as to control its results. Since the offspring of such liaisons had the status of the mother, they remained within the Negro caste, and this usually meant that they could be held as slaves; for most of these relationships involved the sexual exploitation of slave women by masters, overseers, or other whites.

Hence in the southern colonies the fruits of miscegenation did not threaten the hardening line between whites and those with any known or visible African ancestry. But it is probable that the laws, where they existed, or social pressure, where they had not yet been passed, served to curtail significantly the incidence of miscegenation involving white women. Such transgressions continued to occur, more frequently in fact than is generally believed, but the white woman who took a black lover ran very serious risks. If she bore a mulatto child, she could hardly expect to escape legal punishment or at best social ostracism.[25]

When the specific situation that had inspired the early legislation in the Chesapeake area ceased to exist—when, to be more precise, white servant women living and working in close proximity and near equality to black slaves were no longer part of the plantation scene—the laws became more symbolic than instrumental, although a class of "poor whites" living on the fringes of plantation society continued to provide possible female companions for free Negroes in similar straits. But the chances of the wrong kinds of intermixture were certainly reduced, and the prohibitions persisted mainly because they signified that racial caste was an acknowledged principle of social organization. In the South, the caste principle certified that all whites were members of an exclusive and privileged community by virtue of their racial origin, thus establishing a foundation for solidarity in defense of slavery—an institution that brought economic and political privilege to the planters but which in its racial aspect could also be a source of social prestige for the non-slaveholders. If, as Edmund Morgan has argued for Virginia, the freedom and independence of lower-class whites in the eighteenth-century plantation colonies came to depend to some degree on slavery, since slavery meant that there were no servile roles whites had to perform, then it also follows that anti-miscegenation laws and other caste legislation implying that there were no absolute or impermeable barriers to free and intimate associations among whites, whatever their actual differences in wealth, influence, and social status, buttressed the growing sense that all whites were somehow equal.[26]

Persuasive as it may be for Virginia and Maryland, this interpretation does not by itself explain why Pennsylvania and Massachusetts, with their relatively small black populations and limited reliance on slavery, joined the Chesapeake colonies in banning intermarriage in the early eighteenth century, whereas South Carolina, with the largest proportion of blacks and slaves anywhere in North America, failed to do so. What the two northern colonies had in common which may have influenced their miscegenation policies was the combination of a religious conception of community—Puritan or Quaker—and a growing urban center, namely Boston and Philadelphia. The relative moral laxity and heterogeneity of culture and race prevailing in these bustling port cities in the early eighteenth century was undoubtedly perceived as a threat to the ideal of a stable and cohesive Christian commonwealth. Negroes were a highly visible element among an urban lower class that was seemingly getting out of control, and miscegenation was undoubtedly viewed as symptomatic of a loss of moral restraint; hence, laws against race mixture can be seen as part of a larger effort to re-establish cultural uniformity and moral order.[27]

The case of South Carolina is less of a puzzle. Unlike Virginia and Maryland, it never possessed a substantial class of white indentured servants; from the beginnings of the plantation system black slaves were the principal source of domestic as well as field labor. Thus there was little basis for the anxieties about the sexual preferences of white servant women that existed in the Chesapeake area. Furthermore, South Carolina had a less substantial and potentially influential non-slaveholding white element than other slave colonies, and there was less need or occasion for the planter class to encourage caste consciousness by outlawing intermarriage. In the South Carolina low country, as in the plantation societies of the West Indies, the vast social distance between most whites and most blacks made intermarriage so unthinkable that it did not have to be legislated against, while open concubinage between male planters and female slaves could be treated more casually than elsewhere in North America because it presented less of a danger to fundamental social distinctions.[28]

Early Race Mixture: The Permissive South African Pattern

The main external source of attitudes toward race mixture in the early years of the Cape Colony were the precedents deriving from the Dutch experience in Indonesia. Policies in the East were not consistent or uniform, but there was an intermittent trend toward toleration or even encouragement of intermarriage between Dutch colonists and converted indigenous or slave women. As early as 1612, the first Governor General of the Indies recommended marriage with native women as preferable to importing the immoral or "light" women who were the only kind of female colonists that the Company could attract from the Netherlands. In 1617, the ruling Council of Seventeen formally authorized the intermarriage of free burghers with Asian or Eurasian women who had been baptized; although at the same time it acted to inhibit such unions (and inadvertently encourage concubinage) by prohibiting colonists with Asian wives from repatriating to the Netherlands. Johan Maetsuyker, Governor General during most of the initial period of settlement at the Cape, strongly recommended intermarriage as a way of building up the "Dutch" population of the Company's domain. In his opinion, the offspring of mixed marriages were better attuned to the East Indian climate than colonists from Holland and would, as a result of continued intermarriage, be physically similar to Dutch colonists after two or three generations. Since white women continued to be in short supply, such marriages took place fairly frequently under the benign gaze of the officialdom, and the children of these legal unions were, for most purposes, considered Dutch burghers rather than members of an intermediate class or caste. Illegitimate children could achieve the same status if they were "recognized" and offered for baptism by their white fathers. Hence as early as the midseventeenth century, one can discern the beginnings of the assimilationist pattern that would culminate in the formal granting of Dutch citizenship to Eurasians in the nineteenth century.[29]

J. S. Furnivall, the great modern authority on the culture and society of the "plural societies" of Southeast Asia, has viewed the policy of the Dutch, and that of their Portuguese predecessors in the same region, as a variation on the "caste" principle. When the Dutch "assimilated Indos into a superior caste of Europeans," they were following the Portuguese example of "ready acceptance and, indeed, deliberate policy of intermarriage with their native subjects" in an effort "to superimpose on the native social order a new caste of Christians."[30] Furnivall is certainly correct in seeing a clearly defined principle of religious or cultural stratification at work, but his use of the term "caste" might be questioned on the grounds that his own description shows how converted members of the native group could "marry up" into the dominant stratum. Furthermore, it was not only indigenous women who could be thus assimilated but imported slave women as well; indeed in the early Dutch period, when there was little direct rule of indigenous populations, the latter were more readily available to wifeseeking Hollanders.

Some of the children of seventeenth-century mixed marriages actually rose to high positions in the East India Company. Simon van der Stel, the dark-complexioned son of a high company official and his East Indian wife (probably a "half-caste"), was the most notable of the early governors of the Cape Colony, both in his length of service (1679–99) and in his influence on the growth of the settlement.[31] (It is an extraordinary irony that if this revered figure of early South African history were to return from the grave, he might well be classified as "Colored" and forced to use the facilities reserved for nonwhites in the land he helped to colonize.) Hence the system of ethnic stratification that the Dutch were developing in the East Indies, and which provided the initial model for the Cape, sanctioned incorporation of the acknowledged children of Dutch fathers and nonwhite mothers into the dominant or colonizing community. As Furnivall suggests, this pattern of limited assimilation should not be romanticized; it was essentially a pragmatic device to establish hegemony over the indigenous peoples, adopted as a matter of necessity by a colonizing nation whose home sources of manpower, and especially woman-power, were too limited to meet the need for a loyal and reliable "European" population in its eastern colonies. But it also seems evident, and worthy of note, that such a response would hardly have been possible had the Dutch been a people with a highly developed commitment to "racial purity."

Before the late eighteenth century, the Dutch at the Cape responded to questions of intermarriage and ethnic classification in ways generally compatible with the behavior of their compatriots in the East. The only major difference was that they showed less inclination to contract legal marriages with the indigenous women and drew their nonwhite wives almost exclusively from the imported slaves and their descendants. There was, nevertheless, one notable example of marriage between a European man and a Khoikhoi woman: in 1664 the surgeon and explorer Pieter van Meerhoff married Eva, a "female Hottentot" who had lived in Commander van Riebeeck's household, where she had been converted and trained as an interpreter. The nuptials were celebrated with the official blessing of Van Riebeeck's successor, who hosted the bridal feast in his own house. Since Eva had kinship ties with several of the neighboring Khoikhoi groups and had already seen service as an intermediary, the marriage was in part an act of policy designed to cement friendly relations and encourage trade with the indigenous population.[32]

The parallels with the famous union of John Rolfe and Pocahontas in early Virginia are striking: in both instances intermarriage could serve as a useful diplomatic device in a period when the survival of the settlement still depended on the good will of the indigenes; in neither was it the harbinger of things to come. There is no record of another marriage in the Cape between a white and a full-blooded Khoikhoi woman, although there were a few instances much later of legal unions with *Bastaardine*—women of mixed Khoikhoi-white ancestry.[33] In the American colonies, intermarriage with the Indians was limited mainly to traders who lived in Indian villages and generally left their red spouses and "half-breed" children behind when they returned to white society.[34] A major obstacle to such unions in both areas of settlement was the very slow progress of Christianity among the indigenous groups; for it was unthinkable for a Christian to wed a heathen. Intermarriage was also impeded by the lack of close physical proximity between settlers and indigenes, although this pattern of geographical separation eventually broke down more completely in the Cape than in the American colonies. By the eighteenth century, however, when detribalized Khoikhoi women became more accessible to the colonists, they still did not marry them. In the settled portion of colonial North America in the same period, the virtual disappearance of the local Indians and the retrospective improvement of their image enabled writers like the Virginia historians William Byrd and Robert Beverley to rue the fact that whites had not intermarried more extensively with Indians when they had the chance.[35] The implicit context of these endorsements of red-white intermixture was revulsion at the other kind of miscegenation that was occurring, that between whites and blacks. In 1767, a Huguenot immigrant to Virginia made the connection directly when he wrote to his brother in England that the Indian problem could have been resolved by intermarriage, which would have turned the Indians into "staunch friends and good Christians." Instead the colonists had been "guilty of much more heinous practices, more unjustifiable in the sight of God and man . . . ; for many base wretches amongst us take up with negro women, by which means the country swarms with mulatto bastards. . . ."[36]

Hence the difference between the attitudes toward race mixture in English North America and those in the Dutch Cape is more complex than a superficial view would suggest. In neither instance was there extensive intermarriage of a socially sanctioned type with indigenous women; but in the former such unions were not regarded with abhorrence once the Indian had become an "exotic" in the eyes of those not living on the frontier, while in the latter the revulsion persisted or grew even stronger when many Khoikhoi became the servants of whites. But there was a reversal of attitudes when it came to the question of intermarriage with slave women and their mixed offspring. One reason the Dutch colonists did not seek Khoikhoi spouses was that they found more desirable mates among the slave women in the Company's lodge or on the farms. And, even more remarkable from the American perspective, the children resulting from these unions were not invariably stigmatized for life as an "abominable mixture and spurious issue," but had some chance of being assimilated into the dominant group.

The first of these mixed marriages occurred even before the first substantial influx of slaves: in 1656–57, three Netherlanders married Bengalese women, all of whom were freed slaves, and there is no indication that the authorities were either surprised or concerned. Several more such marriages took place during the remaining years of the seventeenth century, and at least three of them founded families that apparently persist among the present-day Afrikaner population.[37] If such marriages had been the only form of miscegenation, it is doubtful if any official concern about race mixing would have developed. But as the number of females in the Company's slave lodge increased, soldiers, sailors, company employees, and even free burghers developed the habit of using the lodge as a brothel. The practice was so extensive that during the first twenty years of the settlement three-quarters of the children born to the Company's slaves had white fathers. Such flagrant immorality could not be condoned by upright Calvinists, and in 1671 a visiting commissioner left behind orders to unite the slaves "as man and wife" in order to put a stop to "the communication between Europeans and female slaves." But little was done, as evidenced by a complaint of 1681 that regular orgies were taking place in the lodge which featured soldiers and burghers dancing naked with slave women.[38]

In 1685, Commissioner H. A. van Rheede ended his tour of inspection by issuing a set of regulations designed to put an end once and for all to what he described as a "public" and "tolerated" concubinage of company slaves and Europeans. Besides ordering that greater efforts be made to induce the slaves to establish settled families among themselves, he sought to prohibit marriages between whites and pure-blooded slave women who were freed for the purpose—although he permitted them for those of mixed origins, a qualification necessitated by his proposals for assimilating half-castes into the European population.[39] Given the context of these recommendations, it seems unlikely that Van Rheede's attempt to ban one form of inter-racial marriage was inspired principally by color prejudice. As his exemption of half-castes makes clear, he obviously lacked any commitment to racial purity or a rigid color line. But it is even doubtful if he objected in principle to the intermarriage of the pure stocks. His professed objective was to improve the sexual morals of both the slaves and the colonists by discouraging white men from seeking the companionship of female slaves. Removing the prospect of finding a permanent partner was one way to weaken the incentive for frequenting the lodge, since most of the adult women were still of unmixed origin. It is also likely that he was concerned about the natural increase of the Company's slave property. Since he was committed to emancipating the mixed children of white fathers and since slave women could not marry Europeans until they had themselves been emancipated, every inter-racial sexual relationship involving company slaves—whether illicit or not—was a potential threat to the reproduction of the company's slave force. If Europeans monopolized the slave women—as they very nearly did in the early years—the male slaves, who outnumbered females in the lodge by more than two to one, would have no one left to mate with, and few slave children would have been born who could have been retained in company service as adults under Van Rheede's proposed emancipation policy.[40] In addition to such pressing ethical and practical concerns, it remains probable that a further impetus for restrictiveness was the conviction that half-castes made better candidates for assimilation and hence more suitable marriage partners; but it would be difficult to determine the extent to which such eligibility was predetermined by racial bias as opposed to a reasonable expectation that those of mixed origin were more fully imbued with European habits and beliefs.

Like most of Van Rheede's instructions, his call for the limitation of intermarriage was never actually enforced at the Cape. Sanctified unions of burghers with freed slave women with no white ancestry continued to occur throughout the entire subsequent period of Dutch rule. A recent survey of Afrikaner ethnic origins records sixty-nine of them contracted between 1688 and 1807 by white immigrants who founded families that apparently persist among the contemporary Afrikaner population. A larger number probably occurred among those whose families died out, emigrated, or became classified as nonwhite. But the same study also suggests that the spirit, if not the letter, of the instruction was being followed; for inter-racial marriages in which the nonwhite partner was of mixed origins were six times more numerous.[41]

Despite the relatively high incidence of intermarriage, concubinage was undoubtedly the most common form of miscegenation. As one observer noted, "female slaves sometimes live with Europeans as husband and wife with the permission of their masters who benefit in two ways: the cost of the upkeep of the slave is reduced through the presents she receives from the man, and her children are the property of her master. . . ."[42] Masters also frequently cohabited with their own slaves. Such illicit relationships were sometimes relatively stable and involved the acceptance of family responsibilities, as revealed by instances when European fathers emancipated their illegitimate offspring, sought to have them baptized, or provided for them in wills and testaments. In addition there were the more casual encounters, such as those that continued to occur at the slave lodge or in certain inns or taverns where slave companions were available to young men with cash in their pockets. According to the report of an Englishman at the end of the century, Cape Town ladies sometimes thrust their slave girls into the bedrooms of house guests with the hope of getting them pregnant.[43] Such flagrant extra-marital miscegenation was, of course, not unique to Cape slave society; similar stories could have been told about Rio de Janeiro, Kingston, Havana, New Orleans, or perhaps even Charleston in the eighteenth century.

What was peculiar about the pattern of race mixture in the Dutch Cape, at least in comparison with North American or even West Indian slave societies, was the surprising frequency and social acceptability of legal intermarriage. Some efforts have been made to quantify the incidence of such unions among selected samples of the white population. The results vary considerably, but they do so within a range that must be considered high by most standards. An investigation of the marriage registers of one of the oldest churches of the Cape for the period 1700–95 led to the conclusion that 10 percent of all marriages were clearly mixed—a conservative figure because "any doubtful cases were classified as European."[44] A study of the records of all the churches except the rural congregations for a shorter period—1757–66—found that about one marriage in sixteen or 6–7 percent were unions of European males "with women who are specifically stated to be of slave, or perhaps other Asiatic, origin."[45] Again this is probably a low figure, because many women of slave ancestry were by this time identified merely by the family names of their white fathers and not by a place of origin (Bengal, Ceylon, Malabar, etc.) for those imported from the East, or by the designation "of the Cape" for those born in South Africa. A sampling of the published *Personalia* for the large number of Germans who immigrated to the Cape between 1652 and 1806 suggests that about one fifth of their marriages were with women who had been born slaves;[46] but this segment of the population probably had a disproportionately high rate of intermarriage. Most of the Germans were company soldiers who had finished their term of service, and their relatively low social, ethnic, and sometimes religious status (many of them were Lutherans) probably put them at a disadvantage in the competition with better-established Dutch or French Huguenot colonists for the limited number of European women. Nevertheless, the figures are significant because almost as many Germans as Dutch migrated to the Cape and most of them were absorbed into the Afrikaner population as soon as they began to speak the local variant of Dutch rather than their original language.

An even more forceful indication of the extent of intermarriage can be found in the genealogist J. A. Heese's recent compilation of data on the ethnic or genetic inheritance of the contemporary Afrikaner population. Heese has listed all the recorded marriages he could find of white immigrants who appear to have been the ancestors of persistent Afrikaner families founded before 1867 and has attempted to calculate the ethnic origin of all the individuals involved. It appears that an extraordinarily high proportion of these unions were inter-racial, at least by the kind of standards that prevailed in English North America. According to calculations based on Heese's data, about 24 percent of the founding marriages taking place between 1688 and 1807 involved one spouse, usually female, who had some known degree of nonwhite ancestry. The rate, furthermore, did not decrease over time, as one might expect, but actually rose steadily during the eighteenth century.[47]

These figures, it must be conceded, are only suggestive and do not clearly reveal the overall incidence of inter-racial marriage. They do not include, as W. M. Freund has pointed out, those legal unions whose offspring were not absorbed into the "white" population but rather provided ancestors for the mixed racial group that later became known as the Cape Coloreds.[48] Also unlisted by Heese are the second- and third-generation Afrikaner marriages—those, in other words, of the children and grandchildren of the family founders that took place during this period. Including unions that did not generate Europeans would raise the proportion, while figuring in subsequent marriages within the white community would presumably lower it, since immigrants were apparently more likely than colonists born at the Cape to take spouses from the nonwhite or mixed population.[49] Another imponderable involves the proper definition of an inter-racial marriage. Although the marriage of a white and a "quadroon" would generally have been considered "mixed" in the American colonies, it is not clear that this was true in eighteenth-century South Africa. Since there were no firm principles of racial classification, those who were mostly white in appearance or ancestry may have simply been regarded as Europeans, as was clearly the case with the two governors Van der Stel.* The fact that it is unclear whether the concept of miscegenation is even applicable to some of the South African unions is itself strong evidence of an attitude toward race mixture that differed substantially from the one that emerged in North America. It is therefore legitimate for comparative purposes to use an American-type definition. Although the data has not been assembled to provide a definitive determination of the total frequency of such intermarriage in the Cape, there can be no doubt that it was remarkably high in comparison to what can be gleaned about the American rate. Using the rough estimate of 10 percent—which may be quite conservative for the incidence of intermarriage by the rigorous American standard of the late colonial and antebellum periods—we would have a frequency equal to that of the contemporary Dominican Republic, where the sociologist Harmannus Hoetink found in the intermarriage of whites and mulattoes strong evidence of the trend toward racial homogenization that he identifies with the Hispanic Caribbean.[50]

Before concluding, however, that the eighteenth-century Cape was a society peculiarly lacking in racial prejudices or preferences—an extremely unlikely situation—one has to look more closely at whom the whites were marrying. In the first place, as has already been suggested, most of the licit unions were with women of mixed origin, usually the offspring of earlier concubinage or casual miscegenation. Hence there was an obvious preference for the part-white as opposed to the purely

---

* Simon van der Stel was apparently one-quarter East Indian and his son Wilhelm Adriaan, who was governor from 1699 to 1707, would thus be one-eighth.

nonwhite. Secondly, the colonists were favoring as marriage partners women descended from only one of the two major racial groups among the slave population. It is usually estimated by historians that the Cape slave force was at most times fairly evenly divided between Asians from India, Ceylon, Malaya, and Indonesia and Africans from Madagascar and Mozambique. Yet a substantial majority of the recorded mixed marriages where the provenance of the woman is indicated involved white males and Asian or Eurasian women.[51] Even though intermarriage was extensive, therefore, it was not occurring in an unbiased way. It is possible that an element in this sexual selectivity was the sense of "somatic norms" or "somatic distance" that Hoetinck has used to distinguish the patterns of race mixture in Western Hemisphere slave societies.[52] In other words, the East Asian women, with their straight hair and quasi-Caucasian facial features, presumably approximated European ideals of feminine beauty to a greater extent than Africans with Negroid characteristics. Those who were already half-white were sometimes said to resemble southern Europeans.

The fact that Africans were discriminated against, not only as marriage partners but also as candidates for "free black" status, is revealed by data on eighteenth-century manumissions. Of the 290 slaves born outside the Cape who were liberated for any reason between 1715 and 1794, 15 were Africans and 275 were Asians, even though the former may have been a majority of the slaves for much of this period.[53] It is obvious, therefore, that the white settlers had some sense of ethnic hierarchy; indeed many contemporaries recorded their opinion that the East Asian slaves were superior in a number of ways to the Africans.[54] One has to wonder whether intermarriage would have been as extensive as it was in the Cape if almost all of the slaves had been Africans, as in the American colonies; or conversely whether the presence of substantial numbers of East Indian slaves in North America would have qualified the opposition to miscegenation. The general explanation to be advanced below will suggest that more tangible, sociohistorical factors are sufficient to explain a considerable difference between the two societies, but it has to be conceded that the extent to which racial attitudes may be affected by inherent preferences for people within a certain "somatic distance" of one's own physical type remains very much an open question for students of human perception and behavior.

No less striking than the comparatively high incidence of intermarriage at the Cape during the seventeenth and eighteenth centuries was the tendency to absorb some of the mixed offspring into the "white" or European population. It appears that the emancipated female children of illicit relationships had a fairly good chance of marrying European men, although they might also establish households with men of color. But the male issue of unsanctified unions were clearly ineligible as suitors for white women. As for those who were the offspring of legal marriages, the girls almost invariably married white, while the boys were likely to do so, and thus move up in the world, only if they were very light or had high-status fathers, a good education, and substantial property. All children of the third generation were likely to be accepted as white without question. A color-conscious Swedish traveler of the 1770s described how the process worked in the female line: "The first generation proceeding from a European male who is married to a tawny slave, that has been made free, remains tawny but approaching to a white complexion; but the third generation, mixed with Europeans, becomes quite white. . . ."[55] The case of the children of Johann Franz Oppenheimer, an ordinary German immigrant who married a free colored woman in 1765, provides striking evidence of the hypergamous tendency. The union produced five daughters, all of whom married whites, but the only son found his bride among the free-colored class. Similarly, the three daughters of Michael Stricker, a button-maker who married a freed slave in 1760, wed white burghers, while his two sons married free women of color. The rarer situation that permitted racial mobility by males is suggested by the family fortunes of Johann Phillip Anhuyser, a "privileged burgher butcher" who apparently married a former slave in 1788 and had a son who was chosen to be "contractor for the new building of the Groote Kerk [Mother Church] in Cape Town" in the early nineteenth century.[56] Just how high the well-connected and unusually successful scion of a mixed marriage could rise, despite noticeably dark pigmentation, was revealed during the period of restored Dutch rule between 1803 and 1806 when a man named Vermaak, the dusky grandson of an East Indian slave woman, served as a member of the Community Council, the highest office to which a burgher could aspire.[57]

In such a society, there was obviously no hard and fast line between white and part-white, although there was a reasonably clear distinction between Europeans and those referred to as "free blacks"—who were mostly emancipated slaves and other nonwhites of relatively unmixed origin or heathen religion. But a marginal group was developing in the mid-to-late eighteenth century whose descendants could, depending on future luck and circumstances, be either fully accepted as white or relegated to the catch-all nonwhite category that became known in the mid-nineteenth century as the Cape Coloreds. The uncertainties of this process are suggested by a traveler's account of two brothers of the 1770s who were "the issue of a Christian man and a bastard negress of the second or third generation." One "did not appear by any means to be slighted in the company of Christian farmers, though at the time he had not been baptized. The other, who was the elder brother, in order to get married and settled in life . . . had been obliged to use all his influence, and probably even bribes, to get admitted into the pale of the church."[58] Apparently both brothers were at least temporarily successful in their quest for social acceptance, either because of personality and appearance or through the application of wealth and influence. One could perhaps even argue that a variation of the process of racial mobility involving the elevation of the mulatto over the black that Carl Degler has called "the mulatto escape hatch" was at work here; but unlike the one Degler found in Brazil, this form of social ascent by people of mixed origin did not involve recognition of a clearly differentiated intermediate class.[59] Those of recent slave ancestry might intermarry with other nonwhites and provide ancestors for the Cape Coloreds of the nineteenth century or be accepted as "Europeans" and thus contribute their genes to the future "whites" of South Africa. J. A. Heese has concluded that the limited inter-racial mobility that has been described resulted in a nonwhite contribution of approximately 7 percent to the "blood units" of the later Afrikaner population.[60] Whether or not this precise proportion is accurate, substantial infiltration of the white population by those of non-European origin obviously occurred, contrary to the myth of Afrikaner race purity that later developed.

The same phenomenon, of course, has occurred to some extent in the United States as a result of the device known as "passing." As Winthrop Jordan has pointed out, the existence of the rigid dichotomy between white and black meant that sometimes a tacit "accommodation had to be made for those persons with so little Negro blood that they appeared to be white, for one simply could not go around calling apparently white persons Negroes." This process began in the colonial period, as Jordan demonstrates by recounting the history of a South

Carolina family named Gibson that succeeded in hurtling the color line during the eighteenth century.[61] But court cases from the antebellum period suggest that South Carolina may have been exceptional in its relatively flexible attitude toward the "whitening" of light mulattoes. It refused, for example, to follow the lead of other states in laying down a firm rule that those with a certain proportion of Negro "blood"—usually one fourth or one eighth—must be classified as black. A court concluded in 1835 that it could not "say what admixture . . . will make a colored person. . . . The condition is not to be determined solely by visible mixture . . . but by reputation . . . and it may be . . . proper that a man of worth . . . should have the rank of white man, while a vagabond of the same degree of blood should be confined to the inferior caste." Elsewhere in the slave South, there was a stronger tendency to relegate all known mulattoes to the free Negro group, and hence "passing" remained primarily a covert violation of the ancestry rule.[62]

Although there is no way that one can calculate the rate of "passing" during the era of slavery in the United States, it seems safe to conclude that a more exclusionary attitude made it substantially less extensive than comparable forms of inter-racial mobility in the Cape. From what has been said it is clear that much of what occurred in South Africa before the post-slavery period should not even be described as "passing." "Selective incorporation through hypergamous intermarriage" would be a more accurate description. The social acceptance by the European population of at least some of the offspring of legal inter-racial unions that were a matter of public knowledge represented a sanctioned form of "whitening" for which there is virtually no parallel in American history. The legitimacy of these children, made possible by a permissive attitude toward intermarriage, was a major factor in giving them better prospects for incorporation into the white group than the normally illicit issue of inter-racial unions had in North America. But the concept of passing would remain applicable to early South Africa for those cases, which undoubtedly occurred, where males of mixed ancestry who were born out of wedlock to white fathers succeeded in concealing the circumstances of their birth and gaining acceptance as whites. The extent of this kind of crossing-over, however, remains as indeterminate as the degree of "passing for white" in the United States.

By the late eighteenth and early nineteenth centuries, there were clear signs at the Cape that prejudice and discrimination against those of mixed origin were on the rise and that many whites hoped to establish a less permeable color line. A trend toward white exclusiveness emerged after 1787, when a special corps of militia was created for "persons here, who though not born in slavery have not been born in wedlock, and for that reason cannot be enrolled among the burghers doing service."[63] The ostensible aim was to cull those of mixed origin who were the illegitimate offspring of white men and free women of color from those who were the product of legal marriages, a policy that was in harmony with the principle of social selection that has been described. But the following year, some white militiamen objected to serving under a corporal who, although apparently of legitimate birth, was "of a black colour and of heathen descent." Although the protesters had no objection to serving with him "as a common soldier," their complaint is evidence that some whites were beginning to question the distinction between those of "heathen descent" who were on the path to assimilation and those who were consigned to a lower status.[64]

Despite the language of the original order segregating the militia, it became apparent in 1791 that some legal heirs of white fathers were in fact being denied access to the burgher corps. In that year, an angry white burgher complained to the authorities that his sons, although "born in lawful wedlock," had been denied enrollment on the grounds that their mother was born a slave. This interpretation of the regulation—which assigned young men who had a married parent born in slavery to the segregated "free corps"—was apparently not being applied in all cases; for the petitioner tried to strengthen his case by pointing to some examples of others of similar origin who were serving in the regular militia. The final disposition of the complaint is unclear from the records, but the incident reflects a growing tendency to discriminate on the grounds of racial origin.[65] Another such straw in the wind was the objection raised by some whites to the appointment of the previously mentioned Vermaak to the Community Council in 1803: "it is truly hard for a citizen to have men of heathen descent for civic leaders," they protested.[66]

This growing undercurrent of objection to the equality and assimilability of those of known "heathen descent" can plausibly be associated with the previously mentioned declaration by a church council in 1792 that it was legally and morally acceptable to hold nonwhite Christians in slavery. This shifting of the ideological basis of servitude tended, as in the American colonies earlier, to legitimize distinctions based on ancestry that went beyond the issue of who could be enslaved. But the early efforts to lump those of mixed origin with their slave ancestors had only a limited success, partly because they ran counter to another peculiar tradition of Dutch slave policy emanating from the East Indies. As we have seen, Van Rheede had attempted in 1685 to provide for the early emancipation of slave children of Dutch fathers; and as recently as 1772 the Council of the Indies had acted in the same spirit by ruling that the children begotten by a master on one of his slaves could not be sold and must be freed, along with their mother, when the father died.[67] Although this law does not seem to have been vigorously enforced at the Cape, those who were seeking to make a kind of caste equivalence between slaves and their mixed descendants must have been aware that they were in conflict with an established tradition.

Some of the other elements involved in the rise of racial consciousness and exclusiveness at the end of the Dutch period and the beginning of the British one can be dealt with more effectively later in discussing the emergence of white supremacy as an ideology or overt pattern of belief.[68] But an obvious development that was peculiar to the settled regions of the western Cape and clearly conducive to a kind of color snobbishness was the emergence of a more complex, hierarchical, and status-conscious society. Descriptions of elaborate jockeying for precedence and place at church, funerals, and other public functions reveal that people with pretensions to social prestige and community leadership were seeking through a variety of devices to distance themselves from those they regarded as their social inferiors. One way to accomplish this was to marry a woman of pure European ancestry and claim an edge over those with spouses of slave or other heathen provenance. Hence the rise of families with quasi-aristocratic pretensions apparently engendered a sensitivity to questions of birth and genealogy that had been lacking in the earlier and cruder stages of the colony's development and made race purity an important status symbol.[69]

But any notion that the white population as a whole needed to be preserved as a matter of policy from the contamination of intermarriage and nonwhite infiltration remained undeveloped until well into the nineteenth century. Heese's data suggest that the incidence of intermarriage among European newcomers who had white descendants declined in the period from 1808 to 1837 but that it was still far from negligible; and no one seems to have seriously considered banning it.[70] A British official, writing of "The State of the Cape of Good Hope in 1822," noted that "the marriages of enfranchised slave girls frequently take place. The 60th regiment, partly Germans, talking the Cape Dutch language, were lately disembodied; and the tradesmen and artificers felt inclined to settle at the Cape. They required a small house or apartment, a little furniture, and a few comforts, all of which the girls possessed. The girls wanted husbands in order to become honest women; and both parties were accommodated, with considerable improvement to their conduct and morals."[71] But by the 1820s obvious intermarriage had become almost exclusively a lower-class white phenomenon, and the children had a decreasing chance of being accepted into white society. Nevertheless, it remained true as late as the era of the Great Trek that white South Africa had not erected a rigid caste barrier—of the kind that had arisen more than a century earlier in North America—against those people of mixed blood who were partly descended from slaves.[72]

By the late eighteenth century, another kind of miscegenation had become common in the rural and frontier areas, with results that were more prophetic of later South African patterns of racial exclusion. Lonely white farmers and trekkers took Khoikhoi concubines to such an extent that a substantial mixed group emerged. The persistence of strong prejudices against the Khoikhoi and the limited progress of Christianity among them meant that it was virtually impossible for these unions to be sanctified and the children legitimized—hence the use of the word *Bastaards* as a blanket term for the progeny. Furthermore, the sons generally could not inherit their fathers' farms or loan places because they were considered to be Khoikhoi, and the right of the indigenes to hold land under European forms of tenure was not clearly recognized. Some did manage to become propertied quasi-burghers, but most were either consigned to the servant class or, if they valued their independence, found it advisable to trek away from their hostile neighbors to regions not favored by white settlers. These "Bastaards," in company with detribalized Khoikhoi and absconding servants or slaves, found havens in the extremely arid northwestern Cape and in what is now South West Africa or Namibia. There they established semi-independent communities that were more European than Khoikhoi in culture and political organization. Their more or less forced migration can be viewed as a disinherited flank of the trekboer expansion of the late eighteenth and early nineteenth centuries, or as an early anticipation of territorial apartheid based primarily on race.[73]

It was in relation to white-Khoikhoi intermixture on the frontier that the government issued its first strong condemnation of miscegenation since the early protests against immorality in the slave lodge. In replying to a burgher petition complaining that "the residents in far distant veld will degenerate into a savage and barbarous people" unless the Company showed greater concern for their welfare, the Council of Policy blamed the colonists themselves for adopting a semi-nomadic way of life that threw them into intimate associations with savage peoples. The only way that the "illicit intercourse of bad men" with indigenous women could be eliminated, it was suggested, was through "an orderly government and the impressions of religion," which would "instill aversion" to "the illicit sexual intercourse" and "prevent the degeneration of these [frontier] residents into a savage horde." This identification of race mixture with a descent into barbarism is perhaps the earliest formal indication in South Africa of the attitude Winthrop Jordan found prevalent in the American colonies—the notion that the mixing of blood signified the loss of civility or even cultural suicide for Europeans settling a wilderness.[74]

The Origins of Difference

Despite tendencies to deplore white-Khoikhoi miscegenation, exclude "Bastaards" from white society, and become more exacting in general about the prerequisites for burgher status, the basic pattern of race mixture and classification in the Cape Colony remained very different from the American tradition until the end of slavery and well beyond. The nub of the difference is not that a larger proportion of the South African whites were involved in inter-racial sexual and familial relationships during the slave era (although this was undoubtedly the case), but rather that so many mixed unions were legalized, were accorded at least some measure of social acceptability, and produced children who had some chance—although a diminishing one—for inclusion within the white or European group. In English North America, on the other hand, intermarriage was formally prohibited in about half the colonies before the Revolution and in a large majority of the states thereafter, and the mulatto offspring of any licit or illicit unions that nonetheless occurred were almost invariably consigned to the free Negro caste unless they succeeded in surreptitiously passing for white.

No simple "one-factor" explanation for this divergence is likely to be persuasive. An interpretation of the facts could be built upon the theory that Europeans responded more readily to the physical attractiveness or compatibility of women of East Indian as opposed to African ancestry. But another explanation, which has the advantage of being more readily supportable from the historical record, can be derived from an analysis of the social and political conditions that provided the context for race mixture.

By the time slaves were introduced in very large numbers into the Chesapeake colonies around the turn of the seventeenth century, a society of established white families had already come into existence. The earlier imbalance of the sexes was beginning to even out in the older settled areas, and it was mainly a diminishing white servant class that faced temporary impediments to entering into regular family relationships with people from the same ethnic background. White males had an increasingly good chance of finding white wives and thus becoming involved in building the closely knit kinship networks that became characteristic of the South. Because other sources of community life— such as the church, the town, and the cooperative business enterprise— were relatively weak in this individualistic agrarian society, family and kinship took on enormous significance. Prohibiting intermarriage was one way to protect the family from entanglements with those of dubious or denigrated social origins that might threaten its cohesiveness and ability to sustain the social order. Furthermore, the presence in most households of white women was a powerful disincentive to the kind of open concubinage that prevailed in plantation societies where single males predominated, such as English Jamaica and Dutch Surinam.[75]

In the non-plantation colonies that took legal action against miscegenation a more broadly cohesive social order had developed on the basis of relatively closed and homogeneous communities that demanded a high level of personal conformity. No one could gain admission to a Massachusetts town, for example, who did not meet rigorous tests of social and cultural acceptability.[76] When Samuel Sewall described Negroes in 1700 as being culturally and physically so different from the white colonists "that they can never embody with us, and grow up in orderly Families, to the Peopling of the Land: but still remain in our Body Politick as a kind of extravasat blood," he intended to make an argument against slavery. But he also expressed the powerful commitment to communal homogeneity that lay behind the Massachusetts anti-miscegenation laws of 1705.[77]

By the early eighteenth century, therefore, many Americans had already developed a strong sense of familial or communal boundaries and feared the intrusion of anyone who was palpably different. Banning or otherwise discouraging intermarriage and miscegenation was one way to stress the necessity for a selective community and to encourage solidarity among those included within its limits. This latter consideration was particularly crucial for the ruling class of the slave South because of their need to insure the loyalty and cooperation of the non-slaveholding class.

Hence the notion was instilled in the psyche of white Americans that all Negroes were permanent aliens who must be strictly excluded from the true community of participating freemen and their families. It was not merely because most Negroes were slaves that this determination was made, although their servitude was clearly a central element in their degradation in the eyes of whites. Also at work was the anxiety of colonists attempting either to replicate what they viewed as the civilized and orderly ways of life they had left behind in England or create a new society superior to any existing in the Old World. There were many threats and dangers to this ideal in the American environment; one was that people might lose control of themselves and intermarry with those whose degradation or inferiority allegedly made them unsuitable to participate in a community-building process which, during and after the Revolution, was transmuted into the deadly serious business of establishing and maintaining a republic of self-governing citizens.[78]

The ethos of South African colonization and early community-building had a rather different character. The original colonists were mostly single men from the social margins of a variety of European nations, and this pattern of immigration persisted until the first substantial influx of British families in 1820. Since few European women could be induced to ship out for the Cape, the immigrants were necessarily dependent on nonwhite women for sexual companionship. Because of the continued influx of single men from Europe, natural increase among whites did not have a substantial effect on the preponderance of white males over females, which persisted at a ratio of about 1.5 to 1 throughout the eighteenth century.[79] Hence many European men would not have found mates at all had they not been willing to establish liaisons with nonwhite women. Under such circumstances, the growth of a society in which an essentially endogamous community of white families was the norm was much slower than in the American colonies. Furthermore, the scarcity of white women meant that there was little real possibility that they would become involved in interracial relationships. They were in fact courted and marched to the altar as soon as they arrived or reached marriageable age by the more successful white burghers. The specific anxiety that fueled the initial antimiscegenation campaign in the Chesapeake colonies—the fear of extensive cohabitation or intermarriage between white servant women and black slaves—could scarcely exist when single white women were almost never placed in situations where they interacted on a basis of virtual equality with nonwhites. The fact that almost all actual or potential miscegenation in South Africa was hypergamous obviously made it more palatable than in the United States, where (even after the decline of indentured servitude) there were enough "poor white" women who might, and sometimes did, take up with blacks to give a limited credibility to fears for "the preservation of white womanhood." South African males had little need to take special measures to monopolize the women of their own ethnic group.

The white colonists were also, for obvious reasons, slower than their much more numerous American counterparts to develop any sense of themselves as belonging to a community with a need for firm boundaries and explicit safeguards against any loss of "civilized" standards of behavior and group cohesiveness. Heterogeneous and uprooted male immigrants were likely to be more interested in freedom from restraint than in hedging themselves in with social taboos. The relatively small size of the white population, the dispersed pattern of settlement that developed in the eighteenth century, the lack of representative political institutions as a vehicle for the expression of common interests, and the limited economic development of the colony all impeded the growth of a collective consciousness of the kind that emerged relatively early in some of the North American colonies. As suggested earlier, the Cape remained a relatively undeveloped frontier society for an extended period; even Cape Town itself was more an international crossroads—a kind of "tavern of the seven seas"—than the hub of a growing and maturing society. Few colonists seem to have been under the illusion that the Netherlands could be re-created in this remote and exotic corner of the world, and until conditions were ripe in the nineteenth century for the emergence of a self-conscious Afrikaner community and culture most whites were relatively unconcerned about defending a communal ideal from alien influence or contamination.[80]

This original pattern and cultural climate did not differ radically from those of several New World "exploitation colonies" where miscegenation was open and extensive. Single men came to Jamaica or Surinam and, in the absence of European women, frequently cohabited openly with female slaves. Conscious of living beyond the pale of European civilization, they came to terms with conditions of life and expectations of community that deviated from what Europeans at home would have regarded as normal and proper.[81] And yet they did not apparently contract legal marriages with women of color to the same extent as the South African settlers. Hence factors like unbalanced sex ratios, frontier-type environments, and an absence of local pride and communal attachments are not sufficient to explain the comparatively high rate of legalized intermarriage, as opposed to concubinage, and the tendency to absorb some of the mixed issue directly into the "white" population rather than giving them a niche as members of a mulatto middle group.

The special factor in the South African case was the attitude of the ruling authorities, at least during the reign of the Dutch East India Company. In the East, the Company had condoned and even at times promoted intermarriage, because it was convinced that too few Europeans were available to man its settlements and that Christianized Dutch-speaking half-castes could take up the slack. The only way to insure the loyalty and reliability of these adopted Netherlanders was to legitimize their origins and see that they were raised within an essentially Dutch cultural milieu. An attempt to apply this policy to South Africa can be seen in Van Rheede's proposal of 1685 for educating and emancipating the slave children of Dutch fathers, "so that in time the whole country may be handed over to the same, together with its cultivation, for which they are better fitted than any one else, since, born in these parts, grown up in its service, having understanding and physical strength, the [Company] would have no better subjects."[82] This vision of a Cape Colony "handed over" to people of mixed race was not, of course, realized. But the subsequent Dutch officialdom tolerated intermarriage beyond what Van Rheede himself would have authorized and apparently acceded only slowly and reluctantly to local pressures for making crucial distinctions between white burghers and those who were of obvious and recent nonwhite ancestry.

After the British took over the colony in 1795, there seems to have been some effort to firm up the permeable color line that the Dutch rulers had usually taken for granted. Some of the special regulations applied to slaves were now imposed not only on the Khoikhoi and the "Bastaards," but also on a generalized category of "colored people."[83] Doubtless this did not apply to those who were already accepted by their neighbors as whites, but it did imply a greater desire to make distinctions among the free population. In the first detailed census that the British took of the colonial population in 1807, "free blacks" were enumerated as an entirely separate category for the first time (under the Company nonwhite freedmen had always been placed on the roll of "free burghers," although usually at the end of the list).[84] The more color-conscious British were apparently uncomfortable with the racial chaos that they found and were trying to establish a clearer basis of stratification. It is a great irony that within a few years, when the pendulum of British opinion swung toward abolition of slavery and equality under the law for nonwhites, they ended up affronting racial sensibilities among their Dutch subjects that their own earlier policies may have helped to encourage.

The Legacy of the Early Patterns

In the period between the ratification of the Constitution and the Civil War, the American tendency to ban intermarriage and classify people of mixed origin with their black ancestors grew in strength and became a rigid orthodoxy in most regions. The new states that entered the Union, slave or free, usually prohibited intermarriage by statute or constitutional provision, and some of the original states amended their laws to make inter-racial unions null and void rather than merely punishable. Only the northeastern states either failed to pass such legislation or repealed earlier laws under the influence of antislavery sentiment. In order to make possible the enforcement of anti-miscegenation and other laws discriminating against free Negroes, more precise definitions of what degree of ancestry placed an individual on the other side of the caste line were formulated. The usual antebellum rule was one fourth or one eighth, meaning that anyone with a black or mulatto ancestor within the previous two or three generations was a Negro.

"Passing" continued, but probably at a diminished rate in comparison to the colonial period because of the heightened caste consciousness of the whites.[85] Of course, free Negroes who actually looked white would have had little difficulty in migrating to a community where they were not known and crossing the line. But this option was not open to many. As Ira Berlin has pointed out for the South, "whites generally lumped mulattoes and Negroes together and treated anyone who looked remotely like a Negro as black." Even phenotypically white people known to have an Afro-American ancestor were often treated no differently from other "Negroes," although the court cases involving racial identity suggest that this situation represented a dilemma for whites and made them acutely uncomfortable. In the port cities of the lower South there was a tendency to treat free mulattoes as a distinct social group in accordance with the West Indian practice, but even there the intensifying racism of the late antebellum period was pushing them downward toward the lower caste.[86] Hence the "two-category" system of racial classification, the ancestry rule for determining who was what, and the erection of caste-like barriers between the "races" were the well-established societal norms throughout the United States at the time of the Civil War.

This situation did not change radically after the emancipation of the slaves. During the period of Radical Republican dominance some southern states and most northern ones dispensed with legal prohibitions on intermarriage, but in the late nineteenth century, when blatant racism was reaching the extreme point of its development, the resurgent white supremacists of the South put new and more stringent laws on the books. Not only were anti-miscegenation statutes re-enacted or reaffirmed, but more rigorous definitions of whiteness were put into effect. By the beginning of the twentieth century most southern states were operating in accordance with what amounted to a "one-drop rule," meaning in effect that a person with any known degree of black ancestry was legally considered a Negro and subject to the full disabilities associated with segregation and disfranchisement. In the North, although mainly in western states that entered the Union after the Civil War, there was also a new wave of legislation against intermarriage. As recently as 1930, twenty-nine of the forty-eight states outlawed marriages between white and Negroes, and strong social pressures in the other states made mixed unions rare.[87]

The effect of persistent or increasing caste exclusiveness and color-line rigidity was to keep most light mulattoes within the Negro caste, where they tended to constitute a relatively privileged group. The predominance of mulattoes among the Negro middle and leadership classes between the Civil War and the modern era was not due to any innate superiority deriving from white genes, as racists claimed, but resulted from an advantaged start—a large proportion of them were descended from antebellum free Negroes rather than slaves—which was perpetuated to some extent by the psychological conditioning imposed by a white-supremacist society. Given the massive efforts of whites to inculcate the notion of racial inferiority into the black population, it is not surprising that some Afro-Americans internalized the idea that the whiter you were the better.[88]

The most obvious legacy of early race mixing in South Africa was to create the distinct population group that became known in the nineteenth century as the Cape Coloreds. In a sense, the very recognition of such a class reflected a movement toward greater racial consciousness and exclusiveness. The gradual emergence of this social category from the intermixture of the various ethnic groups that inhabited the Cape in the seventeenth and eighteenth centuries was in part a by-product of the extension of the eastern Cape frontier and the conquest of Bantu-speaking Africans during the nineteenth century. With the gradual realization that the division that most mattered was between whites and indigenous blacks, the other nonwhites or part-whites whom Europeans had earlier enslaved, conquered, and taken to bed had to be located within the new social structure resulting from the economic incorporation of Bantu-speaking Africans into an expanding settler society. One alternative, for which the early years provided some precedent, would have been to assimilate most of them into the European population, thus strengthening the "white" position in relation to the Bantu-speaking peoples. Another would have been to follow an American-type policy and consign them all to an undifferentiated nonwhite or "black" category. What in fact was done in the Cape Colony, more out of confusion and uncertainty than as a result of fixed policy, was to allow them to find their own level in a prejudiced but not legally segregated society. Hence they became an intermediate group within the broader South African context but functioned as a socially disadvantaged lower class within the western Cape, where most of them were concentrated and where they remained the largest nonwhite element. But white conceptions of their correct position in relation to the black-white dichotomy remained unstable; their *de facto* middle position has rarely been thought of as permanent and desirable, and there has been a perennial debate among white supremacists as to whether they belonged on the European or African side of the main racial divide.[89]

It is therefore somewhat misleading to think of the Coloreds as a mulatto third group in the New World sense. Unlike the latter, they were not the product of direct mixture between two primary racial groups—white and black—that persisted from earliest times as the top and bottom strata of what became a three-tiered hierarchy. They are, for the most part, descendants of the early amalgamation of whites, Khoikhoi, and slaves that preceded the main black-white confrontation. The initial constituent elements were the progeny of unions between whites and slaves or ex-slaves of Asian or East African origin who did not win acceptance into the European group and the offspring of white-Khoikhoi or slave-Khoikhoi intermixture. Eventually the unmixed slaves freed in 1838 and a large proportion of the remaining full-blooded Khoikhoi intermarried with these original Coloreds, thus increasing their nonwhite inheritance. But the white genetic contribution to this population group did not cease with the abolition of slavery; for white men continued to marry or cohabit with Colored women, and most of their children now became part of the mother's racial group.[90]

Although certain sub-groups of the Colored population retained their separate identity, whites in the Cape Colony tended increasingly during the nineteenth century to think of them as an undifferentiated mass, partly because they represented such a range of possible phenotypes that it was increasingly difficult to sort them out on the basis of their ancestry.[91] This homogenization was accompanied by a definite trend toward differentiating the entire Colored group more sharply from whites, as evidenced by the rise of segregation in the Dutch Reformed Church during the 1850s.[92] Yet the tendency toward social discrimination against obvious Coloreds did not lead to anything like the kind of rigid line between whites and mulattoes that existed in the United States. Until well into the twentieth century, distinctions between whites and Coloreds were maintained in the Cape mainly by social convention rather than by law. No laws were passed against intermarriage, and the lack of these and other overtly discriminatory measures made it unnecessary to provide legal definitions for "white" and "Colored." Given the racially mixed ancestry of many families that had earlier been accepted as white, the situation clearly facilitated "passing" on a substantial scale. It was an open secret that this was occurring, and such assimilation was not even universally condemned. In 1876, a Dutch-language Cape Town newspaper boasted that "fortunately in our Colony prejudices of colour have vanished already to such an extent that . . . many people slightly but still unmistakably off-coloured have made their way into the higher ranks of society and are freely admitted to respectable situations and intermarriage with respectable families."[93]

The Coloreds who were most likely to "make it as white" in the late nineteenth century were those who both came close to a not very exacting notion of European appearance and had some degree of wealth or education. A historian of the beginnings of Colored protest activity around the turn of the twentieth century has concluded that crossing-over was of such dimensions that it siphoned off a large proportion of what would otherwise have constituted the leadership class of the Colored community; for "Coloured men who prospered were able to gain readmission into the White population, and some became prominent in the Afrikaner middle class."[94] This situation contrasted sharply with that of the American mulatto elite, who in the same era remained encapsulated within the Negro caste, where they provided much of the leadership. In the era of the First World War, the large-scale urban migration of rural Coloreds and poor Afrikaners, both of whom were being driven off the land, encouraged mixing at a lower socio-economic level and permitted a probable influx of Coloreds into an emerging Afrikaner working class. The fact that the population group defined as Colored by census-takers increased at a rate substantially below that of either whites or Africans in the period from 1911 to 1921 may be attributable in part to such passing.[95]

Clearly the tradition of a permeable color line that emerged during the days of the Dutch East India Company persisted into the twentieth century—some would say even up to the present time—despite the growth of segregationist policies.[96] The American "descent rule" and official dedication to maintaining a fictive "race purity" for whites was never an essential feature of South African white supremacy. Even the Nationalists of the 1950s, who finally banned Colored-white intermarriage and introduced a system of racial registration designed to put an end to most passing, avoided using an unambiguous ancestry rule to determine who was Colored.[97] The problem faced by the Nationalists had been confronted earlier by a government commission set up to consider the desirability of imitating the American anti-miscegenation laws. In its report of 1939 the commission concluded that determining the extent of mixed marriage in South Africa was very difficult and depended on one's definition of a white person. Relying on "general knowledge," the commissioners noted "that a number of persons in the Union, descended only partly from European stock, had in the past been accepted as Europeans by the European population, or had, at any rate, passed as Europeans, either because of their appearance, or because they resided among Europeans and had adopted their habits and standard of living, success or prominence in one or other walk of life having in some cases assisted the process of absorption. When these persons married among the European class, if no question of race was specifically raised at the time, it can easily be understood why they were described in the marriage registers as Europeans. . . ."[98]

Sarah Gertrude Millin, a South African writer of the 1920s, vividly described the difference between the traditional American mode of racial classification and that which then prevailed in her own country. "In the United States," she wrote, "a Coloured person is anyone from a fair-haired type with a tinge of black blood in him to a full-blooded African. And, at the same time, a Negro is anyone from a full-blooded African to a fair-haired type with a tinge of black blood in him. There is no distinction. . . ." In South Africa, on the other hand, "colour is merely a usual definition. A man is as white as he looks." No one is asked "to produce his genealogical table," and light-skinned children of Colored parents are routinely admitted to white schools, even though darker siblings may be denied admission. An individual "suspected of colour but not obviously dark" is "not rejected socially or even matrimonially" by the white community if he can pay his admission fee "in the coinage of success." "South Africa, in short, classes with the white man any person who can conceivably pass as white, where America classes with the Negro any person who can conceivably pass as Negro."[99]

A full explanation of this enduring permissiveness at the lighter end of the chromatic scale would require a detailed examination of the larger pattern of South African race relations in the nineteenth and twentieth centuries. But it is obvious that the intermixture and assimilation that occurred in the earlier period was significant, not so much because it established a consciously affirmed principle as for the fact that it initiated a self-perpetuating set of practical circumstances. Since there were always substantial segments of the white population who knew or strongly suspected that they had nonwhite progenitors, it would have been inadvisable to inquire too closely into the antecedents of others who might have passed over more recently. Such a situation never really developed in the United States, because, from the earliest times, passing has usually been so furtive that most of the descendants have probably known nothing about it.[100] Furthermore, the South African whites have had an incentive for augmenting their own numbers that was usually lacking for the Euro-Americans. Once they had conquered populous African societies and incorporated many of their members into the white economy as laborers, the fear of being overwhelmed by a rebellious black majority became central to their anxieties about their survival as a dominant group. The role of the Coloreds—currently more than half as numerous as the whites and about 10 percent of the total South African population—has inevitably figured in their calculations about the future balance of forces. Since there have been serious proposals in the twentieth century, even within Afrikanerdom, to co-opt the entire Colored minority by granting them European status, or something very close to it, there may also have been a tacit agreement that absorbing its lighter members directly into the white group had certain demographic advantages.[101] In the United States, where whites have heavily outnumbered blacks, except in a few plantation or "black belt" areas of the South, white supremacists have enjoyed the luxury of a kind of exclusiveness that is probably unparalleled in the annals of racial inequality.

IV

Liberty, Union,
and White Supremacy,
1776-1910

White Politics and the Emergence of New Nations

To a casual observer, the political histories of the United States and white South Africa might seem too dissimilar to offer grounds for fruitful comparison. But a search for general patterns or tendencies in the entire period from the eighteenth century to the twentieth suggests a set of common themes. In both instances, political developments involved struggles for freedom from metropolitan or "central" authority on the part of colonists or regionally based segments of the white population. These conflicts generated armed insurrections, new nationalisms, and even full-scale wars to achieve or maintain independence. The outcomes and legacies of movements involving the efforts of some whites to free themselves from the dominance of other whites were historically crucial in both societies because of the way they contributed to the establishment of consolidated nation-states within the current boundaries of the United States and the Republic of South Africa and helped to determine the qualifications for effective citizenship.

The chronological sequences and specific circumstances associated with the achievement of independent white nationhood were, of course, very different. America's formal independence from Great Britain was gained in 1783 after a successful revolutionary war. A self-governing Union of South Africa did not emerge until 1910; and full *de jure* independence from Britain, with all its symbolic trappings, was not achieved until South Africa declared itself a republic in 1961. But the United States of the post-revolutionary era was not yet a consolidated nation. It was a relatively loose federation of former colonies joined for mutual advantage and common defense. Although the Constitution sought to establish "a more perfect union," the states retained considerable autonomy and in times of conflict tended to assert their sovereignty over that of the federal government. It took a second and unsuccessful war for independence—the secessionist rebellion of the southern states—to establish the dominance of a central authority and lay the political and constitutional foundations for a modern nation-state. But the struggle over reconstruction of the Union and the lingering animosities and ideological conflicts left over from the war delayed full sectional reunion and the irreversible triumph of a consolidated spirit of American nationality until late in the nineteenth century.

In South Africa, there was a flurry of settler protests and localized insurrections against imperial authority—first against the Dutch overlords, then against the British—that was roughly contemporaneous with the American Revolution. But these movements were easily suppressed and did not produce even the kind of local self-government that had been enjoyed by the American colonies *before* the Revolution, to say nothing of settler independence. In the period between the 1830s and the 1850s, however, a segment of the Dutch-speaking population of the Cape won its freedom from British rule by trekking beyond the borders of the Cape Colony and establishing independent republics in areas unclaimed by European powers. The imperial authorities recognized the autonomy of the republics in the 1850s, but in 1877 an extension of British ambitions and interests into the interior led to the annexation of the South African Republic of the Transvaal. This highhanded action provoked an upsurge of Afrikaner nationalism, not only in the Transvaal and its sister republic, the Orange Free State, but in the Cape Colony as well. When the Transvaalers regained their independence by a successful revolt in 1881, Afrikaners throughout South Africa found a new source of pride and British imperialists suffered an unprecedented humiliation. But the dreams of a British-dominated confederation of the republics and colonies of southern Africa—which had provoked imperial intervention in the first place—remained alive. When gold was discovered in the Transvaal in 1886 and a pastoral republic began to be transformed into an industrial society, the conflict between Afrikaner republicanism and British imperialism intensified. Pressure on the Transvaal to enfranchise the British immigrants who had come to work the mines and were becoming a substantial minority of the population led to the Second Anglo-Boer War of 1899–1902.

Paradoxical as it may seem, the British victory in this conflict actually played a consolidating role in the development of an autonomous South African nation analogous to the role of the Union triumph in the American Civil War. The entire area of white settlement was brought under one rule and then quickly granted self-government on the model of "settler colonies" like Canada and Australia. For practical purposes, the Union of South Africa that emerged from a constitutional convention in 1910 was an independent nation. Although they had lost the war, the Afrikaners had in effect won the peace; for they remained a majority of the total white population and had the potential capacity, if they could mobilize themselves politically, to establish their ethnic hegemony. Much of twentieth-century South African political history is the story of Afrikaner mobilization and resurgent nationalism. In 1961, with the official establishment of an Afrikaner-dominated Republic of South Africa, they obliterated the last symbolic vestiges of British hegemony.

In neither society were the white settlers or sectionalists who agitated and fought for freedom from what they regarded as alien or external rule inclined to extend the kind of liberty they demanded for themselves to the nonwhites over whom they ruled as slave-owners or conquerors. Sometimes—as in the analogous cases of the Great Trek and southern secession—the cause of white freedom and independence was directly linked with a desire to maintain flagrant forms of racial hegemony. As a general rule, it was the metropolitan or central government that was most likely to be influenced, at least in theory, by a liberal or "modern" conception of a uniform citizenship that denied the legitimacy of ascriptive racial disqualifications. Hence the sectional or ethnic struggles that impeded the course of political consolidation and centralization provoked debates on the legal and political foundations for black-white relations. It was the British who introduced the concept of "equality under the law" into South Africa and sought to impose it on Afrikaners, some of whom found it so alien and intolerable that they emigrated into the wilderness rather than accept it. In the United States, the Republican Party of the 1850s and 60s served as the principal agency for promulgating a concept of individual rights that outlawed slavery and ultimately denied the legitimacy of legalized racial discrimination. When the Republicans won control of the federal government in 1860, the South saw itself as slipping irreversibly into a state of quasi-colonial dependence on a northern "metropole" that had come to embrace liberal-nationalist principles. To avert the danger to its way of life that such dependence entailed, the South adopted the desperate expedient of secession.

Yet the individuals and groups working for the consolidation or unification of disparate sections or white population groups in the nineteenth century—whether they marched under the banner of British imperialism or American Unionism—usually had what they considered to be higher priorities than the achievement of racial justice. With a few exceptions, their own commitments to inter-racial equality were equivocal or unstable, and their basic attitudes toward nonwhites ranged from a kind of liberal paternalism to blatant racism. Their motives for resisting slaveholder or white-settler autonomy were therefore more complex and less purely humanitarian than may appear on the surface. On one level they were simply fervent patriots, adherents of an idealized vision of the British Empire or the American Union that would be besmirched by secession or colonial fragmentation. But they also tended to be ideological proponents of the growth and perfection of capitalistic modes of social and economic organization. Agrarian sections or republics based on racial slavery or the enserfment of indigenous peoples appeared to the nineteenth-century liberal mentality as major obstacles to the extension or preservation of free-market economies capable of rapid commercial and industrial development. And to some extent they undoubtedly were. But after chattel slavery was abolished in the United States and the economic dominance of the industrializing North over the agrarian/South was firmly established, it became possible to make major concessions to southern white supremacists. Similarly, after the British had won the Second Anglo-Boer War, unified South Africa, and opened the way to an untrammeled penetration by metropolitan capital, they found it expedient to give the white inhabitants of the ex-Republics a free hand to rule over blacks more or less according to the settlers' own traditions. In both cases, political consolidation under liberal and capitalistic auspices resulted in the abolition of slavery but stopped far short of substantive racial equality. Providing full citizenship for nonwhites turned out to be less essential for the achievement of more fundamental objectives than it had seemed to an earlier generation.

The political or constitutional divisions and unifications that figure so prominently in American and white South African history are sufficiently analogous, therefore, to justify a comparative analysis of how racial attitudes and ideologies shaped or influenced the nature and outcome of these struggles for power between white groups or sections and were in turn influenced by them. A pursuit of these themes will necessarily take us back to the era of the American Revolution and forward to the unification of South Africa in 1910.

Revolution, Rebellion, and the Limits of Equality, 1776–1820

The late eighteenth century has been accurately described as the "age of democratic revolution" in Europe and America.[1] For the first time in Western history influential groups in several countries forcefully challenged the traditional assumption that a privileged few had the God-given right to rule over the vast majority of the population. The hitherto subversive notion that each member of society had certain natural rights of citizenship—including the right to participate in the choosing of rulers—was insistently proclaimed as the necessary and proper foundation for a new order of human affairs. First elaborated by the theorists of the Enlightenment, the new ideals of liberty, equality, and popular sovereignty became the rallying cries for reformist or revolutionary movements, not only in most Western European societies, but also in their colonial dependencies.

But the new democratic and egalitarian ideologies presented a troublesome, two-edged challenge for Europeans who had settled in the overseas colonies. On the one hand, libertarian doctrines could be used to legitimize the colonists' desire for autonomy or even independence from the mother country. But another possible implication was to call into question the patterns of extreme oppression, especially chattel slavery, that were peculiar to colonial societies. The problem, and it was not an easy one, was how to control the contagion of Enlightenment political thought so that it could underwrite greater freedom for the settlers without weakening their dominance over imported slaves or conquered indigenes. The dilemma was felt most acutely where a heavy reliance on servile nonwhite labor was accompanied by a strong independence movement drawing on the natural-rights philosophy. These conditions were fully met in the American South. In the North, where blacks were few and slave labor was of marginal importance to the economy, the principle of equality could be carried to its logical anti-slavery conclusion without shaking the foundation of society. The dependence on coercive labor systems in the Cape Colony paralleled that of the South, but the doctrine of natural rights penetrated less deeply into the settler consciousness, and the movement for autonomy was relatively weak and unsure of itself. Hence the question of reconciling slavery and natural rights did not emerge in the clear-cut and dramatic way that it did in North America.

The new premise of equality which created the nub of the problem was, and remains, a difficult concept; questions have always been raised about its proper definition and limits of application. The notion that all human beings were equal in some fundamental sense had long been a standard belief of Western Europeans. But before the eighteenth century, universalistic affirmations of equality existed only in forms that had no clear application to the organization of human society. Equality in the eyes of God—an essential Christian belief—was usually seen as no impediment to a hierarchical order in human affairs. It was, in fact, the will of God and a consequence of original sin that some should rule and others be ruled.[2] As John Winthrop had put it on the eve of the Puritan colonization of Massachusetts: "God Almightie in his most holy and wise providence hath so disposed of the Condicion of mankinde, as in all times some must be rich and eminent in power and dignitie, others mean and in subieccon."[3] A century later, despite the growing acknowledgment of a rational faculty shared by all men, Alexander Pope reiterated the premise of inequality in heroic couplets: "Order is Heav'n's first law; and this confest,/Some are, and must be, greater than the rest. . . ."[4] But the general trend of Enlightenment thought was toward the affirmation of a common human nature and the principle that all human beings should, for some purposes at least, be treated alike by the state because they possessed certain "natural rights" that government was bound to respect. This changing assessment of human rights and capabilities reflected a decline in the persuasiveness of traditional concepts of original sin and a corresponding rise in the estimation of the individual's natural ability to reason correctly from experience and to act responsibly and benevolently in accordance with the promptings of an innate moral sense.

Complicating, and to some extent contradicting, this growing assertion of a natural human equality were the beginnings of the scientific study of physical variation among human beings and the growing tendency to classify the types of humanity according to biological race. The great unresolved question was whether alleged differences in intelligence and temperament between Caucasians and various non-European "races" were attributable to their having lived in different environments or reflected the fact that they belonged to what amounted to different species. If the former was true, their subjection to a common set of physical and social circumstances would, sooner or later, erase the differences between them and undermine any justification for differential treatment. But if the latter hypothesis was valid, then it might be justified to limit the "rights of man" to Caucasians, on the grounds that they alone had the ability to fulfill the expectations of human capability upon which the doctrine of equality depended.[5]

For the European thinkers—such as the German naturalist Johann Blumenbach, the French *philosophe* Voltaire, the Scottish philosopher Lord Kames, and the English physician Charles White—who began to address such questions in the late eighteenth century, the issue could be the subject of relatively detached speculation since they did not actually live in multi-racial societies. But for the Jamaican physician Edward Long and the Virginia planter Thomas Jefferson an analysis of race differences was both a reflection of their actual experiences and an urgent and practical question. Long, it can be argued, was the true father of biological racism because in 1774 he presented the case that Negroes were a lower order of humanity than whites and probably a "different species of the same GENUS," strongly implying that this hypothesis provided an adequate justification for slavery.[6] Jefferson's position, as presented in *Notes on Virginia* (1784), was far more equivocal. Although it has become commonplace to view Jefferson's speculations about black inferiority as a direct anticipation of later southern racism, a comparison of his remarks with those of Long suggests that his contribution to a proslavery ethnology has been exaggerated. First of all, Jefferson did not contend that a scientific validation of his strong "suspicion" that blacks were intellectually inferior to whites would justify their enslavement. Indeed, as is well known, Jefferson was incapable of justifying slavery *in principle* on any grounds whatsoever. Secondly, Jefferson differed with Long on the critical question of whether Negroes possessed the same "moral sense" as whites. Where Long had denied "moral sensations" to blacks, Jefferson argued that the alleged moral deficiencies of blacks were a product of nurture and environment, not nature. The key point for the later ethnological

defenders of slavery was the innate inferiority of the black *character*—
as reflected primarily in a constitutional aversion to regular and sustained labor—and it was this judgment, rather than imputation of
mental inferiority *per se,* that set them off from many abolitionists. It
is therefore misleading to regard Jefferson as their direct ancestor. It
makes more sense to view him, despite all his own evasions and compromises, as the spiritual stepfather of an antislavery movement that
did not require the concept of intellectual equality to support the claim
that blacks had natural rights.[7]

It was, of course, the Jeffersonian doctrine of a natural equality of
rights, as set forth in the Declaration of Independence, that was responsible for the original "American dilemma." To assert that "all men are
created equal; that they are endowed by their creator with certain inalienable rights; that among these are life, liberty, and the pursuit of
happiness" was not simply to invoke Enlightenment doctrines as a
justification for American independence; it also implicitly called into
question the institution of slavery within the American colonies. In the
North, where the economic significance of slavery was limited, this
ideology was powerful enough to bring about gradual emancipation in
the post-revolutionary period.[8] In the South, where slavery was a major
interest and a deeply rooted social institution, it was necessary to exploit ambiguities in the natural-rights philosophy or engage in casuistry
in order to rationalize the preservation of what was fast becoming a
"peculiar institution." One approach was to seize on the Whiggish
principle that the protection of private property was the most essential
of natural rights in order to support a claim that the rights of masters
to their human chattel took priority over the slaves' rights to liberty.[9]
Another was to return to the original Lockean conception that natural
rights had their historic origin in a social contract from which slaves
were excluded. The application of the doctrine was thus limited to
those who at the time of the Declaration already possessed the liberties
historically due to all Englishmen and not to those previously excluded
from a social order supposedly based on the contractual agreement of
independent parties.

But these arguments were clearly evasions of the spirit of the Declaration. As J. R. Pole has perceptively pointed out, the radical potential of
the Declaration can be discerned by contemplating the implications of
the assertion that "these truths" were "self-evident": "Every member
of the human race was therefore held to be provided with his own

equipment of moral apprehension; and this statement could be of value only if the truth is universal. It follows that no one could be equipped with the normal moral sense without being accessible to the truth that all men are created equal. This helps to explain why the Declaration was to be of such future potency. It told every individual that he was capable of seeing these things for himself, just as it forbade governments to deny the consequences of that vision."[10]

Since neither Jefferson nor his articulate contemporaries denied that blacks possessed a "normal moral sense," there was really no logical way that the latter could be denied fundamental human rights. Hence a really serious attack on slavery could be countered in only two ways: either by rejecting the philosophy of equality and natural rights on which the American republic was founded or by following the lead of Edward Long and demoting blacks from the category of "men" to whom the Declaration applied—i.e., by defining them as sub-human creatures. But few who were influenced by mainstream Enlightenment thought were prepared to follow either path to its logical outcome. In the absence of a wholehearted and broadly based campaign against southern slavery during the immediate post-revolutionary era, sophisms and pragmatic arguments to the effect that slavery was a "necessary evil" were sufficient to suppress feelings of guilt or ideological dissonance. When pushed unusually hard, either by external critics or by their own consciences, apologists for slavery could appeal to the racial fears and sensibilities shared by most of their countrymen. Jefferson had pointed the way by describing the catastrophic effects of any program of emancipation that did not entail removal of the ex-slaves from American soil. It would be impossible, he wrote in *Notes on Virginia,* to "incorporate blacks into the state," because "deep-rooted prejudices entertained by the whites," the bitterness of blacks against their former masters, and "the real distinctions nature has made" would lead to race war and "the extermination of one or the other race."[11]

Difficult as it was for members of the revolutionary generation to reconcile the institution of slavery with their libertarian ideals, most of them felt safe in assuming that large numbers of blacks could not be assimilated into American society as equal citizens. To sustain this view they needed only to point to the virulent "prejudices" of their fellow whites. Although Northerners emancipated their slaves in the post-revolutionary era, they subsequently treated the freedmen as members of a pariah class.[12] Most of those who advocated gradual emancipation in the South during the early national period conceded that the only practical scheme was one that provided for the immediate deportation or "colonization" of the liberated slaves.[13] Since the Jeffersonian ideal of "a republic of self-governing men" was premised on the existence of a homogeneous and intelligent citizenry, it was confidently predicted that blacks would be a troublesome and corrupting element because whites would never accept them as equals and because they themselves lacked the native intelligence or cultural preparation to perform the duties of citizenship. A successful republic, it was believed, depended on a sense of comity and fellow feeling among its citizens that could not be guaranteed if they were sharply divided along racial or ethnic lines.[14] The assumption that America was meant to be a homogeneous white nation, inhabited chiefly by members of the Anglo-Saxon and closely related "races," was strongly established by the time the Constitution went into effect. One of its most dramatic manifestations was the passage of a naturalization law by Congress in 1790 which expressly limited the acquisition of citizenship to white immigrants.[15]

Like the institution of slavery, such early indications of a racially restrictive conception of American nationality were in potential conflict with the universalistic egalitarianism of the Declaration of Independence. But the practical purpose of the Declaration was more to assert the right of a particular "homogeneous" community to self-determination than to establish a haven of freedom and equality for all types and varieties of people (of whatever race, religion, or culture). White Americans of the post-revolutionary era may have recognized a similar right for other such communities, but they reserved the option to apply tests of cultural and racial compatibility to those who sought admission to their own ranks. Tragically for the blacks (and Indians) already on the ground, all nonwhites were, from the beginnings of nationhood, commonly regarded as "aliens" of the unassimilable kind. It would take a revolution in the American self-image and a new willingness to tolerate racial and ethnic "pluralism" to make the Declaration a charter of equality for those inhabitants of the United States who were not of European ancestry.

The colonists of the Cape of Good Hope also responded to the democratic influences and ideological trends of the late eighteenth century, but in a much less dramatic and effective way than the American patriots. Having a much smaller population, one that was still dependent for its security on European military manpower and materiel, they were, of course, much less likely to develop expectations of independent nationhood. During the era of the American Revolution, however, a movement developed among the burghers of Cape Town and its vicinity protesting the autocratic and monopolistic policies of the Dutch East India Company. In 1778, a pamphlet circulated surreptitiously in the wake of a series of secret meetings warned the authorities that if they failed to carry out their duty of "standing for the people, and defending their lives, property, and liberty," the citizenry would exercise its right to change the government by force. This assertion of the same right of revolution invoked by the American colonists against England may in fact have been influenced by news reaching the Cape about the Declaration of Independence. But the detailed petition of grievances that was signed by 400 free burghers and presented to the governor the following year said nothing about natural rights. It was limited to a catalogue of practical complaints and proposals that amounted primarily to a demand for free trade as a cure for economic privation. Although it gained only minor concessions from the government, the "Cape Patriot" movement persisted into the 1780s, and some of its spokesmen, especially those who traveled to the Netherlands and came into direct contact with Enlightenment ideas circulating there, latched on to the new language of democratic rights and popular sovereignty. But it is doubtful if such notions penetrated deeply into the consciousness of the ordinary burghers at the Cape, most of whom were apparently more interested in being ruled by an authority favorable to their interests than in establishing a model republic.[16]

In 1795, the farmers in the frontier district of Graaff-Reinet rebelled openly against the regime of the Dutch East India Company. As we have seen, their grievances directly involved racial policy—they objected especially to the lack of official sanction for aggressive action against the "Bushmen" and Xhosa and to the fact that the Company's local magistrate, H. D. D. Maynier, interfered frequently in relations between masters and Khoikhoi servants. This rebellion, as well as the similar outbreaks against the British in the same region in 1799 and 1801, had some of the aura of a democratic insurgency. The rebels asserted their right to self-determination in the name of the people (*volk*), and some of them even paraded about in the blue cockade of the French Revolution. But it is difficult to discern a coherent democratic or egalitarian ideology or even an ability to distinguish between democracy and anarchy. Given the inspiration of the revolts, it is clear that any claim of equal rights was for whites only. Despite the fact that the government recognized the burgher status of some inhabitants of mixed blood, none of these participated in the insurrection; and when the rebels referred to themselves as "the burghers" they were apparently using the term as a synonym for white Christians.[17]

Unlike the ideology associated with the Declaration of Independence, therefore, the relatively inchoate set of beliefs and attitudes manifested in these early assertions of settler autonomy in South Africa provided no potential support for a conception of human rights that could cut across racial lines. On the contrary, it was assumed without any doubt or equivocation that individual rights for whites meant unrestrained domination over nonwhites. This was clear even in the Patriot Memorial of 1779, which included objections to governmental restrictions on the right of masters to punish their slaves, to the use of people of color as constables, and to the licensing of Asian immigrants as shopkeepers in Cape Town.[18] Such a yoking of the rights of whites to the rightlessness of nonwhites was even more evident in the Graaff-Reinet rebels' assertion that their own "liberty" meant that they should not be held accountable for their treatment of Khoikhoi servants.

If a conception of equal rights with a potential (if unrealized) application to race relations was an indigenous growth in the United States, it was clearly an exogenous imposition on the settler society of the Cape. The British administration that took over in 1806 after a brief period of restored Dutch rule cannot be described as committed to anything that resembled the natural-rights philosophy of the American Revolution. In fact it was animated initially by the spirit of Tory reaction to the Jacobin democracy of the French Revolution and placed a much higher premium on order than on liberty. But its attempt to impress the rule of law on a colony with a history of weak government and civil disorder involved efforts to establish "equality before the law" in the most conservative British sense of providing all subjects with access to the courts to guarantee that the substantively unequal rights of different status groups were equally enforceable. "We are to bear in view," wrote Governor John Cradock in 1812, "that in the dispensation of justice no distinction is to be admitted, whether the complaint arose with the man of wealth, or the poor man, the master or the slave, the European or the Hottentot, the same patient and equal attention is to be paid to the representation and the most careful inquiry is to ensue, that unbiased justice follow, I will not entertain the doubt." The authorities thus began their reform efforts by attempting to limit the arbitrary and sometimes unrestrained power of masters rather than to remove inequalities of legal status.[19]

The first step in this campaign was to bring the relationship between masters and Khoikhoi servants under the control of the state by providing legal clarification for a form of servitude that had arisen outside the law and often represented little more than the private exercise of despotic power over a weak and vulnerable people. Originating in a form of frontier clientage that involved some degree of reciprocity and mutual advantage, this labor system had, as a result of the weakened bargaining position of the landless and detribalized Khoikhoi, degenerated by the early nineteenth century into what was virtually a form of extra-legal and unregulated slavery. In a proclamation of 1809 the government sought to give Khoikhoi servants the legal rights of indentured laborers while at the same time protecting the interest of masters by requiring the indigenes to have fixed places of abode and carry passes indicating their employment status. In 1812, the "apprenticeship" of Khoikhoi children born and raised on white farms was authorized until the age of eighteen.[20]

Something resembling this general pattern of contract or indentured servitude would, for generations to come, provide white settlers with an effective method for extracting work from conquered Africans— who were essentially given a choice of working for white farmers or being arrested for vagrancy. Contract labor enforced by a pass system was in fact destined to play a central role in the white-dominated societies of southern Africa after the abolition of slavery. But at the time of its initiation, many white employers were offended by the extent to which it limited their authority and provided legal redress to servants who were mistreated or denied their limited contractual rights. In 1812, *landdrosts* (appointed district magistrates) were instructed by the governor that the intent of the new regulations was "to extend to all classes of persons 'equal justice and equal protection'"; and a circuit court actually listened to the complaints of Khoikhoi servants, as well as to some missionaries who had taken up their cause. As a result of these proceedings a few colonists were convicted of violating the rights of their servants by abusing them physically or withholding wages.[21] Three years later, a mini-rebellion broke out on the eastern frontier that originated in the attempt to bring a white farmer to justice for refusing to compensate a Khoikhoi servant. After the burgher—one Frederik

Bezuidenhout—was killed resisting arrest, his relatives and friends tried to organize an insurrection. The government's response to this challenge to its authority was draconian; five of the rebels were hanged, not once but twice (the gallows collapsed on the first attempt).[22]

Even the most limited application of the established British principle of "equality under law" could thus arouse intense opposition among a segment of the colonial population. When the notion of allowing the Khoikhoi access to the courts had been broached during the first British occupation in 1797, the *heemraden* (burgher councilors) of the district of Stellenbosch had protested that this "would open a door and give the Hottentots the idea that they are on a footing of equality with the Burghers."[23] This conviction persisted and became a prime source of grievance when the government made more vigorous efforts to place the Khoikhoi under the rule of law during the early years of the nineteenth century. It could therefore be anticipated that any effort to extend the notion of equality beyond the legal protection of each class in its *particular* rights and toward an equalization of civil status would provoke a major confrontation between a liberalizing state and the colonists' sense of their racial prerogatives.

As of about 1820, therefore, the potential for major disagreements about the civil status of nonwhites existed in both the Cape Colony and the United States. In the American case, an egalitarian creed generally accepted among the white population was still open to an interpretation that undermined the ideological foundations of Afro-American slavery. But implementation of the antislavery implications of this creed had been rendered difficult, if not impossible, by the constitutional compromise involved in the establishment of a federal republic. By making the future of slavery and the determination of citizenship matters of state rather than federal concern, the United States Constitution had, in effect, insulated the southern states from national action against slavery. It had also placed the rights of "free Negroes," in the North and in the South, at the mercy of local white electorates. Pervasive prejudices, taking the form of an implicit understanding that full citizenship was a white prerogative, made the position of free blacks little better than that of the slaves. Furthermore, contrary to some of the expectations of the revolutionary period, the South's commitment to black servitude and subordination had increased rather than declined since the founding of the nation. Not only had the invention of the cotton gin and the expansion of the plantation economy increased the material stake in slavery, but the idea that black emancipation was a practical impossibility, given the allegedly "ineradicable prejudices" of a sovereign white citizenry, had become a settled conviction. The only constitutional outlet for the antislavery convictions of the northern states was the resistance to the extension of slavery into new states and territories that surfaced during the congressional debates over admission of Missouri to the Union as a slave state in 1819–20.[24]

In 1820, the agitation against the expansion of slavery was defused through an adroit political compromise; but as events would prove, the issue was far from being permanently resolved.* As the northern and southern societies diverged—with the former becoming increasingly dedicated to free labor and "equality of opportunity," while the latter sought positive virtues in slavery and hierarchical bi-racialism—a sectional clash over the institutional and ideological destiny of the United States became unavoidable.

White Supremacy and the American Sectional Conflict

In a provocative effort to reinterpret the causes of the American Civil War, the historian Allan Nevins wrote in 1950 that "the main root of the conflict (and there were minor roots) was the problem of slavery *with its complementary problem of race-adjustment. . . .* Had it not been for the difference in race, the slavery issue would have presented no great difficulties."[25] Subsequent scholarship has cast some doubt on this formulation, primarily by plumbing the depths of northern prejudice and discrimination. David Potter, writing in 1968, summed up this work as showing "that the dominant forces in both sections spurned and oppressed the Negro." It was therefore "difficult to understand why the particular form which this oppression took in the South should have caused acute tension, as it did, between the sections."[26] The most compelling recent work bearing on the causes of the sectional struggle has tended to relegate racial attitudes to a subordinate position and has stressed irreconcilable differences in the hegemonic interests and ideologies of the dominant classes of the two sections.[27]

But one does not have to deny importance to these broader con-

* The admission of Missouri as a slave state was balanced by the admission of Maine as a free state; and, more importantly, a line was drawn through the unsettled territories west of Missouri's southern border. North of the line slavery would be prohibited; to the south it would be allowed.

figurations to recognize that racial considerations played a significant role in shaping and intensifying the conflict. The North as a whole may have had little use for blacks, and the dominant planter class of the South may have had a greater stake in slavery than simply racial control. But the question persists as to why the white South as a whole, and not just the slaveholding minority, reacted with such intensity to the prospect of any tampering with slavery or limitation of its expansion. It also remains unclear how the North, with all its Negrophobia, could eventually consent to the sudden liberation of four million slaves on American soil, and, shortly thereafter, to their enfranchisement. Although very few white Americans actually endorsed the principle of racial equality on the eve of the Civil War, significant differences of opinion did in fact exist on the question of what racial differences meant for the future of American society.

One prime source of confusion has been a failure to distinguish between what the psycho-historian Joel Kovel has described as the "dominative" and "aversive" varieties of "racism." "In general," he writes, "the dominative type has been marked by heat and the aversive type by coldness. The former is closely associated with the American South, where, of course, domination of blacks became the cornerstone of society; and the latter with the North, where blacks have so consistently come and found themselves out of place. The dominative racist, when threatened by the black, resorts to direct violence; the aversive racist, in the same situation, turns away and walls himself off."[28] Whatever its validity for other historical periods, this typology can be readily applied to antebellum sectional differences. It was the South that believed it needed blacks as a servile labor force and social "mudsill" (permanent menial class) and developed elaborate rationalizations for keeping them in that position. The North, on the other hand, revealed its basic attitudes in laws that excluded black migrants from entering individual states and in a spate of theorizing, especially in the 1850s, that advocated or prophesied the total elimination of the black population of the United States through expatriation or natural extinction.[29] Some historians have even argued that a principal motive for the northern crusade to prevent the extension of slavery to the federal territories was an aversion to blacks.[30]

But this contrast is misleading, and makes subsequent events incomprehensible, unless another distinction is introduced—namely a crucial difference in the *salience* of the racial attitudes that predominated. "Dominative racism" was a much more significant component of the southern world-view than "aversive racism" was of the northern. Hence it would be an easier matter for Northerners to subordinate their racial sensibilities to other considerations, such as the imperatives of nationalism or the desire for a consistent application of democratic-egalitarian principles. In the South it was necessary to translate all social and political values into racial terms; for it was not just slavery, but *black* slavery, that was the keystone of the social and economic order.

The specific developments leading to the sectional confrontation of 1861 take on an added dimension when viewed in the perspective of comparative racial attitudes. In the 1830s, a northern minority, for whom William Lloyd Garrison was the most prominent spokesman, caused a nation-wide furor by calling for the immediate abolition of slavery and eventual incorporation of freed blacks into American society as full citizens. Spawned by the evangelicalism of the "Second Great Awakening" and its millenarian or perfectionist offshoots, the abolitionist movement was a logical outcome of the spirit of radical reform that constituted one kind of response to the unsettling political, social, and economic changes of the Jacksonian era. As their own relations with blacks sometimes revealed, the abolitionists were not entirely free of the aversive prejudice that was widespread in the North.[31] Where they differed from the majority was in their principled adherence to nonracial principles in the realm of public policy and social organization. The most effective sanction for their position was a literal interpretation of the Declaration of Independence. If "all men are created equal" and "endowed by their creator with certain inalienable rights," it was sheer hypocrisy for Americans to hold blacks as slaves and deny them the essential rights of citizenship. Many abolitionists, perhaps a majority, were not in fact convinced that blacks as a race were intellectually equal to whites. But to them this consideration was basically irrelevant. Like Jefferson, they grounded their belief in equality on the doctrine of an innate moral sense shared by all human beings rather than on an identity of rational capabilities. Furthermore, Christianity taught them that the strong had no right to oppress the weak; and the economic and political liberalism that they shared with most other Americans made no provision for competency tests as a basis for legal equality and participation in a free labor market. Although they condoned such "natural" inequalities as were based on achievement and cultivation, the abolitionists stood firmly against artificial barriers to the advancement of any individual or group. In a real sense, therefore, they represented the egalitarian conscience of the competitive liberal-democratic society that was emerging in the North.[32]

As is often the reaction of those condemned for not living up to their own principles, a northern majority responded to the abolitionist movement of the 1830s with bitter hostility. Antislavery meetings were broken up by mobs, and individual abolitionists were manhandled or even lynched. State legislatures all over the North passed resolutions condemning this new and militant agitation of the slavery issue. The common complaint against the abolitionists, and the one that was most likely to inspire violence, was that they threatened the supremacy and purity of the white race. Charges that the abolitionists promoted inter-racial marriage or "amalgamation" set off two of the most savage riots of the tumultuous 1830s—in New York in 1834 and Philadelphia in 1838.[33] The participation of lower-class whites in these disorders was induced to a great extent by the status anxieties generated by a competitive society. For those who had little chance to realize the American dream of upward mobility, it was comforting to think there was a clearly defined out-group that was even lower in the social hierarchy.

Among the better situated and more thoughtful critics of the abolitionists, another concern was the effect of this new crusade on the preservation of the Union and the success of the republican experiment. Conservative Northerners believed, with considerable justification, that sustained antislavery agitation in their own section would be viewed by the South as a threat to the constitutional "compromise" on slavery and an occasion for "calculating the value of the Union." But there was usually a more profound basis for objecting to the abolitionist program than a purely patriotic devotion to sectional peace and harmony. Since 1817, northern elites had given substantial support to the colonization movement with its unshakable conviction that a combination of white prejudice and black incapacity precluded full citizenship for freed slaves. Hence they endorsed the view that the abolitionist program of "immediate emancipation" would open the doors to the kind of heterogeneity and disorder that was deemed incompatible with the preservation of a stable republican government and a social order dominated by men of property. So long as the blacks remained in the United States in large numbers, they reasoned, it was better that they be firmly enslaved rather than becoming a discontented underclass with just enough freedom to provoke violence and chaos by agitating for their rights.[34]

Despite the widespread northern revulsion to abolitionism in the 1830s and 40s, much of the slaveholding South was thrown into a panic by the very existence of such a movement. Although they clearly exaggerated the extent of northern support for Garrison and his immediate followers, the proslavery polemicists who emerged to do verbal battle with the abolitionists correctly sensed that northern opinion had a potential affinity for antislavery doctrines. Where the abolitionist position seemed most vulnerable was in its prescription of racial egalitarianism as the norm for American society. Partly for strategic reasons, therefore, the earliest defenders of slavery as a "positive good" chose to stress the argument that blacks were a distinct and inferior variety or species of humanity whose innate deficiencies—moral as well as intellectual—made them natural slaves permanently unsuited for freedom or citizenship. It followed that race was a necessary and proper criterion for determining social and legal status in any society that contained a large proportion of such natural "inferiors." This justification of Afro-American servitude as a legitimate application of the quasi-scientific doctrine that there were vast and irremediable differences in the character and capabilities of whites and blacks quickly became the dominant mode of proslavery apologetics in the United States. In his celebrated speech of 1837 defending the South against abolitionist assaults, John C. Calhoun gave central importance to racial distinctions: "where two races of different origin, and distinguished by color, and other physical differences, as well as intellectual, are brought together," he contended, "the relation now existing in the slaveholding states between the two is, instead of an evil, a good—a positive good."[35]

Much of the popularity of the racial defense of slavery stemmed from the fact that its appeal extended far beyond the one-quarter of the southern white population that was actually involved in the ownership of slaves. It is sometimes forgotten that the South turned to a more militant defense of servitude at precisely the time when it was succumbing to Jacksonian pressures to extend the franchise and otherwise increase the democratic rights of the white population. One implication of an appeal to racism by slaveholders was to project an ideal of *"Herrenvolk* equality" by justifying equal citizenship for all whites and a servile status for all blacks on the grounds that there were innate differences in group capacities for self-government. An ideological marriage between egalitarian democracy and biological racism pandered at once to the democratic sensibilities and the racial prejudices of the "plain folk" and was thus well suited to the maintenance of inter-class solidarity between planters and non-slaveholders within the South. It could also create a bond between the southern planter elite and the insecure and often Negrophobic lower-class whites who helped make up the rank-and-file of the Democratic Party in the North. The Alabama "fire-eater" William Yancey summed up the *Herrenvolk* ideology before a northern audience in 1860: "Your fathers and my fathers built this government on two ideas; the first is that the white race is the citizen and the master race, and the white man is the equal of every other white man. The second idea is that the Negro is the inferior race." In such a fashion, the contradiction between the principles of the Declaration of Independence and the practices of slavery and racial subordination—a prime source of the antislavery appeal—could be overcome. Only whites were deemed to be "men" in the sense that they qualified for natural rights. By placing a heavy stress on biological differences whites could conceive of themselves as democratic while also being racially exclusive.[36]

But not all white Southerners were entirely satisfied with such a formulation. There was a tendency among an elite of slaveholding intellectuals to deny the idea of equality more comprehensively. Yet even these unabashed proponents of "aristocracy" as a universally valid basis for social order found an important use for the concept of biological inequality among races. It became a particularly convenient device for sorting out the "mudsill" from the more privileged members of a hierarchical society. If all blacks were naturally "child-like" creatures incapable of taking responsibility for themselves—the standard image of the plantation myth—then it was justifiable to subject them to a form of patriarchal rule inappropriate for adult white males. All white men thereby became potential "aristocrats," and the conservative conception of a rank-ordered society could be preserved without confronting the horrendous task of reducing lower-class but enfranchised members of the dominant race to an inferior civil status. In one fashion or another, therefore, the concept of natural racial inferiority could serve to mitigate the conflict between the paternalistic and pre-modern aspects of the plantation community and the individualistic, formally democratic social and political order prevailing outside its gates. Depending on its context or the audience to which it was addressed, the doctrine that there were innate moral and intellectual differences between whites and blacks could make the latter into perpetual children requiring paternal supervision or into a class of sub-humans who had to be excluded from the community of enfranchised equals prescribed by the liberal-democratic tradition.[37]

If the slavocratic South and its northern sympathizers had remained content with defending slavery where it was already established as a necessary means of disciplining an allegedly inferior race, it is unlikely that such a drastic sectional polarization would have occurred in the 1850s. Abolitionism in its pure form remained unpopular in the North, aversion to blacks continued to be the dominant racial attitude, and it was generally acknowledged that the price of union was a continued respect for the barriers against antislavery action that had been entrenched in the Constitution. But by this time a large number of Northerners had been so antagonized by a southern defense of the principle of slavery that contravened their conception of a democratic society, and so alarmed by what they regarded as the deleterious social and economic consequences of the institution, that they were prepared to resist strenuously any efforts to extend its influence. The abolitionists had failed to arouse much sympathy for blacks as human beings, but their secondary contention that slavery degraded free white labor and retarded capitalistic economic development because it gave slaveholders an unfair advantage in the competition for land, labor, and capital had struck a more responsive chord. Consequently, the issue of the status of slavery in the federal territories, which arose first in connection with the vast areas acquired as a result of the Mexican War and then resurfaced when efforts were made to organize the territories of Kansas and Nebraska in 1854, became the direct source of sectional controversy and conflict.[38]

A northern conviction that Congress had the right and the responsibility to ensure that the territories were "free soil" had first emerged as the platform of a third party in 1848; after the Kansas-Nebraska Act of 1854 opened up the area west of the states of Iowa and Missouri to the possible extension of slavery, this idea became the fundamental tenet of a new sectional party that had already won the support of a majority of northern voters by 1856. The early successes of the Republican Party stemmed in large part from a belief that there was a southern conspiracy to extend slavery, with all its blighting effects on the prospects for a free-labor economy, to frontier areas where it had no con-

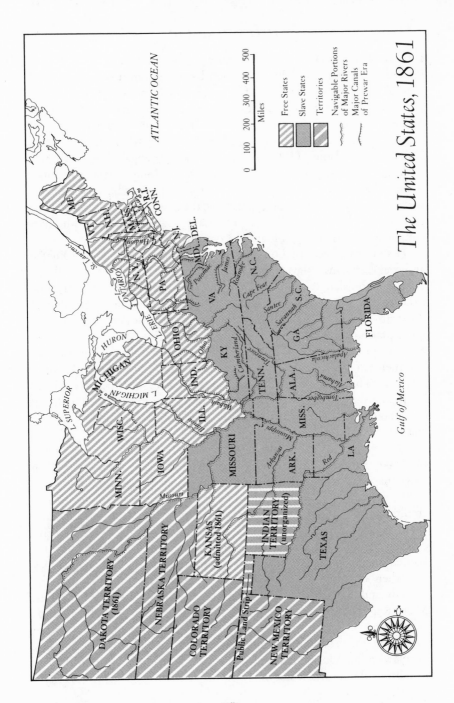

The United States, 1861

Miles

| | 0 | 100 | 200 | 300 | 400 | 500 |

Free States
Slave States
Territories
Navigable Portions of Major Rivers
Major Canals of Prewar Era

ATLANTIC OCEAN

Gulf of Mexico

stitutional right to go. What was more, slavery had been expressly prohibited in the Kansas-Nebraska region by the Missouri Compromise of
1820. Consequently, the fury of Northerners who supported the new
party was aroused by a sense that they were no longer dealing with a
minority section that was simply exercising its constitutional rights by
defending its "peculiar institution" as a local exception to a national
pattern of free labor. They now saw themselves engaged in a struggle
with an aggressive "slave power" that was seeking to make its labor
system the national norm. Such expansionism, Republicans believed,
would directly threaten the capacity of the North—and ultimately the
nation as a whole—to realize its potential as a progressive, middle-class
democracy based on a free-market economy.[39]

Historians have cast doubt on the proposition that a coordinated
and self-conscious "slave-power conspiracy" was actually behind the
Kansas-Nebraska Act, but they are generally agreed that the territorial
issue, once it was raised, provoked a militant response in the South that
drove its leaders to contest every acre of the federal domain, whatever
the actual prospects of slavery being permanently established there, and
even in some cases to call for annexation of new territory south of the
continental United States in the hope of establishing a "Caribbean slave
empire." The logic of the "positive-good" defense of slavery clearly
justified its expansion, and long-standing fears of northern political
dominance dictated efforts to prevent the admission of additional free
states to the Union.

Direct concerns about black-white relations and the destiny of the
black population in the United States affected this sectional quarrel in
ways that may at first glance seem secondary or peripheral. Opponents
of the Republicans, in both the North and South, attempted to dis-
credit the new party by charging that it advocated the equality and
even the amalgamation of the races. But Republican spokesmen, including Abraham Lincoln, generally responded to such demagogic
accusations by professing their own commitment to white supremacy
and then blaming slavery and the South for race mixing and the
growth and spread of a black population within the United States.
Many Republicans, again including Lincoln, advocated colonization or
deportation of blacks as the only solution to the race problem. In the
meantime, they sometimes condoned or even endorsed the discriminatory laws and exclusion from the suffrage that made blacks non-citizens
in most of the northern states.[40]

Despite the Republicans' apparent acquiescence in white supremacy and their repeated disavowal of any attempt to interfere with slavery where it was already established, southern spokesmen and their northern sympathizers continued to invoke the prospect of a collapse of white control, followed by some type of racial cataclysm, as the worst disaster to be anticipated from the Republicans' gaining national power. There is a strong temptation to dismiss such prophecies as either cynical propaganda aimed at a Negrophobic electorate or as the expression of some form of collective paranoia. But there was a strain of realism in the charge that Republicans were covert enemies of the kind of white dominance that the South believed essential to its survival. First of all, it was assumed—with some justification—that the Republican program for containing slavery to its present limits would mean its future demise. Indeed, Republican leaders occasionally admitted that their long-range goal was, in Lincoln's words, to put slavery "on the path to ultimate extinction." The notion that slavery had to expand or die was based partly on the economic imperatives of the institution; it had always required fresh lands to maintain its profitability, and the expectation of further growth of the plantation economy was essential to maintaining the value of the South's enormous investment in human chattel.[41] Any threat to the future of slavery as an institution was *ipso facto* an assault on white supremacy, or so it seemed at the time.

Historians, knowing how the South succeeded in re-establishing black subordination after the Civil War, may be tempted to disassociate racial concerns from the defense of slavery. If the South needed a model for subjugating blacks without owning them, it has been suggested, they needed only to look at the North, with its "black codes," social segregation, and disfranchisement.[42] But this point of view fails to take account of the antebellum perception of the crucial significance of racial demography. The orthodox position on the relationship of slavery and racial control, a view that predominated in the South until it was disproved by the inventiveness of post-war segregationists, was set forth in 1844 by John C. Calhoun when he differentiated between the effects of abolition "where the numbers are few," as in the North, and where blacks were numerous, as in the South. In the former case, the freedmen would rapidly sink to a degraded and "inferior condition." "But . . . where the number is great, and bears a large proportion to the whole population, it would be still worse. It would substitute for the existing relation a deadly strife between the two races, to end in the subjection, expulsion, or extirpation of one or the other. . . ."[43]

The fear that any restriction on the ability of slavery to expand or any weakening of the power or authority of the master class would lead to an inter-racial struggle for survival was close to the heart of southern opposition to Republicanism. As the historian William Barney has pointed out, expansion was viewed not only as an economic necessity but also as "a racial safety valve." To pen up the rapidly growing black population within the existing limits of the South would allegedly fuse a "Malthusian time bomb" and increase the danger of social chaos or even massive slave insurrection. Failure to allow the South to carry its surplus slaves into new territories, Jefferson Davis warned, would "crowd upon our soil an overgrown black population, until there will not be room in the country for whites and blacks to subsist in; and in this way destroy the institution and reduce the whites to the degraded position of the African race."[44]

The lack of Republican sympathy for the white South's racial plight might easily be attributed to a variety of ulterior motives. But, despite the "aversive racism" that Republicans often manifested, their fundamental ideology had no real place for racial domination of a legalized kind, and Southerners were correct in perceiving it as a potential threat to any kind of formalized and rigid racial hierarchy that they might devise. The northern middle-class conception of the good society, as reflected in Republican rhetoric, harbored no justification whatever for the existence of a permanent "mudsill" class; the dominant social and political ideal was "equality of opportunity," or, as Lincoln put it, "equal privileges in the race of life." A competitive society would, of course, result in differences in wealth, power, and social status, but such inequalities would be "natural" and not the "artificial" result of caste distinctions. In the language of modern sociologists, Republicans stood for a social hierarchy based on achievement rather than ascription. This clashed sharply with the southern defense of a social order based, as Barrington Moore has put it, on "hereditary privilege."*[45] To the extent that Northerners repudiated the principle of ascription and defined their own society in opposition to it, they were in effect denying legitimacy to their own practice of legalized discrimination against

---

* Moore's formulation fails to make it clear, however, that the only form of ascription or hereditary privilege that could in fact achieve firm legitimacy in the South was derived from racial criteria.

blacks. Since Republicans had no desire for a subordinated menial class, the only alternatives—at least in theory—were exclusion of blacks and the maintenance of racial homogeneity, or the establishment of a color-blind legal and political system. Clearly the preference in the 1850s was for exclusion or deportation; but when that proved impracticable, and when the North found a need for emancipation and a use for freed blacks during the Civil War, a dominant group was able to sublimate its racial prejudices and make an effort to live up to its egalitarian principles. The final fruit of Republican idealism, and a logical extension of its original principles, was Radical Reconstruction.

The Confederate cause, on the other hand, was not simply the defense of slavery as an institution, but also—and inseparably—a struggle to preserve a social order based squarely on "dominative racism." Slaveholders had many reasons for valuing the peculiar institution; for them it was an obvious source of personal wealth, privilege, and prestige. James L. Roark is probably correct in his assertion that their "commitment to slavery was far more profound than a simple fear of black equality."[46] Nevertheless, the most plausible rationale that they could devise for their practice of enslaving other human beings was that blacks were moral and intellectual inferiors who would lead orderly and productive lives only if under the direct control of white masters. Not only did slaveholders believe this, but the urgent need to ensure the loyalty of the non-slaveholding white majority caused them to emphasize it increasingly as they mobilized the southern states for secession and civil war. As Roark has also pointed out, one of the greatest anxieties of secessionist planters was that class conflict would divide the whites, but they assuaged their fears by appealing to racial solidarity. In his words, "the centripetal force they relied most heavily upon was white supremacy. . . ."[47] Only by stressing the non-slaveholders' social and psychological stake in slavery as a system of racial control could they hope to maintain a united front against a Republican-dominated government that was thought to be bent on the "ultimate extinction" of the institution.

The central role of "dominative racism" as a rationale for secession and a defining feature of southern nationalism was most vividly set forth in Alexander Stephens' famous "cornerstone speech," delivered shortly after his election as Vice President of the Confederacy in 1861. "Many governments have been founded on the principles of subordination and serfdom of certain classes of the same race," he explained; *"such were, and are, in violation of the laws of nature.* Our system commits no such violation of nature's laws. With us, all the white race, however high or low, rich or poor, are equal in the eyes of the law. Not so with the Negro. Subordination is his place. He, by nature, or by the curse against Canaan, is fitted for that condition which he occupies in our system." The basis of the new Confederate government was precisely this great truth: "Its foundations are laid, its cornerstone rests upon the great truth that the Negro is not equal to the white man, that slavery—subordination to the superior race—is his natural or normal condition."[48]

An uncompromising commitment to white supremacy was thus a central and unifying component of the separate southern identity that crystallized on the eve of the Civil War. The North was also a prejudiced society in the sense that its white population was generally hostile to blacks and accepted the prevailing belief that they were inferior to whites. But the legalized racial discrimination that existed in the North created an ideological anomaly because it failed to jibe with a growing commitment to middle-class democracy and an open competitive society. Hence it was peripheral or even contradictory to the larger social and political aims of a reformist leadership and could be jettisoned in good conscience or even with self-righteousness. But without its commitment to hierarchical bi-racialism the South was not the South. Only by drawing on the region's deep and salient sources of racial anxiety could the architects of the Confederacy muster the conviction and solidarity necessary for a sustained struggle for independence.

White Supremacy and the Anglo-Afrikaner Conflict, 1820–77

During the 1820s and 30s, the Dutch-speaking whites of the Cape Colony were exposed to the full force of a new reform impulse, originating in Great Britain, that had much in common with the northern crusade against slavery. Furthermore, a segment of the Afrikaner population, responding in a way comparable to southern secessionism, acted collectively to put themselves beyond the legal or constitutional authority of a government that threatened traditional forms of racial subordination. Here, as in the United States, new demands for the abolition of regressive labor systems and for the implementation of basic human rights provoked stronger affirmations of racial differentiation as a governing principle of society on the part of those who were accustomed to ruling despotically over nonwhite dependents.

Both the British humanitarianism that invaded the Cape and the American abolitionism that inflamed the South were rooted in the changing Anglo-American Protestantism of the late eighteenth and early nineteenth centuries. The rejection of deterministic conceptions of original sin and the concomitant growth of an evangelical commitment to regenerating the most "degraded" specimens of humanity helped undermine traditional sanctions for slavery and gave a new impetus to missionary activity among the heathen. This religiously inspired humanitarianism complemented and helped to legitimize an even more powerful current of thought—a growing commitment to free-labor capitalism and bourgeois conceptions of society and human relationships. If the antislavery Republicans of the 1850s drew to some extent on the moral idealism of the abolitionists to bring an aura of righteousness to their defense of an economic and social system based on free labor, the earlier movements devoted to ending slavery and protecting aborigines throughout the British Empire appealed strongly to liberal principles of political economy and won the support of a substantial segment of the capitalistic middle class.[49]

British humanitarianism, taking the dual form of an attack on slaveholding and a defense of "aboriginal rights" against other forms of settler oppression, had a profound impact on Cape society. In the first place, the campaign directed primarily against West Indian slavery also brought about the reform and eventual abolition of chattel servitude in the Cape. Cape masters, like their Caribbean counterparts, were chagrined by these developments and also felt a special sense of grievance because of the tendency of imperial authorities to disregard peculiar South African conditions in imposing meliorative regulations in the 1820s.* But, in sharp contrast to the American South, no articulate and organized pro-slavery movement emerged to challenge the basic assumption of the emancipators that slavery was an anachronistic institution doomed to extinction. The most common response of Cape slaveholders was sullen acquiescence, and some of them even proposed their own schemes for a very gradual emancipation before the inten-

---

* To take one example, the regulation that most punishments had to be administered by public authorities was a great inconvenience where so many farms were remote from the towns where the responsible officials were located.

tion of the British government to free the slaves after a relatively short period of "apprenticeship" had become clear. It was presumably their lack of a tradition of autonomy and representative government, combined with their sense of powerlessness as a relatively small colonial population contending against the collective will of the British Empire, that led most masters to conclude that a direct defense of slavery would be futile and that they had to make the best of a bad situation. Although the prospect of slave emancipation did not, as in the South, arouse a spirit of die-hard resistance, its actual accomplishment between 1834 and 1838 occurred in such a way as to further antagonize South African masters by denying them the full compensation awarded to West Indian planters.* This pecuniary injustice contributed to a growing feeling of ethnic resentment against British rule; when combined with other grievances involving race policy, it helped fuel the desire of some Afrikaners to escape from the dominance of an alien and autocratic regime.[50]

Another form of liberal-humanitarian interference with white domination, one that played an even greater role than antislavery policies in stimulating Afrikaner discontent and alienation during the 1820s and 30s, stemmed from the efforts of the British missionaries within South Africa to improve the treatment and civil status of Khoikhoi contract laborers or "apprentices." Endeavors that began around the turn of the century to convert the Khoikhoi and organize them into mission communities aroused the hostility of white farmers from the beginning because they often gave the indigenes an alternative to indentured servitude and thus threatened the supply of dependent agricultural workers. The government proclamations of 1809 and 1812 regularizing a contract labor and apprenticeship system had, to a substantial degree, met the needs of farmers for a stable and controlled work force at a time when a recent ban on slave importations was threatening to create an acute labor shortage. But the missionaries, particularly James Read of the nonconformist London Missionary Society, had made use of the new legal rights granted to the Khoikhoi to press

---

* This resulted mainly from the fact that compensation was paid in London, which was no problem for the absentee West Indian planters, but was a grave disadvantage for South African slaveholders, who normally had no occasion to travel to England, lacked commercial contacts there, and either had to work through agents who charged large commissions or sell their claims in the Cape for much less than face value.

charges against individual masters for brutality and violation of contracts.[51]

The smoldering antagonism between Dutch-speaking colonists and British missionaries became a bitter confrontation in the 1820s and 30s, largely as a result of the reformist agitation of the Reverend John Philip, who arrived in the colony in 1819 as superintendent of the London Society missions. Philip came quickly to the conclusion that the Khoikhoi would be more susceptible to the influence of Christianity and "civilization" if they were liberated from special restrictions on their mobility and terms of labor. Philip was in many ways the South African analogue of William Lloyd Garrison, whom he somewhat resembled in his basic beliefs, polemical zeal, and, above all, in the kind of reactions he evoked from the beneficiaries of the racially repressive institutions that he condemned. Philip not only attacked the quasi-servitude of the Khoikhoi as an archaic labor system preventing these dependent workers from bringing "their labor to the best market," but also called for their full legal equality and eventual amalgamation with the white colonists. His forthright views on the potential equality of the races paralleled those of Garrison and the most radical of the American abolitionists. In a letter about his work to the American Board of Missions in 1833, Philip asserted that "the natural capacity of the African is nothing inferior to that of the European."[52]

Philip differed from Garrison, however, in one important respect. The latter's role was almost exclusively that of a moral agitator; his capacity to exert political influence was limited by a Constitution that inhibited direct action against slavery by the federal government, and he himself eschewed politics on principle in favor of "moral suasion," or direct appeals to conscience.[53] Philip, on the other hand, had, or at least appeared to have, real power to shape governmental policy. His close connection with Exeter Hall, the center of British philanthropic activity, and his direct influence on humanitarians in Parliament and the Colonial Office made him a force in South African affairs. The great triumph of his campaign for Khoikhoi rights was the famous Ordinance Number 50 (issued by the Cape Government in 1828), which liberated the indigenes from most restrictions on their economic freedom; no longer did they have to carry passes, apprentice their children for long periods to their masters, or work under contract for more than a year. They thereby, at least on paper, became virtually equal to the European settlers in their civil rights. In 1834, Philip played a major role in persuading the British government to disallow a proposed vagrancy law designed to restore some measure of economic coercion, not merely over the Khoikhoi but also over the slaves, who were about to be emancipated. If Garrisonianism represented an ideological challenge to the southern racial order that was initially backed by little or no political leverage, "Philippianism" was perceived by South African masters as direct and official interference with their system of dominance.[54]

The response of a substantial group of Afrikaners to the doctrine and policies espoused by Philip and his supporters bears some resemblance to the mainstream southern reaction to the abolitionists. In both instances the initial agitation for free labor and equal rights served to make proponents of racial hierarchy more conscious of their own principles. As a result of circumstances and traditions, the "conservative" ideologies that both groups subsequently expressed by word or deed represented a peculiar hybrid of "modern" and "pre-modern" conceptions of social and political organization. Clearly such liberal goals as equal justice under the law, equal status in the eyes of the state, and freedom of contract in the market economy—all strongly espoused by abolitionists and humanitarian reformers—were at war with any social system based on ascriptive inequality. Yet militant white supremacists in both societies claimed for themselves the full range of these rights as something that was due to them as citizens or burghers. Since they acknowledged no clear-cut principle of hereditary privilege that applied to the white population, both Southerners and disaffected Afrikaners tended to defend their special treatment of nonwhites by giving renewed emphasis to race as the one great differentiator and by affirming the ideal of a racially circumscribed democracy—with equality for all whites and rigorous subordination for all nonwhites—that modern scholars have summed up in the phrase *"Herrenvolk* egalitarianism."[55]

The main center of militant opposition to "Philippianism" in the 1820s and early 1830s was the interior or eastern districts of the Cape where a rough equality of circumstances had traditionally prevailed among the white population. The popular belief in these regions was that it was normal for all whites to be pastoralists with large herds or flocks and that the only social or economic division that mattered was between white masters and nonwhite servants or slaves. According to a British traveler in the 1820s, "There is little or no gradation of ranks among the white population. Every man is a burgher by rank, and a farmer by occupation, and there is none so poor that he would not consider himself degraded by becoming the dependent of another."[56] But the increase in population and the pressures on land that accompanied the "closing of the frontier" in these rural areas in the late eighteenth and early nineteenth centuries were beginning to create substantial disparities of wealth among the white settlers.[57] This tendency toward new forms of economic and social stratification presumably aroused strong desires to preserve or recapture an intra-racial egalitarianism that was in danger of being attenuated. If the southern slavocracy sought to defend its peculiar institution against the abolitionists by invoking the image of a *"Herrenvolk* democracy," the Boers responded to the humanitarian assault on their own devices for extracting labor and deference from nonwhites—and to other threats to their customary way of life—by asserting their preference for an equality among whites that required access to new land and their right to a kind of "liberty" that was based on the ethnic domination of indigenous peoples.

The sense of grievance among frontier Afrikaners that led to the organized migration of thousands of *Voortrekkers** in the mid to late 1830s was variously expressed by participants and observers. Major annoyances were the failures of the government to open up new frontiers for pastoralists running short on land and to make life more secure on the ones that existed. But a particularly insistent source of complaint was revulsion against *gelykstelling,* or the equalization of status between black and white. According to one of the early Voortrekkers, "the principal objection against the impending new course of affairs was the *gelykstelling* of the coloreds with the whites."[58]

Like the antislavery doctrines of free labor and equality under law, *gelykstelling* threatened a way of life as well as a system of labor. That way of life might be described as a primitive patriarchalism in which heads of families claimed both personal independence for themselves and arbitrary authority in their "domestic" relations. This spirit of autocratic self-reliance, which a long period of weak government over a far-flung and thinly settled colony had induced in the isolated frontier

---

* *Voortrekkers* were members of organized parties that sought to migrate permanently beyond the borders of the colony and thus escape British jurisdiction. They are usually distinguished in South African historiography from the migratory trekboers, who wandered beyond the borders temporarily or without a secessionist political motive.

farmers, tended to make them natural anarchists in their relations with the outside world. Not only did they distrust all external authority, but they even found it difficult to cooperate with their neighbors and peers in undertakings of common interest. A similar attitude was often found among southern planters, who also tended to be notoriously particularistic in their social and political attitudes. Both planters and Boers were characteristically reluctant to surrender their own "rights" as rulers of small societies to any higher patriarchy that might meddle in their "domestic affairs." In both instances, therefore, the defense of small-scale authoritarianism hindered application of authoritarian principles outside the "family" unit.[59]

There was, nevertheless, a significant difference in the extent to which extreme individualism or claims of patriarchal autonomy actually determined the mode of resistance to a proposed or impending new order of group relations. Until the election of Lincoln in 1860, southern slaveholders not only had control over state and local governments in their own section but also exerted considerable influence over national policy. (It was the loss of the latter that impelled the extreme act of secession.) Hence they possessed a political leverage that enabled them to use constituted authority to buttress their racial dominance and security. They were able to define the status of slaves and free Negroes with great precision and to reinforce the authority of individual masters to any extent that was deemed necessary to prevent slave unrest or rebellion. Laws could even be passed prescribing minimum standards of "humane" treatment for slaves; although these were difficult to enforce in the courts, they did help establish norms that an individual master could violate only at the risk of losing his standing in the community.[60] Despite all its individualistic and particularistic tendencies, therefore, the slave South was capable of acting collectively in accordance with its own conceptions of the rule of law and the need for public responsibility. When secession came, it was the act of constituted political entities and not merely of discontented individuals or *ad hoc* social groupings.

Since they lacked an equivalent influence over the powers that governed them, the frontier Afrikaners came to feel that their best hope of retaining control over their laborers and other nonwhites in the vicinity of their farms or settlements lay in the preservation of a quasi-anarchic freedom of action by individuals, kin groups, or loose associations of friends and neighbors. Constituted authority could not be relied upon to help them; it was either ineffective or, to the extent that the reforms of the 1820s and 30s were actually implemented, a positive hindrance to their customary ways of maintaining discipline. Relatively indifferent to the precise legal status of their nonwhite dependents, they in effect demanded *carte blanche* to treat them in any way that their interests and security seemed to require.

Such an attitude meant that patriarchal rule often became equivalent to arbitrary rule. The cruelty of those masters who either happened to be sadistic or lost their heads under provocation was subject to little or no effective proscription or condemnation from within their own local communities. It could only be reported by hostile missionaries or travelers and promulgated to the English public as evidence of the "barbarism" of the Dutch-speaking colonists. Such accounts could feed the cause of reform but did not affect the attitudes or behavior of the masters themselves. Abolitionist charges of slaveholding atrocities in the American South, on the other hand, may actually have helped ameliorate the physical lot of the slaves because they put a way of life on trial by invoking certain humanitarian values that were shared by both sides in the debate.[61] The missionary-inspired campaign against cruel usage of the "Hottentots," culminating in the liberation of the Khoikhoi in 1828, probably had the opposite effect in that it disrupted a labor system and a social pattern without effectively substituting a new basis for order. It aroused the Khoikhoi laborers to a greater sense of their rights without providing the machinery to enforce them, while at the same time rejecting the masters' demand that they be guaranteed a stable and docile labor force. Hence it confirmed the frontier Boers in their conviction that an unrestrained and (if necessary) brutal use of force was their only salvation. It also emboldened many of them to defy a government that denied their claims to individual autonomy. Their defiance took the form of the Great Trek, a movement that asserted simultaneously their right to rule arbitrarily over nonwhites and their right to be free of any authority over themselves to which they had not given direct assent.[62]

The Afrikaners who trekked away from the Cape Colony beginning in the mid-1830s were thus totally disenchanted with a British reformism that had increasingly weakened the *de jure* power of masters over the servile class. (First there had been the program for the "amelioration" of slavery in the 1820s; then the summary destruction of the legal basis of Khoikhoi quasi-serfdom in 1828; finally the actual beginning of slave emancipation in 1834 and the refusal to pass a vagrancy law to curb the vagabondage resulting from the attempts to introduce a system of "free" wage labor.) But in voting with their feet against such changes—and also in protest of the government's inability to deter devastating frontier wars and otherwise provide security in relations with indigenous societies—the Voortrekkers were reacting to accomplished facts rather than engaging in a prolonged debate about what *might* happen if the humanitarians had their way. Furthermore, they were a semi-literate people who wrote little for publication. The manifesto justifying the Great Trek which appeared in a colonial newspaper in 1837 attacked the new policy on the practical ground that it had done real harm to the interests and safety of the colonists and proclaimed the trekkers' intention "to maintain such regulations as may suppress crime and preserve proper relations between masters and servants."[63] Conspicuously absent was an abstract or theoretical justification for such a pattern of dominance, such as the one that was promulgated to defend slavery in the Old South.

But there is evidence to suggest that the frontier Afrikaners already possessed a body of folk beliefs capable of dispelling any doubts about what role God had prescribed for the nonwhites in their midst. Its inspiration was an Old Testament Christianity of an attenuated Calvinist origin that constituted a prime source of group identity. Because of its lack of theological sophistication, it would be misleading to describe this faith as Calvinist in any sense that an American Puritan or a Scottish Covenanter would have acknowledged, but in its popular form it was basically non-evangelical and thus out of harmony with the proselytizing missionary Protestantism of the nineteenth century.[64]

This simplified and literalistic version of Reformed Protestantism was partly an outgrowth of frontier life. Having trekked in many cases beyond the reach of established congregations, the Boers did most of their worshiping within the patriarchal family. Their only guide was the Bible itself, which they readily interpreted in the light of their own experience as a pastoral people wandering among the "heathen." Inevitably some of them invoked the curse on Ham to justify their dominance over the Khoikhoi. During the brief period of restored Dutch rule from 1803 to 1806, the new governor had been profoundly shocked to encounter a settler who described the "Hottentots" as "descendants of Ham, . . . and thus condemned by almighty God to servitude and abuse."[65] Two years later the same governor received a report from a local official on the treatment of Khoikhoi servants by the colonists. "According to the unfortunate notion prevalent here," the report concluded, "a heathen is not actually human, but at the same time he cannot be classed among the animals. He is therefore a sort of creature not known elsewhere. His word in no wise can be believed, and only by violent measures can he be brought to do good and shun evil."[66] Here are strong indications that "Christian" and "heathen" were functioning as ascriptive categories denoting racial types requiring different kinds of treatment and that what was being justified was not a particular institution of control but the right to apply force in an arbitrary way. It was no giant step from such beliefs to the notion that the Boers were a chosen people, analogous to the ancient Israelites, who had a special and exclusive relationship with God and a mandate to smite the heathen. A Moravian missionary who visited the Cape in 1815 listened to a settler discoursing at length "on the state of the Hottentots and Caffres, whom he considered as the Canaanites of this land, destined to be destroyed by the white people."[67]

By the time of the Trek, therefore, discontented Afrikaners were presumably quite capable of viewing the humanitarian assault on their racial order as a denial of what they took to be firm biblical sanctions for dominating nonwhites by force and formally excluding them from citizenship. In one of the most famous retrospective accounts of the Trek, one of the participants attributed the migration of the Afrikaners partly to "the shameful and unjust proceedings with reference to the freedom of our slaves, and yet it is not so much their freedom that drove us to such lengths, as their being placed on an equal footing with Christians, contrary to the laws of God and the natural distinctions of race and religion."[68] Hence the doctrines and policies of John Philip constituted a religious as well as a social heresy and an affront to some of the most deeply held beliefs of the Afrikaners.

The approximately 10,000 Afrikaners who deserted the Cape Colony between 1836 and 1846 and claimed their freedom from British jurisdiction were thus expressing a world view, as well as reacting to the practical inconvenience and social chaos associated with the new racial policies and with the failure of the British to put a decisive end to African resistance on the eastern frontier. It was a world view akin to that of the Old South in its conviction that white men had an inherent right to rule despotically over people of a darker hue. But unlike southern secessionists, the Voortrekkers had no commitment to slavery as the only effective means of racial control. Their experience with the enserfment of the Khoikhoi had given them a more flexible conception of how to dominate nonwhite dependents; what they wanted was *de facto* power rather than a slave code. To a large extent, this contrast reflected differences between their situation and that of southern slaveholders. As they penetrated more deeply into the interior, they had come to rely less and less on the labor of imported slaves and more and more on that of indigenous peoples who were difficult to enslave in the literal sense but who could be forced into clientage arrangements and ultimately into some equivalent of serfdom. Furthermore, they had little to gain economically from turning their workers into commodities to be bought and sold, because they lacked a plantation system and a developed commercial economy. What they absolutely required was political control over their relationships with the indigenous people, and this was what the Philippian reforms seemed bent on preventing. Hence the aim of their secession, according to a farmer observing the migration of his neighbors in 1838, was to "trek where the authority of Dr. Philip would no longer vex them."[69]

Comparing the proslavery racial arguments that helped to justify southern secession with the white-supremacist attitudes that influenced the Voortrekkers requires juxtaposing a highly developed and relatively sophisticated ideology with a set of communal beliefs that barely reached the level of articulate expression. Relying exclusively on the Bible, and totally out of tune or touch with secular arguments for racial inequality, the Voortrekkers never really developed a "modern" or "scientific" racism. It is not even entirely clear to what extent they considered Africans to be innately inferior in capacity to themselves, as opposed to simply alien, heathenish, and cursed by God for the ancient offenses of Ham or Canaan. Of course the Old Testament curse also played a role as one of the rationalizations of southern slavery.[70] But its use as direct support for permanent black subservience was less frequent and more tentative than is sometimes suggested. As Donald Matthews has shown, the official spokesmen for a predominantly evangelical southern Christianity did not contribute significantly to the case for inherent black inferiority because they concentrated their efforts on converting the slaves to Christianity and the masters to Christian paternalism. Such activities meant that slaves had souls to be saved and implied that their inferiority might be overcome by a lengthy process of Christian nurture and training. The hard racial doctrine that blacks were unalterably inferior and slavish was promulgated primarily by secular defenders of the institution; and it was this secular or naturalistic argument that made the greater contribution to the public ideology of white supremacy.[71]

For the Voortrekkers, on the other hand, religion was the only available source of intellectual authority. But it sufficed for their purposes because it de-emphasized the evangelical implications of the New Testament and stressed Old Testament or Hebraic precedents for the exclusiveness and isolation of a "chosen people." Their mission, as they saw it, was not so much to spread Christianity among the heathen as to preserve themselves as a Christian community amid a horde of savages who needed to be ruled firmly in the name of order and civilization but were unlikely candidates for conversion. Their struggle with the British missionaries in the Cape had in fact encouraged some Boers to take the view that propagating the gospel among the Africans was tantamount to making them their equals—an action that was "contrary to the laws of God." According to a missionary who visited the independent Boer republics in the 1860s, "they have persuaded themselves by some wonderful mental process that they are God's chosen people, and that the blacks are wicked and condemned Canaanites over whose head the divine anger lowers continually."[72]

The self-image of the Boers as a chosen people like the ancient Israelites—with England in the role of the Pharoah, the highveld* as the promised land, and the Africans as the Canaanites—did not spring full-blown from the original trek but became the foundation for a nationalistic mythology only in the wake of events that occurred *after* the Voortrekkers left the colony.[73] The main body of the trekkers who emigrated between 1836 and 1838 moved north and then east, outflanking the Transkei and attempting to settle in the fertile eastern coastal region that was to become the British colony of Natal. But there they collided with the Zulu, who had established a centralized, militaristic empire just to the north of the coveted area. After a party of Voortrekker leaders had been massacred attempting to negotiate for a land grant from the Zulu king, a full-scale war broke out. In the battle of Blood River on December 16, 1838, the greatly outnumbered settlers won a decisive victory leading to Zulu recognition of their territorial

---

* The elevated interior plain of South Africa, comprising much of the Orange Free State and the Transvaal.

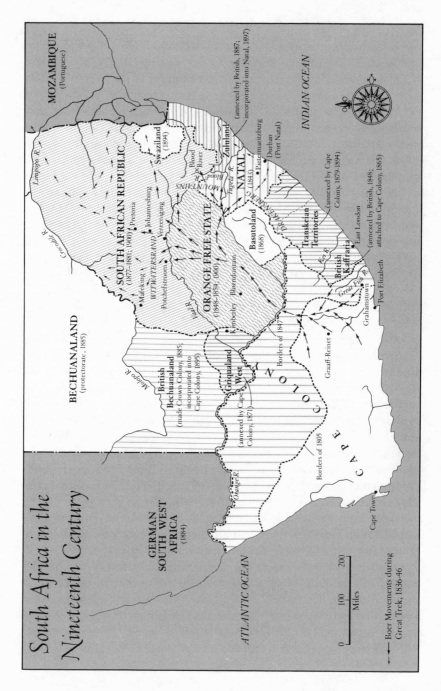

South Africa in the Nineteenth Century

MOZAMBIQUE
(Portuguese)

BECHUANALAND
(protectorate, 1885)

GERMAN SOUTH WEST AFRICA
(1884)

British Bechuanaland
(made Crown Colony, 1885; incorporated into Cape Colony, 1895)

SOUTH AFRICAN REPUBLIC
(1877–1881; 1900)

Mafeking
WITWATERSRAND
Johannesburg • Pretoria
Potchefstroom
Vereeniging

Swaziland
(1884)

Blood River
Blood R.
DRAKENSBERG MOUNTAINS

Zululand
(annexed by British, 1887; incorporated into Natal, 1897)

Pietermaritzburg
Durban (Port Natal)
NATAL (1843)
Tugela R.

ORANGE FREE STATE
(1845–1854; 1900)
Vaal R.
Kimberley • Bloemfontein

Basutoland
(1868)

Griqualand West
(annexed by Cape Colony, 1871)

Borders of 1847

Transkeian Territories
(annexed by Cape Colony, 1879–1894)

British Kaffraria
(annexed by British, 1848; attached to Cape Colony, 1865)

East London

Kei R.
Great Fish R.
Grahamstown
Port Elizabeth
Graaff-Reinet

CAPE COLONY
Borders of 1805

Cape Town

Limpopo R.
Crocodile R.
Molopo R.
Orange R.

INDIAN OCEAN
ATLANTIC OCEAN

0   100   200
Miles

Boer Movements during Great Trek, 1836-46

174

claims. Although it was actually their possession of firearms that gave them the edge, the Voortrekkers were quick to attribute their seemingly miraculous victory to divine intervention. A belief that God had led them into the wilderness and enabled them to smite their heathen enemies would eventually contribute much to their sense of themselves as a chosen people with a special mission.[74]

The republic that the trekkers proceeded to establish in Natal gave a clear indication of their vision of "native policy." The aim was to achieve some kind of balance between the limited need for labor on their farms and the security requirements of a small white settlement surrounded by masses of African tribesmen. Consequently, the highest priority was to exclude most Africans from the areas of white settlement by assigning them reserves or drawing lines of demarcation which they were forbidden to cross. In this way, the Natal republicans helped to establish the enduring South African principle that the only blacks to be permitted to reside in "white areas" were those who performed some essential economic service for the dominant race. To prevent any dangerous and unnecessary concentrations of Africans in the settled regions, the *Volksraad* (assembly) of the Natal Republic decided that no burgher should be allowed to keep more than five African families on his farm. Establishing a pattern that would prevail in subsequent Boer republics, these employed Africans were characteristically bound to their masters by a set of coercive devices that fell short of slavery but bore a strong resemblance to the apprenticeship and indenture arrangements that had bound the Cape Khoikhoi to the soil before the reform of 1828. To acquire additional "apprentices" when they were needed, the settlers sometimes captured allegedly orphaned children in military campaigns and held them in service. According to the law, such apprentices were to be freed at the age of twenty-five for males and twenty-one for females (twenty-five had been the customary age for freeing Khoikhoi apprentices in the Cape before the British lowered it to eighteen in 1812); but lax enforcement and the difficulty of ascertaining or proving correct ages meant that some captives may have served for life. Such a pattern of coerced labor, combined with a method of territorial segregation to relieve whites of the fear of being "swamped" or overwhelmed by vast numbers of "surplus" Africans, became the enduring keystone of South African racial policy.[75]

The closest American parallels were the sporadic efforts of colonies or states to limit the importation of slaves from Africa or other parts of the United States to reduce the possibility of massive slave rebellion. But the problem of security had never become so pressing as to make it seem imperative to restrict by law the number of slaves on each plantation. If the slave South at times resembled an armed camp, it was never to the same extent as the Voortrekker communities; the latter not only needed to keep their laborers under control, but also faced the constant prospect of warfare with the indigenous peoples they were in the process of dispossessing.

The Voortrekker "Republic of Natalia" was short-lived. The British government, responding to its own strategic interests in the area and to fears that the republic's tendency to mount punitive expeditions to secure its southern borders would end up disturbing the Cape's eastern frontier, annexed Natal in 1843, despite some armed resistance by the Afrikaners. The settlers were then offered protection for their actual land holdings and a voice in the determination of new institutions of local government. But they were also required to accept the principle that "there shall not be in the eye of law any distinction of colour, origin, race, or creed; but that the protection of the law, in letter and substance, shall be extended impartially to all alike." This was the hated *gelykstelling* that they had fled the Cape to avoid; consequently most of them chose to trek again, this time to the highveld where other parties of Voortrekkers were in the process of establishing republics that would firmly institutionalize the principle of racial inequality. (Their places were subsequently taken by English colonists, making Natal the most thoroughly British of all the settler societies of South Africa.) The experience in Natal did much to strengthen the Afrikaner conviction that the British not only threatened their desire for independence but persisted in protecting the natives at the expense of the whites by denying to the latter the fruits of their ethnic supremacy.[76]

The republics that were established on the highveld west of the Drakensberg Mountains proved to be a more durable foundation for Afrikaner independence. Individual trek parties founded a number of small republics during the 1840s in scattered locations between the Orange and the Limpopo. In 1848 the British annexed the area between the Orange and Vaal rivers; but in 1852 they formally acknowledged the independence of the 20,000 Voortrekkers who had emigrated beyond the Vaal, and two years later withdrew their claims to the Orange River territory itself, thus permitting the establishment of the

Orange Free State. By 1860, the twin Afrikaner republics of the Free State and the Transvaal (officially known as the South African Republic) had unified the various mini-republics on their respective sides of the Vaal and were independent nations, although the British continued to monitor their external affairs and relations with independent African peoples.[77]

In the constitutions of their highveld republics, the Boers gave formal expression to their revulsion against *gelykstelling* and to their determination that no form of racial equality would be countenanced in their own jurisdictions. The constitution of the Potchefstroom Republic (later to be absorbed into the South African Republic) set the pattern in 1844 by providing that "No persons of mixed race [*bastaards*] shall be able to sit in our meetings as member or judge, down to the tenth degree." In 1858 the *Groundwet* (constitution) of the South African Republic itself made the ringing declaration that there would be "no equality between coloured people and the white inhabitants of the country either in Church or State."[78] These pronouncements signified that a rigorous racial test was now being applied to sanction the differential treatment of all nonwhites, not merely heathen Africans.

The odd-sounding exclusion of Coloreds or "bastaards" "to the tenth degree" apparently reflected an attempt to provide Old Testament support for making racial ancestry a qualification for citizenship. According to Deuteronomy 23, the Israelites had banned bastards, Ammonites, and Moabites from "the congregation of the Lord" to the "tenth generation." As a working principle of racial classification, this test was clearly unenforceable. Many of the trekkers themselves were undoubtedly descended from mixed unions at the Cape that were considerably more recent than ten generations back; furthermore one of the early trek parties may have included a white member with a Colored wife and mixed children.[79] The real purpose of such declarations was probably to prevent any *further* crossing of the color line. This determination to establish a more rigid racial hierarchy than had ever existed at the Cape was in part a fruit of the general heightening of racial consciousness provoked by the earlier humanitarian campaigns on behalf of Colored rights; it was also to some extent the outgrowth of friction in the area just north of the Orange River between white trekkers and previously established communities of Colored emigrants from the Cape (known as Griquas) who for a time enjoyed the protection of British missionaries and colonial officials.[80]

The republics took the constitutional form of "*Herrenvolk* democracies." All white males had the right to vote and hold office, while anyone recognized as nonwhite was denied all perquisites of citizenship—which in the Orange Free State included the right to own fixed property within the borders of the republic. The Free State Constitution, curiously enough, was almost a literal copy of the Constitution of the United States, with the single exception that it explicitly limited the right of citizenship to whites. Inter-racial marriage was banned in the Transvaal—the first time this was attempted anywhere in South Africa—by the simple device of making no provision for the marriage of those who were not white citizens; people of color could not even contract legal unions among themselves, to say nothing of intermarrying with whites. Such extreme applications of a *Herrenvolk* principle of citizenship—which went beyond those affecting free blacks in the Old South—were initially accompanied by a rough equality of social and economic status among white heads of families. What was primarily class ideology in the South—a way of obscuring potentially dangerous inequalities among the white population—was close to being literal reality in the republics before land engrossment began to generate a class of poor whites in the 1880s and 90s.[81]

Compared with the South, however, the republics of the 1860s and 70s manifested relatively little defensive self-consciousness and concern about how to justify or rationalize their practice of *Herrenvolk*ism. The easing of British pressure after the early fifties—as well as the continued absence of a mass of lower-class whites who had to be persuaded of the virtues of a racial order from which they derived no tangible benefits—meant that existing arrangements could usually be taken for granted. It was not even necessary to harp on the innate inferiority of blacks; it was usually enough to rely on the common white perception that Africans were actual or potential enemies and so clearly alien in culture and habits that the idea of assimilating them into white society was unthinkable. Hence racist thinking, in contrast to discriminatory behavior, remained primitive and undeveloped. Defenders of the *status quo* scarcely knew how to respond when a Pretoria newspaper published a letter to the editor in 1875 advocating an extension of some citizenship rights to Africans. The author offered this innovation as the solution to a current labor shortage, a way of raising the morale of African laborers to prevent them from deserting the farms of the Transvaal to work in the diamond diggings that had recently opened up under British jurisdiction in the area around Kimberley. One respondent relied simply on the common assumption that blacks were either equal for all purposes or for none—the basic premise of *Herrenvolk* egalitarianism in South Africa as well as in the South. "Just imagine," he wrote, "seeing a number of kaffirs sitting as members of parliament to make laws for us, or ruling over us . . . even as President." Raising such a prospect was sufficient to demonstrate the absurdity of all forms of *gelykstelling*. Another correspondent trotted out the time-honored argument that "God has distinguished them by their colour, hair, and smell and said that they would be hewers of wood and drawers of water." The advocate of citizenship rights for Africans would "change this and bring me as well to resist God's word and increase the sins of the country."[82]

Among a population of unsophisticated farmers, living in much the same manner as several generations of their ancestors and sharing more or less equally in the benefits of a rigid racial hegemony, there was little need for extended polemic or argumentation to prove that what existed in the republics was right. Antebellum slavocrats, on the other hand, had been forced to defend their way of life against a part of their own tradition that called it into question. They had also been concerned about the loyalty of a non-slaveholding majority that had to be constantly reminded of their status gain from black subordination. Finally, there had been the need for refuting the abolitionists and reducing their effect on northern public opinion, lest the federal government be used as an instrument to contain and weaken the institution of slavery. Pressures of this kind were generally lacking in the Afrikaner republics during the middle decades of the nineteenth century. However much they may have contributed to the mechanics of racial discrimination, the Boers had little need or capacity to participate in the development of racism as an intellectualized doctrine. Their form of white supremacy remained primarily on the level of feeling and instinct, and in this respect at least they clearly differed from the proslavery ideologists who presided over the founding of the southern Confederacy.

Emancipations, Reconstructions, and Political Consolidation

In both the United States and the parts of South Africa that remained under British jurisdiction, the abolition of slavery and other

archaic or pre-capitalist forms of labor coercion was accompanied or
followed by efforts to establish a color-blind legal and political system.
Equality before the law and a uniform or impartial suffrage became
the common goal of Radical Republicans legislating for the conquered
South and British colonial reformers seeking to provide a new order of
public relationships between whites and nonwhites in the Cape Colony.
But the situations differed in their broader historical contexts. In the
United States emancipation and the extension to blacks of the rights of
citizenship occurred in the wake of a civil war and as part of an effort
to unify the nation under northern hegemony. Hence American "Reconstruction" meant both the restoration of a functioning federal union
and the attempt to provide four million freed slaves with the legal and
political rights associated with American nationality. It was the latter
aspect of Reconstruction that aroused intense controversy and provoked
many southern whites into new acts of resistance.

In South Africa, on the other hand, emancipation and efforts to
equalize the civil status of whites and people of color was accompanied
by the political fragmentation of the settler population. Within the
Cape itself, the British were able to give a legal basis to their reforms
with relatively little difficulty or opposition from the local whites
(partly because some of the most intransigent opponents of *gelykstelling*
had trekked away in order to place themselves beyond the jurisdiction
of the new order). Outside the Cape they could not exert this kind of
authority. But the reach of British abolitionism was longer than that
of the equal-rights impulse, and the imperial authorities did manage to
exert enough influence over the republics to prevent the formal re-
establishment of slavery. The Voortrekkers of the 1830s had acquiesced
in emancipation by leaving their slaves behind or giving them the option to return to the colony when asked to do so by British agents; and
it later became an understood condition for the British recognition of
republican independence that the Boers refrain from enslaving indigenous Africans. There was considerable dispute over whether they fully
met these terms, mainly because citizens of the republics not only captured African "apprentices" but also bought and sold them. Nevertheless chattel slavery was officially illegal in both the Transvaal and the
Orange Free State; their labor systems were based primarily on such
quasi-feudal devices as exacting labor as a form of tribute from defeated tribes. But in conceding independence in the 1850s, the British
had obviously given up on any effort to require their former subjects

to provide equal status under the law for nonwhites. Hence the only laboratories that remained for implementing the ideals of civil equality were the Cape Colony and, after 1843, the new colony of Natal.[83]

A major challenge of the post-emancipation era in both the South and the Cape, which was obviously not faced in the republics, was how to guarantee an adequate source of agricultural labor without resorting to coercive devices that were aimed specifically at nonwhites or flagrantly violated the principle of free labor. Southerners attempted to solve the labor problem themselves in 1865–66 by enacting the notorious "black codes" in the all-white state legislatures called into being under President Andrew Johnson's conciliatory plan of reconstruction. What they failed to recognize was that northern public opinion would no longer countenance legalized racial subjugation. By enacting stringent vagrancy and apprenticeship laws that applied only to blacks, Southerners in effect attempted to devise a labor system resembling the one applied to the Khoikhoi in South Africa before 1828. Not surprisingly, the codes were nullified by northern military authority and congressional legislation.[84] Ultimately such open restrictions on the economic rights of blacks were permanently precluded by the ratification of the Fourteenth Amendment. But Northerners as well as Southerners acknowledged that some method was required to ensure an adequate and stable supply of plantation workers. With the aid of military authorities and the Freedmen's Bureau, the ex-slaves were induced to sign annual contracts that were enforced by the withholding of full wages or shares until the end of the growing season. With the rise of the sharecropping system and the demise of Radical Reconstruction in the 1870s, a variety of state laws were passed with the intent to immobilize black tenants for longer periods than a single season. Although most of these enactments were of doubtful constitutionality, they helped to establish an informal quasi-peonage as the new agricultural labor system of the South.[85]

Something analogous occurred at the Cape. Although the vagrancy law of 1834 was disallowed for more or less the same reasons that the southern black codes were nullified, an apparently "color-blind" Masters and Servants Ordinance was passed in 1841 that prescribed criminal penalties for the violation of labor contracts. In 1856, two years after the Cape had been granted representative government, the settler parliament passed a more comprehensive and draconian Masters and Servants Act, lengthening the permissible duration of service and providing severe penalties, not only for such offenses as desertion or absenteeism but also for such breaches of discipline as "disobedience, drunkenness, brawling and use of abusive language."[86] Although such legislation applied to whites as well as nonwhites, the fact that almost all "servants" were Coloreds or Africans meant, in the words of an authority on South African legal traditions, that "the effect of this apparently race-free law was to consolidate rather than weaken race domination."[87] By 1856, therefore, Cape masters actually had a firmer and less ambiguous legal authority over nonwhite workers than southern landlords would ever attain over their tenants. Although laws that in effect made violation of tenancy agreements a criminal offense were enacted by state legislatures in the post-Reconstruction South, they were ultimately held to be unconstitutional by the Supreme Court as a form of the "involuntary labor" prohibited by the Thirteenth Amendment. But it can nevertheless be said of the New South, as of the new order in the Cape, that it fell short of realizing the reformers' ideal of a classic free-labor market.[88]

In the political realm, nineteenth-century liberalism triumphed more decisively over local traditions of racial ascription, at least for a time. The enfranchisement of southern blacks by the Reconstruction Acts of 1867 inaugurated what may have been the most radical experiment in political democracy attempted anywhere in the nineteenth century. Giving the vote to a substantial population of newly freed slaves, most of whom were illiterate and propertyless, seems to represent an extraordinary act of faith in the capacity of every human being to exercise the full responsibilities of citizenship. Examined more closely, however, the black suffrage policy of the Radical Republicans was not so much a manifestation of unadulterated democratic idealism as a desperate northern gamble aimed at establishing an enduring political and cultural hegemony over the South. The preferred program of the most far-sighted and progressive of the Radicals was a long period of direct rule by federal authorities, accompanied by social and economic reform that would include efforts to redistribute land and break up the plantation system. But such policies could not be implemented because they ran counter to the prevailing *laissez-faire* conceptions of the role of government and deviated too sharply from American traditions of federalism and states' rights. Unable to displace the planter elite and transform the economic and social life of the South by direct federal action, the Radicals adopted the expedient of black enfranchisement in an effort to create an electorate that would support the nationalistic and liberal-capitalist aims of the Republican Party and thus help underwrite the political and economic consolidation that constituted the "fruits of victory" in the Civil War.[89]

It would nevertheless be cynical or unfair to ignore the extent to which some of the Radicals were genuinely concerned with what was due to blacks as American citizens and erstwhile contributors to the Union cause. Their argument for black suffrage was that the freedmen could protect their own civil rights against southern white supremacists if they had the ballot and the political influence that went with it. But in the long run voting could have operated as a safeguard against oppression only if there had been firm and consistent federal action to guarantee that the black electorate was not intimidated or terrorized by a hostile white population. To shorten and simplify a long and complex story, the Radical regimes that were established in the southern states under northern Republican auspices in 1868 directly involved blacks as voters, office-holders, and beneficiaries of some of their legislation; but the ultimate unwillingness of the North and the federal government to take the strong measures needed to protect the voting rights of the freedmen against night-riders, "bull-dozers," and white-supremacist paramilitary organizations permitted these interracial governments to collapse after a relatively short time. (They lasted from two to nine years, depending on the balance of political forces within a given state and the proportion of blacks in its population.)

In the Cape, the introduction of a nonwhite franchise was much less traumatic. It did not, first of all, come immediately after the emancipation of the Colored population from slavery or enserfment but had to await the granting of representative government to the colony as a whole. For about two decades the imperial authorities had resisted settler demands for an elected assembly out of seemingly well-founded fears that the white minority would pass laws oppressing the nonwhite majority. When representative government was finally granted in 1854, it was on the condition that the franchise be nonracial. A relatively low property qualification was established that applied to whites and nonwhites alike. The colonists accepted a political arrangement that gave former slaves and indigenous dependents a potential voice in government not so much from egalitarian conviction as because they saw no threat to their social and political dominance from a color-blind franchise. By the 1850s, the master-servant laws and the conditions of economic survival had firmly locked most of the emancipated Coloreds back into their traditional role as laborers and servants. Since the relationship between white and nonwhite corresponded so closely to a European-type class division, the settlers found that they could exercise effective control without legalized racial discrimination. Furthermore, the franchise qualification was just high enough, given the substantial European population and the propertyless condition of most Coloreds and Africans, to ensure that whites remained a firm majority of the electorate.*[90]

Obviously, therefore, the Cape's nonracial franchise did not constitute the direct assault on traditional white prerogatives and sensibilities that black suffrage entailed in the South. Its implementation was eased by the lack of large numbers of enfranchised lower-class whites who derived their sense of status from racial pride rather than real social or economic accomplishment and who might think that their own ballots were devalued if nonwhites were also voting. Furthermore, the color-blind franchise was not forced on the colonists precipitously by an external power and used to establish the hegemony of a political party identified with a former enemy; it was something they acceded to in their own time and under their own conditions. Eventually a limited nonwhite suffrage became the central element in a "Cape liberal tradition" that enjoyed widespread support from both Afrikaner and English-speaking colonists.[91]

In the 1880s, the low franchise qualifications came under increasing attack, mainly because of a vast increase in the potential African vote resulting from the incorporation or annexation of new territories to the east of the old Cape frontier.† Since British politicians representing a minority of the white population were more successful in controlling the African vote than those speaking for the Afrikaner majority and were allegedly using it to help them dominate the responsible cabinet form of government that had existed since 1872, a new Afrikaner po-

---

* The white population at this time was composed of an Afrikaner majority and a substantial British minority. The latter enjoyed a *de facto* privileged position because of their greater average wealth and readier access to governmental and legal institutions.

† The region between the Keiskamma and the Kei, annexed by the British in 1848, was attached to the Cape Colony in 1865. The Transkei was annexed piecemeal by the Cape Colony in the late 1870s and early 1880s.

litical party—the Afrikaner Bond—provided much of the initial support for suffrage restriction. But English-speakers were also becoming anxious about the potential of Africans to outvote Europeans; and, with relatively little white opposition, the voting qualifications were raised and tightened in such a way as to deny the ballot to all but a small fraction of the African population within the expanded borders of the colony. Legislation of 1887 and 1892 increased the qualification, required that the necessary property be held in severalty rather than communally (thus denying the vote to "tribalized" Africans), and imposed a literacy test. But enough nonwhites were left on the rolls to give them the balance of power in several key districts. There were no further efforts by Cape Colonists to limit the franchise; for with the rise of a genuine two-party system in the 1890s, each party found that its hold on certain key seats depended on African or Cape Colored votes. It was in this period that Cecil Rhodes, former Prime Minister of the Colony, described the Cape principle as "equal rights for every civilized man South of the Zambesi." But it is perhaps indicative of the equivocation and pragmatism that lay behind "Cape liberalism" that his original statement, made on the hustings in the election of 1898, was "equal rights for every *white* man. . . ." Only when challenged by Colored voters did Rhodes change the adjective and proceed to define a civilized man as "a man, white or black, who has sufficient education to write his name, has some property or works, in fact is not a loafer."[92]

Even in its attenuated form, Cape liberalism was not synonymous with British practice throughout South Africa in the last half of the nineteenth century. Racial policies in the colony of Natal were closer, in fact if not in theory, to those of the Afrikaner republics than to what prevailed in the Cape. Settled by the British after the humanitarian movement had begun to lose influence and demographically constituted so as to encourage defensive racial policies, Natal rejected the assimilationist doctrine of the Cape in favor of territorial and cultural segregation. The overwhelming African majority was, for the most part, crowded into special reserves and ruled indirectly through chiefs recognized or appointed by the government. Almost all blacks were thus subject to "customary" tribal laws as interpreted ultimately by white magistrates, rather than receiving equal treatment under a common judicial system. The only loophole, which provided a meager kind of lip service to principle of equal rights, was the provision for "exemption" from customary law for those Africans who applied for it on the grounds that they were "civilized." Such exemptions were rarely granted, and a further and more rigorous "civilization" test was required to gain the franchise. Only a handful of Africans had attained this ultimate privilege by 1900. Although culture rather than race *per se* was the only formally acknowledged basis of differentiation, the British settlers revealed by their actions that they were virtually incapable of distinguishing between the two.[93]

The fact that blatantly discriminatory policies could be condoned in a British colony after the 1850s reflected a shift in racial attitudes and doctrines in the mother country that added up to an erosion of support for the principle of equality and a waning of the humanitarianism that had helped inspire emancipation and color-blind legislation in the Cape. A similar upsurge of racist thought and sentiment that occurred in the northern United States during and after Reconstruction helped to rationalize a hands-off policy in the face of resurgent Negrophobia and segregationism in the South. In both cases, the ability of local whites to discriminate against blacks was enhanced by a decline in the humanitarian and egalitarian component in the liberal-capitalist ideology of the metropole.

The extent of this shift should not be overstated. Neither the British nor the northern commitment to racial equality had ever been deeply rooted and unequivocal. Recent scholarship has suggested that the influence of John Philip and the evangelical-humanitarian lobby on British policies in South Africa between 1820 and 1850 has been somewhat exaggerated. Humanitarian reforms were in fact acceptable to the Colonial Office only when they were compatible with financial, commercial, or strategic considerations.[94] In viewing Philip as the principal or sole cause of their misfortunes, the Voortrekkers were engaging in the common practice of attributing a complex series of influences and events to a single malign personality or force: in effect they were developing a "devil" theory of their history. A similar phenomenon occurred in the United States when the slave South responded to Garrison and his radical brand of abolitionism and egalitarianism as if it were the expression of a popular and influential body of northern opinion. Despite the fact that the broader "Free Soil" movement of the 1850s explicitly repudiated Garrison's forthright commitment to racial egalitarianism, southern militants persisted in viewing their opponents as covert supporters of the radical abolitionists. In both instances a distorted view of the lengths to which their enemies would go in destroying the foundations of white supremacy served to strengthen the cohesion and determination of secessionist or separatist elements.

In general and over the long run, neither British imperialists nor northern Republicans proved to be consistent or effective opponents of the general presumption that whites should remain in the dominant position in a multi-racial society. As Robert Ross has pointed out in relation to events in nineteenth-century South Africa, the British as a rule "supported the colonists in their disputes with Africans and 'Coloureds' over land," and the end result of most of their policies was the extension of white "social and political hegemony."[95] Somewhat analogously, the Radical Republicans, when they were in control of the federal government after the Civil War, were unable or unwilling to go beyond recognizing a formal equality of citizenship rights and strike at the social and economic foundations of white dominance in the South.

The real difference between liberal reformers and those engaged in face-to-face racial subjugation was not so much over which race should dominate as over the methods by which that supremacy should be maintained. When Attorney General William Porter of the Cape advocated a low and impartial suffrage requirement for the colony in 1848, he invoked the principle that "no man's station in this free country is determined by the accident of his colour," but went on to imply that such official color-blindness represented no threat to the established social hierarchy, because "the lower orders of this colony are in general an orderly and well conducted class of people and attached to the British government and connexion."[96] Similarly, most northern Republicans of the Reconstruction era did not actually visualize a literal displacement of whites as the dominant racial group in the South. Many of them argued that civil equality would allow the blacks to find their "natural level," which they presumed would be at or near the bottom of the social ladder. Nineteenth-century liberals, therefore, could normally accept a *de facto* white supremacy achieved through what they viewed as a fair competition between groups that were formally equal under the law and in the marketplace. If nonwhites were inherently unequal, as they probably were, they would inevitably remain in the lower class.[97] Still, this *laissez-faire* philosophy of race relations, even when it was accompanied by confident assertions of white superiority, could arouse the intense opposition of employers of black labor in multi-racial colonies or sections. Faced with the proximity of large numbers of nonwhites and imbued with the belief that blacks would not refrain from "crime" or work on their farms and plantations without some form of compulsion, settlers and ex-slaveholders characteristically held out for some new equivalent of the coercive racial control and status rigidity of the pre-emancipation era.

What emerged in the racial thinking of the metropolitan British between the 1850s and the 1880s and in that of the northern middle class between the late 1860s and the 1890s was a greater sympathy, or at least tolerance, for the settler or white southern point of view. The growing popularity of "scientific racism," with its stress on biological differences as determining the natural capacities and destinies of racial groups, was the most obvious manifestation of this tendency. The pseudo-Darwinian conception that the contest of human races entailed a "struggle for existence" leading to the survival or dominance of "the fittest" became a late-Victorian shibboleth in both Britain and the United States. It helped to rationalize the notion that in some instances, especially where Europeans were faced with large populations of racial "inferiors," it might be necessary to rule the latter with a firm hand and deny them access to full citizenship.[98]

But more was involved in this change of attitude than the popularity of "scientific racism" as an intellectual persuasion. Antipathy to people of color and receptivity to the notion that they were incapable of governing themselves was encouraged by a series of apparent setbacks for the liberal-humanitarian program of racial uplift and assimilation to white civilization. The Sepoy Mutiny that broke out in India in 1857 dampened British enthusiasm for educating and "civilizing" indigenous colonial populations, and the insurrection among the freedmen of Jamaica that erupted at Morant Bay in 1865 led many Englishmen to reconsider their belief that ex-slaves were worthy of civil and political rights.[99] In a similar spirit, many Northerners attributed the disorder and corruption associated with Radical Reconstruction in the South to the participation of blacks; when the Radical regimes collapsed, they concluded that the freedmen had demonstrated their incapacity for self-government and could legitimately be consigned to the "guardianship" of their former masters.[100]

A deeper source for the erosion of support for *laissez-faire* colorblindness—but one that cannot be fully explored here—may have been the growth of more intense forms of *class* consciousness among the dominant metropolitan groups. Douglas Lorimer has argued that the efforts of members of the mid-Victorian middle class to heighten the barriers between themselves and "the lower orders," combined with their growing fears of a class struggle in England, sapped the liberal commitment to an open society in ways that strengthened racial prejudice and a tolerance for repression in the colonies.[101] Similarly, as the work of David Montgomery suggests, the middle-class idealism of the Radical Republicans began to founder when the demands of an emerging labor movement and the prospect of class conflict in the North during Reconstruction brought out the ideological limitations of their egalitarianism.[102] Hence the retreat from equality represented something more general than merely an increasing insensitivity to black or brown aspirations for civil and political rights. Hardening attitudes toward the white poor and the working classes in late-nineteenth-century England and America, and an increasing willingness to use force if necessary to keep them under control, presumably led to a less sympathetic view of the plight of nonwhite lower classes in multi-racial colonies or sections.

Nevertheless, official or "enlightened" spokesmen on racial or imperial matters in late-Victorian England and the northern United States usually retained enough respect for the rhetoric of racial benevolence that was part of their traditions to keep from publicly endorsing the most blatant forms of racial discrimination or the brutal application of Darwinian theory that celebrated the extinction of "inferior breeds." Instead, they tended to promulgate the ideology of the "white man's burden," which normally meant that whites had a duty to assume protective "trusteeship" over those farther down the evolutionary scale so that the latter could develop "along their own lines" to whatever level of civilization they were capable of achieving. This doctrine retained some of the sense of paternal responsibility that had been an undeniable component of earlier humanitarian reformism, but its adherents became increasingly vague about whether the beneficiaries of benevolent trusteeship could ever be promoted to equality with the "superior" race. While most southern white supremacists and South African settlers persistently adhered to what Philip Curtin has categorized as "teleological racism"—the idea that blacks "had been created inferior *in order* to serve their white masters"—the proponents of a beneficent guardianship denied any such fixed relationship between the races and endorsed a more flexible and evolutionary variety of racism that al-

lowed for a gradual "elevation" of "uncivilized" peoples that might in
the long run be rewarded by some improvement in their civil and political status.[103]

If "teleological racism" had been suited to the ideological needs of
planters or farmers engaged in face-to-face coercion of nonwhite dependents, "evolutionary racism," especially in its benevolent guise of
trusteeship, was an ideal rationale for imperialists of the post-emancipation era, who sought to establish hegemony over various categories of
non-Europeans by treating them as collective entities subject to white
guidance and administration, rather than as detachable individuals
whose labor could be freely appropriated under some form of slavery
or serfdom. It could also provide the basis for an accommodation between the centralizing efforts of a national or imperial government and
the strong white-supremacist commitments of local whites in newly
subordinated colonies or sections that traditionally excluded nonwhites
from participation in the political process.

In the American case, an acceptance of the failure and futility of
Reconstruction did not utterly obliterate northern concern for the fate
of the freedmen; a lingering sense of responsibility was felt most intensely by those who retained a strong retrospective pride in the Union
cause and the emancipation of the slaves.[104] Hence the growth of legalized segregation and disfranchisement in the South could be a burden
on the conscience unless it could be viewed as part of an evolutionary
process that would result in an eventual improvement in the black
situation. Theodore Roosevelt and other turn-of-the-century northern
"progressives" found the rationale for condoning new forms of southern discrimination primarily in an extension of the same logic that supported imperialist adventures abroad leading to the forced incorporation of nonwhites into a new American empire. If the United States
was justified in exercising protective and educational trusteeship over
"our brown brothers" in the Philippines, then the segregated southern
blacks of 1900 could be viewed as undergoing an analogous and equally
salutory tutelage. One wing of the southern segregation movement explained the "necessity" of social segregation and suffrage restriction in
precisely these terms, and the most prominent black spokesman of the
times, Booker T. Washington, seemed to acquiesce in the concept that
a period of apprenticeship was needed before blacks could legitimately
demand full political equality. Consequently, it became easy for "progressive" Northerners to endorse the idea that southern blacks were not

ready for equal citizenship and should, for their own good, be subjected for an indefinite period to the benevolent guidance of the "best elements" in the white South. Segregation and *de facto* disfranchisement could be countenanced on the assumption that they were needed to keep a "child" race from trying to climb the evolutionary ladder too rapidly.[105]

The northern elite's acceptance of segregationist policies based on this rationale helped provide the foundation for a new national consensus on race policy that constituted a crucial and final step on the long road to sectional "reunion." If the cloud of rhetoric and rationalization is swept away, this last act of the drama of national consolidation that had begun with a struggle to preserve the Union and destroy the "slave power" can be seen for what it really was—a northern betrayal of the blacks who had been emancipated and promised full citizenship. As Paul Buck put it more than forty years ago, "the Negro paid a heavy price" so that whites could be reunited in a common nationality.[106]

South Africa's path to unification was in many ways different from the American "road to reunion," but it was similar in its ultimate betrayal of black hopes and aspirations. The push for consolidation began abortively in the 1870s when the British Colonial Secretary, Lord Carnarvon, proposed a federation of the two British colonies and the two Afrikaner republics. His main motive for confederation was to establish a uniform "native policy" throughout South Africa at a time when the Zulu Kingdom still constituted a threat to white hegemony. One major obstacle to such a union, however, was the adamant isolationism of the South African Republic. The only way to force the Transvaalers into a federation, it seemed, was first to bring them directly under British sovereignty. Taking advantage of the bankrupt and ineffectual government that then existed in the Republic, the British easily and bloodlessly annexed the Transvaal in 1877. But their rule eventually infuriated many Afrikaners, and a resistance movement developed under the leadership of Paul Kruger. In 1880, the Transvaalers rebelled and once again raised the republican flag. In early 1881, they defeated the British troops at the battle of Majuba Hill and regained their independence from a Liberal government that had already concluded that annexation had been a mistake.[107] The "First Anglo-Boer War" was a major setback to hopes for a unification of white South Africa under British auspices, not only because it failed to keep the

Transvaal under the British flag but also because it provided a stimulus for the emergence of a self-conscious Afrikaner nationalism that extended beyond the republics and into the Cape Colony. When the Afrikaner majority in the Cape registered strong support for their embattled brethren in the Transvaal, the possibility that an aroused Afrikanerdom might some day challenge British hegemony in South Africa as a whole first became credible.[108]

As its origins suggest, the new Afrikaner nationalism was more anti-British than distinctively anti-black. Both sides in the Transvaal affair had wanted to bring the Zulu under firm white control, and it is noteworthy that the republicans shrewdly delayed their rebellion until after the British army had disposed of the Zulu threat on their eastern border (something they had been unable to do for themselves). The British incursion had been mounted from Natal—a colony which in its own way was almost as white-supremacist as the Transvaal; and during the period of occupation the new administration had made no move to alter the racially discriminatory policies established by the Republic.[109] Nevertheless, a difference of opinion on precisely how conquered Africans should be treated did give a sharper edge to the Anglo-Boer hostility of the 1870s and 80s (although fundamentally it was really a disagreement between white settlers—British and Afrikaner alike—and the imperial government). After winning major wars against the Zulu and the southern Sotho (or Basuto) between 1877 and 1880, the British authorities refrained from annexing conquered lands for the benefit of the settler population. According to Ronald Robinson and John Gallagher, "Native policy had always been a main source of antagonism to British rule; and in insisting upon large land-reserves . . . for the defeated Zulu and Basuto, the imperial authorities strained their relations with the colonial leaders who were mainly interested in land and labour for Europeans."*[110]

The British policy of allowing conquered Africans to retain much

* Robinson and Gallagher, however, fail to distinguish clearly in this quotation between "land-reserves" in the usual sense of territory reserved for Africans *within* a white colony or republic and conquered African nations ruled separately and indirectly by the British through the agency of compliant kings or chiefs from the established ruling families. Zululand and Basutoland were actually examples of the latter form of white colonial dominance in the period after the wars of the late 1870s. Zululand was eventually incorporated into Natal and the Union of South Africa, but Basutoland retained its status as an indirectly ruled British possession until it became the independent Kingdom of Lesotho in 1966.

of their original territory, where they could be ruled indirectly by an appointed imperial bureaucracy, was contrary to the practice within the Orange Free State, which permitted no native reserves at all, and that of the Transvaal, which tolerated them only as a practical necessity. The republicans wished to keep direct authority over nonwhites in the hands of local farmers and their elected assemblies rather than surrendering it to an alien and independent officialdom; and this was one reason why they valued their freedom so highly. As President Paul Kruger described the Transvaal philosophy of racial control in 1882, its "chief principle" was "that savages must be kept within bounds, and always overruled by justice and morality." The most effective way to accomplish this, he continued, was to rule them directly as "subjects" (but not citizens) of the Republic and see to it that they obeyed the laws governing them and bore "their share of the public burdens."[111] Paternalistic and protective rule by officials not directly responsible to the white settlers or their representatives—the usual pattern for areas of large African concentration under British jurisdiction—was unacceptable to Afrikanerdom.

The abstract difference between British imperial and Afrikaner republican conceptions of how to rule Africans might be described as a conflict between the trusteeship ideal and what the Boers called *Baaskap*—which in essence meant direct domination in the interest of white settlers without any pretense that the subordinate race was being shielded from exploitation or guided toward civilization. Under the leadership and inspiration of President Kruger in the 1880s and 90s, the Transvaalers developed a full-blown nationalistic ideology plainly identifying a sense of national mission with the permanent subordination of Africans as "hewers of wood and drawers of water." Kruger was influenced in his thinking by the rise of an ultra-conservative form of Calvinism in the Afrikaner churches that made it possible to give theological substance to the pre-existing belief that God was on the side of the Boers and had condemned the Africans to perpetual subservience. After his election as President in 1881, Kruger invoked Calvin's conception of the "intermediate election" of a people to carry out some God-given mission to lay the foundation for an Afrikaner "civil religion" that would serve as the wellspring of twentieth-century Afrikaner nationalism. The sociologist T. Dunbar Moodie has described this emerging dogma as a manifestation of the myth of a national covenant: "According to Kruger's understanding of the sacred history, God chose his people (*volk*) in the Cape Colony and brought them out into the wilderness. There he chastised them. . . . God then covenanted with the chastened people and the 'enemies were defeated and the trekkers inhabited the land which God had given them in the rightful manner.' " All Africans and other people of color were implicitly excluded from the covenanted *volk*. As Moodie concludes, "The native Africans were certainly not among the 'elect.' The most definitive experience and powerful traditions of the Boer people labeled them as 'nations without the law.' "[112]

In its practical application, this creed was similar to the "teleological racism" that prevailed in the nineteenth-century South. But in form and intellectual substructure it was less a racism in the narrow sense than an intense ethnocentrism; for it exalted the Boers more than it demeaned the Africans and involved little recourse to the concept of innate biological inferiority that was central to the southern defense of slavery and segregationism. Unlike southern racial ideologists, the Afrikaners were not primarily concerned with defending specific racial institutions and practices; they were asserting their national identity in deeper and more authentic ways than Southerners were able to do even when they were fighting for their independence. What made the Boers white supremacists was their firm conviction that their own safety and survival as a people depended on their freedom to use whatever degree of force was necessary against nonwhites who got in their way or whose labor they required.

It would, however, be grossly misleading to describe the renewed conflict that led to the Second Anglo-Boer War of 1899–1902 as essentially a struggle between benign and oppressive racial ideologies. It was true that British protests and propaganda directed at the Transvaal in the 1890s sometimes used accusations of the mistreatment of Africans and, more particularly, of discrimination against nonwhite British subjects (Cape Coloreds and Indian immigrants) to strengthen a case that republican independence was an affront to Anglo-Saxon principles of justice and equality.[113] But the major British grievance was the denial of political rights to the immigrants, mainly of British origin, who had poured into the Witwatersrand after the discovery of gold in 1886 and might eventually become a majority of the white male population of the republic. It was the desire to control the gold fields and prevent an independent Transvaal from emerging as a wealthy and powerful state that would threaten British hegemony throughout southern Africa that provided the main impetus for the pressure, propaganda, and intrigue that led to war in 1899.[114]

The subsequent military struggle was conducted on the basis of a tacit understanding between the Boers and the British that Africans would not be used to fight for either side.* In fact, as David Denoon has contended, the whites would probably never have allowed themselves the luxury of an intra-racial conflict if all major black resistance to European domination had not already been crushed throughout South Africa.[115] No such gentleman's agreement had been observed during the American Civil War, and the North's emancipation policy and substantial reliance on black troops after 1863 made it inevitable that the war would bring a major transformation in race relations. No basic changes in the relations between whites and blacks resulted from the British victory over the Boers. Indeed, the British quickly reneged on their previous intention to extend the Cape franchise to the Transvaal and the Orange Free State by agreeing in the Treaty of Vereeniging (1902) that "the question of granting the franchise to natives will not be decided until after the introduction of self-government." This provision, in effect, left it up to white settlers rather than imperial "trustees" to determine the extent of black political rights in a British-dominated South Africa.[116]

During the brief period when the Transvaal and the Orange Free State were ruled directly as Crown Colonies, no serious efforts were made to reform or modify the pre-existing policies of racial proscription; and when both colonies were granted responsible self-government in 1907, the whites-only franchise remained in effect.[117] Such a capitulation to white supremacy is not surprising when we consider the basic views of Lord Milner, the British High Commissioner who presided over the "reconstruction" of South Africa in the years immediately following the war. "A political equality of white and black is impossible," he asserted in 1903. "The white man must rule, because he is elevated by many, many steps above the black man; steps which it will take the latter centuries to climb, and which it is quite possible that the vast bulk of the black population may never be able to climb at all."[118] The racial Darwinism of the British imperialists, however softened by the rhetoric of trusteeship, could thus serve as a rationale for conceding to

* This white man's agreement was not always faithfully observed by the British, but their use of Africans as combatants was both limited and covert.

white settlers virtually all the power they desired over Africans and other nonwhites.

Furthermore, the British-dominated South African Native Affairs Commission, which convened in 1903 and reported in 1905, helped set the pattern for future South African racial policies by advocating territorial segregation and a separate and unequal form of representation for Africans in the colonial legislatures.[119] The testimony heard by the commission from prominent English-speaking South Africans reveals the prevalence among them of blatantly racist assumptions. According to an official of the Natal Department of Native Affairs, "No weight should be given to such preposterous notions as equality between Europeans and natives. Equality is a state of affairs which at the present stage of evolution should not be dreamt of. It is an unnatural condition between people so utterly dissimilar in civilization."[120] An Anglophone member of the Transvaal parliament argued that it was not "possible to give the coloured races the franchise in this country unless you wish to make this country intolerable for the white man to live in. . . . Let us keep the two races separate, and let us govern the black races to the best of our ability, because . . . the negro races occupy the lowest position in the evolutionary scale."[121]

The British government's accession to such viewpoints and the policies that they entailed, its hasty retreat from earlier commitments to equal rights under the law and common suffrage qualifications for all races, strongly resembles the North's failure to enforce black suffrage and civil rights in the South after Reconstruction. In both cases, white unity took precedence over the ideal of a nonracial citizenship.

When a convention was assembled in 1908 to attempt the constitutional unification of the South African colonies into a single British Commonwealth, it was virtually inevitable that the interests and racial convictions of the white settler population would be the only ones that counted. The British High Commissioner, Lord Selborne, sent a letter to the delegates suggesting that some provision be made for the enfranchisement of nonwhites who could meet a "civilization" test; but the home government chose not to press the matter.[122] The only racial issue that divided the convention was the question of what should be done about the long-established nonwhite franchise in the Cape. Cape delegates were unwilling to give up their common voters' roll based on a uniform property and education qualification to adopt the "northern" practice of universal manhood suffrage for whites and total exclusion of nonwhites from the electorate. Their spokesmen argued that a qualified suffrage served as a useful "safety valve" for nonwhite discontent. Needless to say, the representatives of the Transvaal and the Orange Free State wanted no part of this "Cape liberal" policy. The compromise that resulted left existing franchise laws in force within the respective provinces. But the fact that the northern tradition was really the ascendent one was revealed in the ban on nonwhite membership in Parliament. Although no Africans or Coloreds had ever actually served in the Cape parliament, they had possessed the right to do so; with the establishment of a new Union parliament the principle that only whites could participate in the governing of South Africa was explicitly affirmed.[123]

Hence the founding of a self-governing South African Union on a constitutional basis that prescribed white dominance and legalized racial inequality occurred almost simultaneously with the completion of a sectional "reunion" process in the United States that also, in effect, compromised or undermined the rights that had previously been granted or promised to blacks. The difference was that segregationism and disfranchisement in the South African case was enshrined in the organic law of the land—with the Cape's mild deviance being tolerated as a local exception—while something like the reverse of this occurred in the United States. The American Constitution, with the addition of the Fourteenth and Fifteenth amendments, explicitly prohibited any denial of civil and political rights on grounds of race. The turn-of-the-century "compromise" was possible because the various "nonracial" subterfuges that had been devised in the South to deny substantive political and civil equality to blacks were condoned by a federal judiciary that took a very narrow and conservative view of the scope of the Reconstruction amendments. A legal-constitutional triumph for white supremacy equivalent to that achieved by white settlers in South Africa would have required repeal of the Reconstruction amendments. Calls for such action were in fact issued from time to time by southern extremists, but their cause failed to attract enough northern support to become more than a white-supremacist pipe dream.[124] Although subject to much *de facto* discrimination, blacks *in the North* were never legally segregated or denied access to the ballot box after Reconstruction. In the United States, therefore, legalized discrimination remained a localized exception rather than a national norm; whereas in South Africa it was the Cape tradition of "equal rights for every civilized man" that represented a provincial divergence from the overt *Herrenvolk* principle that prevailed elsewhere.

Such a difference would have meant little to Afro-Americans in 1910 because 90 percent of them were still in the South. But when they began to migrate in large numbers to the North, beginning in the era of the First World War, they simultaneously rejoined the American electorate. The resulting increase in their political influence and the greater opportunity that they found in the North to organize in defense of their constitutional rights would, after World War II, help to provide the impulse for the "second Reconstruction" that overthrew legalized segregation in the South and restored blacks to their basic rights as citizens.

"Cape liberal" exceptionalism would in the long run suffer a fate similar to that of publicly enforced southern segregationism. At almost exactly the same time that the South was being desegregated, the last frail remnants of the Cape heritage of legal and political "color-blindness" were obliterated by the juggernaut of apartheid. Hence, despite the apparent similarities of a white unification achieved at the expense of nonwhite access to citizenship that occurred at the turn of the century in both the United States and South Africa, it is clear in retrospect that the underlying constitutional and ideological imperatives pointed in opposite directions. To understand fully why this was the case, it is necessary to look beyond politics and examine the changing economic foundations of white supremacy in the late nineteenth and early twentieth centuries.

V

Industrialism, White Labor, and Racial Discrimination

Industrialization and Ethnic Pluralism

Industrial capitalism may be a major cause of social and economic inequality in the modern world, but it makes little historical sense to view it as the source of ideologies directly sanctioning racial discrimination. As we have seen, white-supremacist attitudes and policies originated in preindustrial settings where masters of European extraction lorded it over dark-skinned slaves or servants. The notion that non-whites were created unequal to perform a servile role beneath the dignity of Europeans first became a militant ideology or fighting faith when some of the values associated with the rise of *laissez-faire* capitalism in Great Britain and the northern United States were perceived by the holders of slaves or quasi-slaves as patently antagonistic to their practice of racial subordination. Realization of the nineteenth-century liberal ideal of a totally free labor market, with workers and employers equal under the law and liberated from noneconomic constraints, would in theory have made racial prejudice irrelevant to worldly success. Pursuing their rational self-interest, capitalists would have hired the best individuals for the job regardless of their ancestry, and workers would have freely sought out the best market for their labor. Inequality would have existed, but it would have been purely a matter of class rather than race.

But ideals are not always capable of being realized; and the assumption of antislavery reformers that equal opportunity for nonwhites would result from the substitution of contract for status in the economic realm proved to be utopian. It was based on a conception of progress that underestimated the capacity of the old racial order to adapt to changing economic and legal conditions and failed to foresee how privileged groups within a capitalistic society could accentuate traditional racial divisions and distinctions for their own advantage. If the liberal utopianism of the mid-nineteenth century—the ideology of "free labor and free men"—was instrumental in the abolition of slavery and the discouragement of other kinds of forced labor based openly on conquest or captivity, it was much less effective in averting more subtle forms of labor coercion that had the outward appearance of contractual arrangements freely entered into. Furthermore, even when the structural requirements of a free labor market were roughly approximated, there was still no barrier to private discrimination against those stigmatized by a badge of color that evoked deeply rooted prejudice and recalled their previous condition as slaves or conquered enemies.

Another model for what *should* have occurred is the conventional Marxist theory of class formation. When former slaves or peasants are transformed into wage-earners who lack ownership or control of the means of production and subsist mainly by selling their labor to capitalists, they should, in the long run at least, be able to develop a common class consciousness transcending traditional racial or ethnic divisions. But in societies like the United States and South Africa, where a substantial portion of the industrial work force was composed of alien immigrants or conquered indigenes, this process was impeded by cultural and racial pluralism, and the working population was fragmented along ethnic lines that proved to be durable sources of division and identification.

The initial success of capitalistic industrialization—as we know very well from the British example—depends in large part on a surplus of readily available cheap labor. In the densely populated societies of Western Europe, indigenous peasants driven off the land by the commercialization of agriculture provided much of this exploitable work force. During the formative period of industrialization in the United States, between the 1840s and the 1890s, there was no displaced agricultural population sufficient to man the mines or factories, except on a limited and local basis. Neither the family farms of the Midwest nor the plantations of the South—even after these shifted from slavery to sharecropping—had the capacity to generate the kind of massive labor surplus needed for rapid industrial growth. During the beginning stages of industrial development in South Africa in the late nineteenth century, most of the relatively sparse white settler population had neither the desire nor the need to abandon their agrarian way of life. Large numbers of conquered Africans were potentially available, but, in most cases, they had not been literally uprooted or deprived of their traditional means of subsistence. Living on a constricted land base in the "reserves" to which they had been consigned or on the huge white farms where entire villages were allowed to "squat" in return for sporadic labor services to the owners, they remained reluctant to venture *en masse* into the industrial labor market created by the mining revolution. Hence early industrialists in both countries were compelled to look far afield or adopt special methods to recruit workers. The most obvious possible strategies were to encourage immigration from external areas of labor surplus or to develop non-market devices to extort labor from indigenous rural folk. In the United States, the former policy prevailed, while in South Africa a combination of foreign immigration and domestic coercion was developed to create a strange hybrid of capitalistic "free labor" and indentured servitude.

In the American case, recently arrived European immigrants provided the bulk of the industrial labor force between the mid-nineteenth century and the early twentieth; wave after wave of them met most of the demand for low-paid laborers and factory operatives in the most rapidly developing parts of the nation. According to a clergyman observing the American working class in 1887: "Not every foreigner is a workingman, but in the cities at least, it may almost be said that every workingman is a foreigner."[1] Ethnic differences among workers and the continual influx at the lower occupational levels of aliens from peasant backgrounds were factors that impeded the growth of class consciousness and organization. "Throughout industrial America," John Higham has written, "intricate ethnic divisions dissipated class consciousness. The immigrants tended to identify not with a downtrodden class but with exemplars of success among their own people."[2] Looking at this process of labor recruitment from the perspective of how preindustrial rural folk are transformed into a class of industrial workers, Herbert Gutman has drawn attention to the fact that "the American working class was continually altered in its composition by infusions, from within and without the nation, of peasants, farmers, skilled artisans, and occasional day laborers who brought into industrial society ways of work and other habits and values not associated with industrial necessities and the industrial ethos."[3] Although employers undoubtedly paid an economic price for the inefficiency and preindustrial work habits of each new wave of immigrant workers who entered the economy at the bottom, such losses were greatly outweighed by the fact that such labor was cheap by American standards and remained so for an extended period, partly because of the obstacles to worker organization created by ethnic diversity. The phenomenal rate of capital formation and industrial growth in nineteenth- and early twentieth-century America was due in part to the seemingly inexhaustible supply of low-paid immigrant workers who were in a weak position for improving their collective situation by organizing effective unions or mobilizing politically to compel intervention by the state.[4]

Recruitment of labor for the diamond and gold mines that provided a foundation for South African industrialization occurred on two distinct levels. For the skilled work, immigrant artisans were attracted from Europe by the lure of exceptionally high wages—the only way they could be deflected from more popular areas of settlement like Australia and the United States.[5] For the unskilled and semi-skilled work, large numbers of Africans were recruited, sometimes coercively, from colonized societies all over southern Africa. A substantial minority of these came from areas under Portuguese jurisdiction; others came from regions under British colonial administration that had not been substantially settled by whites. Even more than white immigrants in the United States, these groups functioned as a source of cheap labor that guaranteed a high rate of profit and capital accumulation for the white entrepreneurs. The historian C. W. de Kiewiet has vividly described the crucial importance of such low-paid African workers for South African economic development: "Of the resources that permitted South Africa at long last to take its place beside the Australian colonies, New Zealand, and Canada in the economy of the world, native labor was one of the most important. What an abundance of rain and grass was to New Zealand mutton, what a plenty of cheap grazing land was to Australian wool, what the fertile prairie acres were to Canadian wheat, cheap native labor was to South African mining and industrial enterprise."[6]

The extraordinary initial cheapness of African labor came from the conditions under which the workers were introduced into the mines.

Unlike most of the European immigrants to industrial America, African workers were not normally permitted to bring their families and settle near their places of employment but were signed to contracts of several months' duration and then housed in compounds under direct supervision. They were paid a wage geared to individual rather than family needs and at levels Europeans deemed appropriate for "uncivilized" people inured to a low standard of living. Initially such a system did not conflict seriously with the Africans' own expectations; for most had no desire to separate themselves permanently from their tribal communities and worked only for fixed and limited economic objectives, such as the ability to purchase a gun or acquire enough cattle to provide the "bride-wealth" necessary for traditional marriages. As their aspirations increased and involvement in the industrial economy became a major part of their working lives, a variety of artificial devices were applied to keep their wages at or near the initial low level.[7]

African labor therefore played a role in South African industrialization roughly equivalent to that of white immigrant labor in the United States—but under vastly different conditions. American immigrants settled permanently in industrial areas and, despite initial poverty and economic vulnerability, had some possibility of regular employment and of acquiring property. Their children might move into the ranks of skilled labor or even into the lower middle class, a form of upward mobility that was sometimes facilitated by the arrival of a new unskilled ethnic group to take up the more menial occupations and hence give an upward shove to an earlier generation of immigrants.[8] Because African workers were usually oscillating migrants rather than new members of a settled urban or industrial proletariat, they had little chance to gain any cumulative advantage for their families out of industrial employment. If American immigrants labored under certain handicaps in their efforts to organize in their own interest, the blacks who did most of the industrial labor in South Africa from the beginnings of economic modernization usually had no chance at all to develop class consciousness as workers or proletarians. With the rise of massive government intervention to perpetuate the initial system of migratory labor, low wages, and limited opportunity, Africans were effectively prevented from following the example of working classes in other industrializing nations. Their adaptation to an industrial culture was artificially impeded, their capability to organize in defense of their economic interests was stymied, and their chances for mobility within the industrial order were severely limited. Under these circumstances they could neither partipate in "the making of a working class" nor benefit from the kind of slow upward mobility experienced by proletarian immigrants in the United States.[9]

It may seem peculiar to begin by comparing black South Africans with white immigrants in the United States rather than with Afro-Americans and other victims of palpable racial discrimination in the economic realm. But the comparison is useful as a way of dramatizing the very different economic roles played by American and South African blacks in the industrialization process. If the South African black contribution has been of such significance that it can be likened to that of white immigrants in the United States, that of Afro-Americans has been relatively marginal, at least until very recent times. As slaves, blacks made an enormous involuntary contribution to economic growth, and thus to the capacity of the economy to generate an industrial order, by producing cotton—the commodity that made up more than half the dollar value of all American exports between 1840 and 1860.[10] But after the Civil War most blacks remained tied for half a century to a stagnating and increasingly depressed southern cotton economy and were unable to make substantial inroads into the industrial labor force because of the virtual monopolization of manufacturing jobs by immigrants in the northern states and lower-class native whites in the South.[11] Only with the massive migration to the North which coincided with the decline and restriction of European immigration in the period during and after the First World War did significant numbers of blacks become factory workers.

It follows that the main thrust of economic discrimination as it relates to industrialization has been radically different in the two societies. In the United States the fundamental impulse for an extended period was to exclude blacks from the advanced industrial segments of the economy by keeping them as much as possible in the agricultural and service sectors.* In South Africa the pattern has been one of integrating blacks into the industrial work force as the principal source of labor but under conditions that would prevent them from developing the political and economic leverage that is normally acquired by working classes in a modernizing society. To explain these contrary ten-

---

* The principal exception to this pattern was the extensive employment of blacks as coal miners in Alabama and elsewhere in the deep South in the late nineteenth century.

dencies, it is necessary to acknowledge the role of noneconomic as well as economic influences. My assumption is that economic discrimination along racial lines would not have developed and persisted in the industrial era to the extent that it did if it had not served in some way the material interests of industrial capitalists and skilled white workers. But it is difficult to account for the specific nature of racial caste or exclusion in industry without reference to pre-existing beliefs about the character, capacity, and social status of nonwhites. Furthermore, political and legal developments of a partially autonomous nature could impinge on the economic order in such a way as to influence significantly, for better or worse, the life chances of blacks or other nonwhites in the industrial arena.

The Industrial Legacy of Slavery and the Rise of the Machine

Despite our usual image of the slave as a plantation laborer, there was in fact no inherent obstacle to the employment of slaves in industrial pursuits. In the Old South, slaves frequently worked in iron works, cotton mills, mines, and in a variety of other industrial occupations. In the urban areas, slaves constituted a significant proportion of the skilled artisans.[12] In the Cape Colony, where there was no manufacturing to speak of, virtually all the skilled trades were carried on by slaves, usually under the direction of white master mechanics who were essentially supervisors and small entrepreneurs rather than working artisans. According to a historian of South African slavery, "we find these slaves in all sorts of employments, as shoemakers, coopers, turners, wagon-makers, carpenters, woodcutters, potters, wig-makers, plumbers, thatchers, tin-smiths, tailors. . . . In every trade and pursuit they were adaptable, and many of the more frugal among them were able in the course of the years to save sufficient money to purchase their freedom and, eventually, to have slaves of their own."[13]

Slavery as a labor system may well be incompatible with large-scale industrialization, but one cannot conclusively prove this common assumption from the experience of either the southern United States or South Africa. In the former case, the competitive advantage of a profitable staple agriculture over a nascent and primitive industrial sector may be sufficient in itself to explain why a substantial shift of human and monetary capital from cotton-growing to manufacturing did not take place. Since the Cape Colony obviously lacked the resources, capital, and markets to sustain industrial development, it is bootless to raise the question of whether or not slavery retarded it. Any attempt to resolve the complex issue of whether slavery and economic modernization are necessarily exclusive would go well beyond the scope of this study, but it may be relevant to the debate that when South Africa did industrialize it did so primarily with labor that was not literally enslaved but was nevertheless coerced in ways sometimes more reminiscent of slavery than of a classic "free labor" system. Setting this moot theoretical question aside, it is clear enough that the flexibility in the employment of nonwhite workers during the slave era in both the United States and South Africa should have provided ample evidence to whites that there was no limit to the industrial capabilities of people of color.

In South Africa this proposition was generally accepted. The normative racial division of labor that grew up during the slave era consigned virtually all manual labor, however skilled, to nonwhites. "White man's work" was deemed essentially supervisory or what today would be considered middle class or white collar. In effect, therefore, the concept of a white working class did not even exist, and an image of white men watching while brown or black men toil does not greatly distort the reality of occupational stratification at the Cape. A late-eighteenth-century traveler reported that the white craftsmen in Cape Town never actually labored at their trades but had their slaves do everything, and a burgher memorial of 1784 attributed the popularity of trekking among young colonists to their absolute refusal to seek employment from other whites on the grounds that this put them on the same level as slaves or "Hottentots."[14] Of course white farmers sometimes found it necessary to work with their hands, but they did so as independent individuals, not as employees, and there were almost invariably Khoikhoi servants or imported slaves to do the really arduous tasks. Even after emancipation, skilled freedmen in the Cape benefited to some extent from the ingrained attitude that it was unsuitable for whites to be wage-earners; until well into the twentieth century Colored craftsmen held their own in the skilled trades of the Western Cape partly because massive white competition was slow to develop.[15] By the late nineteenth century, however, the rural areas of both the Cape and the Afrikaner republics had produced a class of landless whites who had no recourse but to depend on other Europeans for their livelihood. But they were often accorded a peculiar status as *bywoners,* which meant that they were permitted to squat on another man's land without a clearly defined dependent status as either tenants or employees. It was understood that they would provide a share of their output and perform certain services in return for their use of the land, but the relationship was apparently kept deliberately vague and informal in order to preserve the fiction that no white man should be directly subservient to another.[16]

In the slave South, the distinction between white and Negro work was not so clear-cut as the differentiation of legal and political status. Of course, field work on plantations and domestic service were slave occupations that no white person could perform, even for wages, without losing caste. But Irish immigrants were sometimes hired to do the heavy work of draining swamps or digging canals, because slaves were considered too valuable to risk in such unhealthful activity.[17] Occupational diversity among the caste of free Negroes was surprisingly extensive. Although they tended to be concentrated in the unskilled, low-paid, menial jobs, some were skilled craftsmen, small businessmen, or even planters. One Louisiana mulatto owned a plantation with seventy-five slaves where he successfully emulated the life-style of the South's ruling class.[18] In the cities, white artisans and laborers were often thrown into direct competition with hired slaves and free blacks; and in the factories blacks and whites were used for the same kind of work, usually on a separate or segregated basis but occasionally side by side.[19] Outside the plantation sphere, therefore, the line between white and Negro work was not rigidly defined for the South as a whole but varied from place to place depending on the extent of white competition and how much popular support white workingmen could arouse for their campaigns to drive Negroes from contested occupations. Free Negroes might dominate a particular trade in one city and be totally excluded from it in another. Nevertheless, as Ira Berlin has indicated, there was a general pattern: "If the specific occupations varied, the character of 'nigger work' was everywhere the same. These occupations were almost all service trades that required little capital and generally depended on white customers. Usually, they were more closely identified with the plantation, where free Negroes had originally learned them, than with the industrializing sector of the economy."[20]

What made this situation different from that of preindustrial South Africa was the presence of a white working-class population that was prepared to work for wages and that struggled, sometimes successfully and sometimes not, to shift the line between white and Negro work in order to include certain trades or occupations within its domain. But the white workingmen lacked substantial political and social power in a planter-dominated society and gained little official or governmental support for their efforts to erect a rigid occupational color bar. Georgia did pass a law in 1845 prohibiting the hiring of black mechanics or masons, but the law failed to cover slave artisans used by white contractors and seems to have been indifferently enforced even against free blacks and slaves hiring out their own time. On the eve of the Civil War, an Alabama lawyer named Robert C. Tharin started a journal to promote the interests of urban non-slaveholders by advocating laws to ban the use of slaves except as plantation workers and servants. But since such a program was obviously against the interests of slaveholders—who received a substantial income from hiring out skilled slaves— he got nowhere and was forced to leave the state.[21]

If blacks in the South had some chance to do industrial work and learn the skills associated with it, those in the antebellum North were effectively excluded from virtually all of the opportunities provided by the beginning of industrialization. Because of powerful prejudices manifested by white workers and employers blacks were, by and large, relegated to menial unskilled labor and service occupations. Even in those areas their precarious economic situation was threatened in the 1840s and 50s by unskilled immigrants, usually from Ireland. The northern predecent suggested that abject poverty and economic marginality would be the fate of most black people in an industrializing America.[22]

Partly because of the North's reputation as a land of opportunity for immigrants but an economic dead end for blacks, most of the freedmen chose to stay in the region of their birth after 1865. It was inevitable that the great majority of them would remain on the land, because the "industrial revolution" that occurred in the post-bellum South was a relatively modest affair. As late as 1900 some 69 percent of the southern working population was still employed in agriculture and only 3.6 percent in manufactures.[23] The transformation of the black slave into the black sharecropper did not alter drastically the antebellum conception of Negro work. According to the predominant white opinion, the most suitable "place" for blacks was as dependent agricultural workers or domestic servants. The role of blacks in skilled crafts or industrial jobs became even more problematical than it had been before the Civil War. In fact there was a stronger impulse than during the slave era to implement the vision of Robert C. Tharin and exclude blacks from the industrializing sector of the economy. One manifestation of this tendency was the declining importance of the black artisan, especially in trades that were modernized through technological advances and the application of machinery. Whites tended to dominate such occupations because of their better training, control of apprenticeship, and ability to organize discriminatory unions. Blacks were more likely to hold their own in fields like the "trowel trades" where mechanization and technological development did not occur.[24]

An even more blatant example of the exclusion of blacks from occupational fields associated with industrialization was the *de facto* bar against their employment in most factory work. In the words of Charles H. Wesley, the pioneer historian of black labor, "With the coming of industry and the factory system, the social code which made manual labor a degrading factor was no longer of binding force. Work in the factories was honorable and it was to be considered as the particular task of white workers. It is not surprising, then, that with exceptions, from the first, the mass of workers in factories and shops were whites."[25] The main event of this post-bellum southern industrialization was the dramatic rise of cotton mills, especially in the Carolinas and Georgia. Between 1880 and 1900, the number of mills increased from 161 to 400, and the number of workers employed grew from 16,741 to 97,559. The promoters of the "cotton mill campaign" helped win popular support and local capital for their enterprises by stressing a "whites-only" employment policy. They argued that a class of whites impoverished by the Civil War and the travails of southern agriculture should be rescued from a brutalizing competition with blacks on the land by being given industrial employment. The result was the almost total exclusion of blacks from the most significant of southern industries. As one manufacturer put it in 1902, the mill-owners "have recognized the fact that the mill is the only avenue open to our poor whites and we have with earnestness and practically without exception kept that avenue open to the white man alone" as a way of safeguarding him from inter-racial competition.[26] Among the rationalizations for this discriminatory policy was the argument that blacks by nature were not adapted to tending machinery. According to the owner of a large cotton mill, they were unsuccessful as operatives because they tended to doze off or daydream. What they lacked was "the faculty of concentrating their attention while quiet."[27]

Like the closing to blacks of trades involving the use of machinery, their exclusion from factories reflected a myth that had been vaguely anticipated during the slave era and became increasingly salient with the rise of post-war industrialization—the belief that, as Gunnar Myrdal put it, "the Negro was inefficient, unreliable, and incompetent to work with machines," and that consequently a principal way of differentiating white from Negro work was the degree of mechanization involved.[28] Such a belief was closely related to the expectation that technological progress would mean the displacement of blacks from their customary menial occupations by white-operated machines. On the eve of the Civil War, Thomas Ewbank, a former United States Commissioner of Patents, had predicted that slavery would wither away when technology made it possible to raise cotton without servile labor.[29] Ewbank was of course wrong about the future of slavery as an institution, but in a broader sense he might be considered a prophet of how, a century later, the mechanical cotton-picker made the black sharecropper obsolete.

The notion that there is an irreconcilable incompatibility between black labor and advanced technology—and that the latter is destined to displace the former—has been one of the most insidious and damaging of American racial myths because it can so easily be made self-fulfilling. Blacks themselves have had a deep awareness of this bitter duality, as reflected in the legend of John Henry's tragic contest with the steam drill. Carried to its logical outcome, the opposition between blackness and mechanization could create a situation where the decline in the importance of the kind of labor traditionally performed by blacks would mean that they no longer had any place at all in the economy. The alternative, of course, would be to end the split between white and Negro work derived from slavery and guarantee equal opportunity within a modernizing society. The story of the struggle for black economic advancement in twentieth-century America might profitably be viewed as a still-unresolved conflict between these two tendencies.[30]

In South Africa, neither the traditional conception of "kaffir work" nor the actual use of black labor in the gold mines provided white supremacists with much basis for regarding blacks and the use of machines as mutually exclusive. In some ways, the Afrikaners may have been even less receptive to the machine age than many Africans. James Bryce noted in 1897 that "the Boers in the two republics and the Boer element in the Cape have neither taste nor talent for [manufacture]."[31]

For the typical Afrikaner the industrial technology introduced into the mines by immigrant capitalists of the late nineteenth and early twentieth centuries must have appeared as an alien intrusion into a pastoral way of life, and his initial reaction was to have as little to do with it as possible. Within the mines themselves the skilled immigrant miners were used mainly for supervision and setting blasting charges; the Africans, in addition to moving ore from the point of extraction to the shaft, operated the machine drills that cut into the wall of gold-bearing rock.[32] A mine owner testified before a commission investigating the Transvaal mining industry in 1907–8 that "some of the Kaffirs are better machine-men than some of the white men . . . they can place the holes, fix up the machine and do everything that a white man can do, but of course, we are not allowed to let them blast." Asked if Africans were capable of blasting as well, he unhesitatingly answered in the affirmative.[33] Such facts must have been obvious even to the white miners, whose allegedly superior skill was the original rationale for their receiving on the average more than ten times the pay of African workers.[34] The pattern that developed in the gold mines and was later extended to other industrial enterprises was not based on any myth that blacks made unsuitable industrial workers; on the contrary, it reflected an awareness that African capabilities were such that the only way that white workers could maintain a privileged position was by erecting artificial barriers against black advancement.

The difference between this ethos of economic discrimination and that which prevailed in the industrializing United States should not be exaggerated. Many white Americans were fully aware that the history of black craftsmanship and industrial employment under slavery made the black worker potentially competitive with the white. But the extent to which blacks actually remained on the land in the early stages of post-war industrialization and continued to be excluded from northern industry during the same period could foster the illusion that Negroes were somehow unsuited to the special kind of discipline imposed by the manufacturing process. Looked at from another angle, the basic contrast was between a situation where semi-skilled work was regarded as an opportunity for whites and one where it was regarded as a role proper for blacks, provided they were supervised by highly skilled Europeans and not permitted to advance to a higher level of competence and remuneration. The character of black-white competition in the industrial sphere was not therefore identical in the two situations.

In the South African case, white workers fought to maintain a pre-existing hierarchy of privilege within the industrial economy; in the American, there was a strong impulse to exclude blacks entirely from areas of mechanized employment where whites had provided the initial source of labor.

The Segmentation of Labor, 1870–1910

In comparing the role of white supremacy in the industrial labor market of the post-emancipation United States and in South Africa during its early and crucial stage of economic development, it is useful to introduce the sociological concept of a "split labor market." According to Edna Bonacich, "ethnic antagonism first germinates in a labor market split along ethnic lines. To be split, a labor market must contain at least two groups of workers whose price of labor differs for the same work, or would differ if they did the same work." Racial or ethnic antagonism is thus aroused by a three-cornered struggle between capitalists desiring the cheapest possible labor, workers of the dominant ethnic group who resist being undercut or displaced by cheaper labor from a minority or subordinate group, and the alien newcomers who are struggling to find a niche in the economy. The outcome of the conflict depends in theory on the extent to which the higher-priced workers can bring pressure to bear on the capitalist class to entrench their advantage either by excluding the lower-priced workers or by establishing some kind of industrial caste system which will allow them to monopolize the best jobs. As applied to our two examples, therefore, this theory would predict that white workers would be the principal agents directly responsible for the growth of regularized patterns of racial discrimination in the industrial sphere, not so much because of prejudiced attitudes *per se* as out of direct self-interest. If left to themselves, capitalists would presumably hire the cheapest workers regardless of color and bring about a situation that would facilitate exploitation of the working class as a whole.[35]

This theory is suggestive and can explain a great deal about the origins of the discriminatory employment policies that developed in the United States and South Africa. But it needs to be combined with a full historical account of how the labor market got split in the first place—the conditions under which one group of workers became cheaper and more exploitable than another. It also requires modification to take account of the semi-autonomous role of the state as a mediating force that may represent other interests and traditions than just those of employers of cheap labor or organized and privileged members of the domestic working class. Contrary to crude Marxist theory, dominant political groups do not simply reflect the economic interests of those who control the means of production. They are also carriers of prevailing cultural traditions and guardians of racial or ethnic identities. Although such concerns are usually compatible with the long-run survival or well-being of the most economically powerful groups in the society, they may conflict with what these groups perceive as their immediate interests.[36]

The post–Civil War labor market in the South was certainly "split," but not in such a way as to provide much scope for direct competition between racial groups. For our purposes, the most important division was between emancipated slaves and working-class whites. Since the South was still a predominantly agricultural society, the main concern of its capitalists at the end of the war was to develop a new system of plantation labor to replace slavery. Since it was widely believed that blacks would not work without coercion, the white-supremacist state governments that came into existence in 1865 enacted the "black codes" whose principal objective was control of black labor by white employers. Vagrancy and apprenticeship laws designed to force blacks to sign contracts with white planters were the core of the system, but restrictions on the right of blacks to buy land or pursue certain occupations were also passed in some states as a way of trying to ensure that the freedmen would remain in the status of unskilled, dependent workers. If the southern economy had been fully restructured on the basis of the black codes, a form of licit serfdom would have replaced slavery, and there would have been no possibility of direct competition between black and white workers. But, as we have seen, the northern Radicals who gained control of the Reconstruction process in 1866–67 were committed to the establishment of a free labor market in the South and through congressional legislation and constitutional amendments overthrew the codes and rendered this form of semi-slavery illegal.[37]

Nevertheless, a resurgent planter class of the post-Reconstruction era developed or perfected a variety of legal or extra-legal devices to limit the economic freedom of blacks. They built upon the pattern of sharecropping and farm credit that had arisen during Reconstruction as a practical compromise between the desire of blacks to work their own land and the unwillingness of planters to surrender ultimate control of staple-crop production even though they lacked the capital to pay wages that would attract and hold a sufficient work force. Despite the fact that true peonage or debt servitude was unconstitutional, ways were soon found to achieve its essential characteristics. Laws subjecting black tenants to criminal penalties for breaking their contracts were justified by defining the advances paid to them as money accepted with the intention to defraud. Sharecroppers were discouraged from moving from one plantation to another by laws prohibiting one employer from "enticing away" his neighbor's tenants. Under the "criminal surety system," a planter paid the fines of blacks guilty of minor public offenses in return for their labor until the debt was discharged. Furthermore, the credit system itself kept black farmers in perpetual debt to local provisioning merchants, who had granted them advances in return for a lien on their crop, because the high rates of interest charged made it almost impossible for sharecroppers to clear their debt at the end of the year; hence they had little choice but to enter into a new agreement on the same disadvantageous terms.[38]

There is considerable debate among historians as to the extent that the black rural labor force actually was immobilized and bound to involuntary labor by this combination of legal and economic constraints.[39] Certainly an absconding tenant farmer had a fairly good chance of escaping if he left surreptitiously enough and traveled a goodly distance. But the floating population of black migrants that resulted was extremely vulnerable to being picked up for vagrancy or petty crime and consigned to a fate that was often worse than slavery. As a device for acquiring cheap and coercible labor for peculiarly laborious quasi-industrial tasks—such as railroad construction, turpentine farming, drainage, and even mining—southern entrepreneurs of the late nineteenth century made substantial use of convict leasing. The contractors relied on the police and the judiciary to crack down on vagrants and impose exorbitant sentences for minor offenses at times when forced labor was needed. Conditions in the convict camps were incredibly harsh, and annual mortality rates could range from 10 to 25 percent. The economic importance of black convict labor has never been systematically calculated, but it was probably of greater significance for the post-Reconstruction development of the South's extractive industries than is generally acknowledged.[40]

What this multi-faceted new system of labor control meant, in relation to our analysis of "split labor markets," was that most blacks in the South between 1865 and 1900 were not yet in a position to compete directly with whites for the same occupations. As already indicated, one area of limited competition was in the urban artisan trades, but there blacks tended to lose ground to better-organized whites. Factory work tended to be a white preserve, while domestic service was obviously a black monopoly where whites had no desire to intrude. The major overlap came in the realm of unskilled or low-skilled manual labor, especially in extractive industries. The impoverishment of large numbers of rural whites in the post-war South drove many of them into types of work where blacks were already employed. As timber workers, coal miners, and longshoremen, blacks and poor whites actually performed similar tasks at similarly low rates of pay. But since the whites in these occupations had scarcely any privileges to protect, the result was not really competition. Mostly the workers were physically segregated without being treated very differently by employers, although whites might have some minor privileges. In times of labor unrest, the collective interests shared by white and black workers could lead to collaboration in the form of bi-racial unions and strikes. The history of inter-racial cooperation in such southern unions as the United Mine Workers, the Brotherhood of Timber Workers, and various longshoremen's associations provides a striking counterpoint to the usual policies of union exclusion and discrimination.[41]

But the basic or characteristic pattern in the South for the half century after emancipation was one of economic segmentation rather than competition or cooperation between white and black workers. This compartmentalization of economic function along racial lines was the result not so much of competitive pressures by lower-class whites as of retarded economic development and cultural continuity. Economic opportunity was severely limited for almost everyone in this society, and the parceling out of low-paying jobs among whites and blacks tended to follow antebellum precedent, where this was possible, or the needs of local employers, where it was not. The general notion that the dirtiest and most unpleasant work should be done by blacks was accepted by almost all whites, but in some areas there were not enough blacks to do it and poor whites had to be recruited. Only with the beginnings of large-scale migration to the industrial North in the period around

World War I did the issue of black-white competition for the same kinds of jobs become a chronic source of racial antagonism in the United States.

In late-nineteenth-century South Africa, the pattern was even more clearly one of segmentation rather than competition. On the farms, as we have seen, Africans and other nonwhites were held to service by even more blatant and obvious forms of labor compulsion than in the American South. In the Cape, master-servant laws carrying criminal penalties for such violations of contract as absenteeism, insubordination, and, of course, desertion gave the employers of African and Colored farm labor many of the day-to-day powers of slave-owners.[42] In Natal, beginning in the 1860s, Indian indentured labor was employed on the sugar plantations, an extension to South Africa of the system of imported compulsory labor that had replaced slavery in some of the plantation colonies of the New World.[43] Africans occupying land within the borders of the Transvaal and the Orange Free State were subject to a kind of *corvée* or labor tax which made them available to white farmers when they were needed. Those who "squatted" on privately owned land—which often meant that they continued to occupy their villages or kraals after some white man had established his claim to their land—were subjected to a form of labor tenancy, a requirement that they work several months of the year for the landlord in return for simply being allowed to remain where they may have lived for generations. A similar system also developed in some districts of Natal.[44] The notion that a nonwhite could be a free worker moving about at will in search of opportunity was as alien to the white farmer in South Africa as it was to most ex-slaveholders in the South, and the former had the legal system behind him in a more direct and unequivocal fashion than the latter. Unlike the republics, the Cape had a theoretically color-blind legal system, but its economic liberalism did not extend to the full "free labor" doctrine that no worker should be subject to criminal action simply because he quit his job.

The notion that the only free worker was a white worker was first applied to an industrial situation in the diamond fields. When white prospectors rushed to the diggings near the Orange River in the 1870s, they found it natural to hire black helpers to do the hardest work. After some blacks attempted to stake out claims of their own, white miners pressured the Cape government to decree that only white men could be granted diggers' licenses.* For a variety of technological and economic reasons, the diamond industry was soon consolidated into a centralized enterprise, and black term laborers were thenceforth housed in closed compounds and subjected to minute personal searches when they departed after a period of service. White employees were allowed to live where they wanted; and when it was proposed in 1883 that they should be stripped and searched for stolen diamonds when they left the fields, they protested the indignity and got the order rescinded. This was perhaps the earliest case of a successful effort by white industrial workers to create a caste-like distinction between white and black employees.[45]

After the discovery of gold on the Witwatersrand in 1886, the segmented South African labor system was fully and systematically extended to what quickly became South Africa's major industry. The basic division between highly paid white skilled workers and low-paid African migrants was originally justified in terms of the peculiar economic circumstances associated with gold-mining on the Rand. The grade of ore in the Transvaal reef is generally very low; it has been the sheer quantity and not the quality of its deposits that has made South Africa the world's leading gold producer. Consequently, profitable mining required a very large capital investment; once the limited surface deposits had been exhausted, it was necessary to dig deep and to apply an elaborate technology to extract the gold from the rock. From the outset, the industry was controlled by combinations of large capitalists who derived much of their initial investment from the bonanza profits of the diamond fields. In the 1890s, the decision was made to exploit the deposits extensively, which meant working not only the richest veins but also many of lower grade that would pay only if costs were kept very low.[46]

For the skilled work in the mines, the owners had no choice but to pay the high wages demanded by experienced European miners. Hence the main cost-saving upon which the viability of the industry depended had to come from a heavy reliance on ultra-cheap African labor. But the recruitment of sufficient African workers and the fixing of their wages at a permanently low level could not be achieved through the

* When Mexican and Chinese prospectors attempted to stake claims in the California gold fields during the 1850s, a similar pattern of discrimination was enforced by vigilante activity.

operation of a free labor market. Most of the potential pool of black workers in southern Africa had not yet been permanently displaced from the land in the manner of the peasant classes of Europe who provided so much of the labor force for the industrial revolution in Europe and America. Although they might be attracted to the mines for short periods, there was no guarantee that Africans would not quickly tire of the unaccustomed regimentation and abysmal work conditions and return to their tribal societies before they had done enough work to justify the expense of their recruitment, training, and accommodation. Of course, Africans might have been encouraged to bring their families and settle permanently in the vicinity of the mines, but such a policy would have required a monetary incentive sufficient to induce a preindustrial folk to make a radical change in their way of life and would also have required a wage scale sufficient for family subsistence. The mining magnates calculated, probably correctly, that this type of recruitment would raise their wage bill to a level that would make it impossible to operate profitably on the scale they desired. They were buttressed in their opposition to bidding for African labor in a conventionally capitalistic way by a belief that "primitive" peoples did not respond to purely economic incentives in the manner of "civilized" workers. It was frequently argued that Africans' aspirations were so limited that they worked only long enough to acquire the wherewithal to meet some immediate and modest need. It followed, according to this theory, that higher wages actually meant less labor since Africans would simply quit sooner if they were paid more.[47]

This witch's brew of rational economic calculation and dubious anthropological theory impelled the founders of South African industrialization to create an elaborate system of labor procurement and control designed to fix the wages of Africans at an ultra-low level and ensure that enough of them would be working for sufficiently long periods to constitute a reliable labor force. To prevent individual mines from bidding up the price of labor, centralized recruiting and industry-wide maximum wage rates were established during the period 1890–1910. The oligopolistic nature of the industry and the emergence of a centralized policy-making body—the Chamber of Mines—made such monopsonistic labor procurement generally effective.* To induce Africans to leave their kraals and go to work for low wages in the mines,

* Monopsony is a market condition that exists when there is only one buyer.

the cooperation of various governments, including the Portuguese co-lonial regime in Mozambique, was enlisted in applying special pressure to tribal societies in order to make them disgorge migrant workers. In Mozambique, the government took direct charge and virtually con-scripted laborers for export to South Africa. In the British colonies, and in the Afrikaner republics before the Anglo-Boer War, the needs of the mines and other employers of native labor were met mainly by the im-position of special taxes that required a family to earn more than its limited agricultural productivity could provide. There was also a vari-ety of land policies, culminating after union in the Native Land Act of 1913, that were calculated to increase the supply of African labor by restricting opportunities for peasant farming.[48]

To ensure labor discipline and prevent excessive turnover in the mines, the coercive features of South African master-servant legislation were applied in industry. Africans were signed to fixed contracts which it was a criminal offense to violate and housed in compounds in order to make possible a kind of total supervision. Once again government collaboration was necessary, this time to prevent these contracts from being broken. In 1895, the Chamber of Mines persuaded the *Volksraad* of the South African Republic to legislate a pass system which would make it easier to identify and apprehend absconding workers. As a spokesman for the mine industry put it in 1897, "the whole intention of the law is to have a hold on the native whom we have brought down, be it from the East Coast, South, or from the North, at a con-siderable outlay to ourselves. . . ." With the coming of a British ad-ministration to the Transvaal after the Anglo-Boer War, the pass sys-tem was not only retained but was more effectively enforced than it had been by the less efficient Afrikaner regime. Holding a pass and be-ing bound to a forced-labor contract were, therefore, integrally related aspects of the same system of labor coercion; and the employer gained additional leverage from the fact that migrant contract laborers or bearers of passes were subject to criminal prosecution if they went on strike for higher pay or better working conditions.[49]

The system that developed for utilization of African labor in the mines was thus distinguished by artificially created restraints on black wages, bargaining power, and personal freedom that required active collaboration between capitalists and the state. Ample precedent for most of these restrictions on economic freedom could be derived from forms of labor control developed earlier in the agricultural sector to meet the needs of farmers after the abolition of slavery and quasi-serfdom. The fact that pass systems, induced migration, and unbreachable contracts were familiar devices made it easier for governments to aid in enforcing such policies in the mines. The co-existence of skilled white worker-supervisors and regimented Africans was reminiscent of farms and plantations where white overseers organized and directed the work of African or Colored laborers. In short, the entire system can be viewed as an adaptation to industry of the traditional pattern of coercing black labor that had its ultimate roots in slavery and Khoikhoi indentured servitude. Clearly the mine owners did not simply invent it out of whole cloth to serve their immediate economic interests, but in fact made business decisions—such as the one to keep low-grade mines in operation—because they knew that the South African context made possible a kind of ultra-exploitation of labor that would have been foreclosed in other industrializing nations. Hence they established the foundations for the twentieth-century South African economy by showing how Africans could be incorporated into the industrial work force without altering traditional patterns of white dominance and black servility.[50]

The contrast with what occurred in the United States is striking. Immediately after the Civil War, southern state governments provided a model for compulsory labor short of slavery that might conceivably have been adapted to industry; but the transition from agrarian to industrial dependency or semi-servitude was never made. If one can imagine what would have happened if the black codes of 1865 had set the pattern for organizing an industrial work force in the South, one has a fairly good comprehension of what occurred in South Africa. One of the most important contributions of the Radical Republicans was to nip this development in the bud. The later revival of some aspects of coercion by contract within southern agriculture did not extend to industry partly because its extra-legal or illegal character, which was relatively easy to obscure in a rural setting, would have been blatant in large industrial enterprises. Furthermore, the availability of cheap white labor that could be paid low wages and worked long hours made it plain to southern industrialists that the classic solution for the labor needs of nascent industry—the landless peasant—now had its local equivalent in the increasing class of rural poor whites. In such a situation the inherited pattern of economic stratification by race could be maintained—and the new order legitimized—by excluding most blacks from the developing sectors of the economy.

The Emergence of Class and Race Conflict

Although the dominant pattern in black-white economic relations up to about 1910 in both South Africa and the United States was non-competitive segmentation of the labor force along racial lines—by industrial caste in the former and *de facto* industrial exclusion in the latter—the end of this era saw an upsurge of white-working-class anxieties about possible displacement by black labor. The primary American arena for competitive race relations in the economic sphere was the North during the early stages of the great black migration from the rural South to the cities of the Northeast and Midwest that began after the turn of the century. Faced with worsening economic conditions and a rising tide of racial persecution, hundreds of thousands of southern blacks decided to take their chances in the urban North between 1900 and 1920. The much smaller influx into northern cities that had occurred in the late nineteenth century had offered no threat to the customary differentiation between white and Negro work. The situation that Stephan Thernstrom found in Boston in 1890 was probably typical. Blacks, in comparison to immigrants, were greatly underrepresented in the skilled trades and "largely bypassed by the Industrial Revolution," in the sense that they found few if any factory jobs open to them.[51] But in the early twentieth century, the combination of organized efforts by white workers to improve their wages and working conditions and the greater availability of black migrants from the South in many areas of the North aroused intense fears of direct competition. The bitter and often violent conflicts between working-class whites and working-class blacks that subsequently erupted were related to a struggle over unionization which enabled employers to play off one racial group against another for their own convenience.

In South Africa there was never any prospect that employers would displace the entrenched immigrant labor aristocracy that engrossed the most highly skilled occupations in the mines. But there was a gray area of semi-skilled work that became a battleground between owners and white workers. When it seemed necessary to reduce costs, the capitalists were tempted to fill these positions with Africans at lower wages than whites had been receiving. But such policies ran up against new pressures to incorporate more whites into industry. The migration to the cities of impoverished Afrikaners who could no longer make a living on the land changed the character of the labor market in the early twentieth century and raised the specter of direct competition between the races not only for semi-skilled but also for unskilled work. These white newcomers to the urban and industrial areas were at a competitive disadvantage in relation to the Africans because they refused to do "kaffir work" or accept "kaffir pay." The crisis generated by the conflict between the demands of a newly augmented and insecure white working class and the established policy of capitalistic reliance on ultra-cheap African labor led to a violent confrontation between capital and white labor. What was common in the American and South African situations, therefore, was the problem presented to a white labor movement by a growing disposition on the part of employers to manipulate the "split labor market."

Despite the fact that the incidence of direct competition between black and white labor in the United States before the turn of the century was quite limited, the working-class leaders and labor reformers who had attempted to form national unions or federations of wage-earners during the late nineteenth century had been unable to avoid the issue of whether blacks should be included. The National Labor Union, organized in 1866 as a loose federation of existing craft unions, local labor assemblies, and labor reform societies, showed an awareness in its deliberations and public platforms of "the danger in the future competition of mechanical Negro labor," but was sharply divided on how to respond to this challenge. Despite declarations of an intention to unite the working class with "no distinction of race and nationality," this short-lived organization proved incapable of implementing this principle or of establishing ties with an emerging group of black labor leaders. The Knights of Labor, founded in 1869 as a class-conscious national membership organization for workers of all kinds, attempted with some success to enlist blacks in its ranks. By 1886, some 60,000 of its 700,000 members were Negroes. But for a variety of reasons the Knights soon went into rapid decline. Their interest in reforming the capitalistic wage system and establishing an alternative economy based on cooperatives was not shared by established craft unions concerned only with the immediate gains that their members might achieve through collective bargaining. In 1886 the craft unions withdrew from the Knights of Labor and joined with other conservative unions to form the American Federation of Labor. The AFL rapidly displaced the Knights at the center of the labor movement.[52]

As a federation of craft unions previously formed in various trades, the AFL was committed to the "bread-and-butter" policy of improving the wages and working conditions of the most skilled segment of the American labor force. Few blacks belonged to these unions because they either lacked the necessary skills or were kept out by discriminatory membership policies. But the notorious reluctance of craft unions to admit blacks was not due exclusively, or perhaps even mainly, to racial prejudice. According to two American labor historians, "Craft unions in the United States looked upon themselves as organizations that could establish and guard a monopoly over particular jobs. By relying on the employer's acceptance of the competence and dependability of skilled workers who were union members, they could exclude outsiders from practicing the trade, maintain control over jobs, and lessen future competition. Racial exclusion was part of a larger program designed to protect them against competition from unskilled workers and to preserve the domination of skilled workers in the labor movement."[53] Although the national Federation paid lip service to the principle that no affiliated body should have an explicit rule excluding blacks, it lacked the power and commitment to prevent discrimination by individual unions and locals. This was especially clear after 1895 when the machinists were admitted to the AFL upon agreeing to remove the color bar from their constitution but not from their ritual for inducting members. Hence in practice the AFL and the craft unions it represented played a significant role in restricting black access to skilled occupations.[54]

Blacks fared somewhat better in industrial unions that sought to organize all the workers in a particular industry. The United Mine Workers not only had a substantial black membership around the turn of the century but even elected blacks to union office and employed them as organizers. The Brotherhood of Timber Workers, organized by the radical Industrial Workers of the World in 1910, eventually enrolled 35,000 members in Louisiana, Texas, and Arkansas, about half of whom were black.[55] The establishment of inter-racial unions was thus a definite and proven possibility in late nineteenth- and early twentieth-century America, even in the deep South, when it was a matter of organizing unskilled or semi-skilled workers in industries where blacks were already entrenched. The ultimate decline or collapse of such unions was due less to racism than to adamant and effective employer opposition to industry-wide unions that included less-skilled workers. The relationship of blacks to organized labor in the United States has, to a large extent, been dependent on the outcome of the conflict between industrial and craft unionism. Or, put another way, when white workingmen have organized to protect their position in skilled crafts they have tended to exclude blacks, but when unskilled or semi-skilled white workers have sought to unionize industries already employing blacks they have sometimes put the needs of labor solidarity above the impulse toward racial exclusiveness. In the former situation racial prejudice and economic self-interest have been mutually reinforcing. In the latter they have been in obvious conflict, and large numbers of working-class whites have historically had the good sense to recognize it.

The traditional Marxist notion that capitalists blind workers to their own interests by cynically playing off one racial group against another does not, therefore, do full justice to the normal perceptiveness and intelligence of working-class whites and, at the same time, probably exaggerates the Machiavellian ruthlessness of management. Yet there have been instances when employers have created genuine conflicts of interest between white and black workers through attempts to undermine the whites' position by using blacks to displace them under conditions that inspired a racist reaction. This is the classic "split labor market" situation which, as we will see, had its clearest manifestation during the outbreak of racial tension and violence that swept through the urban North just before and after World War I. In general, direct confrontation of white and black workers was limited in the nineteenth century by the high degree of segmentation of the labor force; only relatively rarely did members of the two groups actually compete directly for the same jobs under circumstances where the whites could view blacks as weapons used by their employers against them. But when they did, an outburst of racial antagonism was the usual result. The displacement of striking Irish longshoremen by blacks during the Civil War was one of the grievances that provoked the New York "draft riots" of 1863 and made Negroes the principal victims of mob violence. According to the United States Bureau of Labor, there were eight strikes in the 1880s protesting the hiring of blacks and twenty-two in the decade 1890–1900. Blacks were also used occasionally as scabs in late-nineteenth-century strikes, although the more common practice was to pit one white immigrant group against another.[56]

The great nineteenth-century example of large-scale mobilization of white workers against competition from another racial group did not involve blacks at all but was directed against the Chinese in California. When entrepreneurs in the 1860s began to make substantial use of Chinese immigrants as cheap contract labor in mining, railroad construction, and manufacturing, white workingmen perceived a serious threat to their own economic position. Since the Asians were willing to accept wages and working conditions that no white man would tolerate, they provided capitalists with a device for depressing the general wage level and undermining efforts at labor organization. The response was perhaps the most successful labor-based political movement in American history. In this instance, working-class spokesmen could appeal successfully to the xenophobia of middle-class whites who saw their culture threatened by an influx of what Bret Harte called "the heathen Chinee." According to Alexander Saxton, "anti-orientalism furnished a channel of political protest for white labor west of the Rockies" for half a century and "became a building block for labor organization."[57] The movement was kept alive even after the passage of the Chinese Exclusion Act of 1882, and by the turn of the century it fed into a similar labor-supported agitation against Japanese immigration. As a result of this struggle, unionism and working-class politics achieved more legitimacy and influence in some of the industrial regions of the Far West than in most other sections of the country. White workers could, of course, have fought to eliminate the contract labor system instead of the Chinese themselves, and welcomed Orientals into their movement; but the path of least resistance and more immediate advantage was to build worker solidarity and power at the expense of a nonwhite "enemy," who could be characterized both as a tool of greedy capitalists and as a threat to the integrity of the white race.

If western workers resolved the problem of a split labor market by a policy of exclusion, those of the industrial areas of the East and Midwest did not have this option available when faced after 1900 with a growing migration of blacks from the rural South that turned into a mass movement after 1915. Afro-Americans were citizens, and there was no legal way to restrict their internal movement in search of greater economic opportunity. It was a tragedy of major proportions that the first great influx of blacks into the urban industrial market co-incided with a period of labor unrest and became a factor in struggles over the right of workers to organize and strike in some of the new mass-production industries. The persistence of union discrimination against blacks and the unfamiliarity of ex-sharecroppers with the principle of labor organization combined to make blacks prime candidates for use as strike-breakers. In many cases, scabbing was the only way that they could gain access to an industry. But such activity, and the support it received from prominent black leaders (including Booker T. Washington), gave credence to white working-class beliefs that black wage-earners were the traitorous allies of union-busting employers.[58]

The actual employment of blacks as strike-breakers has undoubtedly been exaggerated, but it occurred often enough between 1900 and 1930 to have an intimidating effect on white workers. The knowledge that employers had a reserve army of job-hungry, nonunionized blacks who could displace whites if necessary undoubtedly served both to inhibit strikes and other manifestations of labor militancy and to stimulate racial feeling. In the words of sociologist William Wilson, "the growing presence of black workers in urban industries, coupled with the tendency of management to use blacks as strikebreakers to undercut effective union activity, created a situation where the class conflict between white labor and management produced racial conflict between white workers and blacks."[59]

The great race riots that broke out in East St. Louis in 1917 and in Chicago in 1919 each had as one cause, perhaps the most important one, a local history of industrial conflict that involved the use of black strike-breakers. The East St. Louis riot, which resulted in the deaths of thirty-nine blacks and nine whites, stemmed in part from animosities that arose when the Aluminum Ore Company actively recruited southern blacks in an apparent effort to head off unionization of the work force. A strike was broken shortly before the riot; and despite the fact that most of the scabs were white, it was the black ones who were remembered by the workers who had lost their jobs.[60] In Chicago, blacks had displaced striking whites on several occasions between 1904 and 1919 and had been stigmatized as a "scab race." In the key meatpacking industry, blacks had become a substantial part of the work force by 1917, and labor leaders, who had learned something from previous reverses, began a campaign to organize black workers. But when a major strike broke out in the industry in 1919, three fourths of the blacks were still unorganized and stayed on the job. Blacks had resisted unionization partly because of a traditional distrust of unions and partly because they were offered only second-class membership. Excluded from the craft unions that monopolized the skilled trades in the packing houses, they were consigned to special segregated locals under the direct jurisdiction of the AFL. The fact that membership in these Jim Crow "federal locals" conveyed no real power to participate in union decision-making reduced the incentive for blacks to join them. The bitterness between working-class whites heavily committed to unionization and unorganized blacks who were willing to stay on the job or displace striking whites was a major precipitating factor in the violent racial confrontation that broke out in the summer of 1919 and claimed the lives of twenty-three blacks and fifteen whites.[61]

The three-cornered struggle between employers, white workers, and black newcomers could not be resolved with the brutal finality of the Oriental exclusion policy. In the skilled trades whites remained protected by discriminatory union policies. But in the semi-skilled, mass-production industries there was nothing to stop employers from holding down wages and impeding unionization by hiring blacks from the South. White workers in these industries, most of whom were of immigrant background, lacked the power and prestige to compel preferential treatment from Anglo-American employers. The only alternative was cooperation with blacks in industrial unions, but this required positive support from the government against the awesome power of management and a lessening of the racial tensions associated with the influx of southern blacks into northern cities. The sources of this tension went beyond the struggle for jobs; it also involved the competition for urban space that led eventually to black ghettoization, and it had an important political dimension—white workers tended to be Democrats, while blacks remained loyal to the party of Lincoln and emancipation.[62] With the coming of the New Deal in the 1930s, the government became more sympathetic to the desire of workers in mass-production industries to organize. At the same time working-class whites became somewhat less hostile to blacks because of such developments as the decline in migration from the South during the depression years, the resulting stabilization of the ghetto, and the massive shift of blacks to the Democratic Party. Under these conditions, inter-racial industrial unionism could begin to develop on a substantial scale after 1935 through the agency of the Congress of Industrial Organizations.[63]

In South Africa, the intensification of "split labor market" conditions, the resulting tug-of-war between capital and white labor over the allocation of jobs, and the ultimate intervention of the state to resolve the situation—all of which occurred between the end of the Anglo-Boer War and the late 1920s—was in some ways more analogous to the white workingmen's struggle against Oriental competition on the Pacific Coast than to the conflicts occasioned by the Great Migration to the North. As in the former case, white workers in South Africa felt threatened by a form of labor that was ultra-exploitable because it was carried on by laborers who lacked citizenship rights and were subject to special forms of coercion. Of course the contracts under which Chinese "coolies" were enrolled for gang labor in the Far West, unlike those binding Africans in the gold mines, were not legally enforceable; but the active involvement of Chinese merchant associations in the recruitment and discipline of these workers had made for *de facto* compliance.[64] The fear that nonwhite "slaves" would displace free labor was thus common to the two situations. Indeed Chinese "coolies" figure in the South African story as well; for a temporary shortage of African workers after the Boer War led to the employment of 63,000 indentured Chinese in the mines between 1904 and 1909. The ultimate resolutions of the "Chinese question" were also similar: their increase was prevented in the United States by banning further immigration, while those who had come to South Africa were repatriated, beginning in 1907 when it was also decreed that no more would be introduced.[65] In both instances the vehement protests of white workers were, in large measure, responsible for the policy of exclusion. But the elimination of the Chinese in South Africa left the Africans as potential competitors who could not be excluded because their employment was essential to the functioning of the economic system. Their total displacement by whites would have raised wage levels to a point that would probably have bankrupted the mining industry.

What white mine-workers really feared was not the employment of Africans *per se* but their insidious introduction by management into the more skilled work categories. The owners could thereby reduce costs and increase profits by substituting low-paid Africans for highly paid Europeans. Initially whites had been able to assume their privileged position because they alone possessed the requisite skills. But the emergence of an experienced group of African miners demonstrated that there was no inherent obstacle to their advancement in the job hierarchy. The mine supervisors soon developed a genuine respect for African capabilities: "The African's capacity was never seriously questioned. Engineers and mine managers agreed that selected Africans, adequately trained, could be as competent as the white man for any job including that of mine manager."[66] The white workers, who daily saw Africans perform capably a variety of fairly complex tasks in the mines, were also aware of this truth. Consequently their spokesmen conceived the strategy of erecting an absolute "color bar" against the employment of Africans in skilled jobs. The impulse behind this policy was strikingly similar to that which inspired the racially exclusionary policies of American craft unions. In neither case could the desire for discrimination be ascribed to a conviction that blacks were inherently inferior; it was in fact a recognition of their ability to compete successfully that inspired a desire to establish artificial limits on their opportunities as a way of guaranteeing the security of white jobs.

The legislative history of the color bar began in 1893, when a recently organized white mineworkers' union persuaded the *Volksraad* of the South African Republic to prohibit Africans, Asians, and Coloreds from preparing charges, loading drills, or lighting fuses. In 1896 the explicit racial restriction was eliminated, but a skilled miner was now required to have a blasting certificate, a kind of license that it was understood would only be granted to Europeans.[67] This rudimentary color bar remained in effect under the post-war British administration of the Transvaal. When the importation of Chinese was authorized by the Transvaal Legislative Council in 1904, an effort was made to head off white-worker protests by explicitly barring the newcomers from a broad range of skilled occupations. The South African economist Sheila van der Horst has described the significance of this enactment: "The legal restrictions on the field of employment of the Chinese went far beyond the previous legislation, and are important because the occupations designated by the schedule have continued to be claimed as belonging exclusively to Europeans."[68] It is also worth noting that this action strengthened the precedent that job discrimination would be a matter of governmental policy rather than, as in the United States during the same era, the product of unregulated interaction between management and white workers.

Nevertheless, the decision to phase out Chinese indentured labor led to a period of uncertainty about the future organization of the labor force in the mines during which alternative policies were debated. On the management side considerable sentiment developed for economizing by reducing the number of Europeans. It was argued that there were simply more whites than were needed to perform the essentially supervisory function that characterized most white mine occupations. An implication of this recommendation was that Africans could safely be given greater work autonomy, and it was even suggested that the day would come when they would advance into the skilled ranks. Such thinking aroused strong fears of African competition among white workers. Labor spokesmen and militant white supremacists proposed to go in the reverse direction by shifting the line between white and "kaffir" work downward to permit Europeans to displace Africans in some of the unskilled or semi-skilled work. Such a "white labor policy" now seemed feasible because of the dramatic rise in South Africa since the war of a class of unemployed "poor whites."[69]

The "poor white problem" was the result of a series of developments that eventually drove many Afrikaners off the land and into the industrial regions. Even before the war, a land shortage had developed in the Transvaal that had forced some whites into pauperism. The end of frontier expansion, continued high population growth, engrossment of large holdings by speculators or mining companies, and subdivision of farms into uneconomically small units as a result of the Roman-Dutch tradition of partible inheritance—all had resulted by the nineties in the rise of an Afrikaner lower class unable to subsist by the traditional method of grazing herds of cattle and sheep on large acreages. In the early days of gold-mining on the Witwatersrand many of them had been able to find alternative livelihoods as transport riders or market gardeners, but the coming of the railroads had limited such opportunities. Toward the end of the decade, the problem was exacerbated by an epidemic of cattle disease and a severe drought; and the government of the Republic was finding it necessary to provide relief work for indigent whites. This creeping impoverishment of rural Afrikaners was accelerated by the devastation and dislocation of the Anglo-Boer War, and a mass movement into the urban areas began after the peace of Vereeniging in 1902.[70]

In 1906, the Transvaal government appointed a commission to address the new problem of white poverty. In its report it considered but rejected a policy of direct economic discrimination to protect lower-class whites from African competition on the grounds that this would impede the economic development of the country. But the majority of another commission appointed in 1907 to study the mining industry seemingly came to the opposite conclusion when it denounced "the Coloured labor policy" of the mine-owners and advocated opening up more mining jobs to whites. In 1908, the Rand Unemployment Committee persuaded some mines to hire unemployed whites for unskilled work, but from the point of view of the managers the experiment was a failure because, unlike Africans who were bound by their contracts, Afrikaners had a high rate of absenteeism and a tendency to quit unexpectedly. "There can be little doubt," according to Sheila van der Horst, "of the superior attractions of Native laborers who were bound to long-term contracts and subject to penal prosecution for desertion." Powerful capitalistic interests clearly preferred workers of peasant origin who could be subjected to industrial discipline by force to those who had the freedom to indulge their preindustrial work habits. Hence, the "poor white problem" could not be solved by expanding white employment in the mines.[71]

The rejection of proposals to use unskilled whites in the mines did not resolve the issue of how securely the skilled workers needed to be protected against African encroachment. The Mine and Works Act passed by the new Union Parliament in 1911 gave the government the power to maintain a white monopoly on skilled jobs in the mines by issuing regulations limiting access to a range of occupations, but it did not provide an absolutely iron-clad guarantee against some readjustments that would allow the mines to increase the proportion of blacks in borderline jobs.[72] A white trade union movement, coming into its own in the decade of the First World War, set as one of its major objectives the maintenance of a rigid color bar and the prevention of any reduction in the white proportion of the labor force. On the eve of the war, the Mine Workers' Union set forth its essential position: "The existing colour bar, whether it is justifiable on general grounds or not . . . has always been looked upon by the European worker in these fields as a protection set up by law against the tendency of indentured native labour to encroach on his sphere of livelihood."[73] But the color bar was put under a new strain during the war when a temporary shortage of white workers resulting from enlistments in the army led to the employment of blacks in some semi-skilled jobs previously reserved for whites. Furthermore, rising costs increased the incentive of employers to use Africans wherever possible. As a result of union protests against such tendencies, the industry made a formal commitment to the South African Industrial Federation in 1918 to maintain the status quo in the ratio of white to nonwhite employees.[74]

A major confrontation between white workers and the mining industry became inevitable when the immediate post-war period found the mines in an economic crisis because of a combination of rising costs and declining gold prices. An effort by the Chamber of Mines to abrogate the "status quo agreement" led to the extraordinary series of events that became known as the Rand Rebellion. In December 1921, the Chamber proposed to limit the color bar to skilled work strictly defined and to displace about 2,000 semi-skilled whites by lower-paid blacks. Despite the refusal of the unions to agree, the industry announced plans to go ahead with this reorganization of the labor force beginning on February 1, 1922. In an effort to head off this action the mine unions struck on January 10, joining workers in other Rand industries who were already out in protest against wage reductions. The strike escalated into an insurrection, partly because Afrikaner unionists (who by now constituted the great majority of the white miners) organized themselves into para-military "commandos." In the words of Fredrick A. Johnstone, "the traditional fighting formation of the Afrikaner farmers" was adapted "to a new setting, that of urban, industrial class conflict." The commandos were used to enforce the strike, drive away scabs, and eventually to resist the government troops called out by Prime Minister Jan Smuts. After the strikers had taken full control of the Rand, called for a general strike of white workers to support them in their demands, and begun to launch sporadic attacks on African miners, the government declared martial law on March 10 and moved in 7,000 troops, backed by bombing planes, tanks, and all the paraphernalia of modern warfare. Armed conflict raged for four days, during which between 150 and 220 people were killed and 500–600 wounded. The strike was finally crushed and its leaders arrested; eighteen were condemned to death and four actually executed. The Chamber of Mines then proceeded with its reorganization of the work force by lowering wages and laying off a substantial number of whites. In 1923, a court decision declared the legally enforced color bar *ultra vires,* or contrary to common law, thus providing the industry with a free hand to make further retrenchments in white labor.[75]

The white workers and other defenders of a rigid industrial color bar had lost a battle but not the war itself. In the parliamentary election of 1924, a coalition of Afrikaner Nationalists and the South African Labour Party drove Smuts's South African Party from office by capitalizing on the backlash inspired by the government's fierce repression of the Rand Rebellion and its general record of insensitivity to white-working-class demands for iron-clad protection against African competition. The resulting "Pact Government" under Nationalist Prime Minister J. B. M. Hertzog re-enacted the mining color bar in a more explicit and definitive way in 1926. Addressing the long-festering "poor white problem" more directly, it also inaugurated a set of policies that included displacing black workers with higher-paid whites on government-owned railroads, subsidizing municipalities to permit hiring of white laborers at "civilized" wages, and utilizing minimum-wage determinations and tariff adjustments to force employers in the growing manufacturing sector to increase the proportion of whites in their work force.[76] The industrial color bar and the "civilized labor policy" completed the basic pattern of government-supported discrimination in the South African economy. Whites were to be guaranteed jobs, artificially high wages, and exclusive access to skilled work—all at the expense of African aspirations. The foundations of industrial apartheid were laid.

To put this conflict and its resolution in proper perspective, it is essential to recognize that neither side wanted a free-labor market; hence it was not a contest between equal opportunity and legalized discrimination. The mine-owners and other capitalistic interests were responsible for the primary act of discrimination when they combined forces and called on government support to hold down African wages and bargaining power. They thereby set the stage for a virtually unavoidable conflict between a disfranchised, semi-servile, and ultra-cheap class of workers and another segment of the labor force that had the capacity to organize and exert political influence.[77] As in the case of the Chinese-exclusion movement in the United States, white labor had the one crucial advantage in this struggle. Although their position was not inherently more discriminatory than that of employers who took advantage of the vulnerability of nonwhites to hire them on terms that "free workingmen" would never accept, the struggle inexorably took a form that allowed spokesmen for white labor to identify their cause as that of white supremacy and thus tap the deep wells of prejudice existing in the larger white or European population. If the labor movement in California could appeal to middle-class xenophobia, spokesmen for white workers in South Africa could draw upon the rural Afrikaner's traditional conviction that the white man's privileges and security must be absolutely guaranteed. Hence the immediate material interests of organized labor coincided with traditional racial prejudices in a much more direct and obvious way than those of the employers.

South African industrialists found they could live with the legal color bar—which was eventually extended from mining to other forms of industry—because it turned out to be compatible with their primary concern for maintaining a cheap supply of ultra-exploitable African indentured workers. The surplus of unskilled whites in the 1920s and 30s was only temporary (ending completely with World War II and the subsequent growth of the South African economy) and was largely channeled into state-owned enterprises like the railroads or the iron and steel industry (ISCOR), which could pay "civilized wages" because they did not have to compete directly with private capital and maintain a high rate of profit. Hence there were never enough whites available to displace Africans in low-skilled jobs within private industry. Furthermore, the bar to African advancement into skilled jobs helped rationalize the migratory labor system and denial of African bargaining rights. If blacks had no chance of advancement into the skilled occupations, not much was really lost by shuttling them back and forth in a way that limited their ability to acquire advanced industrial training. The transformation of the entire white working class into a "labor aristocracy" that shared with businessmen and farmers an interest in holding down and exploiting Africans diminished the possibility of class conflict among whites and may have served the interests of South African capitalism better than either a genuinely free labor market—which might have enabled workers to organize across racial lines—or a split, competitive situation that could breed the kind of dangerous and divisive conflict that had erupted on the Rand in 1922.[78]

Why No Industrial Color Bar in the United States?

Although blacks and other racial minorities have often been subjected to flagrant economic discrimination in the United States since the Civil War, there has been no legalized color bar, such as developed in South Africa, explicitly prohibiting anyone from practicing a trade or occupation because of race. Some of the southern black codes of 1865 attempted to impose occupational restrictions through special licensing regulations, but these were quickly nullified by federal civil rights legislation and the Fourteenth Amendment. Similarly, the clauses of the California constitution of 1878 restricting the hiring of Chinese labor were summarily overturned by federal courts.[79] This is not to say that governmental bodies have never played a direct role in job discrimination. State laws requiring the licensing of plumbers were used in the twentieth century to aid and abet the efforts of the exclusionary Plumbers' and Steamfitters' Union to keep blacks out of the trade. Furthermore, city inspectors often refused to approve the work of black plumbers and electricians.[80] Many other examples of such collusion between state or local governments and discriminatory craft unions could undoubtedly be found. But actual legislation putting an official ceiling on black economic opportunities was apparently neither enacted by any law-making body nor even seriously proposed during the era of Jim Crow in the United States. American color bars existed not because government required them but because it did not act, at least until very recently, to prohibit the discriminatory practices of private employers and trade unions.

The most obvious reason why American state and local governments—even in the South at the height of segregation—did not attempt to follow the South African example in this respect was the granting of equal citizenship rights to blacks by constitutional amendment after the Civil War. Formal color bars would have been blatantly incompatible with the equal protection clauses of the Fourteenth Amendment. In South Africa, on the other hand, there was no Constitution, Bill of Rights, or Fourteenth Amendment to provide any rights for blacks that a white parliament was bound to respect; the court decision of 1923 that declared the industrial color bar *ultra vires* was readily overturned by parliamentary legislation.[81]

As in other areas, the promise of equal opportunity for Afro-Americans in the economic sphere remained unfulfilled after emancipation. But unlike the denial in the South of rights to suffrage and equal access to public facilities, job discrimination was not buttressed by legislation circumventing the Reconstruction amendments. Hence an employer who wanted to hire blacks instead of whites for any job had a perfect legal right to do so, and any union that wished to admit blacks on an equal basis would not have violated any law. As we have seen, the trend of South African legislation since the establishment of Union has been to deny these rights. The results of this difference could be disconcerting to a South African visitor to the United States. Maurice Evans was surprised in 1915 to find instances in the South of black and white labor doing the same work at about the same pay, and he noted that "such a thing would be impossible" in South Africa.[82] It is true that the segregation laws of some southern states prohibiting black and white workers from using the same plant facilities or even working in the same areas were significant state-supported impediments to integration of the work force.[83] But it remains somewhat surprising that there was not more of an effort to reinforce by law the distinction between white and Negro work, at least in the South. One can easily conceive of an extensive system of licensing trades or access to industrial occupations that, in the manner of discriminatory legislation in the political and social spheres, would have circumvented the Constitution by making no explicit mention of race, while at the same time allowing a consistent pattern of white preference. Why then, was this not done or even seriously attempted?

An obvious factor was the demographic situation. In contrast to South Africa there were not enough blacks, even in the South, to do all the menial low-status work and too many whites to give all of them a protected or privileged economic status within a capitalistic economy. The magnitude of this difference is evident from gross population percentages. According to the South African census of 1911, the first after Union, whites were only 21.37 percent of the population, a proportion that has declined steadily since that time; in the South of 1900 whites were 68 percent of the total, and by 1930 about 70 percent. Hence there was a necessary overlap in southern occupations and economic levels; a rigid and legalized caste division in industry would have been impracticable.[84]

Another distinguishing feature of the American scene was a peculiarly strong *laissez-faire* tradition that made government regulation of any kind more difficult than in South Africa, where the mining industry had relied from the beginning on an active partnership with the state. The establishment of an economic color bar would have constituted a degree of interference in the "free market" that most businessmen would have found intolerable, at least in the era before the Great Depression. The AFL trade unions also preferred a free bargaining situation to direct government intervention and regulation because their usual experience had been that management had much greater influence in the political arena. Hence neither side welcomed substantial government interference with the conditions of employment; for state action would threaten vested or asserted rights to self-determination and self-regulation. They preferred to work matters out for themselves, which they generally did in a *de facto* discriminatory fashion. But in times of labor shortage, as in the First World War period, blacks could break into types of industrial employment formerly monopolized by whites. If, in other words, the system was sufficiently permeated by prejudice to make a mockery of the concept of equal opportunity, it was also flexible and fluid enough to permit some degree of economic mobility for blacks. In 1910, only 7.9 percent of the black labor force was engaged in skilled or semi-skilled work. By 1930, the proportion had risen to 12.6 percent. Under conditions of industrial unionism and another wartime labor shortage, this proportion rose even more dramatically in the next twenty years, reaching 23.8 percent in 1950.[85] This gradual incorporation of a segment of the black population into the industrial working class at pay levels roughly equivalent to those of whites doing similar work signified a partial breakdown of the dichotomy between white and Negro occupations that had segmented the labor force more rigidly in earlier periods.

The greater rigidity and enforceability of the South African color bar came about because both employers and white workers had involved the government more actively than their American counterparts in efforts to further their own interests at the expense of black labor. After capital had used the state to enforce the contract labor or pass system, thereby guaranteeing the cheapness and powerlessness of African workers, white labor had responded to the threat this system posed to them by engaging in violent industrial conflict. When that failed, they turned to political action, and succeeded in gaining power over the industrial labor market by forging a fateful alliance with Afrikaner Nationalism—a movement that preserved from its agrarian slave-holding past a firm belief that white men should always have the advantage over "kaffirs." Together the two strengthened the pattern of racial segmentation in industry and legitimized the notion that the government had a positive responsibility to establish and maintain a privileged and protected economic status for the entire white community. In so doing, they completed the edifice already partially constructed by white capitalists and bequeathed to contemporary South Africa a coherent system of racial discrimination and control in the economic realm that would provide the lynchpin for an entire social order based on segregation or apartheid.

Behind the contrasting roles of the state—in one case as the prime enforcer of industrial color bars and in the other as either an officially neutral bystander or, at times, an obstacle to economic discrimination— there were additional and perhaps deeper influences that cannot be adequately grasped on the level of economic interests or ideologies. The abolition of slavery in the United States carried with it a certain heritage of moral idealism that might be violated in practice but could not be breached in principle without a catastrophic effect on the national self-image. No strong commitment to racial equality in all of its aspects came out of the struggle, as we saw in the last chapter and will see again in the next, but as a bare minimum the national conscience had absorbed the commitment that slavery, or anything resembling it, would never again be publicly sanctioned. Blacks might not be allowed to associate freely with whites or conceded full access to the suffrage, but to deny them openly the fruits of their labor or the rewards of their own exertions and talents was going too far in the direction of reversing the verdict of the Civil War. Such considerations presumably weighed more heavily in the North than in the South; but even below the Mason-Dixon line it was virtually impossible after emancipation to espouse slavery or forced labor as morally acceptable practices. In South Africa, on the other hand, labor coercion for blacks had never actually been repudiated by the settler population, and the idea that blacks had certain minimal rights had never been instilled into the collective consciousness or official morality of the white community. If the kind of equality under the law that had its most obvious application in the economic sphere became an indelible part of "the American Creed" after the Civil War, a majority of South African whites persisted in denying this principle and in fact derived their sense of identity and security from an opposite premise—that the white man should use all means necessary to maintain his dominance in every sphere, and especially in the realm of work. Hence the essence of the slaveholding mentality retained its legitimacy and helped sustain the new semi-servitude of apartheid.

VI

Two Strange Careers: Segregation in South Africa and the South

Jim Crow and "Native Segregation": A Contrast

Forced racial separation, or *de jure* segregation, has constituted the most striking institutional expression of white supremacy in both the United States and South Africa. Between the 1890s and the 1960s, the notorious Jim Crow laws of the southern states regulated inter-racial contacts in public places or facilities in such a way as to exclude blacks from most accommodations available to whites. The separate amenities or institutions provided for blacks were—despite the legal fiction of "separate but equal"—glaringly inferior and emblematic of a degraded social status. This pattern of mandatory social segregation was paralleled in the political sphere by the exclusion of most blacks from the electorate through a variety of voting restrictions put into effect by state legislation or constitutional provision between the 1880s and 1910. It was not until the rise of a militant and influential civil rights movement in the 1950s and 60s that the walls of legally enforced racial separation and disfranchisement began to crumble.

In South Africa, the emergence of segregationism as a deliberate public policy coincided quite closely with the establishment of a self-governing union in 1910. Although some precedents for this policy can be found in the earlier practices of individual colonies or republics, the full implementation of the principle of racial separation could only be achieved after a centralized and independent white settler state had displaced the British government as the dominant force in the making of "native policy" throughout South Africa. Beginning with the Native Land Act of 1913, a series of laws sought to limit most face-to-face association of Europeans and Africans to the economic realm (where, as we have seen, African labor was indispensable). The principal motive for prescribing separate living areas, public facilities, and political institutions was to restrict the power and privileges of the African majority to such an extent that the preservation of white minority rule would be absolutely assured. But a more idealistic rationale was often provided for the benefit of those who doubted the justice of these policies. It was argued that Europeans and "natives" differed so greatly in cultural backgrounds and levels of civilization that it was best to allow each group to "develop along its own lines." The alternative, according to segregationists, was a cultural "mongrelization" that would deprive both races of the strengths and virtues of their distinctive traditions.

When the Afrikaner-dominated Nationalist Party triumphed in 1948 on a platform of "apartheid" or "separate development," previous trends in white thought and policy were carried to their logical conclusion. Rather than representing a sharp break with a more liberal past— as is sometimes supposed—Nationalist hegemony in the period since 1948 brought to fruition a basic program for racial segregation and dominance that previous white regimes had already initiated or sketched out. The Nationalists closed the remaining loopholes in the system, extended its scope to include some local areas and nonwhite subgroups previously immune from its full rigors, improved and vastly enlarged the centralized bureaucratic machinery used to administer the program, gave to the state new and arbitrary powers to counter resistance and enforce restrictions on black freedom, and promulgated a more elaborate and consistent ideology to justify the established policy of separate and unequal. Building on their own traditions of cultural nationalism, Afrikaner theorists of apartheid applied the notion of a separate and God-given destiny for each *volk* or "nation" to every nonwhite group to which it could assign a distinctive ethnic or tribal origin. Eventually, the Nationalist regime pushed the pre-existing ideal of territorial separation to the point of advocating political "independence" for the various African groupings within their own "homelands" or reserved areas. For most comparative purposes, therefore, it is not necessary to make a sharp distinction between what was called "native segregation" between 1910 and 1948 and what became known as "apartheid" or "separate development" thereafter. The latter was essentially an outgrowth of the former; the basic content and direction of white racial policies remained the same.

The term "segregation" came into common use in both South Africa and the American South at about the same time—in the early years of the twentieth century. South African white supremacists may in fact have borrowed the term from their American counterparts. But a close examination of the two modes of legalized discrimination reveals some major differences in how they worked and in the functions they performed. Both, of course, were necessarily based on separatism; but the specific kinds of separation that were stressed and regarded as crucial for maintaining white privilege and furthering white interests were not the same. Despite some resemblances in practice and a good deal of similarity in ideology and spirit, the institutional foundations and socio-economic implications of the pattern of social discrimination and political exclusion that is usually summed up by the term "Jim Crow" differed substantially from those of "native segregation" and apartheid. Indeed, these differences are of such degree as to cast doubt on the value of a detailed comparison of the unequal treatment of southern blacks during the Jim Crow era and the lot of Africans under segregation or apartheid since 1910.

The crux of "native segregation" and some of the reasons why it is not strictly comparable with Jim Crow have already been suggested by the preceding discussion of how it sustained a labor system and provided a foundation for economic development. The most important *spatial* aspect of white minority rule in twentieth-century South Africa has been the territorial division of the country on the principle of "possessory segregation" as originally mandated by the Native Land Act of 1913. This legislation prohibited Africans from purchasing land outside designated native reserves and even from entering into sharecropping arrangements in the "white" agricultural areas.[1] Its larger implication, made clearer in subsequent legislation, was that the reserves were the only places where Africans could reside except to the extent that the interests and convenience of the whites required them to be elsewhere. African laborers were needed on farms outside the reserves, but their status was to be that of contract wage laborers or labor tenants rather than sharecroppers or "squatters." Similarly their presence was required in urban-industrial areas, where they became the majority of the work force; but the principle was established in the 1920s that the influx should be limited, as much as possible, to those who were absolutely essential to the economy. Furthermore, their usual status was to be that of migrant workers or provisional sojourners who could be shunted back to the reserves when their contracts were fulfilled or their labor was no longer required locally. According to the Native Affairs Commission of 1921, "It should be understood that the town is a European area in which there is no place for the redundant native who neither works nor serves his or her people. . . ." The following year, the Transvaal Local Government Commission concluded "that it should be a recognized principle of government that natives—men, women, and children—should only be permitted within municipal areas in so far and for so long as their presence is demanded by the wants of the white population."[2]

Such considerations created the impetus for the Natives (Urban Areas) Act of 1923 and its many subsequent amendments. This body of legislation attempted to regulate the flow of Africans into the cities by such devices as requiring them to have jobs or granting them only a limited time to look for work; it also discouraged male workers from bringing their families and directed that new arrivals be housed in controlled "locations" or compounds. The authorities were empowered to expel the economically "redundant" (unemployed), and by an amendment of 1937 the right of blacks to acquire urban freehold property was restricted. In 1959, in the wake of a rash of additional legislation denying Africans a permanent foothold in the cities, one of the principal theorists of modern apartheid reaffirmed their status as temporary urban sojourners: "*All* the Bantu have their permanent homes in the reserves and their entry into other areas or urban centres is merely of a temporary nature and for economic reasons. In other words they are admitted as workseekers, not as settlers."[3]

To enforce the maze of "influx controls," the government required that Africans carry passes indicating, among other things, their current employment status. Since the 1920s, the South African police have devoted a major portion of their time and energy to checking passes and arresting those whose papers were not in order. The fate of offenders has varied over time and from place to place in accordance with changing laws, regulations, and labor requirements. An African without credentials or who violated other restrictions on personal freedom

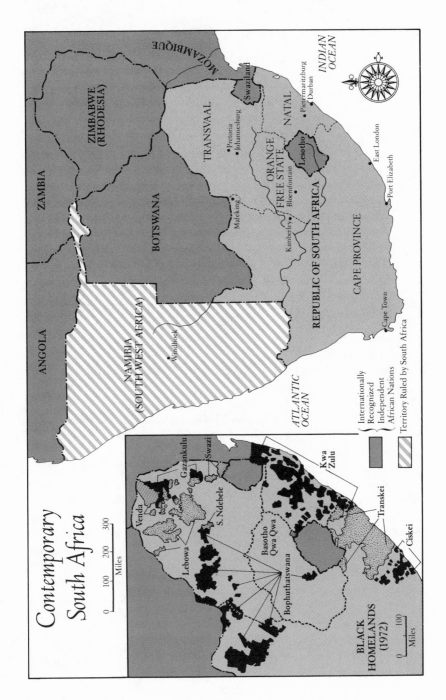

Contemporary South Africa

0 100 200 300
Miles

ANGOLA

ZAMBIA

ZIMBABWE (RHODESIA)

MOZAMBIQUE

NAMIBIA (SOUTH WEST AFRICA)

Windhoek

BOTSWANA

Mafeking

TRANSVAAL

Pretoria
Johannesburg

ORANGE FREE STATE

Bloemfontein

Kimberley

Swaziland

Lesotho

NATAL

Pietermaritzburg
Durban

INDIAN OCEAN

East London

Port Elizabeth

REPUBLIC OF SOUTH AFRICA

CAPE PROVINCE

Cape Town

ATLANTIC OCEAN

Internationally Recognized Independent African Nations

Territory Ruled by South Africa

BLACK HOMELANDS (1972)

0 100
Miles

Venda

Gazankulu

Swazi

S. Ndebele

Lebowa

Basotho Qwa Qwa

Bophuthatswana

Kwa Zulu

Transkei

Ciskei

243

might be ordered to return to his or her native reserve or "homeland," imprisoned, subjected to forced agricultural labor under conditions resembling the southern convict-lease system, or, in recent years, sent to remote "resettlement" camps or villages where "superfluous" blacks can be gathered until the government decides how to dispose of them.[4]

What has made "possessory segregation" contribute so enormously to the advantage of whites and to the disadvantage of Africans has been the grossly inequitable division of territory between races. The Land Acts have allotted only about 13 percent of the country as "reserves" or "homelands" for the African majority. In these areas, certain African "rights" have been recognized by the government. In addition to access to land ownership on an individual or communal basis, there has been a trend toward conceding some forms of political autonomy or self-government; between 1976 and 1979 this was carried to its logical outcome by the granting of "independence" to the Transkei, Bophuthatswana, and Venda.[5] But, despite the hopes of some utopian theorists of apartheid, the politicians responsible for segregation have never really intended to bring about a total separation of the white and African populations. The need for black labor in the "European areas" has always existed and has increased greatly over time. Reflecting this long-range trend, 58 percent of the African population resided, either permanently or temporarily, outside the reserves in 1950; by 1960 the proportion had grown to 63 percent.[6] The architects of the Land Act of 1913 had certainly not envisioned a total and permanent partition of population; in fact their main concern was to increase the supply of labor available to white farmers and industrialists by stifling the incipient growth of an African peasant class outside the reserved areas.[7] In 1931, Jan H. Hofmeyr, a relatively liberal politician who was to become deputy prime minister in the 1940s, described the aim of "constructive segregation" as "a white nation and a black nation dwelling side by side in the same land." But, he was quick to add, "it is inconceivable that the white man should be able completely to dispense with the black man's labor on his farms, in his mines, in his factories; it is just as inconceivable that there should be set aside for the black man's occupation land sufficient to provide for all his needs independent of the white man's wages."[8]

The reserves were thus never intended as a permanent domicile for all or even most of the African population. Already overcrowded in

1913, they have, despite some minor enlargements, become increasingly inadequate even for the maintenance of a minority. Their actual function has been to provide a reservoir of cheap and coercible labor for the rest of the country—labor that does not have to be paid a family wage or provided with many of the usual social services, because part of its subsistence and most of its "social security" is theoretically provided by a family holding in one of the homelands. At any given time, a large proportion of the male population of the homelands is actually working outside these areas under the migrant labor system; only in this way can many Africans earn enough to provide a bare subsistence for their families.[9]

Despite all the influx restrictions, a substantial minority of the African population has, in fact if not in law, established itself as an urban lower class with no real home except in the cities. By 1960, some 3.4 million Africans, out of a total of 10.9 million, were urban residents, and most of these were not oscillating migrants. Furthermore, their numbers exceeded those of urban whites by over a million.[10] Under these circumstances, the fictive norm of territorial segregation has been invoked to deprive even the most detribalized urban Africans of any of the civil and political rights that might otherwise have accompanied such a change of residence and style of life. According to the segregation or apartheid laws, all Africans, wherever they may have spent most of their lives, can be treated as temporary and provisional sojourners in the white areas. Any confusion or disagreement about their status that might have existed before 1948 was decisively resolved by the Nationalist regime. It was now clearly and explicitly established that the only place where any African could hope to enjoy most of the political and civil rights accorded to white citizens was in a homeland. The fact that many urban Africans had been born outside these areas or had weak or nonexistent ties to them did not exempt them from a kind of resident alien status. It did not even guarantee they would not be declared "redundant" to the economy of cities or towns that they had come to regard as their homes and sent "back" to "homelands" they may have never seen.[11] The effort that began in the 1960s to induce the "Bantu Homelands" to accept the government's offer of "independence" is a logical outgrowth of these policies; for if all Africans can be assigned "citizenship" in a homeland on the basis of tribal ancestry, the government can strengthen its claim that they are alien sojourners with the same essentially rightless status as temporary "guest workers" in some other industrial nations.*

The policies that have been described—and which consitute the essence of "native segregation" and apartheid or "separate development"—seem calculated to serve two major purposes. The first is the continued political dominance of a white oligarchy that now constitutes about 17 percent of the total population. The territorial division also helps sustain the white monopoly on political power by deflecting African ambitions into the comparatively safe terrain of homeland politics. Furthermore, it is an apparently adroit application of the divide-and-conquer strategy often employed by ruling minorities, for it serves to impede the development of a unified African nationalist movement by encouraging the development of the separate tribal nationalisms associated with each of the nine homelands, no one of which has the potential capability to challenge the white regime in a decisive or effective way.[12] The second objective, less emphasized by government spokesmen but nevertheless a vital consideration for many white South Africans, is the continued assurance of a supply of cheap and coercible African labor as a source of growth and prosperity for the white economy. Even the granting of genuine independence to the homelands is not likely to interfere drastically with the traditional pattern of labor procurement and use, since, for the foreseeable future, these overcrowded and impoverished "nations" will be able to sustain themselves economically only by exporting labor to the industrial regions of South Africa on the white government's terms.†[13]

Translating this form of "segregation" into an American context requires a counter-factual flight of imagination. Assume for a moment that the American Indian population had not been decimated and that the number of European colonists and immigrants had been much less than was actually the case—creating a situation where the Indians, al-

* The question of citizenship rights for Africans residing permanently outside their "homelands" has, however, become a bone of contention between the Pretoria regime and the homeland governments. When the Transkei became "independent" in 1976, the white government moved to divest the million Transkeians residing permanently in "white" areas of their South African citizenship. But the Transkei government itself, with the support of other homeland authorities, has tried to resist the full implementation of this decision.

† The economic subservience of Lesotho, an independent African nation encapsulated within South Africa, foreshadows the fate of the homelands once they are free of direct South African rule.

though conquered, remained a substantial majority of the total population of the United States. After the whites had seized the regions with the most fertile land and exploitable resources, the indigenes were consigned to a fraction of their original domain. All one has to envision here are greatly enlarged versions of the current Indian reservations. Then suppose further that Indians were denied citizenship rights in the rest of the country but nevertheless constituted the main labor force for industry and commercial agriculture. It is hardly necessary to continue; for one immediately thinks of the kinds of devices a white minority might adopt to insure its hegemony under conditions where a majority of the Indians in fact work off the reservation and even outnumber the whites outside these designated areas. The twin objectives of white supremacy would then be, as in South Africa, to maintain direct minority rule over most of the country and some kind of indirect rule over the reservations, while at the same time providing for a controlled flow of Indian workers for industry and agriculture in the white regions. Under these circumstances, it would clearly be advantageous for the whites to encourage tribal cultures and "separate development"—conceive, for example, a more self-interested and sinister motive for the apparently benevolent reversal of the traditional Indian "acculturation" policy that actually occurred in the 1930s. Promoting tribal distinctiveness and autonomy would help prevent the growth of a Pan-Indian nationalism with the chance to regain through a revolutionary struggle most of what had been lost during the period of white colonization and frontier expansion.

This imaginary but not inconceivable scenario is useful not merely to make the essential features of apartheid explicable to Americans, but also to help deflate any notion that white Americans have a kind of innate moral superiority over white South Africans. Given the actual history of Indian-white relations in the United States, such a counter-factual turning of the demographic tables—with the defeated Indians retaining the capacity to overwhelm the whites in terms of sheer population—could well have resulted in territorial segregationist policies roughly similar to those that have evolved in South Africa.

The aspect of segregation most familiar to Americans—the social separation of racial groups that reside permanently in relatively close proximity, or at least within the same metropolitan areas—also has a history in South Africa, but only as a relatively minor or superficial aspect of the larger pattern of African-European relations. What is currently described in South Africa as "petty apartheid"—the separate provision of public facilities and amenities necessarily required by both whites and blacks—has been the usual practice there since Union; but before 1953 the precise character and degree of separation was left up to local governments and reflected standards that varied in different sections of the country. The situation as it existed on the eve of World War II was described by R. F. A. Hoernlé, a liberal commentator on South African race policies. He noted that separate hospitals and cemeteries were the rule, that the state railways provided separate first- and second-class cars for nonwhites, but that the poorest or third-class accommodations were not technically segregated (although "in practice" they were "used almost exclusively by natives"). "The regulations for the use of municipal transport facilities (buses and trams) vary somewhat from municipality to municipality and from province to province. E.g. there is no colour-bar in Cape Town, whereas Johannesburg provides separate buses and trams for non-Europeans, while elsewhere occasionally separate sections of the same vehicle are allocated to non-Europeans." Most hotels and restaurants excluded blacks but a few of the latter accommodated them at separate tables.[14]

The South African courts never challenged the legality of social separation *per se,* but in decisions of 1934, 1943, and 1950 they held that segregation in public places was valid only if the facilities for nonwhites could be considered equal to those provided for Europeans. To obviate the need for equal accommodations and to make social separation uniform and comprehensive throughout the country, the Nationalist government pushed through Parliament the Reservation of Separate Amenities Act of 1953. This law not only required segregation in all public facilities and accommodations but explicitly authorized inferior amenities for nonwhites.[15]

Whether applied somewhat capriciously by municipalities or more systematically and rigorously by the central government after 1953, petty apartheid has never loomed very large as an element of white dominance over Africans. For the whites, the use of facilities designated "for Europeans only" was mainly a symbolic reflection of a more fundamental pattern of legally entrenched political and economic privilege. For Africans, the use of separate restaurants, hotels, waiting rooms, toilets, buses, railroad cars, and places of recreation could be vexing and inconvenient; but it was a minor irritant when compared to the pass system and the industrial color bars. Because of their extreme poverty and lack of economic and residential freedom—most urban Africans have always resided in separate "locations" and "townships" or in the closed compounds or hostels set aside for male migrants—the occasions when whites and Africans could actually come together in situations where petty apartheid was needed to maintain social distance have been comparatively infrequent, except perhaps in public transportation. Segregation laws of the Jim Crow type, therefore, represented a relatively superficial complement to the more fundamental aspects of "native segregation" or apartheid and added little to them. For this reason, as recent developments have shown, they are the most expendable part of the system and can in fact be easily relaxed or even eliminated in response to international criticism. Americans in particular are likely to make too much of these "reforms" because of our rather different experience of what constitutes the essence of segregation.[16]

Beyond legalized social separation, disfranchisement was the second main feature of the Jim Crow order that emerged in the South between 1890 and 1910. Exclusion of blacks from the electoral system and hence from influence over government policy can certainly be viewed as a common and centrally important feature of institutionalized white supremacy both in South Africa today and in the South before the 1960s. But disfranchisement, in the strict sense of taking away suffrage rights previously granted, has only a limited applicability to the historical development of African segregation in South Africa. Except in the Cape Province (where natives who met a property qualification could vote on the common roll until 1936 and for three specially designated white M.P.s until 1960), the indigenous black majority was never enfranchised in the first place. The Transvaal and the Orange Free State explicitly excluded Africans from the suffrage during the republican period and, by the indulgence of the British, continued to do so after their reconstitution as colonies and then as provinces of the Union. In Natal, as we have seen, there was a pale ghost of an African suffrage that was little more than a convenient fiction. The most meaningful political life available to most Africans after Union was in some of the reserves, where councils that were partly elected were given limited responsibilities, and some of the forms of traditional tribal governance and decision-making were adapted to the needs of white rule as part of the "native segregation" policy. This partial autonomy was extended and regularized as an aspect of "separate development" in the 1950s and 60s.[17]

Despite some superficial similarities, therefore, the differences between Jim Crow and "native segregation" or "separate development" are too great, in terms both of underlying structures and patterns of historical development, to sustain an elaborate comparison based on analogy. First, the southern mode, except on a local level, was directed at a minority rather than a majority. Hence, despite the rhetoric of white supremacists raising the specter of "black domination," legalized discrimination was not really a requirement for the maintenance of white pre-eminence. Even during Radical Reconstruction blacks did not dominate politics on a state level, except perhaps in South Carolina, where they were the majority in one house of the state legislature.[18]

Second, the Afro-American freedmen and their descendants were more influenced by white culture than the majority of twentieth-century black South Africans. Despite their participation in a rich and distinctive folk culture of their own, southern blacks of the Jim Crow era had much more in common with their white oppressors in language, religion, social values, and life-style than all but a small minority of black South Africans had with theirs during the period when the foundations of "native segregation" were being laid. Hence there was little basis in the South for the characteristic South African reliance on cultural pluralism as both a rationale for segregation and a desired consequence of its operation. Unlike apartheid, Jim Crow was never intended to preserve and accentuate cultural differences of a fundamental sort. It was the basis of a much more nakedly and overtly *racial* form of domination. The subcultural differences that actually existed between the races were not usually recognized as such by whites but were generally attributed to genetically determined characteristics and capacities.

A third difference was that southern blacks were theoretically citizens of a democratic nation and not conquered aliens. This meant that they could be consigned to separate and inferior facilities, disfranchised, and denied economic opportunities only by legal subterfuge or extralegal community pressure. Such a difference in legal status from *officially* rightless Africans did not save them from the ravages of Negrophobia during the heyday of Jim Crow, but it did give an aura of tenuousness and illegitimacy to the whole segregationist enterprise that would help make it vulnerable to the successful assault of the 1950s and 60s.

Finally, blacks and whites in the South had never been geographically separated; hence there was no basis for employing the notion that each race had its own natural territories as a rationale for determining status by real or fictive location. Ironically enough, the only serious suggestions that pointed in this direction in the twentieth century have come from the extreme left or from black nationalist sources. The Communist Party's ill-fated call of the late twenties and the thirties for "self-determination for the black belt" and the Black Muslims' more recent demand that a portion of the United States be set aside for a black nation came closer to the South African program of territorial division than any proposal of the white segregationists. The fact that the objectives sought from these separatist proposals were radically different from those intended by the architects of apartheid simply draws attention to the fundamental contrast between the two situations.[19]

The significance of all these differences can perhaps be summed up by stating that blacks of the post-emancipation era in the South were, despite all the discrimination and *de facto* or *de jure* segregation and disfranchisement, much more integrated into the white-dominated society and culture than most Africans have ever been in South Africa. Hence segregation could not so readily be perceived as a form of internal colonialism that involved regimenting a mass of conquered "aliens." It was more a problem of how to erect a set of barriers to the social and political inclusion of a population group that was by the late nineteenth century willing and able to participate in a common society.*

Before segregation laws and suffrage restrictions had apparently put southern blacks "in their place," anxieties about how to maintain total dominance over a group that persisted in asserting its claim to civil and political equality helped provoke an epidemic of lynchings and pogrom-type "race riots" in the South.[20] Even after the full array of discriminatory legislation was on the books, extra-legal violence, or the threat of it, continued to play an important role as a device for intimidating blacks and shoring up the color line. Besides being symptomatic of pathological Negrophobia, these brutal vigilante tactics also reflected a persistent insecurity about the effectiveness of white dominance and a lack of faith in the full adequacy of legal or institutional controls over blacks. In South Africa, on the other hand, lynching has been virtually unknown, and other forms of private collective violence against blacks have been relatively rare. This difference can best be

---

* It is only since the Second World War that this situation has to some extent been replicated in South Africa as a result of the emergence of a substantial class of urbanized or "Westernized" Africans.

explained in terms of institutions rather than attitudes. Just as the lynching of blacks in the Old South was rendered infrequent and unnecessary by the disciplining effect of slavery, so the element of direct regimentation and effective police power built into the segregation-apartheid system made it possible for South African whites to trust the authorities to do their repressive violence for them. If white vigilante action does not figure prominently in the history of South African race relations, the police or the army have been used to bolster white authority by a massive show of force against Africans several times. The Sharpeville massacre of 1960, in which approximately 70 Africans were killed and more than 180 wounded, and the firing on black schoolchildren during the Soweto riots of 1976 are only the most recent and notorious of a series of such incidents.[21]

The fact that the prime agents of white-supremacist terror have been different in the two cases—mobs in the South and the police or the army in South Africa—provides telling evidence of the basic contrast in the two situations. In the southern case, the structure of white power was relatively fragile, for all its apparent effectiveness, because it did not incorporate the kind of systematic authority over black residence, movement, and labor allocation that has existed in South Africa. One manifestation of this tenuousness of control was extra-legal violence. Another was the much greater stress placed on social segregation. The very fact that blacks could not be sharply differentiated from whites in terms of formal legal status or ascriptive economic roles put a high premium on forms of social discrimination designed to inculcate feelings of inferiority and deference—devices that were to some extent a substitute for more thoroughly institutionalized and comprehensive patterns of dominance such as those that exist in contemporary South Africa or prevailed under slavery.

Southern segregation, therefore, was an effort to establish and maintain a rigid caste division between racial groups that were inextricably involved in the same culture, society, economy, and legal system. "Native segregation," on the other hand, was an effort to perpetuate a post-conquest pattern of vertical ethnic pluralism that initially involved major cultural differences, divergent social institutions, and even separate legal codes governing Europeans and Africans. Only as workers were Africans meant to have a place in the common life of the South African nation, and their separateness and inferiority in that role were maintained primarily by the contract labor system, influx controls, and industrial color bars. The ultimate rationalization—false at bottom for South Africa but utterly and obviously implausible for the South—was that whites and blacks did not really inhabit the same nation and that an inequitable territorial division could somehow be made the basis of a "multi-national" solution to the race question.

Despite the patent impossibility of such a "solution" in the South, there were at least two serious proposals to adopt something like the South African version of segregation. The first was the plan of a northern Republican politician, General Jacob Cox, to reconstruct the South after the Civil War by separating the races geographically and ruling the black areas as federal territories. Had such a program been adopted— and for a time it was seriously discussed although never widely supported—it might conceivably have created a situation similar in some ways to the South African one. Since Cox recommended that blacks be granted political rights only in their own enclaves, it is easy to imagine them working in the white areas as rightless semi-aliens.[22] The second proposal was directly inspired by the emergence of the South African form of segregationism. In 1912, Clarence Poe of North Carolina, the editor of *The Progressive Farmer,* encountered Maurice S. Evans, a leading South African politician and early theorist of "native segregation," in London. Impressed with the thinking behind the Land Act of 1913, Poe became a vigorous proponent of dividing the rural South into areas where only one of the two races could purchase land. But the proposal met substantial opposition and had to be abandoned, partly because of fears that the resulting relocation of population would deprive white farmers and planters of easy access to black labor. The traditional southern rural pattern was not based on physical segregation and might even be described as "integrated but unequal." Hence wholesale territorial separation could be seen as a substantial departure from the local white-supremacist tradition.[23]

If proposals to separate whites and blacks into geographically distinct rural areas never really got off the ground, another form of areal segregation—the urban residential type—not only aroused great interest but was actually implemented in several southern cities between 1910 and 1915. Most of the residential segregation ordinances passed during this period prohibited whites and blacks from living on the same block as a way of establishing firm boundaries between existing neighborhoods; but Virginia went further by passing a state law authorizing the systematic division of entire cities or towns into "segregation districts," within which only one race could legally reside. At least two cities, Roanoke and Portsmouth, attempted to put this scheme into effect. The Virginia plan and the intent, if not the precise form, of many of the local ordinances bear a strong resemblance to the South African Group Areas Act of 1950. Building upon a series of earlier laws and regulations limiting the rights of Africans and Indians to reside or trade outside certain designated districts or "locations," this act was designed to confine each racial group—including the Coloreds, who had previously been immune from this kind of treatment—to its own clearly delineated residential areas. (One consequence was severe economic loss for members of the designated groups; for they lost the right to trade or operate businesses outside their own areas.) Such legalized separation, which was ruthlessly carried out in South Africa in the 1950s and 60s, was aborted in the United States by a Supreme Court decision of 1917. The Court held that a Louisville residential segregation law was unconstitutional because it interfered with the legal right of an owner to dispose of his real estate as he saw fit.* Here, as in the case of the industrial color bar, the Fourteenth Amendment and the powerful American commitment to economic *laissez-faire* combined to inhibit the legalization of racial discrimination. Other ways were found to create a high degree of *de facto* residential separation and ghettoization in American cities, but the comprehensiveness and efficiency of a governmentally supported and centrally planned program were never attained.[24]

In conclusion, therefore, it can be said that the areal aspect of segregation—the determination of where people have a right to live, either permanently or temporarily—has been central to modern South African race policy. Combined with limitations on the economic freedom of Africans and deliberate efforts to impede their acculturation to a modern industrial society, it has provided the framework for a uniquely rigid and thorough-going system of social segmentation. In the South, on the other hand, the essence of segregation was not geographical or even spatial but was rather an effort to maintain hierarchical social distance between racial groups that were too much involved with each other to be separated by sharply drawn territorial, cultural, or economic boundaries.

* Despite this decision, several American cities attempted to enact residential segregation laws in the 1920s and 30s; but all these efforts were declared unconstitutional by lower courts.

A Closer Parallel: Southern Blacks and Cape Coloreds

If the situations and historical experiences of the Afro-American minority and the black South African majority differ in some fundamental ways, there is another important racial group in South Africa that has had a changing relationship with the dominant whites that more closely parallels the "strange career of Jim Crow" in the South. The history of the Cape Coloreds since the era of emancipation is comparable to that of southern blacks in that it involved an early movement toward equality followed by a rise or extension of segregation and disfranchisement culminating in full legalization of a separate and inferior status. More than the contrast with "native segregation," such a comparison can shed light on some of the circumstances likely to promote the emergence of legalized caste distinctions based exclusively and unambiguously on racial criteria. The cultural divergence between whites and those Africans who maintained strong ties with a traditional culture—a factor that complicates any effort to see the European-African confrontation as purely or simply a race struggle—is not an element here, any more than it was a central and defining feature of black-white relations in the South.

The common or analogous elements of the Afro-American and Cape Colored experiences are numerous. Both groups are descended to a large extent from slaves or quasi-slaves rather than from indigenous groups that were conquered and allotted reservations under conditions that permitted them to retain substantial elements of their traditional culture.[25] Both are of racially mixed origin, although there is a difference of degree. Studies of gene frequency among contemporary Afro-American population samples give a wide range of results for the apparent percentage of white admixture, but the best estimates are between 4 and 11 percent for southern blacks and 19 to 26 percent for nonsouthern. Uncalculated and indeterminate are the effects of black-Indian intermixture.[26] Hence Afro-Americans, while far from being purely African in descent, are predominantly so. Cape Coloreds, according to one recent study, are more clearly tri-racial in origin; indeed "the Cape Coloured population in Cape Town . . . are constituted by approximately equal proportions of European, Asian, and Southern African genes."[27]

Moving from the realm of genetic intermixture to that of cultural adaptation, one finds that both southern blacks and Cape Coloreds have been profoundly influenced by white or European culture—an inevitable result of two or three centuries of close interaction with the dominant group. It is not accurate to say that they have undergone total cultural assimilation; for Afro-Americans have adapted some of their African heritage to American conditions to create a distinct and vital subculture of their own, and certain elements among the Cape Coloreds, most notably the Muslim community known as the Cape Malays, have retained living ties to a non-European tradition.[28] But in comparison to most indigenous Africans or American Indians, they have become substantially "Western" in their cultural orientations. Both groups, for example, are predominantly Christian and speak no languages other than those also spoken by whites.

They also represent similar proportions of the total population of the nations in which they reside—about 10 percent or slightly more in recent decades. Another striking demographic similarity is revealed by comparing their numbers relative to the whites in South Africa as a whole and in the American South during the segregation era. In both cases, these racial minorities are about one-half as numerous as the whites. The western Cape, where most of the Coloreds have remained concentrated, can be likened to the deep South or the cotton belt before the Great Migration. Here one is dealing with something close to demographic parity between whites and Afro-Americans or Coloreds.[29]

Of greatest significance for our purposes, however, are the comparable historical experiences of emancipation from thralldom, being granted equality under the law and access to the suffrage, and then losing most of these rights as the result of an upsurge of white supremacy. What happened to Afro-Americans in the period 1890–1910 was not fully experienced by Cape Coloreds until the 1940s and 50s, but in both instances there was a prior history of partial or customary segregation and an erosion of political and civil rights that anticipated formal and complete disfranchisement and the legalization of separate and unequal treatment in virtually every aspect of social activity.

Of course the profound differences in the larger national and social context must be borne in mind in making the comparison. As a denigrated minority in an overwhelmingly white nation, Afro-Americans became the major scapegoat for majority prejudices and served as the lowest-ranking reference group for the society as a whole. As a minority within a society with a larger white minority and a black majority, the Coloreds have sometimes been in a position to enjoy the relative advantage of intermediate or buffer status, which has shielded them from some of the racial hostility vented on Afro-Americans. Where blacks have been the main object of white antagonism in the United States, it is the Africans and not the Coloreds who have been most feared by Europeans in South Africa. Hence the status and situation of the Coloreds have been determined as much by how whites perceived their role in African-white relations as by the intrinsic character of their own relationship with the dominant racial group.

The Era of Laissez-Faire Segregation

The kind of separation that guarantees "social distance" in situations that would otherwise be ambiguous or implicitly egalitarian was unnecessary on plantations or farms where a clear-cut status difference between white master and nonwhite dependent made possible a physical closeness and intimacy that in no way threatened the status hierarchy. But even when the South and the western Cape were slave societies there were certain types of interaction that provoked sorting-out by color and ancestry and thus anticipated the more comprehensive segregation of the post-emancipation era. Mostly this primitive segregationism involved free people of color, but there were times when masters and slaves congregated in ways that required special adjustments. The earliest instance of what appears to be social segregation in both the South and South Africa was the practice that developed in most eighteenth-century churches of seating people of color in a separate section of the church. By the middle of the century it was the general practice in the Cape Dutch Reformed churches to seat nonwhites in the back pews. In colonial America, blacks were frequently consigned either to the rear or the balcony.[30] Such policies were undoubtedly inspired in part by the desire to counteract some of the egalitarian implications of common worship and Christian brotherhood, and it is significant that this most primitive form of separation occurred in the midst of a process of acculturation that could, if unchecked or unstructured, have logically led to full assimilation.

But one should not make too much of the purely racial implications of this pattern. As Winthrop Jordan has pointed out, "seating in most colonial churches was partly governed (whether formally or not) by accepted social distinctions; the town drunk did not occupy a prominent pew even when sober. The meaner sort of people accepted seats at the back or in the gallery, and Negroes, even Negroes who owned some property, were patently of the meaner sort. Here lay the makings but not the actuality of a radical separation."[31] In the Cape churches an extremely elaborate hierarchy of seating by social status existed, and it seems likely that those in the back were mainly slaves and freedmen of unmixed or illegitimate ancestry and little or no property. It was no violation of normal Protestant practice to give the lowest social class the worst pews. Church members of part-slave or other nonwhite ancestry who were full-fledged burghers were presumably accommodated, like those with purely European antecedents, according to a ranking based mainly on wealth and public position.[32]

The first really significant and clear-cut manifestation of segregationism in the American South occurred in the antebellum cities. Richard Wade has described how blacks, both slave and free, were normally excluded from taverns, inns, hotels, public conveyances, and parks or other public grounds. In hospitals, jails, cemeteries, and places of public amusement like theaters and opera houses they were provided separate and inferior accommodations. Mostly this was accomplished by custom, but some forms of segregation were mandated by local ordinance. These efforts to impede the promiscuous mixing of people that is a normal feature of city life might suggest that the Jim Crow type of segregation is a characteristically urban phenomenon and could be regarded as the natural response of a racially segmented society to the socially leveling effects of such an environment.[33]

But one cannot apply this hypothesis to the Cape without some qualifications. If the South began as an essentially rural society that only slowly and gradually developed urban centers, the Cape Colony originated from an urban base. As a "tavern of the seven seas" and a crossroads for people of diverse races and cultures, Cape Town long maintained such reputation for race mixing and fluidity that its customs came to be regarded as an abomination by a rural (or *platteland*) population committed to firmer racial barriers.[34] The closest American parallel is New Orleans, a city with a tradition of cosmopolitanism, cultural diversity, and miscegenation that made it more difficult to segregate than other southern cities.[35] In general, fraternization between racial groups in Cape Town remained relatively free and unimpeded by laws or even strong and consistent patterns of customary exclusion until well into the twentieth century.[36] Hence cities *per se* can scarcely be regarded as inevitable breeding grounds for social segregationism. It is perhaps more accurate to say that cities which emerge *after* a pattern of racial caste has already been established in the larger society tend to reflect that pre-existing reality by initiating segregationist or exclusionary practices that make sense only in an urban setting.

In one important realm, that of education, the early Cape went beyond a lack of enforced separation and demonstrated a capacity for what in today's parlance might be described as racial integration. The government-authorized and supported schools established in the eighteenth century were open on a nondiscriminatory basis to whites, free blacks, and even slaves whose masters would pay their fees. Substantial numbers of both of the latter groups attended and received as good an education as was available to the offspring of most white burghers.[37] According to a contemporary description, a school in Stellenbosch in the late eighteenth century was "occupied by all colours, some paying, others admitted gratis—the latter chiefly from the poor maintained by church funds."[38] Nothing could have differed more from the situation in colonial and pre–Civil War America, where blacks were, with very few exceptions, excluded from white-supported educational institutions. What education free Negroes received in the antebellum South was limited mainly to separate "African schools" supported largely by the free blacks themselves.[39] But the contrast should not be too sharply drawn; for the Dutch tradition of mixed education did not survive intact into the period of British rule. Although there was no formal color bar, the new schools established by the government in 1822 to teach English to the Dutch-speaking population appear to have been almost exclusively white. Some slaves and other nonwhites continued to be instructed in the less-favored Dutch-medium schools, but a trend had clearly been established toward limiting nonwhites to an inferior grade of education.[40]

Some of the reasons why social separatism was less highly developed in the Cape than in the South before emancipation have been suggested by earlier discussions of racial attitudes and policies. The lack of a clear differentiation between white and light Colored would have made segregation difficult to implement, and the relative absence of institutions of local self-government meant that prejudiced attitudes among the colonists had relatively little effect on public policy in many areas where color lines could have been drawn. In addition, the Cape

Colony of the early to mid nineteenth century was such a rudimentary society in terms of the growth of public institutions and facilities that there were many fewer situations than in the South where segregation could conceivably have been introduced. Aside from Cape Town with its special tradition of multi-racialism, there was little urban development to arouse tensions about access to places of public accommodation.

After emancipation, there was a period in both the Cape and the South during which a large part of the racial separatism that existed was informal, voluntary, or even, in some cases, relatively benign in the sense that it helped meet the special needs of the newly freed. "Cape liberalism" and the southern "paternalism" that dominated thinking about race relations for about fifteen years after the fall of Radical Reconstruction were similar ideologies in that they condoned, or at least paid lip service to, an essentially *laissez-faire* approach to the regulation of contacts between racial groups. In both cases there was a strong reliance on custom and an avoidance of overtly discriminatory legislation that would flout the principle of legal equality established by the North and the British as part of the emancipation process. In the new sphere of inter-racial politics, underwritten by the "color-blind" franchise of 1854 in the Cape and by the Fifteenth Amendment in the South, the right of Afro-Americans and Cape Coloreds to vote was acknowledged or at least tolerated as a necessary evil.[41]

But a closer look at what occurred in the South reveals that a general pattern of *de facto* social separation developed between 1865 and 1890 that was well on its way to crystallization by the end of Reconstruction. One of the most important aspects of this development was the growth of parallel communal institutions. Blacks seceded from the white churches as soon as they had the chance, seeking in their own congregations and denominations the religious autonomy and full membership privileges that had previously been denied them. Racial co-education was never really tried, except in New Orleans from 1868 to 1877. The first schools started by the Freedmen's Bureau and the northern freedmen's aid societies were meant to meet the special needs of ex-slaves, and when the Radical regimes established the South's first authentic public education systems, they were too eager to win support for any kind of public schooling that could accommodate blacks to jeopardize the effort by enforcing integration and arousing the bogey of "social equality." The need to provide welfare services for a mass of ex-slaves previously "cared for" by their masters was more easily met by the establishment of special hospitals, orphanages, or asylums than by enlarging existing facilities meant for whites.[42]

In the realm of social intercourse, laws were passed in some states during Reconstruction providing for equal access to public facilities, but little was done to enforce them, and blacks were often effectively excluded from establishments or conveyances accommodating whites even before such legislation was repealed or ignored by the "Redeemer" governments.[43] But the pattern was not yet Jim Crow in the full sense. Not only was much of this discrimination extra-legal or even illegal before the 1890s, but in many cases it was not yet accompanied by the provision of separate facilities reserved exclusively for blacks. A common practice was to relegate blacks to second-class accommodations that were also used by some whites. These whites might be there because they chose to be—you could smoke, spit, and behave raucously in second-class railroad cars—or because they could not afford to be anywhere else. Class and race distinctions were therefore both involved. The injustice to blacks was not so much that they were rigorously separated from whites but that they were usually treated as lower class whatever their actual social attainments. Furthermore, there were exceptions to the general practice. In some places in the 1880s blacks were served along with whites in restaurants or rode the street cars in an unsegregated fashion. It was a crazy-quilt pattern, involving a good deal of informal, customary discrimination but not yet fixed into a rigid and comprehensive system of enforced separation.[44]

The most significant change occurring in southern race relations between the end of Reconstruction and the 1890s—during the "Bourbon" or "Redeemer" era—was in the political sphere. Black suffrage was impeded, more seriously in some states than others, by a variety of methods, ranging from vigilante intimidation ("bull-dozing") to the enactment of complex and onerous registration and voting requirements aimed at discouraging poor and illiterate freedmen from casting their ballots. A majority of eligible black males voted in most southern states as late as 1880, and a majority of these voted Republican in defiance of white-supremacist Democratic regimes which were then seeking to control rather than eliminate their suffrage. But the trend thereafter was toward reduction of the black electorate by one means or another. By the nineties, the black vote had been substantially cut in most states, although in some it was still large enough to make the difference in close elections involving competing white parties or factions.

Black office-holding, of course, dropped off drastically after the fall of the Radical governments, but did not disappear. The last black United States congressman did not lose his seat until 1901.[45]

What is often described as the first real Jim Crow law was passed in 1881 when the Tennessee legislature required that separate first-class facilities be provided for blacks on the railroads. Although it was an important step toward total segregation and away from merely permitting discriminatory access to favored accommodations, this law "did not require complete separation of the races on the railroads."[46] Laws prohibiting blacks and whites from mingling in any cars were not enacted until the following decade. Meanwhile, black education suffered from the financial retrenchment and parsimoniousness of the "Redeemer" governments, and a gap began to develop between the amounts appropriated per pupil for the two races. But the disparity was considerably less than it would be in the early twentieth century.[47] The Bourbon era was not a golden age of race relations, but it can nevertheless be characterized as a time when much separatism retained an informal and *laissez-faire* quality. In addition, the parallel black institutions that were firmly established—such as schools and welfare or correctional facilities—were not so radically inferior to those serving whites as they would later become, nor did they carry such strong implications of social inferiority.

A roughly comparable pattern developed at the Cape after the era of emancipation and the Great Trek, but it persisted much longer than the *laissez-faire* phase in the South and evolved more slowly and uncertainly toward the kind of parallel communal institutions that emerged very rapidly during the Reconstruction period. A major reason why independent churches, separate schools, and special eleemosynary institutions for the Colored population failed to develop in a substantial way until the twentieth century was that the Cape did not experience anything like a Radical Reconstruction. The initial growth of *de facto* institutional parallelism in the South came about partly as a result of the more or less benevolent attempt of northern Radicals to provide certain essential services for the freedmen as a way of equipping them to take better advantage of their freedom. As Howard Rabinowitz has suggested, this early segregation was often the honest expression of a "separate but equal" philosophy and was a step up from the *exclusion* from public services that had been characteristic of the slave era.[48] Furthermore, the aspirations aroused in blacks by emancipation and Reconstruction, combined with their recognition of the persistent hostility of southern whites to "social equality," fostered their own inclination to develop separate and independent religious, fraternal, and self-help organizations.

In the Cape, on the other hand, the liberation of the Khoikhoi from quasi-serfdom in 1828 and the emancipation of the slaves in 1838 neither involved a substantial political commitment to their subsequent welfare that went beyond "equality before the law" in the most rudimentary sense nor occurred in such a way as to inspire the newly freed with the kind of communal pride and ambition that would lead them to develop institutions of their own when those of the whites proved inadequate or discriminatory. On a deeper level, the proto-nationalism or community consciousness that historians like Eugene Genovese, John Blassingame, and Herbert Gutman have found among Afro-American slaves—and which prepared them for autonomous activity after emancipation—could scarcely have existed among such a fragmented servile community as the progenitors of the Cape Coloreds.[49] Divided by race, religion, and even conditions of servitude, they had little capacity to mobilize for independent communal action when freed from bondage. The result was that the Coloreds accepted the crumbs that fell from the white man's table, and for a long time this meant a combination of indifference and paternalism that made for a relaxed and casual but ultimately debilitating system of race relations—one in which the Coloreds were neither rigorously segregated nor provided with anything remotely resembling equality of opportunity.

As in the American case, the first clear signs of social parallelism appeared in religion. Church separation began innocently enough with the rise of missionary activity in the early nineteenth century. Although some Coloreds were full members of white churches, the vast majority of slaves and Khoikhoi were heathens, and churchmen interested in proselytization determined that the best way to reach the latter would be to hold separate services for their benefit. At the same time, mission stations were being established by such external religious bodies as the Moravians and the London Missionary Society to reach the outlying Khoikhoi who were not permanently in the service of white farmers. After emancipation many ex-slaves took up residence in these missions and intermarried with the original Khoikhoi residents. The missionaries who administered these separate Cape Colored communities usually regarded the segregationist aspect of their endeavors as a temporary form of protection against white exploitation and a way of encouraging Colored self-reliance. That no notion of permanent or racially invidious separation was originally involved is suggested by the fact that neighboring white farmers attended services at some of the stations, especially at the Moravian community of Genadendal. But the farmers apparently stopped coming after emancipation.[50]

It was also during the era when the slaves and Khoikhoi were being freed from economic bondage and given a semblance of legal equality that whites first demanded separate services for nonwhites who were already members of the regular churches. In 1829, a synod of the Dutch Reformed Church was confronted for the first time with requests that Colored parishioners be barred from taking communion at the same time as whites. In response to petitions from two congregations, the synod ruled that such religious exclusiveness was contrary to the Bible and the spirit of Christianity. Such requests continued to be made, however, and in 1857 another synod capitulated, permitting separate celebrations of the Lord's Supper in cases where common worship, "as the result of the weakness of some [members], might impede the progress of the cause of Christ among the heathen." This practical concession to a form of prejudice that was still rejected in principle opened the way to almost total segregation of the Coloreds into separate but white-controlled "missionary" churches.[51]

In contrast to the Afro-American case, therefore, separation was instigated almost exclusively by the whites and did not lead to ecclesiastical independence but rather to a kind of dependent or satellite religious status. On only two relatively recent occasions did Coloreds on their own initiative successfully found separate independent denominations equivalent, for example, to the African Methodist Episcopal Church (AME) in the United States. In 1922, the Volkskerk van Afrika was founded by a renegade Colored Methodist, and in 1950 a secessionist Dutch Reformed body, the Calvyn Kerk, was established. Colored acquiescence in white religious hegemony was also broken in part by successful proselytization by AME missionaries from the United States in the early twentieth century; but clearly the Coloreds as a group have lacked the same sense of community consciousness or quasi-national identity that sustained black-initiated religious separatism in the United States.[52]

Developments in Colored education after emancipation followed a slightly different pattern. Full school segregation was not achieved until the early twentieth century, but there was a clear pattern of differential access to educational opportunity. As previously mentioned, the government schools established by the British in 1822 tended to exclude nonwhites, although this was not an official policy. When a dispute arose in Stellenbosch in 1832 as to the right of Colored children to attend one of these schools, the precedent of the past ten years was used as a basis for denying them admission. But the government schools were essentially elite institutions requiring fees that most whites could not afford. Hence a general system of public education was not really provided for the majority of either racial group during the middle decades of the nineteenth century. As an adjunct to their purely religious endeavors, the churches took up the slack by establishing mission schools originally intended for the Coloreds (as in the United States, educating the newly freed was seen as a challenging field for benevolent activity). Beginning in the late 1830s, therefore, mission schools proliferated and large numbers of Colored children were given at least a rudimentary education. But the paucity of schooling available to the poorer class of whites led them to seek admission to these institutions as well. B. M. Kies, a Colored historian of educational segregation, has estimated that during the period 1839 to 1859 there were actually more white children in the mission schools established for the Coloreds than in the state-supported institutions. In some of them, Colored pupils predominated, in others the majority was actually white; but almost all of them were integrated. He concludes that "Coloured, White, and Native mixed quite freely in the schools, which were very cheap, and contained roughly two-thirds of the white school-going population. Colored (and Native) children seldom found their way into the Established schools, because of the economic barrier. Even if they overcame this, they would very likely, especially outside the Cape Peninsula, have met with a social bar." In 1863, the government belatedly recognized the key role that mission education was playing for all racial groups in the colony and began to provide these schools with direct state aid.[53]

This peculiar episode in the history of Colored-white relations lasted until the end of the century. As late as 1885, there were still 9,235 whites in the mission schools, where they represented about one fourth of the students, as opposed to 12,358 in the public schools. (The latter, it should be added, were not themselves rigorously segregated; for they then had a token enrollment of 355 nonwhites.)[54] Apparently many whites could overcome their fears of "social equality" when their only access to schooling was in a mixed setting. Perhaps something similar would have occurred in the South if the only free education available during Reconstruction had been in schools designed primarily for the freedmen but also open to poor whites. This two-tiered educational system is also suggestive of the way that class considerations could subsume, or at least modify, those of race in the nineteenth-century Cape. If there was some tendency during the Bourbon era in the South to provide racial exclusivity only for whites who could afford first-class facilities, leaving the others to mingle with blacks in smoking cars or cheap restaurants and taverns, the nineteenth-century Cape carried the class-race feedback principle to its logical outcome, at least in educational policy. As a general rule, Coloreds were *ipso facto* lower class and were therefore customarily excluded from an education intended for a social and economic elite. But many whites were also relatively poor and hence could not claim the advantages of a segregated education. Whether one chooses to call this a class system with a racial qualification or a race system with a class qualification, it clearly will not do to think of it exclusively in terms of either socio-economic or color stratification.

There is relatively little hard information available concerning *de facto* discrimination against Coloreds in public accommodations in the late nineteenth century. Presumably they were sometimes turned away from private establishments catering to a white elite on the grounds that they were presumptively of "the meaner sort." But a first-hand description of a day in the life of an inn in Caledon, an establishment grand enough in 1863 to accommodate an English lady, suggests that a good deal of inter-racial fraternization or at least common eating and imbibing was possible during that period even outside Cape Town. Lady Duff Gordon observed with great interest a drunken fight between a "Hottentot" and an Irishman, the dignified conduct of an "Othello-looking" black customer, and the general spectacle of cheerful service being provided to patrons of all hues and ethnic origins.[55] Half a century later, a Natalian visiting Cape Town—the same Maurice Evans who influenced Clarence Poe—was struck by "a toleration of colour and social admixture to which he is quite unaccustomed; it is evident in the streets, the tramways, in the railroad stations, public offices and places of entertainment. . . . As a rule whites and Coloured keep apart and do not mix, but there are a great many exceptions. . . .

Young white men will be seen walking with well-dressed coloured girls, and an older European may often be seen with coloured wife and children of varying shades, taking the air and gazing in shop windows. The doors of a bioscope are open and the crowd waiting admission and jostling each other as they get tickets includes representatives of every colour, . . . and if he enters the overcrowded room, . . . he will find no distinctions made, all and any colour occupy the same seats, cheek by jowl, and sometimes on each others' knees. . . ."*[56]

Cape Town was exceptional, even for the western part of the Cape Province, in its traditional toleration of white-Colored intermingling in public places, but it is still significant that as late as the early twentieth century there was apparently nothing resembling the southern effort to keep blacks "in their place" by limiting their access to public accommodations or requiring them to use separate facilities. Perhaps, as Evans' description suggests, it was the persistence of a certain tolerance of miscegenation, as well as the notorious permeability of the color line, that made segregated accommodations in the heart of Cape Town not only contrary to local traditions but impracticable.

If they often mixed more freely in public with whites, the Coloreds of the late nineteenth and early twentieth centuries were at a disadvantage as compared with southern blacks of the period from 1865 to 1900 in one crucial area of common involvement, namely the political sphere. Although they had the vote after 1854 on the same basis as whites, they made little effective use of it. Partly this was due to the general property qualification; most Coloreds were simply too poor to vote. Although there was no legal barrier to their electing one of their leaders to Parliament, they never succeeded in doing so. In 1893, the Colored community of Cape Town made a serious effort to take advantage of a form of cumulative voting to elect a prominent Malay,† but Parliament avoided integrating its membership—as the Congress of the United

* To some extent this fluid pattern of race relations still existed in Cape Town as recently as the 1950s. According to a sociologist writing in that decade, "The descendants of the Trekkers . . . feel ill at ease in a city where liberalism lingers to the extent that Coloured people sit on the municipal council and on the same park bench or bus seat, where a motorist may be directed or even corrected by a Coloured policeman, and where a tourist may find Coloured people using the same piece of beach or sea."[57]

† Cape Town had four representatives in Parliament who were elected at large. Each elector had four votes and could cast them all for a single candidate if he chose.

States had done during and after Reconstruction—by changing the voting procedures to preclude this possibility.[58] The political impotence of the Coloreds, even compared to the eastern Cape Africans who also had the vote, can be attributed in part to the fact that no white-supported political movement or party, comparable to the Radical Republicans in the South, ever sought to mobilize them on behalf of policies that spoke to some of their real interests. Some white politicians did pander to the Colored vote at election time, as others did to the African, but they provided little or nothing in return.

Of at least equal importance was the archaic political culture that existed in the Cape. It resembled British politics before the Reform Acts or the American pattern of the colonial period; its key elements were faction, property, and deference. Since only the propertied could vote and only the wealthy and prominent could expect to be elected to office, the possibility of genuine democracy did not exist. Hence a predominantly nonwhite lower class could be excluded from power or meaningful participation without an overt application of racial criteria. Under such a political and social system, many Coloreds who actually qualified for the vote would find it natural to cast it the way white patrons, employers, or local notables counseled. Furthermore, since voting was public, more substantial sanctions than those of customary deference were often involved. For most purposes, Coloreds could be kept in *their* place, not so much by instilling the notion that they were racially inferior, as by convincing most of them that they were social inferiors in a perfectly proper kind of class society, and that they had no business interfering with the right of their "betters" to rule over them.[59]

The Emergence of Legalized Segregation and Disfranchisement

In the period from 1890 to 1910, southern state legislatures passed a panoply of laws requiring separation of the races in virtually all possible areas of social interaction. The path for Jim Crow was cleared by the Supreme Court's decision of 1896 that racial segregation did not violate the Fourteenth Amendment if the facilities provided were equal. In fact, they generally turned out to be glaringly unequal; but parity of accommodations was patently unenforceable during an era when the national climate of opinion was strongly racist and federal courts were inclined to intervene on behalf of blacks only in cases where discrimination was peculiarly flagrant and overt. During the same period, the process of divesting southern blacks of their right to vote was carried to completion. Local registrars were empowered by new provisions and amendments in state constitutions to apply a variety of tests to prospective voters—mostly involving literacy, ability to understand the constitution, and personal character or reputation—that enabled them to turn away all or most black voters while allowing at least some white illiterates to continue on the rolls.[60]

In somewhat less dramatic fashion, the Cape Coloreds were increasingly subjected to differential treatment by public authorities beginning around the turn of the century. Besides being denied full access to new welfare and educational services being offered to the whites, they saw a gradual erosion of their political status as a result of the establishment of the Union and the application to whites only of changes in the suffrage requirements that broadened the electorate. It was not until the 1950s, however, that the Coloreds experienced the full brunt of legally enforced social segregation and elimination from the common voters' roll. As an adjunct of the larger apartheid program, the government carried out a policy of separation or exclusion that went beyond the southern Jim Crow system in its rigor and comprehensiveness. In essence it constituted an effort to relegate Coloreds to a social and political status similar in most ways to that of the African population.[61]

Recent historians of American and South African race relations have so stressed the disabilities imposed by the customary, *de facto,* or partial segregation and disfranchisement that existed before the onslaught of full legalization that they may have raised doubts about the significance of the ultimate phase. There is currently an understandable temptation to view the Jim Crow laws and constitutional changes in the South as well as the full implementation of Colored apartheid in South Africa as nothing more than the ratification of pre-existing patterns of social separation and exclusion from power. This emphasis on *de facto* discrimination has served as a useful corrective to somewhat romantic or nostalgic views of earlier race relations, but it can be misleading if pushed too far.

There are several reasons why the stage of comprehensive legalization can still be considered important. In the first place, it removed most of the anomalies, loopholes, and confusions of class and race discrimination that had characterized the more informal or *laissez-faire* stage of black-white and Colored-white relations. No longer would it be possible for lower-class whites, in particular, to mingle freely with non-whites in certain social situations or institutions. The privilege of full racial exclusivity was thus extended down the social scale to include all of the white population, even some who may not have desired it. The phasing out in South Africa of integrated mission schools in the early twentieth century and mixed working-class neighborhoods during the later apartheid era was paralleled by an end to the integrated use of some second-class public facilities in the South. Legislation served the function of insulating all whites, regardless of class, from inter-racial contact of a potentially egalitarian kind and thereby unequivocally enshrined the *Herrenvolk* principle in place of a dialectic of class and race that could sometimes lead to situations where the former overshadowed the latter in group encounters. Oddly enough, the "separate but equal" concept that justified the earliest Jim Crow laws in the South may have been calculated in part to protect the principle of class or status differentiation *within* each racial group by providing some semblance of first-class accommodations for blacks on a segregated basis.[62] But in fact it was economically and politically impossible to duplicate the middle-class amenities of a substantial group of privileged whites for the benefit of a relatively small black elite. Hence the more fundamental tendency was toward relegating all blacks to accommodations that were simultaneously inferior and separate. By 1914, when the full implications of the Jim Crow system had become apparent, a southern educator could sum up the essence of the new "race orthodoxy" in the following terms: "in matters of civil rights and legal adjustments give the white man, as opposed to the colored man, the benefit of the doubt and under no circumstances interfere with the prestige of the white race"; "let the lowest white man count more than the highest negro."[63]

In South Africa, systematic discrimination against the Coloreds was long impeded by the tradition of "passing" and imprecise racial classification described earlier. The first attempt to define white and Colored for public purposes occurred in a Cape Supreme Court decision of 1911 in which the right of local school boards to exclude Colored children from public schools was upheld. Noting that the enabling legislation failed to provide adequate definitions of the groups affected, the judges wrestled with the problem but were unable to agree on exactly how to differentiate between whites and light-skinned Coloreds. A majority concluded that there could be no hard and fast rule and that school committees were not required to examine the ancestry of a child who appeared to be white. As a result, the infiltration of light Coloreds into schools that were now supposedly restricted to "Europeans" continued to occur.[64]

In 1950, as a necessary step in introducing a comprehensive scheme of segregation for the Coloreds, the Nationalist government passed a Population Registration Act which ultimately required everyone to carry an identity card indicating his or her racial classification. Although this legislation followed the South African tradition to the extent that it put more emphasis on associations, reputation, and community acceptance than on ancestry or even color *per se,* it did provide the bureaucracy with a device for assigning each person a definite racial status that would permit the application of segregation laws to anyone who was not "obviously white in appearance" or "by general repute and acceptance." When in doubt, as they often were, officials could now ask to see a certificate of identity.[65] Because of its traditional "descent rule," the South had less of a problem in this regard; but it also had some borderline cases, and the obsessive concern with "race purity" associated with the full elaboration of Jim Crow led Georgia in 1927 and Virginia in 1930 to attempt a form of mandatory racial registration, based on the "one-drop rule." The thought that light-skinned people with black ancestors might be availing themselves of facilities "for whites only" was apparently disturbing to the guardians of white supremacy. Even more upsetting, of course, was the possibility that they might intermarry with whites.[66]

By extending the caste principle into previously ambiguous social situations, making segregation all-inclusive and systematic, and providing more precise determinations of who was to be affected by it, Jim Crow for blacks and apartheid for Coloreds each attempted to transform a previously informal and unstable pattern of separation into a fixed and rigid system of differentiation. If left to itself, the old order might conceivably have evolved in a different direction. As C. Vann Woodward has argued, southern discussions of race relations in the 1880s and early 90s were characterized by genuine debate on alternative approaches to the "Negro problem." In addition to the emerging Negrophobes who prepared the way for Jim Crow, there were a few opponents of segregation, and a large number of paternalistic conservatives who accepted the general principle of racial separation but sought some way to apply it that would not stifle the economic and social advancement that they believed was occurring among blacks.[67] But a racist reaction developed in the nineties that was fueled by frustrations arising from a depressed economy and the renewed fears of black political influence engendered by the emergence of the Populist Party as a rival of the Democrats. Consequently, the belief that blacks were immutably inferior and retrogressing toward savagery or even ultimate extinction became so dominant in southern thinking that other perspectives receded into the background. After about 1915 the extreme racist tide receded somewhat and moderate efforts at racial amelioration again became respectable. But there was little if any questioning of the basic structure of legalized Jim Crow and disfranchisement until the 1950s.[68]

In South Africa, the anomalous position of the Coloreds in the context of the "native segregation" of the 1920s encouraged thoughts of incorporating them, for some purposes, on the white side of the European-African division. Prime Minister J. B. M. Hertzog, the leader of Afrikaner Nationalism and a major architect of segregationist policies directed at Africans, was also a proponent for a time of economic and political integration of the Coloreds with the whites, although he drew the line at "social equality." Coloreds were expressly exempted from Hertzog's industrial "color bar" legislation, and on two occasions he advocated extending the limited franchise rights they enjoyed in the Cape to the other provinces of South Africa.[69] After Hertzog and his Nationalist supporters merged with Jan Smuts's South African Party in the early depression years to form the United Party, a new and "purified" Nationalist Party emerged in opposition to Hertzog's coalition government; as part of its hard-line defense of white supremacy, the new party developed the alternative Colored policy that was implemented after it came to power in 1948.[70] The Hertzogian approach of treating the Coloreds more as Europeans than as "natives" contained elements of opportunism and hypocrisy; but if it had come to fruition as a full acceptance of Colored equality the racial balance of forces in South Africa would have been significantly altered. The severe repression that the Coloreds have experienced under the Nationalist regime has rendered any future rapprochement of the white and Colored minorities—who together form almost 30 percent of the South African population—much more difficult than it would have been at an earlier time.

In both instances, therefore, the full legalization and systematic application of segregation served to narrow the racial alternatives available to the white supremacists. Southern blacks had acquiesced in a general pattern of parallel institutions before the era of Jim Crow, and they might even have embraced separate schools as permanently desirable had these been equal to the ones provided for whites and susceptible to control by the black community. But after the full implementation of Jim Crow, almost all forms of social separateness took on an invidious character and became, as many were indeed intended to be, patent symbols of racial inferiority. Hence the decision came down in the 1950s and 60s to a choice between the legalized racism of the segregation laws and comprehensive integration. The possibility of a consensual type of pluralism in the social realm accompanied by substantive legal and political equality was effectively ruled out as a compromise solution that (whatever its abstract merits) might have prevented the need for nonviolent resistance by blacks and forcible intervention by the federal government.

In South Africa, the alienation and humiliation of the Coloreds since 1948, as well as the similar treatment of the smaller Indian minority, has probably created a situation where the whites must either extend basic civil rights to *all* nonwhites or face the prospect of their combined resistance to an entrenched white presence in southern Africa. If the ruling whites had moved in the 1940s and 50s toward equal rights for Coloreds, Indians, and detribalized Africans—rather than going in the reverse direction—and at the same time provided a more adequate land base for the Africans who still had strong roots in the tribal areas, it is conceivable that the later policy of granting independence to the homeland areas would have been acceptable to world opinion as a legitimate form of decolonization and that a racially diverse nation of essentially European culture (with the whites securely entrenched as a major population group) would have been in a strong position to survive indefinitely in much of what is now South Africa. But that alternative has probably been precluded by the effort of the past thirty years to apply the rigors of apartheid to all nonwhites regardless of culture or geographical origin.

Some sense of the circumstances and motivations involved in these fateful efforts to push segregation or exclusion to an extreme point of inflexibility can be obtained from examining parallel developments in the crucial areas of education and political participation. Despite all the demoralization and inconvenience created by separation in public accommodations and amenities, the most damaging forms of Jim Crow or Colored segregation were the institutionalization of separate and grossly inferior education and exclusion from the general electorate. Unequal education severely limited the ability of Afro-Americans and Coloreds to compete economically with whites and attain a higher standard of living, as well as making it more difficult for them to internalize a system of values conducive to high levels of achievement in a modern society. Disfranchisement removed the possibility that members of either group could exert influence over public decisions affecting their own vital interests.

The comparable educational trends that occurred around the turn of the century in the Cape and the South both involved successful campaigns for school reform that ended up benefiting whites only. Although segregation already existed in southern public education before 1900, it was not as decisive a source of unequal opportunity as it would later become; the public schools provided for both races during the Bourbon era were of generally low quality, and large numbers of poor whites, as well as blacks, lacked any access at all to sustained schooling. Educational segregation became a more serious cause of relative black disadvantage in the period between 1900 and 1915 when the "public school campaigns" upgraded white schools and increased per pupil expenditures for white pupils while leaving the funding of black education unchanged or actually reducing it. Furthermore, most southern states passed compulsory attendance laws that were, by the clear intention of the framers, enforced only against whites. Louis Harlan has told this story in considerable detail for the seaboard states; he notes that "in South Carolina in 1915 the average white child of school age received twelve times as much from the school fund as the average Negro child," a disparity that had doubled since 1900.[71] In the Alabama black belt county of Wilcox, to take an even more extreme example, total expenditures for teachers' salaries in 1890–91 were $4,397 for 2,482 white children and $6,545 for 9,931 black pupils; by 1907–8, they had risen to $28,108 for 2,285 whites and actually declined to $3,940 for the 10,745 blacks then attending school.[72] Given the fact that unequal education was such a major impediment to black economic and social advancement, it is not surprising that the struggle for integrated schools assumed such crucial importance in the 1950s and 60s. By that time there had been a reduction of the statistical gap, but the South as a whole still provided patently inferior schools for blacks.[73]

An even more devastating development occurred in Colored education at about the same time. An indication of things to come was provided in 1890 by Sir Langham Dale, the Superintendent-General of Education for the Cape Colony, when he recommended not merely educational segregation but radically different types of schools for whites and nonwhites. Europeans, he argued, should be trained to be employers of labor, while Coloreds needed only to be educated to perform manual work. Since most of the latter were destined to be artisans, farm laborers, or domestic servants, it was absurd to give them the kind of literary education suitable for Europeans. He then inaugurated a campaign to establish a new grade of government schools as a way of providing an alternative and segregated educational opportunity for the poorer whites who were still enrolled alongside Coloreds in the mission schools. Around the turn of the century, the lack of adequate education for lower-class whites, of a kind that would prepare them to be masters of servants and exemplars of "European supremacy," became an object of great concern among the leadership class; and compulsory schooling for whites only was suggested as a solution. In 1905, a School Board Act was passed by the Cape Parliament providing for local taxation to support the education of children of European ancestry or parentage and introducing the principle of compulsory attendance. Despite the problems of racial classification that made rigorous separation virtually impossible, this legislation had the effect of excluding most Coloreds from a newly established system of general public education. Consequently, they were left to learn what they could in generally inferior mission schools that were now thoroughly segregated. Furthermore, since they were not subject to the compulsory attendance law, many of them, especially in rural areas, continued to receive no formal education whatsoever. Provision was made for the establishment of some public or "nondenominational" schools for the Coloreds, but as late as 1921 only 17 of the 413 primary schools serving the Colored community were of this character. Colored leaders justifiably complained that local school boards appropriated tax revenues, including those received from nonwhites, almost exclusively for white education. In 1925 when the central government began to give per-pupil subsidies to provincial schools, the principle of separate and unequal was given further recognition: the initial grants were £14 for each white student and only five guineas for each Colored one.[74]

Differential education for Coloreds turned out to be a convenient device for discriminating against them in other ways without specifically establishing a racial test. In 1922, the setting of an educational requirement for apprenticeship in the skilled trades dealt a savage blow to the previously entrenched Colored position in these crafts by requiring completion of a higher grade level or "standard" than Colored schools generally offered.[75] Hence, even more dramatically than in the South, educational segregation and inequality served to limit economic opportunities for a subordinate racial group and caused a deterioration in their economic and social position relative to the dominant whites.

These two patterns of educational discrimination arose out of analogous circumstances and provided equivalent advantages for the white community. First of all, substantial white interests were directly served by limiting the quality and extent of nonwhite schooling. There was a continuing need for a class of menial laborers, especially in agriculture, and it was widely believed that their willingness to work for low wages and under somewhat coercive conditions would be disturbed by the aspirations that expanded education was likely to arouse. Furthermore, whole families were needed for farm work, especially at harvest time, and it would not do to have too many children in school for extended periods. Hence the persistence of a system of agriculture that was dependent on cheap and unskilled family labor militated against extending the benefits of a compulsory modern education beyond the white community.[76]

But a simple aversion to improving nonwhite education does not explain the new urge to provide decent schooling for all whites, regardless of class or economic position, which was the main source of an increasing inequality of opportunity. In part this impulse was due to the upsurge of ideological racism described earlier. The perceived need to prepare every white person to assume the burdens of ethnic hegemony in the era of racial Darwinism—a time when all were allegedly needed in the front lines of imperial consolidation or on the watch towers of "race purity"—demanded a kind of training clearly distinguishable from that offered to "lesser breeds." Beyond that, there was the practical problem of how to develop modern institutions in societies where the underlying economic and social system had a very limited capacity to generate the resources necessary for progressive reform. Per capita wealth in both the Cape and the South at the start of the twentieth century was too low to sustain an adequate system of publicly supported education for the entire population.[77] Under such circumstances the impetus to create modern institutions could only work in a segmental or discriminatory fashion, and the traditional racial division provided the most popular and convenient way to allocate the fruits of progress. By limiting access to newly emerging institutional roles and opportunities to a favored group that also regarded itself as the true or essential community, the South and the Cape could lay claim to being "progressive" or modernizing societies despite the persistence of backwardness and underdevelopment. The outgroups, who allegedly impeded a more general progress, could—by another turn of racist logic—be blamed for their own relative lack of accomplishment.

A similar pseudo-modernization might be seen operating in the political sphere as well; for the rise of self-conscious concern with the kind of electorate appropriate to a modern society was accompanied by restrictions on the Afro-American and Colored franchise. But the comparison here is complicated by the fact that a suffrage based on citizenship rather than property was accepted as the norm in the United States almost a century earlier than at the Cape. While the expansion of the white electorate during the Jacksonian era was accompanied by the reduction or elimination of black suffrage in several states, the second disfranchisement during the era of Jim Crow took place in the context of a general reaction against an unlimited suffrage, with the result that many poor or illiterate whites lost the vote along with blacks. The process was rationalized as an attempt to certify an electorate that had the education or capacity to deal with what the "progressive" proponents of suffrage restriction described as "the complex problems of modern life." The fact that blacks as a group were the most conspicuous victims of the new suffrage laws can be attributed in part to the prevailing ideology of genetic inferiority and partly to a realization that they were potential collaborators with poor whites in movements, such as Populism, that resisted the kind of "progressive" change under capitalistic auspices that was prescribed by the dominant elements of the society.[78]

"Progressivism for whites only" was not, however, the whole story of southern disfranchisement; as J. Morgan Kousser has shown, political partisanship also played a very important role. Most major restrictive legislation occurred at times when the Democrats were facing a challenge from other parties: "Their sponsors . . . knew that the bills would disfranchise a larger portion of potential opposition voters than of their own."[79] Since the one thing that held the post-Reconstruction Democratic Party together was a commitment to maintaining white supremacy, the issue of franchise restriction was simultaneously a way of re-emphasizing the party's central issue and source of white electoral support and a method for reducing the actual or potential opposition, especially by eliminating the black Republicans. The success of the Democrats' efforts to convince whites that they alone could be trusted to prevent "Negro domination"—or more accurately the chance that blacks might hold the balance of power in close elections—resulted in saddling the South of the first half of the twentieth century with a one-party system that helped retard the region's economic and social development. Hence the aim of modernization through "purification" of the electorate was thwarted by the kind of politics used to pursue this end. The promise of some suffrage reformers that the whites could divide in a "safe" and normal way after the "corrupting" influence of the black vote had been removed was not realized: either Democratic machines continued to rule over a diminished electorate or political competition degenerated into a clash of factions or personalities within the segregated confines of "white primaries."[80]

In some ways the decline of Cape Colored political rights and potential influence paralleled the first or Jacksonian pattern of disfranchisement more than that of the Jim Crow era. As the white electorate was broadened in the twentieth century, traditional qualifications or restrictions remained in effect for Coloreds only, thus reducing their capacity to influence the outcome of elections. The first act of overt political discrimination against Coloreds occurred when the National Convention of 1908 and 1909, which assembled to unify South Africa, not only failed to extend the nonwhite franchise of the Cape to the other provinces but explicitly barred Coloreds from sitting in the central Parliament. Although their presence on the common voters' roll in the Cape was made an "entrenched" clause of the Constitution, meaning that it could only be eliminated by a two-thirds vote of both houses of Parliament, this provision in fact made the Colored franchise vulnerable to future reduction or elimination whenever a substantial white majority favored such a step. In 1930 the vote was granted to white women in South Africa, and the following year educational and property qualifications were eliminated for Europeans in the Cape Province and Natal, thus extending universal white suffrage throughout the

Union. These racially discriminatory extensions of the suffrage did not diminish the Colored vote absolutely but they did drastically reduce its relative importance. In the parliamentary election of 1929 approximately 25,000 Coloreds voted as compared to 410,000 whites; in 1932 the Colored vote remained almost the same but the European electorate had swollen to 850,000. Hence the establishment of a modern system of universal suffrage for South African whites was directly responsible for a decline in the political status and influence of the Coloreds.[81]

It might appear from the above figures that the Colored vote could not possibly weigh very heavily in parliamentary elections, especially after 1931. Yet the heavy concentration of the Colored electorate in a few districts in the western Cape gave them the capacity to determine the results in some key constituencies. This situation was roughly analogous to that which existed in some southern states in the 1890s when the black vote, although reduced, could still be decisive in determining the outcome of close elections between Democrats and their Populist or Populist-Republican opponents. The refusal of most blacks to vote for Democrats provided that party with a substantial incentive to disfranchise them as a way of eliminating the possibility of successful opposition. The Colored vote of the 1930s and 40s was not of equivalent importance in the calculations of white politicians in South Africa; but it nevertheless became a matter of considerable irritation to the Nationalists that the Coloreds voted overwhelmingly for the opposition United Party. After it won a narrow parliamentary majority in 1948, the Nationalist government undertook to fulfill a campaign pledge to remove the Coloreds from the common roll in the Cape. After a protracted constitutional struggle necessitated by the special entrenchment of Colored voting rights, the Nationalists attained their objective in 1956.[82] According to a prominent South African sociologist and student of the Colored community, "the major reason for the removal of the Coloured people from the common voters roll during the fifties was the fear that a solid mustering of Coloured voters by the Opposition could result in a defeat by [*sic*] the Nationalist Party."[83] Hence, as in the South, political partisanship played a major role in disfranchisement.

But more than normal partisanship was involved. Since both the Democrats in the period 1890–1910 and the Nationalists in the late forties and fifties considered themselves to be the only party that could save the whites from some kind of racial catastrophe (or so at least their rhetoric proclaimed), their actions pointed toward a *de facto* system of one-party rule—on the state and local level in the South and on the national level in South Africa. Furthermore, both parties made nonwhite suffrage a symbolic issue that served to crystallize a broader racial philosophy and program. In South Africa the full logic of apartheid seemed to require political as well as other forms of segregation for the Coloreds; and in the South the assumptions behind the rise of Jim Crow made black voting incompatible with the abject inferiority of status implied by social separation. Beyond its partisan purposes, therefore, disfranchisement implied much the same thing as social segregation—in some ways even more dramatically. It meant that full citizenship, community acceptance, and enjoyment of the fruits of economic and social progress was limited to those who were recognized as white. By being excluded from the suffrage, blacks and Cape Coloreds were not only subjected to one additional form of humiliation, they were also denied rights previously enjoyed and supposedly protected by earlier constitutional acknowledgments of their membership in the political community. In addition, they were prevented from exerting future influence over the allocation of resources and opportunities in a developing society and thus denied full access to the new services and advantages being provided to the enfranchised segment of the population.

Southern blacks were, of course, re-enfranchised and protected against legalized segregation in the wake of the changed climate of American opinion and the rising black assertiveness that developed after the Second World War. In South Africa second thoughts have developed about the segregation and disfranchisement of Coloreds; in 1976 a government commission actually recommended the repeal of most of the apartheid legislation directed specifically at them.*[84] One might be tempted to suppose, particularly as a result of American developments, that the legal segregation and disfranchisement of racial minorities like the Afro-Americans and the Cape Coloreds represent temporary departures from some larger process of integration. But the persistence of *de facto* segregation in the United States, particularly in the allocation of urban space and in education, makes it clear that equality and fraternity do not result automatically from the elimination of Jim Crow laws and practices. In the South African case, the larger

* The government turned a deaf ear to the commission's more radical recommendations, such as abolition of anti-miscegenation laws, but a trend toward some relaxation of Colored apartheid appears to be developing.

European-African confrontation makes the future of Colored-white relations extremely problematic. The whites may be tempted to incorporate the Coloreds into the ruling group as a defensive measure—this would make the current argument that apartheid is a matter of culture rather than race slightly more credible; but they are unlikely to do so in a more than symbolic fashion at a time when there is growing agitation for citizenship rights among urbanized Africans. Significant concessions to the Coloreds would probably increase the level of African frustration. Furthermore, there have been indications that the Coloreds are increasingly disposed to side with the Africans and take their chances under the black majority rule that will surely emerge, sooner or later, in all or most of what is now South Africa.

If the trend in the United States is for blacks and whites to participate on a more equitable basis in a common society, the long-run destiny of the Coloreds would seem to lie in the direction of integration, on some levels at least, with the African majority rather than the white minority. Total assimilation is unlikely in either case; for the divergent historical experiences that provide a basis for ethnic identity, even when the factor of race *per se* loses some of its importance, are very durable. But equality of essential rights and a free choice about their destiny as communities or population groups is not an impossible hope for blacks in a predominantly white America or for Coloreds in the new "South Africa for the Africans" that will ultimately come into being.

That other sizable minority of the South African population—the whites—may also have a place in the new South Africa of the future. But the nature of this place will depend on the decisions that the white leadership makes in the years to come when faced with increasing pressures from within South Africa and without to dismantle apartheid and enfranchise the African majority. Intransigent opposition to these demands for basic change will only invite race war and could ultimately result in the oppression or even the expulsion of the white community by victorious African nationalists. Accommodation—a willingness to share political power and economic resources in an equitable way—might still enable the whites to survive as members of a permanent and useful minority within a multi-racial state. As the preceding pages have shown, the history of white supremacy in South Africa provides little hope for such an outcome. But one of the more general lessons of history is that human groups can sometimes transcend the past and adapt to circumstances in unanticipated ways. If enlightened self-interest can induce whites to abdicate their privileged position, they may still be able to call themselves South Africans twenty-five, fifty, or even a hundred years hence. Otherwise they may end up in the same situation in which nonwhites now find themselves—as disenfranchised aliens in the land of their birth.

Chronology of Major Events

South Africa

1652	First settlement at the Cape of Good Hope.
1657	Dutch East India Company frees a few servants, creating the nucleus for a burgher class.
1658	First substantial importation of slaves.
1659–60	First Khoikhoi-Dutch War.
1673–77	Second Khoikhoi-Dutch War.
1688	Arrival of 200 French Huguenot settlers.
1717	Company decides against encouraging European immigration and reducing dependence on slavery.
1779–81	First Frontier War with Xhosa.
1793	Second Frontier War.
1795	Burgher rebellions on the eastern frontier. First British occupation of the Cape.
1799	Renewed burgher rebellion on the eastern frontier. Third Frontier War.
1803	Cape restored temporarily to Dutch rule.
1806	Second British occupation.
1807	Abolition of the slave trade.
1809	Ordinance issued regulating Khoikhoi contract labor.
1812	First circuit court hears complaints of brutality against masters of Khoikhoi servants.
1814	British acquire permanent sovereignty over the Cape.

1815   Slagter's Nek rebellion.

1820   Arrival of 5,000 British immigrants.

1828   Ordinance No. 50 relieves Khoikhoi of restrictions on their economic freedom.

1834   Beginning of slave emancipation.

1834–35   Major war with Xhosa on the eastern frontier.

1836–38   The Great Trek.

1838   Trekking Boers defeat the Zulu at the Battle of Blood River.
          Founding of Boer Republic in Natal.
          Completion of slave emancipation in the Cape Colony.

1843   British annexation of Natal.

1848   British government proclaims its sovereignty between the Orange and Vaal rivers.

1852   British recognize the independence of the Boers in the Transvaal.

1854   British grant independence to the Orange Free State.
          Cape Colony granted representative government; establishment of nonracial franchise.

1858   Founding of the South African Republic by the Boers in the Transvaal.

1860   Indian indentured laborers introduced into Natal.

1867   Discovery of diamonds near the confluence of the Orange and Vaal rivers.

1872   Cape Colony granted responsible, cabinet government.

1877   Annexation of the Transvaal by the British.

1879   British-Zulu War.

1880   First Anglo-Boer War.

1881   Transvaal republic regains its independence.

1884   Discovery of the first important gold field in the Transvaal.

1886   Founding of Johannesburg.

1893   Natal granted responsible government.

1895   The Jameson Raid—an abortive effort by pro-British interests to overthrow the Transvaal government.

1899   Outbreak of the Second Anglo-Boer War.

1902   End of the Boer War; peace of Vereeniging.

1905   South African Native Affairs Commission advocates territorial segregation of whites and Africans.

1907   Cape Colony School Board Act restricts access of nonwhites to public education.
          Attainment of responsible government by the Transvaal and the Orange Free State.

1908   Convention assembles to plan for South African union.

1910   Establishment of the Union of South Africa.

1911   Mine and Works Act of Union Parliament sanctions an industrial color bar.

1913   Native Land Act provides for territorial segregation.

1922   Strikes and rebellion on the Witwatersrand (the Rand Rebellion).

1924   Smuts's South African Party defeated in parliamentary elections; establishment of a Nationalist-Labour coalition government under Hertzog.

1926   Colour Bar Act secures a monopoly on skilled jobs for white mine-workers.

1930   White women enfranchised.

1933   Coalition government formed by Hertzog and Smuts.

1934   Founding of Purified Nationalist Party by Afrikaner opponents of Hertzog's coalition policy.

        Founding of United Party by supporters of Hertzog and Smuts.

1936   Africans removed from the common voters' roll in the Cape Province.

1948   Nationalist victory over the United Party in parliamentary elections.

1949   Prohibition of Mixed Marriages Act.

1950   Population Registration Act; Group Areas Act.

1951   Bantu Authorities Act establishing a new system of government for African reserves.

1953   Reservation of Separate Amenities Act.

1956   Coloreds removed from the common voters' roll in the Cape Province.

1960   Sharpeville massacre.

1961   South Africa severs its ties with the British Commonwealth and becomes a republic.

1976   Soweto riots.

        Transkei declared independent.

United States

1607	Settlement at Jamestown.
1619	First blacks arrive in Virginia.
1622	Indian attack on the Virginia settlement provokes a massive retaliation.
1644	Second Indian uprising in Virginia.
1667	Virginia legalizes slavery for converted blacks.
1675–76	Bacon's Rebellion in Virginia.
	King Philip's War ends Indian resistance in southern New England.
1691	Inter-racial marriage banned in Virginia.
1711–12	Tuscarora Indian War in North Carolina.
1715	Yemasee War in South Carolina.
1763	Pontiac's Conspiracy in the Ohio Valley.
	British proclamation restricts westward movement of settlers.
1776	Declaration of Independence.
1783	International recognition of American independence.
	Beginning of gradual emancipation of slaves in the North.
1787	Northwest Ordinance prohibits slavery in the territories north of the Ohio River.
	Constitutional Convention compromises on slavery.
1790	First federal naturalization law reserves citizenship for whites.
1793	Invention of cotton gin strengthens economic basis for southern slavery.
1808	Closing of the international slave trade.
1811	Battle of Tippecanoe breaks resistance of Ohio Valley tribes.
1813–14	Creek War leads to cession of most Creek lands in Alabama.
1820	Missouri Compromise establishes dividing line between slave and free territory.
1830	Indian Removal Act.
1831	Beginning of abolitionist agitation in the North.
1838	Removal of the Cherokees by federal troops.
1850	Compromise of 1850 temporarily resolves controversy over extension of slavery into the territories.
1854	Kansas-Nebraska Act revives sectional controversy.
1857	Dred Scot decision nullifies the Missouri Compromise and denies all blacks the right to U.S. citizenship.
1860	Election of Lincoln.

1860–61	Secession of the southern states.
1861	Outbreak of the Civil War.
1863	Emancipation Proclamation.
1865	End of the Civil War.
	Ratification of Thirteenth Amendment prohibiting slavery.
	Beginning of presidential Reconstruction; passage of black codes by southern state legislatures.
1866	Congress passes Civil Rights Act over President Johnson's veto.
1867–68	Radical Reconstruction begins; enfranchisement of southern blacks.
1868	Ratification of Fourteenth Amendment extending citizenship rights to freedmen.
1870	Ratification of Fifteenth Amendment designed to protect voting rights of blacks.
1877	End of Radical Reconstruction.
1881	First state law segregating the races in public transportation is passed in Tennessee.
1882	Exclusion Act prohibiting immigration of Chinese.
1887	Dawes Severalty Act provides for individual allotment of land on Indian reservations.
1890	Mississippi becomes the first state to disfranchise blacks by constitutional convention.
1896	*Plessy* v. *Ferguson* decision of Supreme Court authorizes segregation of public accommodations.
1917	Supreme Court outlaws residential segregation.
	Race riot in East St. Louis.
1919	Chicago race riot; similar outbreaks in several other cities.
1934	Indian Reorganization Act grants greater autonomy to tribes on reservations.
1954	Supreme Court bans segregation in public schools in *Brown* v. *Board of Education of Topeka*.
1960–64	Sit-ins and mass demonstrations against legalized segregation in the South.
1964	Civil Rights Act requiring equal access to public facilities.
1965	Civil Rights Act providing strong protection for black voting rights.
1967	Supreme Court declares state laws banning inter-racial marriage unconstitutional in *Loving* v. *Virginia*.

Notes

INTRODUCTION

1. On the concept of *Herrenvolk*ism, as applied to the United States and South Africa, see Pierre L. van den Berghe, *Race and Racism: A Comparative Perspective* (New York, 1967), 18, 29, 77, 101.
2. For discussion of the concept of racism, see Michael Banton, *Race Relations* (New York, 1967), 7–8, and *passim; idem,* "The Concept of Racism," in Sami Zubaida, ed., *Race and Racialism* (London, 1970), 17–34; John Rex, "The Concept of Race Sociological Theory," in *ibid.,* 35–55; *idem, Race Relations in Sociological Theory* (London, 1970), 136–61; Van den Berghe, *Race and Racism,* 11, and *passim;* and William J. Wilson, *Power, Racism, and Privilege: Race Relations in Theoretical and Sociohistorical Perspectives* (New York, 1973), 30–35, and *passim.* My own effort to provide a critical analysis of the concept can be found in an unpublished paper, "Social Theory and the Historical Study of Racism," presented at the 1975 meeting of the Organization of American Historians.
3. See my essay "Comparative History," in Michael Kammen, ed., *The Past Before Us: Contemporary Historical Writing in the United States* (Ithaca, N.Y., 1980).
4. Some notable examples are Louis Hartz, *The Founding of New Societies: Studies in the History of the United States, Latin America, South Africa, Canada, and Australia* (New York, 1964)—although this volume includes chapters on individual societies written by historians; Barrington Moore, *Social Origins of Dictatorship and Democracy: Lord and Peasant in the Making of the Modern World* (Boston, 1966); Eric

R. Wolf, *Peasant Wars of the Twentieth Century* (New York, 1969); Immanuel Wallerstein, *The Modern World-System: Capitalist Agriculture and the Origins of the Modern World-Economy in the Sixteenth Century* (New York, 1974); James Lang, *Conquest and Commerce: Spain and England in the Americas* (New York, 1975); and Reinhold Bendix, *Kings or People: Power and the Mandate to Rule* (Berkeley and Los Angeles, 1978).

5. Cyril E. Black, who is the author of *The Dynamics of Modernization: A Study in Comparative History* (New York, 1966), and one of eight authors from various disciplines who collaborated to produce *The Modernization of Japan and Russia: A Comparative Study* (New York, 1975).

6. See Carl Degler, "Comparative History: An Essay Review," *The Journal of Southern History*, XXXIV (1968), 425–30, for a good statement of the centrality in comparative history of finding and explaining differences.

7. This point is made very effectively by Fritz Redlich in "Toward a Comparative Historiography: Background and Problems," *Kyklos*, XI (1958), 379–80.

8. For the debate on New World slavery, see Frank Tannenbaum, *Slave and Citizen: The Negro in the Americas* (New York, 1946); Stanley Elkins, *Slavery: A Problem in American Institutional and Intellectual Life* (Chicago, 1959), 27–80; Herbert S. Klein, *Slavery in the Americas: A Comparative Study of Cuba and Virginia* (Chicago, 1967); Marvin Harris, *Patterns of Race in the Americas* (New York, 1964), 65–94; David Brion Davis, *The Problem of Slavery in Western Culture* (Ithaca, N.Y., 1966), 223–88; Franklin W. Knight, *Slave Society in Cuba during the Nineteenth Century* (Madison, Wis., 1970); Carl N. Degler, *Neither Black Nor White: Slavery and Race Relations in Brazil and the United States* (New York, 1971), 25–92; and H. Hoetink, *Race Relations in the Americas: An Inquiry into their Nature and Nexus* (New York, 1973), 3–86.

9. See especially Degler, *Neither Black Nor White*, 95–264; and essays in David W. Cohen and Jack P. Greene, eds., *Neither Slave Nor Free: The Freedmen of African Descent in the Slave Societies of the New World* (Baltimore, 1972).

10. A recent historical work on American race relations that has benefited substantially from a concern with the questions raised by comparative studies in Ira Berlin, *Slaves Without Masters: The Free Negro in the Antebellum South* (New York, 1974).

11. For representative statements of these interpretive perspectives, see Tannenbaum, *Slave and Citizen;* Harris, *Patterns of Race;* Eugene D. Genovese, *The World the Slaveholders Made: Two Essays in Interpre-*

tation (New York, 1969), 1–113; Degler, *Neither Black Nor White,* 245–56; and Hoetink, *Slavery and Race Relations,* 192–209.

12. This comparison will in fact be pursued by a number of scholars in a forthcoming volume of essays on the American and South African frontiers edited by Howard Lamar and Leonard Thompson.

13. See especially the work of Edna Bonacich: "A Theory of Ethnic Antagonism: The Split Labor Market," *American Sociological Review,* XXXVII (1972), 547–59; "Abolition, the Extension of Slavery, and the Position of Free Blacks: A Study in Split Labor Markets in the United States, 1830–1863," *American Journal of Sociology,* LXXXI (1975), 601–28; "Advanced Capitalism and Black/White Relations in the United States: A Split Labor Market Interpretation," *American Sociological Review,* XLI (1976), 34–51; and "Capitalism and Race Relations in South Africa: A Split Labor Market Analysis," forthcoming in Maurice Zeitlin, ed., *Political Power and Social Theory.*

14. For a provocative discussion of these issues, see Eugene D. Genovese, "Materialism and Idealism in the History of Negro Slavery in the Americas," in *In Red and Black: Marxian Explorations in Southern and Afro-American History* (New York, 1971), 23–52. The classic sociological analysis of race relations as determined by economic class interest is Oliver Cromwell Cox, *Caste, Class, and Race: A Study in Social Dynamics* (Garden City, N.Y., 1948). For an example of the argument that "race consciousness" was more fundamental than "class consciousness" in the history of the American South, see Carl N. Degler, *The Other South: Southern Dissenters in the Nineteenth Century* (New York, 1974), 7, and *passim.* For a discussion from a Marxist perspective of the class-race issue in South African historiography, see Martin Legassick, "The Frontier Tradition in South African Historiography," in *Collected Seminar Papers on the Societies of Southern Africa in the 19th and 20th Centuries,* Vol. II (London: Institute of Commonwealth Studies, 1971), 1–33.

15. Robert Ross, *Adam Kok's Griqua: A Study of the Development of Stratification in South Africa* (Cambridge, Eng., 1975), 3.

16. See Gwendolen M. Carter, *The Politics of Inequality: South Africa since 1948,* 2nd ed. (New York, 1959), 16–17. For a detailed account of the role of physiographic features in South African history, see N. C. Pollock and Swanzie Agnew, *An Historical Geography of South Africa* (London, 1963).

I. SETTLEMENT AND SUBJUGATION

1. See Donald Noel, "A Theory of Ethnic Stratification," *Social Problems,* XVI (1968), 137–72; and William J. Wilson, *Power, Racism, and*

Privilege: Race Relations in Theoretical and Sociohistorical Perspectives (New York, 1973), 16–28.

2. Quoted in Francis Jennings, *The Invasion of America: Indians, Colonialism, and the Cant of Conquest* (Chapel Hill, N.C., 1975), 4. On the medieval crusading tradition and its impact on American colonization, see *ibid.*, 3–14, and Wilcomb E. Washburn, *Red Man's Land/White Man's Law: A Study of the Past and Present Status of the American Indian* (New York, 1971), 3–6.

3. Quoted in Lewis Hanke, *Aristotle and the American Indians: A Study of Race Prejudice in the Modern World* (Bloomington, Ind., 1959), 19.

4. *Ibid.*, 44–45, 86–87, and *passim*.

5. J. H. Elliott, *The Old World and the New, 1492–1650* (Cambridge, Eng., 1970), 41–42. See also Richard Bernheimer, *Wild Men in the Middle Ages: A Study in Art, Sentiment, and Demonology* (Cambridge, Mass., 1952).

6. Nicholas P. Canny, "The Ideology of English Colonization: From Ireland to America," *William and Mary Quarterly*, XXX (1973), 585–86; Washburn, *Red Man's Land*, 22; Margaret T. Hodgen, *Early Anthropology in the Sixteenth and Seventeenth Centuries* (Philadelphia, 1964), 234–35. Boemus was translated into English in 1555.

7. Hodgen, *Early Anthropology*, 405.

8. *Ibid.*, 405–26.

9. Richard Hakluyt, *Voyages and Discoveries,* ed. Jack Beeching (Harmondsworth, Eng.: Penguin Books, 1972), 278.

10. *Ibid.*, 402.

11. Hodgen, *Early Anthropology*, 411–12.

12. *The Complete Works of Montaigne* (Stanford, 1957), 153. Thomas Cavendish contributed to the primitivist as well as the bestial image of the Indian. He found some of the North American Indians that he encountered on his voyage of 1587 to be "most gentle, loving, and faithful, void of all guile and treason, and such as live after the manner of the golden age." (Hakluyt, *Voyages,* 274.) See also Gary B. Nash, "The Image of the Indian in the Southern Colonial Mind," *William and Mary Quarterly*, XXIV (1972), 201–3; and Henri Baudet, *Paradise on Earth: Some Thoughts on European Images of Non-European Man* (New Haven, 1965).

13. Elliott, *Old World and New,* 103.

14. Quoted in Roy Harvey Pearce, *Savagism and Civilization: A Study of the Indian and the American Mind* (Baltimore, 1965), 6. See also Charles M. Andrews, *The Colonial Period of American History,* Vol. I (New Haven, 1934), 65–66.

15. Quoted in J. H. du Plessis, *A History of Christian Missions in South Africa* (London, 1911), 23.

16. Canny, "Ideology of Colonization," 575–98; James Muldoon, "The Indian as Irishman," *Essex Institute Historical Collections,* CXI (1975), 267–89; David Beers Quinn, *The Elizabethans and the Irish* (Ithaca, N.Y., 1966), 106–22.

17. Canny, "Ideology of Colonization," 576–79.

18. Hodgen, *Early Anthropology,* 213–14; Winthrop D. Jordan, *White over Black: American Attitudes Toward the Negro, 1550–1812* (Chapel Hill, N.C., 1968), 3–11. The innumerable descriptions of Indians and Asians found in Hakluyt, *Voyages,* make relatively little of color or physical characteristics and much of habits and customs. On the question of the American Indian's pigmentation, Wesley Frank Craven contends that "the view best suited to the European's preconceptions was one holding that the native American was born white and that the distinctive complexion of his skin was artificially achieved." (*White, Red, and Black: The Seventeenth-Century Virginian* [Charlottesville, Va., 1971], 40.) For an expression of the belief that the "Hottentots" were naturally white, see the quotation from John Maxwell in Eric Walker, *A History of Southern Africa,* 3rd ed. (London, 1957), 35.

19. Canny, "Ideology of Colonization," 580–95 (quotes from p. 588); Muldoon, "Indian as Irishman," 274–77.

20. The parallel with North American Indian policy is noted by W. C. MacLeod, *The American Indian Frontier* (New York, 1928), 164. On the savage war that led to the English conquest of Ulster in 1603, see Quinn, *Elizabethans and the Irish,* 134–41.

21. On this neglected topic, see Michael Hechtor, *Internal Colonialism: The Celtic Fringe in British National Development, 1536–1966* (Berkeley, Calif., 1975); and Quinn, *Elizabethans and Irish,* 7–9.

22. On the economic interests involved, see Theodore K. Rabb, *Enterprise and Empire: Merchant and Gentry Investment in the Expansion of England, 1575–1630* (Cambridge, Mass., 1967).

23. The population situation and its impact on the thinking of Elizabethan expansionists is well summed up by Edmund Morgan, *American Slavery—American Freedom: The Ordeal of Colonial Virginia* (New York, 1975), 30–31, 65. See also E. A. Wrigley, *Population and History* (London, 1969), 78–80; Christopher Hill, *The Century of Revolution, 1603–1714* (London: Sphere Books, 1969), 31; and *idem, Change and Continuity in Seventeenth-Century England* (Cambridge, Mass., 1975), 188–89.

24. The standard account of this period of Dutch history is found in Pietr Geyl's works, in *The Revolt of the Netherlands, 1555–1609,* rev. ed. (London, 1966), and *The Netherlands in the Seventeenth Century, Part One,* rev. ed. (London, 1961).

25. See Violet Barbour, *Capitalism in Amsterdam in the Seventeenth Century* (Baltimore, 1950), 138–39.
26. C. R. Boxer, *The Dutch Seaborne Empire, 1600–1800* (New York, 1965), 20–24.
27. *Ibid.*, 94; Gerrit Schutte, "Company and Colonists at the Cape," in Richard Elphick and Hermann Giliomee, eds., *The Shaping of South African Society, 1652–1820* (Cape Town, 1979), 175, 182.
28. J. H. Parry, *The Age of Reconaissance* (Cleveland and New York, 1963), 254. C. R. Boxer presents a somewhat harsher general evaluation of the racial attitudes that the Dutch manifested in the East (*Dutch Seaborne Empire,* 233); but his assertion that their Calvinism made them peculiarly discriminatory is undocumented, and he presents much evidence on specific policies that could be used to support Parry's generalizations.
29. Boxer, *Dutch Seaborne Empire,* 99; George Masselman, *Cradle of Colonialism* (New Haven, Conn., 1963), 416–23, 456–57, 460–61.
30. Boxer, *Dutch Seaborne Empire,* 58, 216–22; Bernard H. M. Vlekke, *Evolution of the Dutch Nation* (New York, 1945), 215–16.
31. Immanuel Wallerstein, *The Modern World-System: Capitalist Agriculture and the Origins of the European World-Economy in the Sixteenth Century* (New York, 1974), ch. 6.
32. Nash, "Image of the Indian," 205–6.
33. Quoted in Wesley Frank Craven, *The Southern Colonies in the Seventeenth Century, 1607–1689* (Baton Rouge, La., 1949), 44.
34. Nash, "Image of the Indian," 202–3.
35. *Ibid.,* 208–9.
36. *Ibid.,* 216, and *passim;* Craven, *Southern Colonies,* 75–82.
37. Craven, *Southern Colonies,* 81–82, 115–16; Nash, "Image of the Indian," 214–17. See also Morgan, *American Slavery,* 71–81.
38. Quoted in Nash, "Image of the Indian," 211.
39. Craven, *Southern Colonies,* 137, 123–24. On Indian responses, see Nancy Lurie, "Indian Adjustment to European Civilization," in James M. Smith, ed., *Seventeenth-Century America* (Chapel Hill, N.C., 1959), 33–60.
40. Nash, "Image of the Indian," 217–19 (quote from 218); Craven, *Southern Colonies,* 146, 172–73.
41. Gary B. Nash, *Red, White and Black: The Peoples of Early America* (Englewood Cliffs, N.J., 1974), 82–84; Alden Vaughan, *New England Frontier: Puritans and Indians, 1620–1675* (Boston, 1965), 189; Pearce, *Savagism,* 19–31; Jennings, *Invasion,* 241–42.
42. Walter T. Hagan, *American Indians* (Chicago, 1961), 14; Vaughan, *Frontier,* 320; Wilcomb E. Washburn, *The Indian in America* (New York, 1975), 131–32.

43. Washburn, *Indian in America*, 113; Vaughan, *Frontier*, 288–95, 315–20; Nash, *Red, White, and Black*, 127.

44. For a good brief discussion of the Tuscarora and Yamasee wars in the Carolinas, see Nash, *Red, White, and Black*, 145–51. Werner W. Crane also deals with these conflicts and the circumstances surrounding them in *The Southern Indian Frontier, 1670–1732* (Durham, N.C., 1928).

45. M. F. Katzen, "White Settlers and the Origin of a New Society, 1652–1778," in Monica Wilson and Leonard Thompson, eds., *The Oxford History of South Africa*, Vol. I (New York and Oxford, 1969), 189, 194.

46. Richard Elphick, "The Khoisan to c. 1770," in Elphick and Giliomee, *South African Society*, 10–11; *idem, Kraal and Castle: Khoikhoi and the Founding of White South Africa* (New Haven, 1977), 205–7.

47. Elphick, *Kraal*, 95–116; *idem*, "Khoisan," 9–12.

48. Elphick, "Khoisan," 10, 13–17; *idem, Kraal*, 99–103, 130–34, 151–70.

49. Elphick, *Kraal*, 170–74, 217–34; *idem*, "Khoisan," 18–23; Shula Marks, "Khoisan Resistance to the Dutch in the Seventeenth and Eighteenth Centuries," *Journal of African History*, XIII (1972), 69–71.

50. See Elphick's summary of how this occurred (*Kraal*, 237–39).

51. Katzen, "White Settlers," 208–13. The standard detailed account of Trekboer expansionism is still P. J. van der Merwe, *Die Trekboer in die Geskiedenis van die Kaap Kolonie* (Cape Town, 1938). See also Leonard Guelke, "The White Settlers, 1652–1780," in Elphick and Giliomee, *South African Society*, 58–67.

52. On the white image of the Khoikhoi, see Elphick, *Kraal*, 193–200; and I. A. MacCrone, *Race Attitudes in South Africa: Historical, Experimental and Psychological Studies* (London, 1937), 22, 46–49, 100–101, 118–20 (quote from 22).

53. On eastern Indian landholding forms, see Washburn, *Indian*, 32–33; and Harold E. Driver, *Indians of North America*, 2nd ed. (Chicago, 1969), 278–79.

54. Jennings, *Invasion*, 82–84, 128–45; Albert K. Weinberg, *Manifest Destiny* (Baltimore, 1935), 72–99; Pearce, *Savagism*, 66–104.

55. Richard Elphick and Robert Shell, "Intergroup Relations: Khoikhoi, Settlers, Slaves, and Free Blacks, 1652–1795," in Elphick and Giliomee, *South African Society*, 157–58; Schutte, "Company and Colonists," 190, 191–92.

56. F. le Vaillant, *Voyages dans l'intérieur de l'Afrique, 1781–1785* (Paris, 1932), 233. Translation is mine.

57. For comparable descriptions of American frontiersmen, see Arthur K. Moore, *The Frontier Mind: A Cultural Analysis of the Kentucky Frontiersman* (Lexington, Ky., 1957), 54. But Moore also shows that the frontiersman was viewed as an "agent of progress"; his prescribed

role was to prepare the way for civilization and then disappear like the Indian before him.

58. See MacCrone, *Race Attitudes,* 125–31.

59. See Chapter IV, below.

60. See Almon W. Lauber, *Indian Slavery in Colonial Times within the Present Limits of the United States* (New York, 1913).

61. Monica Wilson, "The Hunters and Herders," in Wilson and Thompson, *Oxford History,* 68.

62. Elphick, *Kraal,* 173–80; *idem,* "Khoisan," 28–30; S. Daniel Neumark, *Economic Influences on the South African Frontier, 1652–1836* (Stanford, Calif., 1957), 74; Monica Wilson, "Cooperation and Conflict: The Eastern Cape Frontier," in Wilson and Thompson, *Oxford History,* 246–49.

63. According to Neumark (*Economic Influences,* 113): "It is doubtful . . . whether the colonists could have defended themselves against the attacks of the Bushmen and other hostile native tribes without the help of their numerous and faithful Hottentot servants." See also Martin Legassick, "The Northern Frontier to 1820," in Elphick and Giliomee, *South African Society,* 260. But the Khoikhoi were not all collaborators, as Marks forcefully demonstrates in "Khoisan Resistance."

64. On the origins of the Cape Coloreds, see J. S. Marais, *The Cape Coloured People, 1652–1937* (Johannesburg, 1968); and Chapter III below.

65. For some anticipations of the "noble savage" theme in the colonial period, see Wilbur R. Jacobs, *Dispossessing the American Indian: Indians and Whites on the Colonial Frontier* (New York, 1972), 107–25. On the later development of the image, see Pearce, *Savagism,* 135–50, 169–95; and Bernard W. Sheehan, *Seeds of Extinction: Philanthropy and the American Indian* (Chapel Hill, N.C., 1973), 87–116.

66. See James Axtell, "The Scholastic Philosophy of the Wilderness," *William and Mary Quarterly,* XXIX (1972), 354; and Nash, "Image of the Indian," 227–28.

67. For examples of this derogatory physical stereotype of the Khoikhoi, see I. Schapera, ed., *The Early Cape Hottentots* (Cape Town, 1933), 43–45; Peter Kolb, *The Present State of the Cape of Good Hope* (New York and London, 1968; orig. pub. 1731), 52 ff.; C. P. Thunberg, *Travels in Europe, Africa and Asia,* Vol. II (London, 1795), 73, 186–87; and Andrew Sparrman, *A Voyage to the Cape of Good Hope, 1772–1776,* Vol. I (Dublin, 1785), 182–83.

68. For a general summary of Indian history during this period, see Washburn, *Indian,* 146–69; or Hagan, *American Indians,* 22–65.

69. Monica Wilson, "The Nguni People," in Wilson and Thompson, *Oxford History,* 85, 102, 107, 118–19, and *passim.*

70. See Hagan, *American Indians,* 26–27; Nash, *Red, White, and Black,*

304; and James H. O'Donnell III, *Southern Indians in the American Revolution* (Knoxville, Tenn., 1973), 6.

71. See Herman Giliomee, "The Eastern Frontier, 1770–1812," in Elphick and Giliomee, *South African Society,* 292–337; Wilson, "Eastern Cape Frontier," 233–46, 250–256; and W. M. Macmillan, *Bantu, Boer, and Briton: The Making of the South African Native Problem,* rev. ed. (Oxford, 1963), 38–52.

72. D. K. Fieldhouse, *The Colonial Empires from the Eighteenth Century* (New York, 1966), 79, 107; John C. Miller, *Origins of the American Revolution* (Boston, 1943), 74–77, 373–76.

73. See Herman Giliomee, "The Burgher Rebellions on tht Eastern Frontier," in Elphick and Giliomee, *South African Society,* 338–43; and J. S. Marais, *Maynier and the First Boer Republic* (Cape Town, 1944).

74. See Reginald Horsman, *Expansion and American Indian Policy, 1783–1812* (East Lansing, Mich., 1967); and Sheehan, *Seeds of Extinction.*

75. Reginald Horsman, *The Origins of Indian Removal* (East Lansing, Mich., 1970), 16–17, and *passim.*

76. For general accounts of Indian removal, see Ronald N. Satz, *American Indian Policy in the Jacksonian Era* (Lincoln, Neb., 1975); Dale van Every, *Disinherited: The Lost Birthright of the American Indian* (New York, 1966); and Grant Foreman, *Indian Removal: The Emigration of the Five Civilized Tribes,* rev. ed. (Norman, Okla., 1953).

77. Wilson, "Eastern Cape Frontier," 253–56; Macmillan, *Bantu, Boer, and Briton,* 73.

78. *Ibid.,* 82–84; Arthur Keppel-Jones, *South Africa: A Short History,* 4th ed. (London, 1968), 53–54.

79. See Macmillan, *Bantu, Boer, and Briton,* 95–193.

80. Macmillan *(ibid.)* stresses the philanthropic motive. John S. Galbraith acknowledges that Glenelg's decision was influenced by missionary and humanitarian pressure but asserts that it "was more significantly the result of economic considerations." *(Reluctant Empire: British Policy on the South African Frontier, 1834–1854* [Berkeley, Calif., 1963], 127–28). Galbraith's general thesis is that a desire for "rigorous economy" was the main factor limiting British expansionism in South Africa during the period of his study.

81. Macmillan, *Bantu, Boer, and Briton,* 195–200. For more on the causes of the Great Trek, see C. F. J. Muller, *Die Oorsprong van die Groot Trek* (Cape Town, 1974); and Chapter IV below.

82. For a comparative analysis that comes to similar conclusions, see Richard Ford, "The Frontier in South Africa: A Comparative Study of the Turner Thesis" (Ph.D. diss., University of Denver, 1966), 257–88, 107–38, 469–71.

83. For a general account of the Trek, see E. A. Walker, *The Great Trek* (London, 1934).

84. W. H. Macmillan, *The Cape Colour Question: A Historical Survey* (London, 1927), 233-46; *Bantu, Boer, and Briton,* 195-201. C. F. J. Muller emphasizes physical and economic insecurity as a major cause of the Trek but also acknowledges the political and ideological component. (*Oorsprong,* 171-222.) Actually the two cannot be clearly disassociated; for the *Voortrekkers* (members of organized parties that participated in the Great Trek) viewed their problems of survival and safety through an ideological lens that posited a certain pattern of race relations as just and proper.

85. On the nature and causes of British reluctance to support a moving frontier in this period, see Galbraith, *Reluctant Empire;* on the Great Trek as a manifestation of "sectionalism," see Ford, "Frontier in South Africa," 454-55.

86. See Macmillan, *Cape Colour Question,* 174-75.

87. Robert F. Berkhofer, *Salvation and the Savage: An Analysis of Protestant Missions and American Indian Response* (Lexington, Ky., 1969), 100-106; Satz, *Indian Policy,* 54-56.

88. Michael Rogin, *Fathers and Children: Andrew Jackson and the Subjugation of the American Indian* (New York, 1975), 166-69.

89. Satz, *Indian Policy,* 54.

90. See T. R. H. Davenport, "The Consolidation of a New Society: The Cape Colony," in Wilson and Thompson, *Oxford History,* 287-97; and C. W. de Kiewiet, *A History of South Africa: Social and Economic* (Oxford, 1941), 56-59. In a bold effort at revisionism, Neumark argued in 1957 that the trekboers were significantly involved in market relationships and that their movements were motivated primarily by rational expectations of profit. (*Economic Influences.*) But this view has been cogently criticized and modified by Guelke ("The White Settlers," 67-71), who concludes that the trekboer environment "offered few prospects for sustained growth," that the economy was "primitive," and that "a large proportion of its goods and services" were "produced and consumed at the same point" (70).

II. THE RISE OF RACIAL SLAVERY

1. See H. J. Nieboer, *Slavery as an Industrial System: Ethnological Researches* (The Hague, 1900); W. Kloosterboer, *Involuntary Labour Since the Abolition of Slavery: A Survey of Compulsory Labour Throughout the World* (Leiden, 1960); H. Hoetink, *Slavery and Race Relations in the Americas: An Inquiry into Their Nature and Nexus*

(New York, 1973); 65–83; and Evesey C. Domar, "The Causes of Slavery and Serfdom: A Hypothesis," *Journal of Economic History,* XXX (1970), 18–31.

2. Peter Kolb, *The Present State of the Cape* (New York and London, 1968; orig. pub. 1731), 46. On the early use and non-use of Khoikhoi labor see Richard Elphick, *Kraal and Castle: Khoikhoi and the Founding of White South Africa* (New Haven, 1977), 175–77, 102.

3. An example is the devastation associated with the enslavement of the basically nomadic Brazilian Indians by the Portuguese. See Gilberto Freyre, *The Masters and the Slaves: A Study in the Development of Brazilian Civilization,* tr. Samuel Putnam (New York, 1956), 154–58; and Alexander Marchant, *From Barter to Slavery: The Economic Relations of Portuguese and Indians in the Settlement of Brazil* (Baltimore, 1942).

4. On Indian slavery generally, see Almon Wheeler Lauber, *Indian Slavery in Colonial Times Within the Present Limits of the United States* (New York, 1913). On South Carolina, see Werner W. Crane, *The Southern Frontier, 1670–1732* (Durham, N.C., 1928), 109–14.

5. On Indian work patterns, see Wilcomb E. Washburn, *The Indian in America* (New York, 1975), 30; and Francis Jennings, *The Invasion of America: Indians, Colonialism, and the Cant of Conquest* (Chapel Hill, N.C., 1975), 60–69. On Indian craftsmen in South Carolina, see Crane, *Southern Frontier,* 113.

6. For other attempts to explain why Indians, as compared with blacks, were not more extensively and systematically enslaved, see Winthrop D. Jordan, *White Over Black: American Attitudes Toward the Negro* (Chapel Hill, N.C., 1968), 89–91; and David Brion Davis, *The Problem of Slavery in Western Culture* (Ithaca, N.Y., 1966), 176–81.

7. See Richard S. Dunn, *Sugar and Slaves: The Rise of the Planter Class in the English West Indies, 1624–1713* (Chapel Hill, N.C., 1972), 73, 264; and Carl Bridenbaugh, *No Peace Beyond the Line: The English in the Caribbean, 1624–1690* (New York, 1972), 263–64.

8. Edmund S. Morgan, *American Slavery—American Freedom: The Ordeal of Colonial Virginia* (New York, 1975), 65, 235–36, 295, and *passim;* Marcus Wilson Jernegan, *Laboring and Dependent Classes in Colonial America, 1607–1783* (New York, 1965), 45–56.

9. John Codman Hurd, *The Law of Freedom and Bondage in the United States,* Vol. I (New York, 1968; orig. pub. 1858), 138–39; Morgan, *Slavery—Freedom,* 126–29; James Curtis Ballagh, *White Servitude in Virginia: A Study of the System of Indentured Labor in the American Colonies* (Baltimore, 1895), 45.

10. Christopher Hill, *The Century of Revolution, 1603–1714* (London: Sphere Books, 1969), 33, 47–49; Morgan, *Slavery—Freedom,* 319–26.

11. See E. P. Thompson, *The Making of the English Working Class* (New York, 1963), 356–58; and *idem,* "Time, Work-Discipline, and Industrial Capitalism," *Past and Present,* XXXVIII (1967), 56–97. On the rise of the "free-market" ideology, see Karl Polanyi, *The Great Transformation* (Boston, 1957).

12. T. H. Breen, "A Changing Labor Force and Race Relations in Virginia," *Journal of Social History,* VII (1973), 3–25; Morgan, *Slavery—Freedom,* 215–70.

13. On efforts to extend the terms of service, see Morgan, *Slavery—Freedom,* 216–18. For a discussion of the conditions that led to an improvement in the status of white servants and increased the attractiveness of a slave labor system, see Oscar and Mary F. Handlin, "Origins of the Southern Labor System," *William and Mary Quarterly,* VII (1950), 210–14. The decline of British concern for overpopulation is described in Hill, *Century of Revolution,* 136–37, 182.

14. Donald Moodie, ed. and trans., *The Record; or a Series of Official Papers Relative to the Condition and Treatment of the Native Tribes of South Africa* (1838–41; reprint ed., Amsterdam and Cape Town, 1960), 95.

15. G. D. Scholtz, *Die Ontwikkeling van die Politieke Denke van die Afrikaner,* Vol. I (Johannesburg, 1965), 109; I. D. MacCrone, *Race Attitudes in South Africa: Historical, Experimental and Psychological Studies* (London, 1937), 30; C. R. Boxer, *The Dutch Seaborne Empire, 1600–1800* (New York, 1965), 79–83, 247; Leonard Guelke, "The White Settlers, 1652–1780," in Richard Elphick and Hermann Giliomee, eds., *The Shaping of South African Society, 1652–1820* (Cape Town, 1979), 43; A. J. Boëseken, *Nederlandske Commissarissen van de Kaap, 1657–1700* (The Hague, 1938), 62.

16. George Masselman, *The Cradle of Colonialism* (New Haven, Conn., 1963), 343, 358, 361, 428; James C. Armstrong, "The Slaves, 1652–1795," in Elphick and Giliomee, *South African Society,* 75–76.

17. MacCrone, *Race Attitudes,* 27–28; Moodie, *Record,* 90; Boxer, *Seaborne Empire,* 247.

18. MacCrone, *Race Attitudes,* 30–32; Moodie, *Record,* 125; A. J. Boëseken, *Slaves and Free Blacks at the Cape, 1658–1700* (Cape Town, 1977), 5–23, 74–75, and *passim;* Armstrong, "Slaves," 96, 107; Gerrit Schutte, "Company and Colonists at the Cape," in Elphick and Giliomee, *South African Society,* 187.

19. M. Whiting Spilhaus, *The First South Africans* (Cape Town and Johannesburg, 1949), 121–23; MacCrone, *Race Attitudes,* 49–50; Boxer, *Seaborne Empire,* 258–60.

20. M. F. Katzen, "White Settlers and the Origins of a New Society," in

Monica Wilson and Leonard Thompson, eds., *The Oxford History of South Africa*, Vol. I (New York and Oxford, 1969), 196–201; Victor de Kock, *Those in Bondage: An Account of the Life of the Slave at the Cape in the Days of the Dutch East India Company* (Pretoria, 1963), 63–64; *The Reports of Chavonnes and His Council and Van Imhoff at the Cape* (Cape Town, 1918), 87, 121, 126, and *passim*.

21. *Reports of Chavonnes*, 137.
22. Breen, "Changing Labor Force," 7–11; Morgan, *Slavery—Freedom*, 327–28.
23. See South Africa Archives Commission, *Kaapse Plakkaatboek*, Vol. II (Cape Town, 1948), 95–97.
24. Morgan, *Slavery—Freedom*, 338–62.
25. Armstrong, "Slaves," 97–98.
26. Davis, *Slavery in Western Culture*, 119–20.
27. *Ibid.*, 130; Morgan, *Slavery—Freedom*, 9; Daniel P. Mannix, in collaboration with Malcolm Cowley, *Black Cargoes: A History of the Atlantic Slave Trade, 1518–1865* (New York, 1962), 23–25.
28. Boxer, *Seaborne Empire*, 21, 238–39; Armstrong, "Slaves," 74.
29. Hurd, *Freedom and Bondage*, 161, 278.
30. See Davis, *Slavery in Western Culture*, 181–96, 207–8.
31. See *ibid.*, 85–90, 98–101, 198–99; and Lester B. Scherer, *Slavery and the Churches in Early America, 1619–1819* (Grand Rapids, Mich., 1975), 34–38.
32. Lorenzo Johnston Greene, *The Negro in Colonial New England* (New York, 1968), 167–90, 261–62; Robert C. Twombley and Robert H. Moore, "Black Puritan: The Negro in Seventeenth-Century Massachusetts," *William and Mary Quarterly*, XXIX (1967), 224–42.
33. H. P. Cruse, *Die Opheffing van die Kleurlingbevolking* (Stellenbosch, 1947), 224 and 224 n.; Richard Elphick and Robert Shell, "Intergroup Relations: Khoikhoi, Settlers, Slaves, and Free Blacks, 1652–1795," in Elphick and Giliomee, *South African Society*, 120.
34. See Jordan, *White Over Black*, 3–43; James Walvin, *Black and White: The Negro and English Society, 1555–1945* (London, 1973), 23–27; Davis, *Slavery in Western Culture*, 449–50.
35. See Eldred D. Jones, *The Elizabethan Image of Africa* (Charlottesville, Va., 1971), 48–49.
36. For a further discussion of the role of color in precolonization attitudes toward Africans, see George M. Fredrickson, "Toward a Social Interpretation of the Development of American Racism," in Nathan I. Huggins, Martin Kilson, and Daniel M. Fox, eds., *Key Issues in the Afro-American Slave Experience*, Vol. I (New York, 1971), 242–43.
37. On the preference for Asian over African slaves, see De Kock, *Those in*

Bondage, 53; Robert Percival, *An Account of the Cape of Good Hope* (New York, 1969; orig. pub. 1804), 285–88; and William J. Burchell, *Travels into the Interior of South Africa,* Vol. I (Cape Town, 1967; orig. pub. 1822), 32–33.

38. Hurd, *Freedom and Bondage,* 161, 169, 202, 205–7, 321.

39. See especially Handlin and Handlin, "Southern Labor System." A more carefully qualified version of the gradualist hypothesis can be found in Jordan, *White Over Black,* 71–82.

40. See Joseph Boskin, *Into Slavery: Racial Decisions in the Virginia Colony* (Philadelphia, 1976), 38–40; Jordan, *White Over Black,* 71–82; and Warren M. Billings, ed., *The Old Dominion in the Seventeenth Century: A Documentary History of Virginia, 1606–1689* (Chapel Hill, N.C., 1975), 148–50.

41. Wesley Frank Craven, *White, Red, and Black: The Seventeenth Century Virginian* (Charlottesville, Va., 1971), 81. For a somewhat different interpretation of the early census data, see Alden T. Vaughan, "Blacks in Virginia: A Note on the First Decade," *William and Mary Quarterly,* XXIX (1972), 469–78.

42. Helen Tunnicliff Catterall, *Judicial Cases Concerning American Slavery and the Negro,* Vol. I (Washington, D.C., 1926), 55–56, and 55n; Vaughan, "Blacks in Virginia," 470.

43. See Fredrickson, "American Racism," 244–45.

44. On these cases, see Catterall, *Judicial Cases,* 58; Boskin, *Into Slavery,* 40–42; Billings, *Old Dominion,* 152, 165–69; and *idem,* "The Cases of Fernando and Elizabeth Key: A Note on the Status of Blacks in Seventeenth Century Virginia," *William and Mary Quarterly,* XXX (1973), 467–73 (quote from 469–70).

45. Hurd, *Freedom and Bondage,* 232, 233, 235. Emphasis added.

46. Jordan, *White Over Black,* 96–97.

47. Morgan Godwyn, *The Negro and Indian's Advocate, Serving for their Admission into the CHURCH or a Persuasive to the Instruction and Baptising of the Negroes and Indians in our Plantations* (London, 1680), 36.

48. Fredrickson, "American Racism," 240–51.

49. This is the judgment of Edmund Morgan, *Slavery—Freedom,* 299.

50. Catterall, *Judicial Cases,* 57; Jernegan, *Laboring and Dependent Classes,* 26; Wilbert E. Moore, "Slave Law and Social Structure," *Journal of Negro History,* XXVI (1941), 174–75.

51. On slavery in New Netherlands, see Edgar J. McManus, *A History of Negro Slavery in New York* (Syracuse, N.Y., 1966), 1–22, 79–80. The Cape Slave Code, promulgated in 1754, is printed in South Africa Archives Commission, *Kaapse Plakkaatboek,* Vol. III (Cape Town,

1949), 1–6. On Dutch use of the Roman law of slavery, see Hurd, *Freedom and Bondage*, 277 n; and the letter from the Court of Justice to Major General Craig, 14 January 1796, *Records of the Cape Colony*, Vol. I (London, 1897), 304.

52. Elphick and Shell, "Intergroup Relations," 120.
53. Cruse, *Opheffing*, 245–47; MacCrone, *Race Attitudes*, 76–77; Elphick and Shell, "Intergroup Relations," 121; for the Dutch text of Van Rheede's instructions on slavery, see George McCall Theal, ed., *Belangrijke Historische Dokumenten Verzameld in de Kaap Kolonie en Elders*, Vol. I (Cape Town, 1896), 25–28.
54. Cruse, *Opheffing*, 250, 258; C. Spoelstra, *Bouwstoffen voor die Geschiedenis der Nederduitsch-Gereformeerde Kerken in Zuid-Africa*, Vol. I (Amsterdam and Cape Town, 1906), 65.
55. O. F. Mentzel, *A Geographical and Topographical Description of the Cape of Good Hope*, Vol. II (Cape Town, 1925; orig. pub. 1787), 131.
56. Andrew Sparrman, *A Voyage to the Cape of Good Hope . . . 1772–1776*, Vol. I (London, 1786), 58.
57. Jernegan, *Laboring and Dependent Classes*, 34–44.
58. Bernard Krüger, *The Pear Tree Blossoms: A History of the Moravian Mission Stations in South Africa* (Genadendal, South Africa, 1967), 101; British Parliament, *Papers Relative to the Condition and Treatment of the Native Inhabitants of the Cape of Good Hope or Beyond the Frontiers of that Colony*, Vol. I (London, 1835), 207–8; De Kock, *Those in Bondage*, 107; Elphick and Shell, "Intergroup Relations," 123–25.
59. Elphick and Shell, "Intergroup Relations," 122; De Kock, *Those in Bondage*, 112, 214–15.
60. MacCrone, *Race Attitudes*, 135.
61. *Records of the Cape Colony*, Vol. VIII (London, 1901), 490.
62. See Scherer, *Slavery and the Churches*, 82–103, 143–44; Gerald Mullin, *Flight and Rebellion: Slave Resistance in Eighteenth-Century Virginia* (New York, 1972); 17–18, 128–30; and Donald Matthews, *Religion in the Old South* (Chicago, 1977), 62–80, 136–50.
63. See Ch. IV below.
64. De Kock, *Those in Bondage*, 200–201; Elphick and Shell, "Intergroup Relations," 135–36.
65. Elphick and Shell, "Intergroup Relations," 136; Cruse, *Opheffing*, 253; Sheila Patterson, "Some Speculations on the Status and Role of the Free People of Colour in the Western Cape," in Meyer Fortes and Sheila Patterson, eds., *Studies in African Social Anthropology* (London, 1975), 72 (table). The exact number emancipated is uncertain: Elphick and Shell counted 1,075 apparently successful applications for manu-

mission while Cruse found only 893. Patterson's 1807 census figure for "free blacks" does not, of course, include the indeterminate number of people of part-slave ancestry who had been absorbed into the "white" population. (See Ch. III below.)

66. Hurd, *Freedom and Bondage,* 65.

67. Ira Berlin, *Slaves Without Masters: The Free Negro in the Antebellum South* (New York, 1974), 3–4, 137 (table), and *passim.*

68. See David W. Cohen and Jack P. Greene, eds., *Neither Slave Nor Free: The Freedmen of African Descent in the Slave Societies of the New World* (Baltimore, 1972); and Carl Degler, *Neither Black Nor White: Slavery and Race Relations in Brazil and the United States* (New York, 1971), especially 39–47, 88–92.

69. For more on caste and caste consciousness in the United States, see Chapters III and IV below. On the relative lack of status conflict between slaves and free Negroes in the United States, see Eugene D. Genovese, "The Slave States of North America," in Cohen and Greene, *Neither Slave Nor Free,* 272.

70. *Plakkaatboek,* II, 93–94; De Kock, *Those in Bondage,* 219; MacCrone, *Race Attitudes,* 70–73, 133–36; Elphick and Shell, "Intergroup Relations," 145–46. For more on intermarriage, see Ch. III.

71. For a fuller development of the argument that this was essentially a class society, see W. M. Freund, "Race in the Social Structure of South Africa," *Race and Class,* XVIII (1976), 53–67.

72. See W. H. Macmillan, *The Cape Colour Question: A Historical Survey* (London, 1927), 34–37, 71–72; and *idem, Bantu, Boer, and Briton: The Making of the South African Native Problem* (Oxford, 1963), 6. A fuller discussion of Khoikhoi indentured servitude is contained in Ch. IV below.

73. On some of the economic and geographical factors limiting the spread of a slave-based agriculture, see Katzen, "New Society," 202, and *passim;* and Guelke, "White Settlers," 51–67. On how slaves were employed, see De Kock, *Those in Bondage,* 53–70.

74. See Ch. IV below for a fuller discussion of white responses to emancipation.

75. De Kock, *Those in Bondage,* 153–56, 167–69, 189; *Plakkaatboek,* II, 149–50; H. C. V. Leibbrandt, *Précis of the Archives of the Cape of Good Hope: Requesten,* Vol. I (Cape Town, 1905), 20–22; Armstrong, "Slaves," 89, 103.

76. On the laws and enforcement policies relating to the killing of slaves in the South, see Eugene D. Genovese, *Roll, Jordan, Roll: The World the Slaves Made* (New York, 1974), 37–39; and Kenneth M. Stampp, *The Peculiar Institution: Slavery in the Ante-Bellum South* (New York, 1956), 221–24.

77. See Cruse, *Opheffing,* 205–22, and Mentzel, *Description of the Cape,* 129.

78. De Kock, *Those in Bondage,* 173–85; Lewis J. Greenstein, "Slave and Citizen: The South African Case," *Race,* XV (July, 1973), 37–38; Mentzel, *Description of the Cape,* 133.

79. See Greenstein, "Slave and Citizen," for an argument that the Cape's reputation for comparatively mild treatment was undeserved. But a case can still be made that the conditions faced by the typical Cape slave, bad as they were, were still not as harsh as those confronting slaves in most New World plantation societies. Cape masters did not usually have the same economic incentives to overwork their slaves and did not have access to the cheap replacements that were available to planters in the Americas so long as the West African trade was open.

III. RACE MIXTURE AND THE COLOR LINE

1. See the following comparative and theoretical discussions of miscegenation: Pierre van den Berghe, "Hypergamy, Hypergenation, and Miscegenation," *Race and Ethnicity: Essays in Comparative Sociology* (New York, 1970), 54–63; R. A. Schermerhorn, *Comparative Ethnic Relations: A Framework for Theory and Research* (New York, 1970), 204–6; Philip Mason, *Patterns of Dominance* (London, 1970), 87–103, and *passim;* and Noel P. Gist and Anthony Gary Dworkin, eds., *The Blending of Races: Marginality and Identity in World Perspective* (New York, 1972), 1–23.

2. Louis Wirth and Herbert Goldhamer, "The Hybrid and the Problem of Miscegenation," in Otto Klineberg, ed., *Characteristics of the American Negro* (New York, 1944), 253–54.

3. For attempts by social scientists to explain the North American descent rule, see Marvin Harris, *Patterns of Race in the Americas* (New York, 1964), 56, 79–94; H. Hoetink, *The Two Variants of Caribbean Race Relations: A Contribution to the Sociology of Segmented Societies* (London, 1967), 46–47, and *passim;* and *idem, Slavery and Race Relations in the Americas: An Inquiry into Their Nature and Nexus* (New York, 1973), 9–20, and *passim.*

4. Edward Bryon Reuter, *Race Mixture: Studies in Intermarriage and Miscegenation* (New York, 1968; orig. pub. 1931), 3.

5. In addition to the works cited in note 3, see Carl Degler, *Neither Black Nor White: Slavery and Race Relations in Brazil and the United States* (New York, 1971); David W. Cohen and Jack P. Greene, eds., *Neither Slave Nor Free: The Freedmen of African Descent in the Slave Societies of the New World* (Baltimore, 1972); and

Donald L. Horowitz, "Color Differentiation in the American Systems of Slavery," *Journal of Interdisciplinary History*, III (1973), 509–41.

6. See Elizabeth P. Wittermans, "The Eurasians of Indonesia," in Gist and Dworkin, *Blending of Races*, 79–102; Amory Vandenbosch, *The Dutch East Indies: Its Government, Problems and Politics* (Berkeley, Calif., 1944), 7–10; Justus M. van der Kroef, "The Eurasian Minority in Indonesia," *American Sociological Review*, XVIII (1953), 484–93; and Paul W. van der Veur, "The Eurasians of Indonesia: A Problem and Challenge in Colonial History," *Journal of Southeast Asian History*, IX (1968), 191–207.

7. For a systematic elaboration of a similar typology, see Mason, *Patterns of Dominance*, 90–91.

8. The literature of "caste" is enormous. But see especially W. Lloyd Warner, "American Caste and Class," *American Journal of Sociology*, XLII (1936), 234–37; John Dollard, *Caste and Class in a Southern Town*, 3rd ed. (New York, 1957), 61–96; Edward W. Pohlman, "Evidences of Disparity Between the Hindu Practice of Caste and the Ideal Type," *American Sociological Review*, XVI (1951), 375–79; and Michael Banton, *Race Relations* (New York, 1967), 142–62, and *passim*. For an excellent discussion of how bans on intermarriage function as central features of a caste hierarchy, see David Fowler, "Northern Attitudes Towards Interracial Marriage: A Study of Legislation and Public Opinion in the Middle Atlantic States and States of the Old Northwest" (Ph.D. diss., Yale University, 1963), 10–20. The following discussion of American attitudes toward intermarriage owes much to Fowler's work. I am grateful to him for allowing me to use his manuscript.

9. See Winthrop D. Jordan, *White Over Black: American Attitudes Toward the Negro, 1550–1812* (Chapel Hill, N.C., 1968), 32–43, for a discussion of these Elizabethan attitudes towards black sexuality. On the growing sexual repressiveness of the early seventeenth century, see Lawrence Stone, *The Family, Sex, and Marriage in England, 1500–1800* (London, 1977), 523, 603–5, 615, 623–24.

10. John Codman Hurd, *The Law of Freedom and Bondage in the United States*, Vol. I (New York, 1968; orig. pub. 1858), 229; Edmund S. Morgan, *American Slavery—American Freedom: The Ordeal of Colonial Virginia* (New York, 1975), 333, 155–56.

11. Jordan, *White Over Black*, 79; Hurd, *Freedom and Bondage*, 249–50, 236; Eugene Irving McCormac, *White Servitude in Maryland, 1634–1820* (Baltimore, 1904), 67–69; Fowler, "Attitudes Towards Interracial Marriage," 45.

12. Fowler, "Attitudes Towards Interracial Marriage," 50–62; Jordan, *White Over Black*, 139.

13. Hurd, *Freedom and Bondage,* 249, 236. Emphasis added in second quotation.
14. Fowler, "Attitudes Towards Interracial Marriage," 37–41. In the long footnote on pages 38–39 Fowler documents fifteen cases of intermarriage or open cohabitation reported during the colonial period. Only two were unions of white men and black women. But Edmund Morgan has uncovered four cases in Virginia before the prohibition of 1691, two involving white males and black females. (*American Slavery—American Freedom,* 334.)
15. Fowler, "Attitudes Towards Interracial Marriage," 37–39.
16. James Walvin, *Black and White: The Negro and English Society* (London, 1973), 52, 57, 99–100.
17. See Marcus Wilson Jernegan, *Laboring and Dependent Classes in Colonial America, 1607–1683* (New York, 1965), 55, 151; and Warren Billings, ed., *The Old Dominion in the Seventeenth Century: A Documentary History of Virginia, 1606–1689* (Chapel Hill, N.C., 1975), 131, 144.
18. See John H. Russell, *The Free Negro in Virginia, 1619–1865* (Baltimore, 1913), 91, 123–25, and *passim;* Jordan, *White Over Black,* 78–80, 122–28, 136–44; Fowler, "Attitudes Towards Interracial Marriage," 78–79; Morgan, *American Slavery—American Freedom,* 335–36.
19. Hurd, *Freedom and Bondage,* 250. For a provocative discussion of the anxieties that may have lain behind the use of castration, see Jordan, *White Over Black,* 154–59.
20. See Jordan, *White Over Black,* 167–78.
21. Horowitz, "Color Differentiation," 526–30.
22. Quoted in Herbert S. Klein, *Slavery in the Americas: A Comparative Study of Virginia and Cuba* (Chicago, 1967), 232–33.
23. Horowitz, "Color Differentiation," 530–38.
24. Klein, *Slavery in the Americas,* 232. On the fear of free Negroes as instigators of rebellion in the antebellum period see Ira Berlin, *Masters Without Slaves: Free Negroes in the Antebellum South* (New York, 1974).
25. On patterns of miscegenation in the South from the seventeenth century to the Civil War, see especially James Hugo Johnston, *Race Relations in Virginia and Miscegenation in the South* (Amherst, Mass., 1970), 163–314. Johnston documents the persistence of sexual relations between white women and black men, as well as the pressures that inhibited them (250–68).
26. See Morgan, *American Slavery—American Freedom.*
27. On the probable relationship between Puritan fears of "social disorder" and repressive legislation against free Negroes, including the

anti-miscegenation laws of 1705, see Robert C. Twombley and Robert H. Moore, "Black Puritan: The Negro in Seventeenth Century Massachusetts," *William and Mary Quarterly,* XXIV (1967), 238–42. For a description of the Massachusetts and Pennsylvania legislation, see Fowler, "Attitudes Towards Interracial Marriage," 48–55.

28. Fowler, "Attitudes Towards Interracial Marriage," 60–61, 68–70. For an excellent general account of the plantation society of colonial South Carolina, see Peter H. Wood, *Black Majority: Negroes in Colonial South Carolina from 1670 through the Stono Rebellion* (New York, 1974).

29. See C. R. Boxer, *The Dutch Seaborne Empire, 1600–1800* (New York, 1965), 216–21; Vandenbosch, *Dutch East Indies,* 8; Van der Veur, "Eurasians of Indonesia," 191; Wittermans, "Eurasians," in Gist and Dworkin, *Blending of Races,* 81–82.

30. J. S. Furnivall, *Netherlands India: A Study of Plural Economy* (Cambridge, Eng., 1944), 465.

31. Eric A. Walker, *A History of Southern Africa,* 3rd ed. (London, 1959), 48.

32. I. A. MacCrone, *Race Attitudes in South Africa: Historical, Experimental and Psychological Studies* (London, 1937), 43; Richard Elphick, *Kraal and Castle: Khoikhoi and the Founding of White South Africa* (New Haven, 1977), 201–2.

33. J. A. Heese, *Die Herkoms van die Afrikaner, 1657–1867* (Cape Town, 1971), 10.

34. See Wilbur Jacobs, *Dispossessing the American Indian: Indians and Whites on the Colonial Frontier* (New York, 1972), 116–19.

35. William K. Boyd, ed., *William Byrd's Histories of the Dividing Line between Virginia and North Carolina* (Raleigh, N.C., 1929), 3–4; Robert Beverley, *The History and Present State of Virginia: A Selection,* ed. David Freeman Hawke (Indianapolis, 1971), 18–19, 150.

36. Ann Maury, *Memoirs of a Huguenot Family* (Baltimore, 1967), 349–50.

37. MacCrone, *Race Attitudes,* 42; George McCall Theal, *History of South Africa Under the Administration of the Dutch East India Company,* Vol. I (London, 1897), 58; Heese, *Herkoms,* 63–65.

38. Boxer, *Seaborne Empire,* 263–64; MacCrone, *Race Attitudes,* 68–69; Donald Moodie, ed. and trans., *The Record: Or a Series of Official Papers Relative to the Condition and Treatment of the Native Tribes of South Africa* (1838–41; reprinted, Amsterdam and Cape Town, 1960), 309.

39. George McCall Theal, ed., *Belangrijke Historische Dokumenten Verzameld in de Kaap-Kolonie en Elders,* Vol. I (Cape Town, 1896),

25–28, 40–41; MacCrone, *Race Attitudes,* 69; H. P. Cruse, *Die Opheffing van die Kleurlingbevolking* (Stellenbosch, 1947), 247.

40. See Chapter II above for an account of Van Rheede's proposals for manumission of children of mixed parentage. For evidence of the unbalanced sex ratio of company slaves, see A. J. Böeseken, *Slaves and Free Blacks at the Cape, 1658–1700* (Cape Town, 1977), 52–53.

41. Heese, *Herkoms.* According to this source book for Afrikaner genealogy, there were, by my count, 69 founding marriages involving unmixed nonwhite women between 1688 and 1807, out of 500 in which one spouse had some nonwhite ancestry.

42. O. F. Mentzel, *A Geographical and Topographical Description of the Cape of Good Hope,* Vol. II (Cape Town, 1925), 130.

43. *Ibid.,* 81, 109–10; Robert Percival, *An Account of the Cape of Good Hope* (New York, 1969; orig. pub. 1804), 291–92. J. Hoge's *Personalia of the Germans of the Cape, 1652–1806* (Cape Town, 1946), a compendium of the recorded information on approximately 4,000 German immigrants, contains 106 cases of concubinage which came to public attention, usually because the fathers offered their children for baptism or sought to provide for their mistresses and/or children in their wills.

44. "The Origin and Incidence of Miscegenation at the Cape during the Dutch East India Company's Regime, 1652–1795," *Race Relations Journal,* XX (1953), 27. The reliability of this study might be questioned because of the anonymity of the author. But the article has all the earmarks of having been written by a competent historian. Such information as can be checked against other sources is reasonably accurate, and a possible explanation for the author's concealing his identity is the sensitive nature within South Africa of the question of white racial ancestry.

45. M. C. Botha, in association with Judith Pritchard, *Blood Group Gene Frequencies: An Indication of the Genetic Constitution of Population Samples in Cape Town,* supplement to the *South African Medical Journal,* 1 April 1972, 5.

46. Hoge, *Personalia.* For the approximately 4,000 Germans listed, 288 racially mixed marriages are recorded. The total number of marriages was of course much higher. Of the 100 recorded marriages that I sampled (pp. 314–35), 21 were classified as mixed because they were with women of slave origin, as indicated by the absence of a last name and the substitution of a non-European society of origin or "of the Cape" for slaves born in South Africa.

47. Heese, *Herkoms,* 67–170. The actual figures (by my count) can be seen from the following table:

Period	No. of founding marriages	No. involving nonwhite spouse	Percentage
1688–1717	326	54	16.6
1718–1747	382	80	20.9
1748–1777	594	145	24.4
1778–1807	820	221	27.0
	2,122	500	23.6

48. W. M. Freund, "Race in the Social Structure of South Africa 1652–1836," *Race and Class*, XVIII (1976), 57.

49. This problem of second- and third-generation marriages was suggested to me in a personal communication of August 21, 1978, from Hermann Giliomee of the University of Stellenbosch. Dr. Giliomee cites an estimate that the total of all marriages at the Cape from 1652 to 1807 was somewhere between 5,500 and 7,000 and notes that Heese's approximately 2,000 founding marriages are thus a minority of the total. But presumably some of the other marriages resulted in "Coloreds" rather than Afrikaners. Furthermore, even if the 506 mixed marriages occurring before 1807 (this figure includes the 6 recorded between 1657 and 1687) were all the mixed marriages that occurred (which is clearly not the case), they would still constitute somewhere between 7.2 and 9.2 percent of all marriages, an obvious undercount that is nevertheless not very far out of line with some of the estimates given above. Hence I cannot agree with the conclusion in Richard Elphick and Hermann Giliomee, eds., *The Shaping of South African Society, 1652–1820* (Cape Town, 1979), that recent scholars have tended to overestimate the rate of mixed marriages and that such unions were "fairly rare" (130, 372). But the question is of course a relative one, and I am aware that my perspective of a comparison with the United States draws attention to a phenomenon that might be less striking in other contexts.

50. Hoetink, *Slavery and Race Relations*, 105.

51. See Heese, *Herkoms*, 19, 34.

52. See Hoetink, *Caribbean Race Relations*, 120–60.

53. Cruse, *Opheffing*, 266–67.

54. See note 37 to Chapter II, above.

55. Carl Pehr Thunberg, *Travels in Europe and Asia, Made Between the Years 1770 and 1779*, Vol. I (London, 1795), 112. On the ease with which women of mixed blood found European husbands, see "Miscegenation at the Cape," 24–25; Percival, *Cape of Good Hope*, 292; and Heese, *Herkoms*, 13.

56. Examples are from Hoge, *Personalia*, 302–3, 416–17, 8.

57. Hermann Giliomee, *Die Kaap Tydens die Eerste Britse Bewind, 1795–1803* (Cape Town, 1975), 22.

58. Andrew Sparrman, *A Voyage to the Cape of Good Hope . . . 1772–1776*, Vol. I (London, 1786), 284–85.

59. Degler, *Neither Black Nor White*.

60. Heese, *Herkoms*, 21, 36, 56 (table).

61. Jordan, *White Over Black*, 171–73.

62. Helen Tunicliff Catterall, *Judicial Cases Concerning American Slavery and the Negro*, Vol. II (Washington, 1929), 358; Berlin, *Slaves Without Masters*, 97–99, 161–65.

63. H. C. V. Leibbrandt, *Précis of the Archives of the Cape of Good Hope: Requesten*, Vol. I (Cape Town, 1905), 170–71.

64. MacCrone, *Race Attitudes*, 133.

65. Leibbrandt, *Précis: Requesten*, 221–23.

66. Giliomee, *Die Eerste Britse Bewind*, 22.

67. Victor de Kock, *Those in Bondage: An Account of the Life of the Slave at the Cape in the Days of the Dutch East India Company* (Pretoria, 1963), 122.

68. See Chapter IV below.

69. For a vivid description of the jockeying for status that occurred around the turn of the eighteenth century, see Petrus Borchardus Borcherds, *An Autobiographical Memoir* (Cape Town, 1861), 193–94. On the general tendency of elite Europeans to encourage racial stratification, see Hermann Giliomee and Richard Elphick, "The Structure of European Domination at the Cape, 1652–1820," in Elphick and Giliomee, *South African Society*, 376, and *passim*.

70. Of the Afrikaner founding marriages between 1808 and 1837, 132 out of 1,079 were inter-racial. (Heese, *Herkoms*, 171–222.)

71. W. Bird, *The State of the Cape of Good Hope in 1822* (Cape Town, 1966; orig. pub. 1823), 76–77.

72. See Freund, "Race in the Social Structure of South Africa," for the development of a similar argument.

73. *Ibid.*, 59–61; Martin Legassick, "The Northern Frontier to 1820: The Emergence of the Griqua People," in Elphick and Giliomee, *South African Society*, 256–57, 259–61, and *passim*; J. S. Marais, *The Cape Coloured People, 1652–1937* (Johannesburg, 1968), 10–12, 32–73. See also Robert Ross, *Adam Kok's Griquas: A Study in the Development of Stratification in South Africa* (Cambridge, Eng., 1975).

74. Leibbrandt, *Précis: Requesten*, 293. Jordan, *White Over Black*, 543, and *passim*.

75. On the weakness of most forms of community in the colonial and antebellum South, see David Bertelson, *The Lazy South* (New York,

1967). Bertelson, however, does not deal with the way in which an exceptional stress on family and kinship partially compensated for the loss of other forms of cohesion and stability. The remarkable extent to which eighteenth-century Virginia society was family-centered is well conveyed in Edmund S. Morgan, *Virginians at Home* (Williamsburg, Va., 1952). On the ability of white women to discourage open concubinage in the North American colonies, see Degler, *Neither Black Nor White*, 235-39.

76. See Michael Zuckerman, *Peaceable Kingdoms: New England Towns in the Eighteenth Century* (New York, 1970), 102-18. As partial explanation for the very small percentage of blacks in New England as compared with other colonies, Zuckerman notes "the deliberate policy of the communities of the region. Committed to a conception of social order that precluded pluralism, the men of Massachusetts offered the chilliest reception to men who were so clearly not of their own kind" (180).

77. Samuel Sewall, *The Selling of Joseph: A Memorial* (Northampton, Mass., 1969; orig. pub. 1700), 10.

78. See Jordan, *White Over Black*, 579-81, and *passim*; and Ronald T. Takaki, *Iron Cages: Race and Culture in Nineteenth-Century America* (New York, 1979), 11-15.

79. Robert Ross, "The 'White' Population of South Africa in the Eighteenth Century," *Population Studies*, XXIX (1975), 221 (table); Leonard Guelke, "The White Settlers, 1652-1680," in Elphick and Giliomee, *South African Society*, 41.

80. According to the Dutch historian P. J. Idenburg, the efforts of the government around 1800 to create strong communal bonds among the colonists were, on the whole, unsuccessful: "Even the common interests of the various groups did not constitute a strong tie in view of the size of the country and the spread of population." (*The Cape of Good Hope at the Turn of the Eighteenth Century* [Leiden, Neth., 1963], 111-12.)

81. An indication of casual Jamaican attitudes toward concubinage can be found in Edward Long, *The History of Jamaica . . . ,* Vol. II (London, 1774), 328 (quoted in Jordan, *White Over Black*, 140). The "Surinam marriage" as a customary but unsanctified union between Europeans and black or mulatto women is described in J. G. A. Stedman, *A Narrative of a Five Year's Expedition, against the Revolted Negroes of Surinam. . . .* (London, 1813), 2 vols.

82. Quoted in MacCrone, *Race Attitudes*, 76-77.

83. Giliomee, *Eerste Britse Bewind*, 258-59.

84. Sheila Patterson, "Some Speculations on the Status and Role of the Free People of Colour in the Western Cape," in Meyer Fortes and

Sheila Patterson, eds., *Studies in African Social Anthropology* (London, 1975), 172; James C. Armstrong, "The Free Black Community at the Cape of Good Hope in the Seventeenth and Eighteenth Centuries" (unpublished paper), 5.

85. See Fowler, "Attitudes Towards Interracial Marriage," 82–219; John Hope Franklin, *The Free Negro in North Carolina, 1790–1860* Chapel Hill, N.C., 1943), 35–37; Berlin, *Masters Without Slaves,* 97–99, 161–63.

86. Berlin, *Masters Without Slaves,* 163, 214–16, 364–67. For evidence of the growing white antipathy to the lower South's free Negroes (who were mostly mulatto) and the resulting negation of any "three-category" tendencies, see Marina Wikramanayake, *A World in Shadow: The Free Black in Antebellum South Carolina* (Columbia, S.C., 1973), 169–70.

87. See Reuter, *Race Mixture,* 82–98; Charles S. Magnum, Jr., *The Legal Status of the Negro* (Chapel Hill, N.C., 1940), 236–73; and Fowler, "Attitudes Towards Interracial Marriage," 220–334.

88. Although seriously flawed by its racial biases, Edward Bryon Reuter's *The Mulatto in the United States* (Boston, 1918) remains the major study of the widely acknowledged phenomenon of mulatto pre-eminence among black leadership in the early twentieth century. See E. Franklin Frazier, *The Negro Family in the United States* (Chicago, 1966), 295–333, for a discussion of color consciousness and status as it existed in the black community of the 1930s and earlier.

89. On the history of the Cape Coloreds and their problematical situation in the South African socio-racial structure, see Marais, *Cape Coloured People;* Sheila Patterson, *Colour and Culture in South Africa: A Study of the Status of the Cape Coloured People within the Social Structure of the Union of South Africa* (London, 1953); H. P. Dickie-Clark, *The Marginal Situation: A Sociological Study of a Coloured Group* (London, 1966); D. P. Botha, *Die Opkoms van Ons Derde Stand* (Cape Town, 1960); and Michael G. Whisson and Hendrik W. van der Merwe, eds., *Coloured Citizenship in South Africa* (Cape Town: The Abe Bailey Institute of Interracial Studies, 1972). On the segregation of Coloreds, see Chapter VI below.

90. See Marais, *Cape Coloured People,* 9–13; and Michael G. Whisson, *The Fairest Cape: An Account of the Coloured People in the District of Simonstown* (Johannesburg, n.d.), 5–14.

91. Although the Cape census of 1865 continued to enumerate "Hottentots," they were outnumbered (132,655 to 81,598) by "others" who were neither European nor "Kaffir" (Bantu-speaking African). *Census of the Cape Colony—1865* (Cape Town, 1866), 7–11.

92. See Chapter VI below.

93. *Het Volksblad,* 15 July 1876, translated and reprinted in André du Toit, *Roots of Afrikaner Political Thought* (Cape Town: Center for Extra-Mural Studies, 1977), pt. IV, 19.

94. Stanley Trapido, "The Origin and Development of the African Political Organization," *Collected Seminar Papers on the Societies of Southern Africa in the Nineteenth and Twentieth Centuries,* I (London: Institute of Commonwealth Studies, 1970), 90–91.

95. See George Findlay, *Miscegenation: A Study of the Biological Sources of Inheritance of the South African European Population* (Pretoria, 1936), 22.

96. For evidence of recent passing of a quasi-institutionalized nature, see Graham Watson, *Passing for White: A Study of Racial Assimilation in a South African School* (London, 1970).

97. For a brief discussion of the principles of racial classification under apartheid, see Chapter VI, below.

98. Union of South Africa, *Report of the Commission on Mixed Marriages,* U.G. 30 (1939), 1.

99. Sarah Gertrude Millin, *The South Africans* (London, 1926), 199–200.

100. But the fact that such passing has occurred is suggested by a physical anthropologist's calculation that "approximately 23% of the persons classified as white in 1960 have an African element in their inherited biological make-up." (Robert P. Stuckert, "Race Mixture: The African Ancestry of White Americans," in Peter B. Hammond, ed., *Physical Anthropology and Archaeology* [New York, 1964], 195.) One suspects, however, that most of these people would be unaware of any African genetic inheritance, which would normally be of remote origin. The South African proportion of nonwhite ancestry among whites would appear to be much higher, as suggested by Botha and Pritchard, *Blood Group Frequencies.* Botha and Pritchard found that the whites sampled drew roughly 7 percent of their blood-group genes from non-European sources (21–24). The comparable figure for sampled white populations in the United States is less than 1 percent. (Laurel Newell Morris, ed., *Human Populations, Genetic Variation, and Evolution* [San Francisco, 1971], 448.) It is difficult for a scholar not trained in population genetics to evaluate these figures or extrapolate from them; but, for what it's worth, it seems likely to me that if a nonwhite genetic contribution of less than 1 percent can be shared by 23 percent of the population, then one of 7 percent could well mean that a majority of South African whites have some degree of nonwhite ancestry.

101. Proposals to co-opt the Coloreds are discussed briefly in Chapter VI below.

IV. LIBERTY, UNION, AND WHITE SUPREMACY

1. See Robert R. Palmer, *The Age of Democratic Revolution: A Political History of Europe and America, 1760–1800,* 2 vols. (Princeton, N.J., 1959–64).
2. For an incisive discussion of these beliefs, as they related specifically to the institution of slavery, see David Brion Davis, *The Problem of Slavery in Western Culture* (Ithaca, N.Y., 1966), 62–90, and *passim.*
3. John Winthrop, "A Modell of Christian Charity," in Perry Miller and Thomas H. Johnson, eds., *The Puritans* (Boston, 1938), 195.
4. Alexander Pope, *Essay on Man,* IV, lines 49–50.
5. An excellent account of the eighteenth-century debates on the meaning of racial diversity can be found in Winthrop D. Jordan, *White Over Black: American Attitudes Toward the Negro, 1550–1812* (Chapel Hill, N.C., 1968), 216–65, 482–511.
6. *Ibid.,* 492–94.
7. Thomas Jefferson, *Notes on Virginia* (1784), in Adrienne Koch and William Peden, eds., *The Life and Selected Writings of Thomas Jefferson* (New York, 1944), 261; Jordan, *White Over Black,* 439, 492. Gary Wills has recently argued that the central role of the moral sense in Jefferson's social philosophy meant that he was according blacks the most essential kind of equality when he distinguished between their apparent intellectual limitations and their innate moral capabilities. (*Inventing America: Jefferson's Declaration of Independence* [Garden City, N.Y., 1978], 218–28.) On Jefferson's complex legacy to the later slavery controversy, see Merrill D. Peterson, *The Jefferson Image in the American Mind* (New York, 1960), 164–89. Support for the argument that moral rather than intellectual inferiority was the main point at issue in the antebellum controversy can be found in George M. Fredrickson, *The Black Image in the White Mind: The Debate on Afro-American Character and Destiny, 1817–1914* (New York, 1971), 43–164, *passim.* A recent re-evaluation of Jefferson's attitudes on slavery and race that is both thorough and judicious is John Chester Miller, *The Wolf by the Ears: Thomas Jefferson and Slavery* (New York, 1977).
8. This process is described in Arthur Zilversmit, *The First Emancipation: The Abolition of Slavery in the North* (Chicago, 1967).
9. Duncan J. MacLeod, *Slavery, Race, and the American Revolution* (Cambridge, Eng., 1974), 75–76; Miller, *Wolf by the Ears,* 13.
10. J. R. Pole, *The Pursuit of Equality in American History* (Berkeley, 1978), 25, 52.

11. Jefferson, *Notes on Virginia,* 256.

12. Zilversmit, *First Emancipation,* 222–26; Leon F. Litwack, *North of Slavery: The Negro in the Free States, 1790–1860* (Chicago, 1961), 3–29, and *passim.*

13. Fredrickson, *Black Image,* 6–12. The best account of the colonizationist impulse is P. J. Staudenraus, *The African Colonization Movement, 1816–1865* (New York, 1961).

14. See Ronald T. Takaki, *Iron Cages: Race and Culture in Nineteenth Century America* (New York, 1979), 36–64.

15. Litwack, *North of Slavery,* 31; Takaki, *Iron Cages,* 15.

16. Gerrit Schutte, "Company and Colonists at the Cape," in Richard Elphick and Hermann Giliomee, eds., *The Shaping of South African Society, 1652–1820* (Cape Town, 1979), 198–202. See also Schutte, *De Nederlandse Patriotten en de Koloniën: Een Onderzoek naar hun Denkbeelden en Optreden, 1770–1800* (Groningen, 1974), 60–87; and Coenraad Beyers, *Die Kaapse Patriotte* (Cape Town, 1930).

17. See Hermann Giliomee, "The Burgher Rebellions on the Eastern Frontier, 1795–1815," in Elphick and Giliomee, *South African Society,* 338–54; and J. S. Marais, *Maynier and the First Boer Republic* (Cape Town, 1944), 89–90.

18. See the Patriot Memorial of 1779 in Beyers, *Kaapse Patriotte,* 9–37.

19. W. M. Macmillan, *The Cape Colour Question: A Historical Survey* (London, 1927), 39–48; Circular from Sir John Cradock to the Landdrosts, April 20, 1812, *Records of the Cape Colony,* Vol. VIII (London, 1901), 380.

20. J. S. Marais, *The Cape Coloured People, 1652–1937* (Johannesburg, 1968), 121–29; Macmillan, *Cape Colour Question,* 161–62.

21. *Records of the Cape Colony,* VIII, 380; Macmillan, *Cape Colour Question,* 99.

22. See Giliomee, "Burgher Rebellions," 348–51.

23. Letter from Landdrost van der Riet and Heemraden of Stellenbosch, 6/2/1797, published in André Du Toit, *Roots of Afrikaner Political Thought* (Cape Town: Centre for Extra-Mural Studies, 1977), pt. II, 8.

24. For an account of the constitutional compromises on slavery and the background of the Missouri debate, see Donald L. Robinson, *Slavery in the Structure of American Politics, 1765–1820* (New York, 1971).

25. Allan Nevins, *The Emergence of Lincoln,* Vol. II (New York, 1950), 468.

26. David Potter, *The South and the Sectional Conflict* (Baton Rouge, La., 1968), 114–16.

27. See especially works by Eugene Genovese—*The Political Economy of Slavery: Studies in the Economy and Society of the Slave South* (New

York, 1965), and *The World the Slaveholders Made: Two Essays on Interpretation* (New York, 1969); and Eric Foner—*Free Soil, Free Labor, Free Men: The Ideology of the Republican Party before the Civil War* (New York, 1970) and "Politics, Ideology, and the Origins of the American Civil War," in George M. Fredrickson, ed., *A Nation Divided: Problems and Issues of the Civil War and Reconstruction* (Minneapolis, 1975), 15–34. Also in a neo-Marxist vein is the provocative interpretation of the Civil War in Barrington Moore, Jr., *Social Origins of Dictatorship and Democracy: Lord and Peasant in the Making of the Modern World* (Boston, 1966), 111–55.

28. Joel Kovel, *White Racism: A Psychohistory* (New York, 1970), 32.
29. See Fredrickson, *Black Image,* 43–70, 130–64, 323–24.
30. See Eugene H. Berwanger, *The Frontier against Slavery: Western Anti-Negro Prejudice and the Slavery Extension Controversy* (Urbana, Ill., 1967); and James A. Rawley, *Race and Politics: "Bleeding Kansas" and the Coming of the Civil War* (Philadelphia, 1969).
31. See William H. and Jane H. Pease, "Antislavery Ambivalence: Immediatism, Expediency, and Race," *American Quarterly,* XVII (1965), 682–95.
32. Fredrickson, *Black Image,* 27–42, 51, and *passim;* Ronald G. Walters, *The Antislavery Appeal: American Abolitionism after 1830* (Baltimore, 1976), 54–69, and *passim.* See also Gilbert Hobbs Barnes, *The Antislavery Impulse, 1830–1844* (New York, 1964); and Lewis Perry, *Radical Abolitionism: Anarchy and the Government of God in Antislavery Thought* (Ithaca, N.Y., 1973).
33. Leonard L. Richards, *"Gentleman of Property and Standing": Anti-Abolition Mobs in Jacksonian America* (New York, 1970), 35–36, 42, 165–66. Another study of anti-abolitionism that stresses race prejudice as a motivation is Lorman Ratner, *Powder Keg: Northern Opposition to the Antislavery Movement, 1831–1840* (New York, 1968). For a general discussion of the susceptibility of lower-class northern whites to extreme racist appeals, see Fredrickson, *Black Image,* 90–96.
34. See Fredrickson, *Black Image,* 16–19. The full range of explicit anti-abolitionist concerns is covered in Ratner, *Powder Keg.* In *"Gentleman of Property and Standing,"* Richards stresses elite fears of a loss of control resulting from the mode of abolitionist agitation.
35. See Fredrickson, *Black Image,* 43–96. (Quote from Calhoun on p. 47.)
36. *Ibid.,* 61–70, 90–96. (Quote from Yancey on p. 61.)
37. See George M. Fredrickson, "Masters and Mudsills: The Role of Race in the Planter Ideology of South Carolina," *South Atlantic Urban Studies,* Vol. II (Columbia, S.C., 1978), 34–48.
38. The best account of the political crises of the 1850s is David Potter,

The Impending Crisis, 1848–1861, comp. and ed. Don E. Fehren-
bacher (New York, 1976).

39. On the ideological affirmations and responses of the Republican Party,
see Foner, *Free Soil.*

40. See George M. Fredrickson, "A Man but Not a Brother: Abraham
Lincoln and Racial Equality," *Journal of Southern History,* XLI
(1975), 40–58; *idem, Black Image,* 138–59; Foner, *Free Soil,* 261–300.

41. For a recent analysis of the plantation South's economic stake in the
protection and unfettered expansion of slavery, see Gavin Wright,
*The Political Economy of the Cotton South: Households, Markets,
and Wealth in the Nineteenth Century* (New York, 1978). See also
Genovese, *Political Economy,* 243–74.

42. Eugene Genovese argues that "the War for Southern independence"
cannot be interpreted "from the point of view of the race question"
because "racial hegemony did not require slavery, as many contemporaries clearly understood." (*World the Slaveholders Made,* 103.) My
quarrel is with the final clause of this statement.

43. Calhoun to Mr. King, August 12, 1844, *The Works of John C. Calhoun,* ed. Richard K. Crallé, Vol. V (New York, 1858), 391.

44. William L. Barney, *The Road to Secession: A New Perspective on the
Old South* (New York, 1972), 63–66. (Davis quoted on p. 65.)

45. Moore, *Social Origins,* 121. My view of Republican ideology has been
strongly influenced by Foner, *Free Soil.*

46. James L. Roark, *Masters Without Slaves: Southern Planters in the
Civil War and Reconstruction* (New York, 1977), 23.

47. *Ibid.,* 22.

48. Quoted in Fredrickson, *Black Image,* 63–64.

49. For a provocative discussion of the relationship between British antislavery thought and bourgeois ideological "hegemony," see David
Brion Davis, *The Problem of Slavery in the Age of Revolution, 1770–
1823* (Ithaca, N.Y., 1975), 346–73.

50. Isobel Edwards, *Towards Emancipation: A Study in South African
Slavery* (Cardiff, 1942), 111–37, 169, 188–95, 197–204.

51. See Macmillan, *Cape Colour Question,* 87–94; Bernhard Krüger, *The
Pear Tree Blossoms: A History of the Moravian Mission Stations in
South Africa, 1737–1869* (Genadendal, South Africa, 1967), 63–67;
Jack Boas, "The Activities of the London Missionary Society in South
Africa, 1806–1836: An Assessment," *African Studies Review,* XVI
(1973), 420–24; and William M. Freund, "The Cape under the Transi-
tional Governments, 1795–1814," in Elphick and Giliomee, *South
African Society,* 224–28.

52. John Philip, *Researches in South Africa,* Vol. I (London, 1828), 402,
xxx–xxxi, and *passim.* Philip's letter affirming racial equality is re-

printed in Julius Lewin, *The Struggle for Equality* (London, 1967), 29–31. For general accounts of Philip's work, see Macmillan, *Cape Colour Question,* 95–140, and *passim;* and Boas, "London Missionary Society."

53. On Garrison's career and influence, see especially John L. Thomas, *The Liberator: William Lloyd Garrison* (Boston, 1963).

54. A debate has in fact developed among South Africanists on how much of a role Philip actually played in bringing about the reforms traditionally associated with his name. Macmillan (*Cape Colour Question*) established the orthodox view. But this position has been challenged by John S. Galbraith in *Reluctant Empire: British Policy on the South African Frontier, 1834–1854* (Berkeley and Los Angeles, 1963). Galbraith argues that the "philanthropic" influence on official policy, although "powerful," has been exaggerated by historians like Macmillan. (See n. 80 to Ch. I.) Leslie Clement Duly, in "A Revisit with the Cape's Hottentot Ordinance of 1828," in Marcelle Kooy, ed., *Studies in Economics and Economic History* (London, 1972), notes that a Cape colonist, Andries Stockenstrom, "was in fact the real author of the Fiftieth Ordinance" (p. 31). But Duly fails to confront the strong argument of Harry A. Gailey, Jr., in "John Philip's role in Hottentot Emancipation," *Journal of African History,* III (1962), 419–33. Gailey argues that Philip was instrumental in securing ultimate ratification of Khoikhoi emancipation from the King in Council and that he and his co-workers had in fact prepared the ground in England before the ordinance was issued in the Cape. No one seems to have disputed Macmillan's claim (233–46) that Philip was influential in the campaign leading to the disallowance of the Vagrancy Act in 1834. Perhaps the safest conclusion that a non-specialist can reach was that Philip was not the mover and shaker that his most fervent detractors and supporters have tried to make him out to be, but that he nevertheless had considerable influence on policy, especially if our vantage point is a comparison with the role of Garrison and the American abolitionists. A good statement of this compromise position is Boas' conclusion that "the role of the missionaries from 1806 to 1836 was neither peripheral nor all decisive." ("London Missionary Society," 431.) Furthermore, the most important consideration, for our present purposes, is not so much what Philip actually accomplished in his own right as how the effects of his activities were perceived by the white colonists.

55. On the concept of *"Herrenvolk* equality" as applied to the United States and South Africa, see Pierre L. van der Berghe, *Race and Racism: A Comparative Perspective* (New York, 1967), 17–18; Fredrickson, *Black Image,* 61; and Kenneth P. Vickery, " 'Herrenvolk' Democracy

and Egalitarianism in South Africa and the U.S. South," *Comparative Studies in Society and History*, XVI (1974), 309–28.

56. George Thompson, *Travels and Adventures in South Africa* (London, 1827), 324. See also: Vickery, " 'Herrenvolk' Democracy," 314–15; I. A. MacCrone, *Race Attitudes in South Africa: Historical, Experimental and Psychological Studies* (London, 1937), 127–28; Leonard Guelke, "The White Settlers, 1652–1780," in Elphick and Giliomee, *South African Society*, 63; and P. J. van der Merwe, *Trek: Studies oor die Mobiliteit van die Pionersbevolking aan die Kaap* (Cape Town, 1945), 6.

57. On the effects of "a closing frontier," see Hermann Giliomee, "The Eastern Frontier 1770–1812," in Elphick and Giliomee, *South African Society*, 322–24.

58. Quoted in C. F. J. Muller, *Die Oorsprong van die Groot Trek* (Cape Town, 1974), 200. (My translation.)

59. This patriarchal individualism is well described in Richard Ford, "The Frontier in South Africa: A Comparative Study of the Turner Thesis" (Ph.D. diss., University of Denver, 1966), 154–71. See also R. Cole Harris and Leonard Guelke, "Land and Society in Early Canada and South Africa," *Journal of Historical Geography*, III (1977), 148–50. For a graphic, if perhaps somewhat exaggerated, description of southern individualism or particularism, see W. J. Cash, *The Mind of the South* (New York, 1941), 32–46.

60. For a brilliant discussion of the complex relationship between law and social norms in southern slave society, see Eugene D. Genovese, *Roll, Jordan, Roll: The World the Slaves Made* (New York, 1974), 25–49.

61. See *ibid.*, 54–55. Among the most influential British observations of Boer mistreatment of nonwhite dependents were those found in John Barrow, *An Account of Travels into the Interior of Southern Africa, in the Years 1797 and 1798*, 2 vols. (London, 1801); Philip, *Researches*; and S. Bannister, *Humane Policy: Or Justice to the Aborigines of New Settlements* (London, 1829). Although these accounts undoubtedly contain exaggerations, they cannot be totally disregarded; for there is independent documentation for many of the practices they describe. More important for our purposes, there is no evidence that they had any appreciable effect on the behavior of Boer masters toward their Khoikhoi servants or that there was an autonomous movement for more humane treatment among the frontier Afrikaners themselves.

62. On the lack of effective local enforcement of the Fiftieth Ordinance of 1828, see Duly, "Revisit," 34–46. On the disruption of the labor system that nevertheless occurred and its role in precipitating the Great

Trek, see C. F. J. Muller, *Die Britse Owerheid en die Groot Trek* (Cape Town and Johannesburg, 1948), 60–62.

63. The manifesto is reproduced in Manfred Nathan, *The Voortrekkers of South Africa* (South Africa and London, 1937), 16–18.

64. The precise role of Calvinism as a source of Afrikaner racial attitudes has recently become a matter of controversy. Some difficulties in the standard argument are raised in Hermann Giliomee and Richard Elphick, "The Structure of European Domination at the Cape, 1652–1820," in Elphick and Giliomee, *South African Society*, 362–64. In an unpublished paper, "Dutch Calvinism and the Development of Afrikaner Nationalism" (1974), Irving Hexham has argued that Calvinism did not influence Afrikaner society before 1870. But his definition of Calvinism is a very narrow one. Surely it can still be held that the Voortrekker religion was more in the Calvinist than in the evangelical-Arminian tradition. The case for Calvinism as a formative influence is presented most fully in Gerhard Beckers, *Religiöse Factoren in der Entwicklung der Sudafrikanischen Rassenfrage* (Munich, 1969). The whole issue clearly requires further study.

65. Governor Janssens, as quoted in Dutch in M. Boucher, *The Frontier and Religion: A Comparative Study of the United States of America and South Africa in the First Half of the Nineteenth Century,* Vol. II of *Archives Year Book of South African History* (Cape Town, 1968), 4. (Translation is mine).

66. Landdrost Albert to Gov. Janssens, as quoted in Marais, *Maynier,* 73 n.

67. C. I. Latrobe, *Journal of a Visit to South Africa in 1815* (New York, 1969; orig. pub. 1818), 287.

68. As quoted in Macmillan, *Cape Colour Question,* 81.

69. Quoted in Boucher, *Frontier and Religion,* 34. (My translation.)

70. A recent study of this myth in the Old South, which in my view somewhat exaggerates its importance, is Thomas Virgil Peterson, *Ham and Japheth: The Mythic World of Whites in the Antebellum South* (Metuchen, N.J., 1978).

71. Donald G. Matthews, *Religion in the Old South* (Chicago, 1977), 171–73, and *passim.* See also H. Shelton Smith, *In His Image, But . . . : Racism in Southern Religion, 1780–1910* (Durham, N.C., 1972), 130–32, 152–53; and Lewis M. Purifoy, "The Southern Methodist Church and the Proslavery Argument," *Journal of Southern History,* XXXII (1966), 328–29. My sense that the curse on Ham was used infrequently, in comparison to other arguments for slavery and racial inferiority, is based on an extensive survey of proslavery literature. On the pre-eminence of the secular racist argument in the period between 1845 and 1860, see Ralph E. Morrow, "The Proslavery Argument Revisited," *Mississippi Valley Historical Review,* XLVIII (1961), 90.

72. John MacKenzie, *Ten Years North of the Orange River, 1859–1869* (London, 1971; orig. pub. 1871), 50. On characteristic Boer attitudes toward missions, see MacCrone, *Race Attitudes,* 128–30; and J. A. I. Agar-Hamilton, *The Native Policy of the Voortrekkers; An Essay in the History of the Interior of South Africa, 1836–1858* (Cape Town, 1928), 115–32. Agar-Hamilton, however, shows that hostility to missionary work among Africans was not absolute and was principally directed against English societies.

73. On the nature and development of this mythology, see F. A. van Jaarsveld, *The Afrikaner's Interpretation of South African History* (Cape Town, 1964), 1–32.

74. See Leonard Thompson, "Cooperation and Conflict: The Zulu Kingdom and Natal," in Monica Wilson and Leonard Thompson, eds., *The Oxford History of South Africa,* Vol. I (New York and Oxford, 1969), 355–64.

75. See *ibid.,* 367–68; Edgar Brookes, *White Rule in South Africa, 1830–1910* (Pietermaritzburg, 1974), 37–38; and Agar-Hamilton, *Native Policy,* 37–48. For a primary account of the workings of the apprenticeship system in Natal, see Captain Smith to Sir George Napier, Sept. 29, 1842, in John Bird, *Annals of Natal, 1495 to 1845,* Vol. II (Pietermaritzburg, 1888), 118–19.

76. See Thompson, "The Zulu Kingdom and Natal," 370–73.

77. See Leonard Thompson, "Cooperation and Conflict: The High Veld," in Wilson and Thompson, *Oxford History,* 416–25; and Arthur Keppel-Jones, *South Africa: A Short History* (London, 1968), 70–74.

78. Quoted in Agar-Hamilton, *Native Policy,* 88.

79. Eric A. Walker, *The Great Trek* (London, 1934), 109.

80. On antagonism and conflict between the Boers and the Griqua, see Robert Ross, *Adam Kok's Griquas: A Study in the Development of Stratification in South Africa* (Cambridge, Eng., 1976), 84–86.

81. For a summary of white citizenship policies in the republics see C. M. Tatz, *Shadow and Substance in South Africa: A Study in Land and Franchise Policies Affecting Africans, 1910–1960* (Pietermaritzburg, 1962), 4–5. On the Transvaal marriage law, see N. J. Rhoodie and H. J. Venter, *Apartheid: A Socio-Historical Exposition of the Origins and Development of the Apartheid Idea* (Cape Town, 1959), 97; and Albie Sachs, *Justice in South Africa* (Berkeley and Los Angeles, 1973), 82–83. For a revisionist account of social and economic relationships in the South African Republic which makes a case for the emergence, especially after 1880, of an intra-Afrikaner class division between landowning "notables" and poor whites, see Stanley Trapido, "The South African Republic: Class Formation and the State, 1850–1900," in *Collected Seminar Papers on the Societies of*

Southern Africa in the 19th and 20th Centuries, Vol. III (London: Institute of Commonwealth Studies, 1972), 53–65.

82. Correspondence in *De Volksstem* (Pretoria), 1875–76, as translated and reprinted in Du Toit, *Roots of Afrikaner Political Thought,* pt. IV, 1–10. (Quotes on pp. 4 and 8.)

83. On forms of labor coercion in the early republics and the dispute over whether they constituted enslavement, see especially Agar-Hamilton, *Native Policy,* 169–205. See also Thompson, "High Veld," 435–37, and Edwards, *Towards Emancipation,* 201–2. For more on the labor system of the republics, see Ch. V below.

84. See Theodore B. Wilson, *The Black Codes of the South* (University, Ala., 1965); and Leon F. Litwack, *Been in the Storm So Long: The Aftermath of Slavery* (New York, 1979), 364–71.

85. See Litwack, *Been in the Storm,* 374–86, 408–49; and William Cohen, "Negro Involuntary Servitude in the South, 1865–1940: A Preliminary Analysis," *Journal of Southern History,* XLII (1976), 30–60. For a discussion of the economic aspects of labor coercion in the post-bellum South, see Ch. V below.

86. H. J. and R. E. Simons, *Class and Colour in South Africa, 1850–1950* (Harmondsworth: Penguin Books, 1969), 19–20, 24.

87. Sachs, *Justice in South Africa,* 40.

88. See Pete Daniel, *The Shadow of Slavery: Peonage in the South, 1901–1969* (New York, 1973), 25, 76–77; Cohen, "Involuntary Servitude," 42–43.

89. See Fredrickson, *Black Image,* 183–86. For conflicting interpretations of the motivation for black enfranchisement, see William Gillette, *The Right to Vote: Politics and the Passage of the Fifteenth Amendment* (Baltimore, 1965); and Lawanda and John H. Cox, "Negro Suffrage and Republican Politics: The Problem of Motivation in Reconstruction Historiography," *Journal of Southern History,* XXXIII (August 1967), 303–30. On the reasons why a more radical reform program was not enacted, see Phillip S. Paludan, *A Covenant with Death: The Constitution, Law, and Equality in the Civil War Era* (Urbana, Ill., 1975), 49–60; and Wilbert H. Ahern, "Laissez Faire vs. Equal Rights: Liberal Republicans and Limits to Reconstruction," *Phylon,* XL (1979), 52–65.

90. See J. L. McCracken, *The Cape Parliament, 1854–1910* (Oxford, 1967), 62–70; Arthur Keppel-Jones, "A Case of Minority Rule: The Cape Colony, 1854–1898," *The Canadian Historical Association, Historical Papers* (1966), 98–101.

91. See Phyllis Lewsen, "The Cape Liberal Tradition—Myth or Reality," in *Collected Seminar Papers,* I (1970), 72–88.

92. Rhodes is quoted in Marais, *Cape Coloured People,* 277 n. Emphasis

added. On the politics of suffrage restriction, see McCracken, *Cape Parliament,* 71–104; Stanley Trapido, "White Conflict and Non-White Participation in the Politics of the Cape of Good Hope" (Ph.D. diss., University of London, 1969), 110–94; T. R. H. Davenport, *The Afrikaner Bond: The History of a South African Political Party, 1880–1911* (Cape Town, 1966), 118–23; and Keppel-Jones, "Minority Rule," 103–4.

93. See David Welsh, *The Roots of Segregation: Native Policy in Natal, 1845–1910* (Cape Town, 1971).

94. See n. 54, above, and n. 80 to Ch. I.

95. Ross, *Adam Kok,* 48.

96. Quoted in G. D. Scholtz, *Die Ontwikkeling van die Politieke Denke van die Afrikaner,* Vol. II (Johannesburg, 1970), 175.

97. See Fredrickson, *Black Image,* 178–83.

98. See *ibid.,* 228–55; Christine Bolt, *Victorian Attitudes to Race* (London, 1971), 75–108, 206–18; and Richard Hofstadter, *Social Darwinism in American Thought,* rev. ed. (Boston, 1955), 170–200.

99. Bernard Porter, *The Lion's Share: A Short History of British Imperialism, 1850–1970* (London and New York, 1975), 37; Bolt, *Victorian Attitudes,* 102–8.

100. See Fredrickson, *Black Image,* 197; and Victor P. De Santis, *Republicans Face the Southern Question—The New Departure Years, 1877–1897* (Baltimore, 1959), 44–45, 49–52.

101. Douglas A. Lorimer, *Colour, Class, and the Victorians: English Attitudes to the Negro in the Mid-Nineteenth Century* (Leicester and New York, 1978).

102. David Montgomery, *Beyond Equality: Labor and the Radical Republicans* (New York, 1967).

103. Philip D. Curtin, *The Image of Africa: British Ideas and Actions, 1780–1850* (Madison, Wis., 1964), 380, 415, 422–28. See also Fredrickson, *Black Image,* 305–11.

104. See James M. McPherson, *The Abolitionist Legacy: From Reconstruction to the NAACP* (Princeton, N.J., 1975).

105. See Fredrickson, *Black Image,* 283–319.

106. Paul Buck, *The Road to Reunion, 1865–1900* (New York: Vintage Books, n.d.; orig. pub. 1937), 300. See also Rayford W. Logan, *The Betrayal of the Negro: From Rutherford B. Hayes to Woodrow Wilson* (New York, 1965).

107. Keppel-Jones, *South Africa,* 95–101; Porter, *Lion's Share,* 95–97.

108. See F. A. van Jaarsveld, *The Awakening of Afrikaner Nationalism, 1868–1881* (Cape Town, 1961).

109. On the relationship of Transvaal annexation to the Zulu War, see David Denoon, with Balans Nyeko and the advice of J. B. Webster,

Southern Africa Since 1800 (New York, 1973), 69–71; on the British administration of the Transvaal, see Leonard Thompson, "Great Britain and the Afrikaner Republics, 1870–1899," in Monica Wilson and Leonard Thompson, eds., *The Oxford History of South Africa,* Vol. II (New York and Oxford, 1971), 298.

110. Ronald Robinson and John Gallagher, *Africa and the Victorians: The Climax of Imperialism in the Dark Continent* (New York, 1961), 63.

111. *The Memoirs of Paul Kruger* (New York, 1969; orig. pub. 1902), 41 n.

112. T. Dunbar Moodie, *The Rise of Afrikanerdom: Power, Apartheid, and Afrikaner Civil Religion* (Berkeley and Los Angeles, 1975), 26–29.

113. See J. S. Marais, *The Fall of Kruger's Republic* (Oxford, 1961), 180–83, 235–36, 258–62; and G. B. Pyrah, *Imperial Policy and South Africa, 1902–1910* (Oxford, 1955), 91, 97–98.

114. See Robinson and Gallagher, *Africa and the Victorians,* 410–68; and Marais, *Kruger's Republic,* 325–31.

115. Denoon, *Southern Africa,* 100–107.

116. Leonard Thompson, *The Unification of South Africa, 1902–1910* (Oxford, 1960), 11–12; Pyrah, *Imperial Policy,* 91–92.

117. See David Denoon, *A Grand Illusion: The Failure of Imperial Policy in the Transvaal Colony during the Period of Reconstruction, 1900–1905* (London, 1973), 96–126; Pyrah, *Imperial Policy,* 98–99; and Thompson, *Unification,* 26–28.

118. Quoted in Thompson, *Unification,* 6.

119. Tatz, *Shadow and Substance,* 6–11.

120. Quoted in Welsh, *Roots of Segregation,* 232.

121. Quoted in Tatz, *Shadow and Substance,* 9.

122. Thompson, *Unification,* 217–18.

123. *Ibid.,* 212–26.

124. See Paul Lewinson, *Race, Class, and Party: a History of Negro Suffrage and White Politics in the South* (New York, 1965), 84 n, 85; and C. Vann Woodward, *Origins of the New South, 1877–1913* (Baton Rouge, La., 1951), 480.

V. INDUSTRIALISM, WHITE LABOR, AND RACIAL DISCRIMINATION

1. Samuel Lane Loomis, quoted in Herbert G. Gutman, *Work, Culture, and Society in Industrializing America* (New York, 1976), 40.

2. John Higham, *Send These to Me: Jews and Other Immigrants in Urban America* (New York, 1975), 24.

3. Gutman, *Work, Culture, and Society,* 15.

4. See Higham, *Send These to Me,* 22–25. On the vital contribution of cheap immigrant labor to the industrialization of one major American city, see Oscar Handlin, *Boston's Immigrants: A Study in Acculturation* (Cambridge, Mass., 1941), 79–88.

5. On the role of white immigration in the industrialization of South Africa, see especially Lawrence Saloman, "Socio-Economic Aspects of South African History, 1870–1962," (Ph.D. diss., Boston University, 1962), 6–16.

6. C. W. de Kiewiet, *A History of South Africa: Social and Economic* (Oxford, 1957), 96.

7. See Sheila T. van der Horst, *Native Labour in South Africa* (London, 1971), 59–153, and *passim;* and Frederick A. Johnstone, *Class, Race, and Gold: A Study of Class Relations and Racial Discrimination in South Africa* (London, 1976), 26–45.

8. On immigrant mobility, see especially the work of Stephen Thernstrom: *Poverty and Progress: Social Mobility in a Nineteenth Century City* (Cambridge, Mass., 1964), and *The Other Bostonians: Poverty and Progress in the American Metropolis, 1880–1970* (Cambridge, Mass., 1973), 111–44, 250–56.

9. The specific restraints on African economic freedom will be described in more detail below. My conception of working-class formation is influenced by E. P. Thomson, *The Making of the English Working Class* (New York, 1963).

10. On the central role of slave-grown cotton in American economic development, see Douglass C. North, *The Economic Growth of the United States, 1790–1860* (New York, 1966), 67–76, and *passim.*

11. On the economic stagnation of southern agriculture in the post-bellum period, see Roger L. Ransom and Richard Sutch, *One Kind of Freedom: The Economic Consequences of Emancipation* (Cambridge, Eng., 1977), 9–12. Exclusion of blacks from industry is discussed more fully below.

12. See Robert S. Starobin, *Industrial Slavery in the Old South* (New York, 1970); and Claudia Dale Goldin, *Urban Slavery in the American South, 1820–1860: A Quantitative History* (Chicago, 1976), 42–46.

13. Victor de Kock, *Those in Bondage: An Account of the Life of the Slave at the Cape in the Days of the Dutch East India Company* (Pretoria, 1963), 62.

14. G. D. Scholtz, *Die Ontwikkeling van die Politieke Denke van die Afrikaner,* Vol. I (Johannesburg, 1965), 111; P. J. van der Merwe, *Die Trekboer in die Geskiedenis van die Kaap Kolonie* (Cape Town, 1938), 187.

15. See J. S. Marais, *The Cape Coloured People, 1652–1937* (Johannesburg, 1968), 259–60.

16. See De Kiewiet, *South Africa: Social and Economic*, 162–64.

17. See Ulrich B. Phillips, *Life and Labor in the Old South* (Boston, 1929), 86.

18. Ira Berlin, *Slaves Without Masters: The Free Negro in the Antebellum South* (New York, 1974), 217–49, 275.

19. Starobin, *Industrial Slavery*, 137–45.

20. Berlin, *Slaves Without Masters*, 236.

21. Sterling D. Spero and Abram L. Harris, *The Black Worker: The Negro and the Labor Movement* (New York, 1968; orig. pub. 1931), 7–10.

22. See Leon F. Litwack, *North of Slavery: The Negro in the Free States, 1790–1860* (Chicago, 1961), 153–86.

23. C. Vann Woodward, *Origins of the New South, 1877–1913* (Baton Rouge, La., 1951), 140.

24. Paul B. Worthman and James R. Green, "Black Workers in the New South, 1865–1915," in Nathan I. Huggins, Martin Kilson, and Daniel M. Fox, eds., *Key Issues in the Afro-American Experience*, Vol. II (New York, 1971), 54; Gunnar Myrdal, *An American Dilemma* (New York, 1944), 286–87.

25. Charles H. Wesley, *Negro Labor in the United States* (New York, 1927), 227.

26. Woodward, *Origins*, 132–34; Broadus Mitchell, *The Rise of Cotton Mills in the New South* (Baltimore, 1921), 132–37, 210–21. (Quote from pp. 136–37.) Woodward casts some doubt on the full sincerity of the "philanthropic" motive behind racial exclusion stressed by Mitchell, but there can be little doubt that the policy of black exclusion added to the popularity of the movement and probably enhanced the attractiveness of mill employment for southern whites, despite the low wage scales that prevailed. For an instance where white workers sacrificed their own economic interests to keep blacks out of a mill, see Philip S. Foner, *Organized Labor and the Black Worker* (New York, 1974), 86.

27. James L. Orr, "The Negro in the Mills," *The Independent*, LIII (April 11, 1901), 845–46. I am indebted to Joel Williamson for calling this article to my attention.

28. Myrdal, *American Dilemma*, 282–83.

29. See George M. Fredrickson, *The Black Image in the White Mind: The Debate on Afro-American Character and Destiny* (New York, 1971), 143.

30. The self-fulfilling myth of "blacks vs. machines" deserves further study. Myrdal briefly discusses the adverse effect of mechanization on black opportunity in the twentieth century (*An American Dilemma*, 282–83), and Dale T. Hiestand deals with the subject somewhat more fully in *Economic Growth and Employment Opportunities for Minorities*

(New York, 1964), 114–19. Hiestand notes that as late as the 1940s and 50s there was a tendency for whites to monopolize fields "where the technology is most advanced," and contends that the problem of black employment will be solved only when it becomes possible for black labor to "leapfrog from the backward to the more advanced fields." To what extent this situation has simply been the result of white economic and educational advantages and to what extent it has been influenced by deeply rooted cultural preconceptions or racial mythologies is a question worthy of serious examination.

31. James Bryce, *Impressions of South Africa* (New York, 1898), 459.

32. For a description of these processes, see Francis Wilson, *Labour in the South African Gold Mines* (Cambridge, Eng., 1972), 16–22.

33. Quoted in Van der Horst, *Native Labour,* 175.

34. See *ibid.,* 127–28, for the initial wage differentials of the 1890s, which appear to have been on the order of 7 or 8 to 1. In *Labour in the Gold Mines,* Wilson gives figures from 1911 to 1969. The 1911 ratio was 11.7 : 1 (46).

35. Edna Bonacich, "A Theory of Ethnic Antagonism: The Split Labor Market," *American Sociological Review,* XXXVII, 549, 553–58. See also *idem,* "Capitalism and Labor Relations in South Africa: A Split Labor Market Analysis," forthcoming in Maurice Zeitlin, ed., *Political Power and Social Theory.*

36. For a brilliant critique of economic determinist interpretations of class formation in South African society, see Heribert Adam, "Perspectives in Literature," in Heribert Adam and Hermann Giliomee, *Ethnic Power Mobilized: Can South Africa Change?* (New Haven, 1979), 47–50.

37. See n. 84 to Ch. IV, above.

38. William Cohen, "Negro Involuntary Servitude in the South, 1865–1940: A Preliminary Analysis," *Journal of Southern History,* XLII (1976), 30–60. See also Pete Daniel, *The Shadow of Slavery: Peonage in the South, 1901–1969* (Urbana, Ill., 1972); Daniel A. Novak, *The Wheel of Servitude: Black Forced Labor after Slavery* (Lexington, Ky., 1978); Jonathan M. Wiener, *Social Origins of the New South: Alabama, 1860–1889* (Baton Rouge, La., 1978), 35–73; and Ranson and Sutch, *One Kind of Freedom,* 149–70.

39. For the argument that blacks were not sufficiently immobilized or coerced to invalidate a free labor market analysis, see Robert Higgs, *Competition and Coercion: Blacks in the American Economy, 1865–1914* (Cambridge, Eng., 1977), 58–59, and *passim.* The thesis that the post-bellum system of agricultural labor was fundamentally "coercive" or "labor-repressive" has recently been presented in different forms by Wiener in *Social Origins* and by Jay Mandle in *The Roots of Black*

Poverty: The Southern Plantation Economy After the Civil War (Durham, N.C., 1978). From a less theoretical perspective, Pete Daniel demonstrates the widespread incidence of debt peonage (*The Shadow of Slavery*), while William Cohen argues in "Involuntary Servitude" that the system of labor-repressive legislation he documents was selectively applied, being relaxed when there was a surplus of labor and vigorously enforced when there was a shortage (59–60).

40. On convict leasing, see Cohen, "Involuntary Labor," 55–56; Woodward, *Origins*, 212–15; and Vernon L. Wharton, *The Negro in Mississippi, 1865–1890* (Chapel Hill, N.C., 1947), 234–42.

41. On inter-racial unionism among coal miners, see Gutman, *Work, Culture, and Society*, 123–208. On the timber workers, see Spero and Harris, *Black Worker*, 331–33. Cooperation among longshoremen is described in Worthman and Green, "Black Workers," 62–63.

42. See Ch. IV, above.

43. See Hugh Tinker, *A New System of Slavery: The Export of Indian Labor Overseas, 1830–1920* (London, 1974); and Robert A. Huttenback, *Racism and Empire: White Settlers and Coloured Immigrants in the British Self-Governing Colonies, 1830–1910* (Ithaca, N.Y., 1976), 52–58.

44. See Van der Horst, *Native Labour*, 98, 283–84; and n. 83 to Ch. IV, above.

45. G. V. Doxey, *The Industrial Colour Bar in South Africa* (Cape Town, 1961), 27–32.

46. On the economic constraints on the mining industry, see Johnstone, *Class, Race, and Gold*, 13–20; and Alan Jeeves, "The Controls of Migratory Labour on the South African Gold Mines in the Era of Kruger and Milner," *Journal of African Studies*, II (1975), 5–8.

47. See Johnstone, *Class, Race, and Gold*, 13–25; Jeeves, "Migratory Labour"; and Van der Horst, *Native Labour*, 164–65, 197–99.

48. See Johnstone, *Class, Race, and Gold*, 26–34; Jeeves, "Migratory Labor," 8–29; Van der Horst, *Native Labor*, 110–16, 128–38, 151–53, 199; and Wilson, *Labour in the Gold Mines*, 2–5.

49. See Johnstone, *Class, Race, and Gold*, 34–39; and Jeeves, "Migratory Labor," 11–12. Quote from Van der Horst, *Native Labor*, 133.

50. For a theoretical and comparative development of the argument that industrialization adapts to pre-existing patterns of race relations rather than radically transforming them, see Herbert Blumer, "Industrialization and Race Relations," in Guy Hunter, ed., *Industrialization and Race Relations: A Symposium* (London, 1965), 220–53. The universal validity of this hypothesis might be questioned, but it applies reasonably well, in my view, to the case of early industrialization in South Africa.

51. Thernstrom, *The Other Bostonians*, 192–93.

52. Spero and Harris, *Black Worker,* 23–48 (quote from p. 24); Ray Marshall, *The Negro Worker* (New York, 1967), 16–17 (quote from p. 16).

53. Worthman and Green, "Black Workers," 59.

54. On early AFL race policies, see Bernard Mandel, "Samuel Gompers and the Negro Workers, 1886–1914," *Journal of Negro History,* XL (1955), 34–60.

55. See Gutman, *Work, Culture, and Society,* 121–208; and Spero and Harris, *Black Worker,* 331–33, 352–82.

56. See David Montgomery, *Beyond Equality: Labor and the Radical Republicans* (New York, 1967), 102–6; Spero and Harris, *Black Worker,* 131, 162; and Worthman and Green, "Black Workers," 55–56.

57. See Alexander Saxton, "Race and the House of Labor," in Gary B. Nash and Richard Weiss, eds., *The Great Fear: Race in the Mind of America* (New York, 1970), 107–14 (quote from p. 112); and *idem, The Indispensable Enemy: Labor and the Anti-Chinese Movement in California* (Berkeley and Los Angeles, 1971).

58. For a general discussion of black strike-breaking and reactions to it, see Spero and Harris, *Black Worker,* 128–46. For a graphic example, see Allen H. Spear's account of the Chicago stockyards and teamsters' strikes of 1904–5 in *Black Chicago: The Making of a Negro Ghetto* (Chicago, 1967), 36–41.

59. William Julius Wilson, *The Declining Significance of Race: Blacks and Changing American Institutions* (Chicago, 1978), 73.

60. See Elliott Rudwick, *Race Riot at East St. Louis, July 2, 1917* (Cleveland, 1966), 16–20, 218, and *passim.*

61. See William M. Tuttle, "Labor Conflict and Racial Violence: The Black Worker in Chicago, 1894–1919," in Milton Cantor, ed., *Black Labor in America* (Westport, Conn., 1969), 86–110; and *idem, Race Riot: Chicago in the Red Summer of 1919* (New York, 1970), 108–56.

62. On conflict over neighborhoods and the divisive effect of political affiliations, see Tuttle, *Race Riot,* 157–207; Spear, *Black Chicago;* Gilbert Osolfsky, *Harlem: The Making of a Ghetto* (New York, 1966); and Rudwick, *East St. Louis,* 10–15, 24, 70.

63. For a summary of the changes in black political affiliation and relationship to organized labor in the 1930s, see John Hope Franklin, *From Slavery to Freedom: A History of American Negroes,* 2nd ed. (New York, 1963), 512–19, 528–33. For more detailed accounts of race relations in this period, see Raymond Wolters, *Negroes in the Great Depression: The Problem of Economic Recovery* (Westport, Conn., 1970); and Harvard Sitkoff, *A New Deal for Blacks: The Emergence of Civil Rights as a National Issue* (New York, 1978).

64. Saxton, "Race and the House of Labor," 108.

65. See Van der Horst, *Native Labour,* 171–72.
66. H. J. and R. E. Simons, *Class and Colour in South Africa, 1850–1950* (Harmondsworth, Eng., Penguin Books, 1969), 92.
67. *Ibid.,* 55–57.
68. Van der Horst, *Native Labour,* 171–72.
69. *Ibid.,* 175–79.
70. On the origins of the South African "poor white problem," see Francis Wilson, "Farming, 1866–1966," in Monica Wilson and Leonard Thompson, eds., *Oxford History of South Africa,* Vol. II (New York and Oxford, 1971), 126–27; De Kiewiet, *South Africa: Social and Economic,* 181–86, 191–97; Saloman, "Socio-Economic Aspects of South African History," 29–40.
71. Van der Horst, *Native Labour,* 176–79. See also Saloman, "Socio-Economic Aspects of South African History," 77–78, 83–84.
72. On the provisions of the Mine and Works Act, see Van der Horst, *Native Labour,* 179–80; and De Kiewiet, *South Africa: Social and Economic,* 166.
73. Quoted in Johnstone, *Class, Race, and Gold,* 73. See also Simons and Simons, *Class and Colour,* 88–90.
74. Van der Horst, *Native Labour,* 181.
75. This account of the Rand Rebellion and its consequences is based mainly on Johnstone, *Class, Race, and Gold,* 125–50 (quote from p. 132). But see also Simons and Simons, *Class and Colour,* 271–99; Edward Roux, *Time Longer than Rope: A History of the Black Man's Struggle for Freedom in South Africa,* 2nd ed. (Madison, Wis., 1964), 143–53; and Van der Horst, *Native Labour,* 182–83.
76. See Johnstone, *Class, Race, and Gold,* 150–67; De Kiewiet, *South Africa: Social and Economic,* 223–28; and Saloman, "Socio-Economic Aspects of South African History," 95–96.
77. On the basic distinction between "ultra-exploitable" and expensive, enfranchised labor, see Johnstone, *Class, Race, and Gold,* 20–25, and *passim.*
78. For an incisive development of the argument that South Africa has developed a forced-labor economy that is compatible both with capitalistic interests and those of an entrenched white labor aristocracy, see Martin Legassick, "South Africa: Forced Labor, Industrialization, and Racial Differentiation," in Richard Harris, ed., *The Political Economy of South Africa* (Cambridge, Mass., 1975), 229–70. But Legassick, in my view, pursues his economic interpretation a bit too single-mindedly and thus underplays the autonomous tradition of white-supremacist belief and attitude that was essential for legitimizing the new order. On the economic benefits to employers of the migratory system, see Wilson, *Labour in the Gold Mines,* 136–39.

79. See Saxton, *Indispensable Enemy*, 128–29.

80. Spero and Harris, *Black Worker*, 59, 121.

81. On the consequences for nonwhites of parliamentary supremacy and the lack of a bill of rights, see Albie Sachs, *Justice in South Africa* (Berkeley and Los Angeles, 1973), 132, and *passim;* and D. V. Cowen, *The Foundation of Freedom: With Special Reference to South Africa* (Cape Town, 1961).

82. Maurice S. Evans, *Black and White in the Southern States: A Study of the Race Problem in the United States from a South African Point of View* (London, 1915), 261.

83. See Foner, *Organized Labor and the Black Worker*, 123.

84. This explanation is stressed by Kenneth P. Vickery in "'Herrenvolk' Democracy and Egalitarianism in South Africa and the U.S. South," *Comparative Studies in Society and History*, XVI (1974), 321. The percentages are from Leonard M. Thompson, *The Unification of South Africa, 1902–1910* (Oxford, 1960), 486 (table); Francis Butler Simkins and Charles Pierce Roland, *A History of the South*, 4th ed. (New York, 1972), 492; and Howard Odum, *Southern Regions of the United States* (Chapel Hill, N.C., 1936), 88. By 1950, the percentage of blacks in the South had declined to 21 (Simkins and Roland, 492), and the 1970 percentage of whites in South Africa was 17.5. (Heribert Adam, *Modernizing Racial Domination: The Dynamics of South African Politics* [Berkeley and Los Angeles, 1971], 3.)

85. Hiestand, *Employment Opportunities*, 43.

VI. TWO STRANGE CAREERS: SEGREGATION IN SOUTH AFRICA AND THE SOUTH

1. On the provisions and implications of the Land Act of 1913, see T. R. H. Davenport, *South Africa: A Modern History* (Toronto, 1977), 334–39; Francis Wilson, "Farming, 1866–1896," in Monica Wilson and Leonard Thompson, eds., *The Oxford History of South Africa*, Vol. II (New York and Oxford, 1971), 127–31; and Peter Walshe, *The Rise of African Nationalism in South Africa: The African National Congress, 1912–1952* (Berkeley and Los Angeles, 1971), 44–46. The original Land Act was not applied to the Cape Province because of its incompatibility with the land ownership provisions of the Cape African franchise.

2. Quoted in David Welsh, "The Growth of Towns," in Wilson and Thompson, *Oxford History*, 187.

3. *Ibid.*, 197–99, 238; Davenport, *Modern History*, 340–47; Dr. W. W. M. Eiselen, as quoted in C. M. Tatz, *Shadow and Substance in South*

Africa: A Study of Land and Franchise Policies Affecting Africans, 1910–1960 (Pietermaritzburg, 1962), 166.

4. See Welsh, "Towns," 196–202; Davenport, *Modern History,* 345–47; Francis Wilson, "Political Implications for Blacks of Economic Changes," in Leonard Thompson and Jeffrey Butler, eds., *Change in Contemporary South Africa* (Berkeley and Los Angeles, 1975), 181; Albie Sachs, *Justice in South Africa;* and Joel Carlson, *No Neutral Ground* (New York, 1973).

5. See Muriel Horrell, *The African Homelands of South Africa* (Johannesburg, 1973); Gwendolen M. Carter, Thomas Karis, and Newell M. Stultz, *South Africa's Transkei: The Politics of Domestic Colonialism* (Evanston, Ill., 1967); and Stultz, *Transkei's Half Loaf: Race Separatism in South Africa* (New Haven, Conn., 1979).

6. Carter *et al., Transkei,* 5.

7. See F. Wilson, "Farming," 127–29; Davenport, *Modern History,* 334–35.

8. Jan H. Hofmeyr, *South Africa* (London, 1931), 313–14, as quoted in Carter *et al., Transkei,* 34.

9. On the function of the reserves as labor reservoirs, see Welsh, "Towns," 181–82; and Martin Legassick, "South Africa: Forced Labor, Industrialization, and Racial Differentiation," in Richard Harris, ed., *The Political Economy of Africa* (Cambridge, Mass., 1975), 247–51. On the migrant labor system, see especially Francis Wilson, *Migrant Labour* (Johannesburg, 1972).

10. Carter *et al., Transkei,* 5.

11. For a good description of the current status of urban Africans, see Peter Randall, ed., *South Africa's Political Alternatives: Report of the Political Commission of the Study Project on Christianity in Apartheid Society* (Johannesburg, 1973), 36–38.

12. For a particularly good statement of the aims of the policy of separate development in the "real-politik sense," see Lawrence Schlemmer and Tim J. Muil, "Social and Political Change in the African Areas: A Case Study of Kwazulu," in Thompson and Butler, *Contemporary South Africa,* 108.

13. Legassick stresses the labor requirements of South African capitalism as a foundation of separate development in "South Africa: Forced Labor, Industrialization, and Racial Differentiation," 229–70. On the homelands' lack of economic viability and their current and projected need to provide workers for the white South African state, see Randall, *South Africa's Political Alternatives,* 34–36.

14. R. F. A. Hoernlé, *South African Native Policy and the Liberal Spirit* (Johannesburg, 1945; orig. pub. 1939), 31–32.

15. D. V. Cowen, *The Foundations of Freedom: With Special Reference*

to South Africa (Cape Town, 1961), 27, 129; Gwendolen M. Carter, *The Politics of Inequality: South Africa since 1948,* 2nd ed. (New York, 1959), 96–100.

16. Writing in Thompson and Butler, *Contemporary South Africa* (1975), Albie Sachs ("The Instruments of Domination in South Africa") and Heribert Adam ("Internal Constellations and Potentials for Change") both anticipated the probable relaxation of petty apartheid, or what they call "symbolic" discrimination, as a way of deflecting international criticism from the more vital or "instrumental" aspects of apartheid which sustain the economy and the security of white rule (248, 312). Newspaper reports in the late 1970s indicated that these prognostications were correct and that many of the petty apartheid policies were being phased out.

17. On the Cape African franchise and its elimination, see Edward Roux, *Time Longer than Rope: A History of the Black Man's Struggle for Freedom in South Africa,* 2nd ed. (Madison, Wis., 1964), 57–77, 286–301. On the forms of self-government that have evolved in one of the homelands, see Carter *et al., Transkei,* 92–110, and *passim.*

18. See Thomas Holt, *Black Over White: Negro Political Leadership in South Carolina during Reconstruction* (Urbana, Ill., 1977); and J. G. Randall and David Donald, *The Civil War and Reconstruction,* 2nd ed. (Lexington, Mass., 1969), 622–23.

19. See Wilson Record, *The Negro and the Communist Party* (New York, 1971), 54–119; and E. U. Essien-Udom, *Black Nationalism: A Search for Identity in America* (New York: Laurel Edition, 1964), 284–87.

20. See C. Vann Woodward, *Origins of the New South, 1877–1913* (Baton Rouge, La., 1950), 350–52; and Mary Frances Berry, *Black Resistance/White Law* (New York, 1971), 110–37.

21. Sachs, *Justice in South Africa,* 70–71; *idem,* "Instruments of Domination," 226–29.

22. George M. Fredrickson, *The Black Image in the White Mind: The Debate on Afro-American Character and Destiny* (New York, 1971), 175–77.

23. See Jack Temple Kirby, *Darkness at the Dawning: Race and Reform in the Progressive South* (Philadelphia, 1972), 119–30, for an account of Poe's program and its South African antecedents.

24. See Charles S. Johnson, *Patterns of Negro Segregation* (New York, 1943), 173–76; and Roger L. Rice, "Residential Segregation by Law, 1910–1917," *Journal of Southern History,* XXXIV (1968), 179–99. On the Group Areas Act, see Carter, *Politics of Inequality,* 84–91.

25. See Chapter II, above, on the origins of the Cape Coloreds.

26. Laura Newell Morris, *Human Populations, Genetic Variation, and Evolution* (San Francisco, 1971), 417–21.

27. M. C. Botha, in association with Judith Prichard, *Blood Group Gene Frequencies: An Indication of the Genetic Constitution of Population Samples in Cape Town,* supplement to *South African Medical Journal,* 1 April 1972, 20.

28. An excellent historical study of Afro-American folk culture is Lawrence W. Levine, *Black Culture and Black Consciousness: Afro-American Folk Thought from Slavery to Freedom* (New York, 1977). On the Cape Malays, see I. D. du Plessis, *The Cape Malays* (Cape Town, 1944).

29. For recent Colored population figures and percentages, see C. D. Cilliers, *Coloured People: Education and Status* (Johannesburg: S.A. Institute of Race Relations, 1971), 1, 4.

30. Susan Rennie Ritner, "The Dutch Reformed Church and Apartheid," *Journal of Contemporary History,* II (October 1967), 18n; Lester B. Scherer, *Slavery and the Churches in Early America, 1619–1819* (Grand Rapids, Mich., 1975), 101–2.

31. Winthrop D. Jordan, *White Over Black: American Attitudes Toward the Negro, 1550–1812* (Chapel Hill, N.C., 1968), 132.

32. See Chapter III, above, for a discussion of the social status of converted individuals of mixed origin who were considered part of the burgher class.

33. Richard C. Wade, *Slavery in the Cities: The South, 1820–1860* (New York, 1964), 266–71.

34. For a provocative sociological analysis of the difference between the racial attitudes traditionally associated with Cape Town and those of the rural or frontier areas, see Gerhard Beckers, *Religiöse Factoren in der Entwicklung der Südafrikanischen Rassenfrage* (Munich, 1969), 34–41.

35. See John W. Blassingame, *Black New Orleans, 1860–1880* (Chicago, 1973), 208–10, and *passim;* and Roger A. Fischer, *The Segregation Struggle in Louisiana, 1862–1877* (Urbana, Ill., 1974), 3–20.

36. See the testimony from Maurice Evans as quoted below and referenced in note 56.

37. Edgar Lionel Maurice, "The History and Administration of the Education of the Coloured Peoples of the Cape, 1652–1910" (B.Ed. thesis, University of Cape Town, 1946), 32–33, 41; B. M. Kies, "The Policy of Educational Segregation and Some of Its Effects upon the Coloured People of the Cape" (B.Ed. thesis, University of Cape Town, 1939), 7–10. Maurice and Kies are the pioneer Cape Colored historians of the educational experience of their population group. I have made substantial use of their unpublished theses and dissertations.

38. Petrus Bochardus Borcherds, *An Autobiographical Memoir* (Cape

Town, 1861), 18, as quoted in Maurice, "History and Administration," 51.

39. See Jordan, *White Over Black*, 354–56; Ira Berlin, *Slaves Without Masters: The Free Negro in the Antebellum South* (New York, 1974), 74–78.

40. Maurice, "History and Administration," 105–6, 113.

41. For more on these suffrage policies, see Chapter IV, above.

42. On the general pattern of *de facto* segregation that developed during and immediately after Reconstruction, see Joel Williamson, *After Slavery: The Negro in South Carolina, 1861–1877* (Chapel Hill, N.C., 1965), 274–99; and Howard Rabinowitz, *Race Relations in the Urban South, 1865–1890* (New York, 1978), 127–254. On the experiment with integrated schools in New Orleans, see Fischer, *Segregation Struggle*, 110–32.

43. See Williamson, *After Slavery*, 287; and Rabinowitz, *Race Relations*, 183.

44. See Rabinowitz, *Race Relations*, 183–97; George W. Cable, *The Negro Question*, ed. Arlin Turner (Garden City, N.Y., 1958), 102–6; and C. Vann Woodward, *The Strange Career of Jim Crow*, 3rd rev. ed. (New York, 1974), 31–44.

45. On "bull-dozing," see Nell Painter, *Exodusters: Black Migration to Kansas after Reconstruction* (New York, 1977). On the various electoral laws and devices employed to limit black voting prior to the disfranchisement laws and conventions, see J. Morgan Kousser, *The Shaping of Southern Politics: Suffrage Restriction and the Establishment of the One-Party South, 1890–1910* (New Haven, 1974). (Figures on black voting in 1880 are from Kousser, 14–15.) For a good account of black voting and suffrage restriction in one state, see George B. Tindall, *South Carolina Negroes, 1877–1900* (Columbia, S.C., 1952), 54–91.

46. Joseph H. Cartwright, *The Triumph of Jim Crow: Tennessee Race Relations in the 1880s* (Knoxville, Tenn., 1976), 106.

47. For figures showing this trend in South Carolina in the 1880s and 90s, see Tindall, *South Carolina Negroes*, 214–16. See below for an account of the dramatic acceleration of the difference in the early twentieth century.

48. Rabinowitz, *Race Relations*, 127, 165, 185–86, 332–33.

49. See Eugene D. Genovese, *Roll, Jordan, Roll: The World the Slaves Made* (New York, 1974); John W. Blassingame, *The Slave Community: Plantation Life in the Antebellum South* (New York, 1972); and Herbert G. Gutman, *The Black Family in Slavery and Freedom, 1750–1975* (New York, 1976).

50. C. J. Kriel, *Die Geskiedenis van die Nederduitse Sendingkerk in Suid-*

Afrika, 1881–1956 (Paarl, 1963), 54–55; Bernard Krüger, *The Pear Tree Blossoms: The History of the Moravian Church in South Africa* (Genadendal, 1967), 79–80, 196–97, 212–19; Peter Hinchliff, *The Church in South Africa* (London, 1968), 46.

51. See G. D. Scholtz, *Die Ontwikkeling van die Politieke Denke van die Afrikaner,* Vol. II (Johannesburg, 1970), 73–75, 246–48; D. P. Botha, *Die Opkoms van Ons Derde Stand* (Cape Town, 1960), 70–80; J. S. Marais, *The Cape Coloured People, 1652–1937* (Johannesburg, 1968); Kriel, *Nederduitse Sendingkerk,* 54–62.

52. On Colored religious separatism, see Sheila Patterson, *Colour and Culture in South Africa: A Study of the Status of the Cape Coloured People within the Social Structure of the Union of South Africa* (London, 1953), 158–59; and R. E. van der Ross, "A Political and Social History of the Cape Coloured People," 2 vols., unpublished ms. (1973), Centre for Intergroup Studies, University of Cape Town, II: 740–48, 763–68.

53. Kies, "Educational Segregation," 18–26 (quoted from p. 26).

54. *Ibid.,* 32.

55. Lady Duff Gordon, *Letters from the Cape* (London, 1927), 82–83.

56. Maurice S. Evans, *Black and White in South East Africa: A Study in Sociology* (London, 1911), 296–97.

57. Sheila Patterson, *The Last Trek: A Story of the Boer People and the Afrikaner Nation* (London, 1957), 83.

58. See Arthur Keppel-Jones, "A Case of Minority Rule: The Cape Colony, 1854–1898," *Canadian Historical Association, Historical Papers* (1966), 102; and Stanley Trapido, "White Conflict and Non-White Participation in the Politics of the Cape of Good Hope" (Ph.D. diss., University of London, 1969), 154–58.

59. See Keppel-Jones, "Minority Rule," 101–2, 113–14; and Trapido, "White Conflict," 186–94, 395ff, and *passim.*

60. For descriptions and interpretations of these developments, see Woodward, *Jim Crow,* 67–109; and Kousser, *Shaping of Southern Politics,* 139–223.

61. The only detailed and thorough historical account of this process is to be found in Van der Ross's unpublished "Political and Social History." But see Carter, *Politics of Inequality,* for evidence that discrimination against the Coloreds was a major element in early apartheid legislation.

62. See Cartwright, *Triumph,* 165–69.

63. Thomas Pearce Bailey, as quoted in Fredrickson, *Black Image,* 297–98.

64. Edgar Lionel Maurice, "The Development of Policy in Regard to the Education of Coloured Pupils at the Cape, 1880–1940" (Ph.D. diss., University of Cape Town, 1966), 311–16; Graham Watson, *Passing for*

White: A Study of Racial Assimilation in a South African School (London, 1970), 32.

65. Carter, *Politics of Inequality,* 81.
66. Charles S. Mangum, Jr., *The Legal Status of the Negro* (Chapel Hill, N.C., 1940), 6–7.
67. Woodward, *Jim Crow,* 31–65.
68. See Fredrickson, *Black Image,* 228–82, and Woodward, *Jim Crow,* 67–109, for discussions of the retrogressionist thought and Negrophobic climate of opinion that prevailed between 1890 and World War I. On the growth of a moderate "separate-but-equal" reformism in the twentieth century, see Morton Sosna, *In Search of the Silent South: Southern Liberals and the Race Issue* (New York, 1977).
69. See Botha, *Derde Stand,* 100–102; H. J. and R. E. Simons, *Class and Colour in South Africa, 1850–1950* (Harmondsworth, Eng., Penguin Books, 1969), 341–42; Leonard Thompson, *The Cape Coloured Franchise* (Johannesburg: 1949), 20–24; and Van der Ross, "Political and Social History," I: 130–45.
70. David Welsh, "The Politics of White Supremacy," in Thompson and Butler, *Contemporary South Africa,* 61; Newell M. Stultz, *Afrikaner Politics in South Africa, 1934–1948* (Berkeley and Los Angeles, 1974), 56–57, 136–37.
71. Louis R. Harlan, *Separate and Unequal: Public School Campaigns and Racism in the Southern Seaboard States, 1901–1915* (New York, 1968), 11, 15, and *passim.*
72. Horace Mann Bond, *Negro Education in Alabama: A Study in Cotton and Steel* (New York, 1969), 162 (table).
73. See Benjamin Muse, *Ten Years of Prelude: The Story of Integration Since the Supreme Court's 1954 Decision* (New York, 1964), 6–7.
74. Maurice, "Development of Policy," 65–66, 77–79, 195–96, 203, 249–50, and *passim;* Marais, *Cape Coloured People,* 270–73.
75. Marais, *Cape Coloured People,* 262.
76. For evidence of such a perspective in the South, see Harlan, *Separate and Unequal,* 125, 194.
77. See Maurice, "Development of Policy," 156, 178–79; and Harlan, *Separate and Unequal,* 251–53, for discussions of the effect of poverty and underdevelopment on educational policy in the South and the Cape.
78. See Kousser, *Shaping of Southern Politics.* On the earlier disfranchisement in the United States, see Kenneth Vickery, "'Herrenvolk' Democracy and Egalitarianism in South Africa and the U.S. South," *Comparative Studies in Society and History,* XVI (1974), 311–12; and Fredrickson, *Black Image,* 90–91.
79. Kousser, *Shaping of Southern Politics,* 259.

80. *Ibid.*, 36–38, 224–65. See also V. O. Key, Jr., *Southern Politics in State and Nation* (New York, 1949).

81. Marais, *Cape Coloured People,* 278–80. Figures are from Van der Ross, "Political and Social History," I: 157. For a short general account of the Colored franchise before the era of apartheid, see Thompson, *Cape Coloured Franchise.*

82. As David Welsh has pointed out, the Nationalists were strengthened in their resolve by their loss in the provincial elections of 1949 of two Cape districts that they had won in '48, a reversal that they attributed to "the registration of new Colored voters." They became convinced that they could lose a close election "through the addition of a few thousand extra Colored voters." ("Politics of White Supremacy," 61–62.) For an excellent account of the constitutional struggle over the Colored franchise, see Carter, *Politics of Inequality,* 121–41.

83. C. P. Cilliers, "The Concept of Citizenship and the Future of the Coloured Community," in Michael G. Wisson and Hendrik W. van der Merwe, eds., *Coloured Citizenship in South Africa* (Cape Town: The Abe Bailey Institute of Interracial Studies, 1972), 118.

84. See South African Institute of Race Relations, *A Survey of Race Relations in South Africa (1976)* (Johannesburg, 1977), 10–12.

Index